The Media Revolution in America and in Western Europe

COMMUNICATION AND INFORMATION SCIENCE

A series of monographs, treatises, and texts
Edited by
MELVIN J. VOIGT
University of California, San Diego

William C. Adams • Television Coverage of the Middle East
William C. Adams • Television Coverage of International Affairs
William C. Adams • Television Coverage of the 1980 Presidential Campaign
Alan Baughcum and Gerald Faulhaber • Telecommunications Access and Public Policy
Mary B. Cassata and Thomas Skill • Life on Daytime Television
Hewitt D. Crane • The New Social Marketplace
Rhonda J. Crane • The Politics of International Standards
Herbert S. Dordick, Helen G. Bradley, and Burt Nanus • The Emerging Network Marketplace
Glen Fisher • American Communication in a Global Society
Oscar H. Gandy, Jr. • Beyond Agenda Setting
Oscar H. Gandy, Jr., Paul Espinosa, and Janusz A. Ordover • Proceedings from the Tenth
  Annual Telecommunications Policy Research Conference
Edmund Glenn • Man and Mankind: Conflict and Communication Between Cultures
Gerald Goldhaber, Harry S. Dennis III, Gary M. Richetto, and Osmo A. Wiio • Information
  Strategies
Bradley S. Greenberg • Life on Television: Content Analyses of U.S. TV Drama
Bradley S. Greenberg, Michael Burgoon, Judee K. Burgoon, and Felipe Korzenny • Mexican
  Americans and the Mass Media
Cees J. Hamelink • Finance and Information: A Study of Converging Interests
Heather Hudson • When Telephones Reach the Village
Robert M. Landau, James H. Bair, and Jean Siegman • Emerging Office Systems
James Larson • Television's Window on the World
John Lawrence • The Electronic Scholar
John S. Lawrence and Bernard M. Timberg • Fair Use and Free Inquiry
Robert G. Meadow • Politics as Communication
William H. Melody, Liora R. Salter, and Paul Heyer • Culture, Communication, and Dependency:
  Vincent Mosco • Broadcasting in the United States
Vincent Mosco • Policy Research in Telecommunications: Proceedings from the Eleventh Annual
  Telecommunications Policy Research Conference
Vincent Mosco • Pushbutton Fantasies
Kaarle Nordenstreng • The Mass Media Declaration of UNESCO
Kaarle Nordenstreng and Herbert I. Schiller • National Sovereignty and International
  Communication
Harry J. Otway and Malcolm Peltu • New Office Technology
Ithiel de Sola Pool • Forecasting the Telephone
Everett Rogers and Francis Balle • The Media Revolution in America and in Western Europe
Dan Schiller • Telematics and Government
Herbert I. Schiller • Information and the Crisis Economy
Herbert I. Schiller • Who Knows: Information in the Age of the Fortune 500
Jorge A. Schnitman • Film Industries in Latin America
Indu B. Singh • Telecommunications in the Year 2000
Jennifer Daryl Slack • Communication Technologies and Society
Dallas W. Smythe • Dependency Road
Sari Thomas • Studies in Mass Media and Technology, Volumes 1-3
Barry Truax • Acoustic Communication
Georgette Wang and Wimal Dissanayake • Continuity and Change in Communication Systems
Janet Wasko • Movies and Money

In Preparation:

William Dutton and Kenneth Kraemer • Modeling as Negotiating
Fred Fejes • Imperialism, Media, and the Good Neighbor
Howard H. Fredericks • Cuban-American Radio Wars
Kenneth Mackenzie • Organizational Design
Armand Mattelart and Hector Schmucler • Communication and Information Technologies
Keith R. Stamm • Newspaper Use and Community Ties
Robert S. Taylor • Value-Added Processes in Information Systems
Tran Van Dinh • Independence, Liberation, Revolution

The Media Revolution in America and in Western Europe

Volume II in the Paris–Stanford Series

Edited by

Everett M. Rogers
Stanford University

Francis Balle
Université de Paris II

Ablex Publishing Corporation
Norwood, New Jersey 07648

Printed in the United States of America.

Library of Congress Cataloging in Publication Data
Main entry under title:

The Media revolution in America and in western Europe.

   (Volume II in the Paris-Stanford series) (Communication and information science)
   Bibliography: p.
   Includes index.
   1. Mass media—History. 2. Communication—Research. I. Rogers, Everett M. II. Balle, Francis. III. Series IV. Series: Communication and information science.
P90.M372   1983   001.51   84-21680
ISBN 0-89391-258-1

Ablex Publishing Corporation
355 Chestnut Street
Norwood, New Jersey 07648

Contents

Preface

At present, a gap exists between Western European and American scholars of mass communication in understanding each other's work. The present volume is organized by Francis Balle, Director of the Institut Français de Presse et des Sciences de l'Information, Université de Paris II, and by Everett M. Rogers, Institute for Communication Research, Stanford University. Our purpose is to improve the knowledge of European and American scholars of mass communication about research in their field, with emphasis upon the work being done on both sides of the Atlantic. We particularly stress the communication research presently under way on the new communication technologies of computers, satellites, and cable that are bringing about an Information Revolution in America and Europe.

Most Americans know that important communication research is going on in Europe, and they may know of such scholars as Osmo Wiio, Dennis McQuail, Hilde T. Himmelweit, Karl Erik Rosengren, Jacques Ellul, and Elizabeth Noelle-Neumann, for example. But other than understanding that such communication research is somewhat different than its U.S. counterpart, they do not know the up-to-date details of European communication research, other than that it provides certain alternatives to the main U.S. approaches. On their side, leading European scholars of mass communication are generally well-acquainted with U.S. research, in part due to their greater language facility and to wider travel and participation in international conferences. But because the United States and Western Europe are the two most important locales for mass communication research, many European scholars feel that a comparison of American and European approaches has long been needed.

Our emphasis in this book is upon mass communication, rather than upon interpersonal communication, because: (a) the study of communication in Europe mainly is the study of the mass media (this stress on the media by European communication researchers may be due to their greater interest in the societal context of communication, including its political aspects), (b) the tilt in both of the editors' institutes is toward mass communication, and (c) the Information Revolution is occurring in the mass media, making them become more like interpersonal communication (due to the interactivity of these communication systems, because they include a computer as one component). Perhaps in the future, as the Information Revolution marches forward, the essential differences between mass and interpersonal communication (which have been basic divisions in the field of communication research) will gradually fade, as the new media become more and more interactive.

We hope that the present volume is a step toward the greater internationalization of mass communication research, while recognizing the important differences that exist between the mass media of North America and those of Western European countries. Such contrasts provide a basis for comparative analyses that illuminate how cultural-linguistic-political differences in national mass media systems can contribute toward, rather than detract from, intellectual understanding of human communication behavior.

To quote from a later chapter in this volume, the world of communication scholarship can be divided for certain purposes into two main "schools", based on the nature of their ideologies, assumptions, and methods of conducting communication research. The two schools are commonly referred to as the empirical school and the critical school. The *empirical school* is characterized by quantitative empiricism, functionalism, and positivism. In the past this school generally emphasized study of the effects of communication, while often paying less attention to the broader context in which such communication is embedded. The *critical school* is more philosophical, focuses on the broader social-structural context of communication system, and has drawn on Marxist thought (although many critical scholars today are not Marxists). Critical scholars believe that a theory of communication is impossible without a theory of society, so the scope of their analysis is much wider than that of empirical scholars. The critical school traces its origins to the Frankfurt Institute for Social Research, founded in 1923.

Although having roots in Europe, the empirical school really began in the United States, and grew to intellectual strength in the past 35 years or so. But it is a gross simplification to refer to the critical school as the European approach, and the empirical school as the American approach. In fact, today there are probably more empirical than critical scholars in

Europe. And there may even be more critical scholars in America than in Europe. Several of the leading European empirical scholars are represented as chapter authors in the present volume. Interest in the critical school is now becoming more widespread in the United States.

Fortunately for the field of communication research, the critical and empirical schools are now beginning to learn from each other, leading to a hybrid approach that differs in important ways from either of its intellectual parents. The continental boundaries once separating competing schools of thought in communication research are presently breaking down. Perhaps a pluralistic accommodation will eventually prevail. Perhaps not.

No complete communication scholar today can understand only his own nation's viewpoint in communication research. The present volume is dedicated to the objective of furthering the intellectual merger of the differing European and North American viewpoints by facilitating improved understanding of each other. With this goal in mind, a leading group of European and American scholars agreed to contribute chapters toward the present volume. Their work is a symbol of this commitment to improve interchange across the Atlantic. All royalties earned by sales of this book will be used by the University of Paris and by Stanford University to encourage improved understanding of European-American approaches to mass communication. We hope that the next generation of students will thus benefit from the earnings of this book, as well as from its contents.

The co-editors chose Ablex as publishers of the English language edition of this book because of its strong interests (a) in the field of communication, and (b) in European-American academic exchanges. Ablex has been unusually pluralistic in publishing books that represent a wide range of intellectual positions, both European and American. We selected Dunod in Paris as publisher of the French edition of this book, which will be published as a co-edition with the Canadian publisher Stanke. Ev Rogers is listed as the first co-editor of the English edition, and Francis Balle as the first co-editor of the French edition.

We acknowledge the helpfulness of Melvin Voigt, Editor of the Communication and Information Science Series at Ablex, and of Laurent du Mesnil, Editor at Dunod. Invaluable assistance with the translation of certain chapters was provided by Ms. Christine N'Cho-Oguie and by Dr. Faustin Yao at Stanford University. We tried to preserve the original meanings of these translated chapters, so they are more than just direct translations of the original words.

A second theme of this book, in addition to its Euro-American comparative aspects, is its stress on new communication technologies. One cannot fully understand the mass media of communication today without recognizing that a tremendous revolution is getting underway. Leading the Information Revolution are such technologies as microcomputers, satellites, and fiber optics. Unlike the recent generation of electronic broadcasting, dominated by the one-way media of radio and television, newer communication systems are interactive. Herein we emphasize the trend toward interactive communication systems, which are presently getting underway in Europe and America. Such interactivity in communication systems promises to generate major rethinking about the nature of communication theories and research methods for the investigation of human communication behavior.

The collaboration represented in this book is a product of an agreement between the co-editors' two institutions. The Paris-Stanford relationship began in the early 1960s as a means of exchanging professors, students, and academic viewpoints. The first volume in this series, *Paris-Stanford Studies in Communication,* was published in 1961. Interchange between the University of Paris and Stanford University then was renewed under this agreement in 1980. Each of the co-editors has taught at the other's institute, thanks to the Fulbright Program, an experience leading to the present product.

We hope there will be many others.

Everett M. Rogers
Stanford, California
Francis Balle
Paris, France

About the Contributors

Elie Abel is Harry and Norman Chandler Professor of Communication at Stanford University. Formerly a correspondent with *The New York Times* and Dean of the Columbia Journalism School, Abel is now Chairman of the Department of Communication at Stanford University. He was a member of the 16-nation MacBride Commission of UNESCO, which investigated the nature of international news flows. Abel's most recent book is *What's News: The Media in American Society.*

Francis Balle is Professor and Director of the Institut Français de Presse et des Sciences de l'Information (the French Press Institute), Université de Paris II. Balle is best-known for two of his books, *Profit d'Une Oeuvre: McLuhan* (Profile of a Work: McLuhan) in 1972, and *Medias et Sociaté* (Media and Society) in 1979. His latest book, *Les Noveaux Medias* (The New Media) is co-authored with Gérard Eymery. Balle is the founder and co-editor (with Jean-Marie Cotteret) of *Les Cahiers de la Communication,* a journal of communication research.

Claude-Jean Bertrand is Maitre-Assistant at the Université de Paris X, and also teaches in the French Press Institute of the Université de Paris II. He authored the book *Les "Mass Media" aux Etats-Unis* (The Mass Media in the United States) in 1974, and *Les Etats-Unis: Histoire et Civilisation* (in 1983).

Jay Blumler is Director of the Centre for Television Research at the University of Leeds in England, where he also holds a Personal Chair in the Social and Political Aspects of Broadcasting. He has been a visiting professor at the University of Wisconsin and at the University of Southern California, and now spends a semester annually at the University of Maryland. One of his principal research interests is the role of the mass media in politics. Blumler is especially known for several influential writings on U.S.–European differences in mass communication research. His most recent books are *The European Voter* (1983) and *Communicating to Voters* (1983).

Denise Bombardier is a noted Canadian communication scholar, who has written about the role of French-language television in Quebec. Bombardier earned her Ph.D. from the Université de Paris, and has authored a book about the French broadcasting system, *La Voix de la France* (1975). She is in charge of an international news program (''Noir sur Blanc'') broadcast by Radio-Canada, the French-language television network in Quebec.

Henry Breitrose is Professor and former Chairman of the Department of Communication at Stanford University. He facilitated the Paris-Stanford agreement for academic exchange that led to the present volume. Breitrose's interest is in the inpacts of the new communication technologies. During 1983–84, Breitrose was on sabatical leave from Stanford, lecturing at European and Asian universities.

Steven Chaffee is Professor and Director of the Institute for Communication Research at Stanford University. A former President of the International Communication Association, Chaffee is best known for his research on political communication. He co-authored (with M. Petrick) *Using the Mass Media: Communication Problems in American Society*, and (with George Comstock, Natan Katzman, Maxwell McCombs, and Donald Roberts) *Television and Human Behavior* (in 1980).

Jacques Ellul is Professor at the Université de Bordeaux and is one of the best-known French scholars of communication. Among his several important books is *Propaganda*. Most recent of his books is *In Season, Out of Season* (1982).

Bradley Greenberg is former chairman of the Department of Communication and Professor of Communication and Telecommunication, at Michigan State University. Known for his long interest in the mass media in America, Greenberg recently published *Life on Television* and *Mexican Americans and the Mass Media*.

Axel Gryspeerdt is Professor in the Département de Communication Sociale at the Université Catholique de Louvain, in Louvain, Belgium. He has a long interest in the changes underway in the mass media, and especially in the move toward audience participation and decentralization of the media in European nations. His recent books include *Les Nouveaux Courants de la Presse Francophone en Belgique après Mai 1968* (1979), and *Les Media à l'école* (1981).

John Hochheimer is Assistant Professor in the School of Journalism and Mass Communication at the University of Iowa. Previously, Hochheimer taught at San Francisco State University and at Stanford University, where he studied for his Ph.D. degree. His central research interest is in political communication.

Bella Mody is Assistant Professor of Broadcasting at San Francisco State University. She is authoring *Communication Technology in Third World Contexts*. Mody's interest in this topic stems from her experience as one of the project leaders in the social evaluation of the Indian Satellite Instructional Television Experiment (SITE) from 1974–77; SITE broadcast television messages to 2,400 Indian villages to promote development and national integration.

Arnold Picot is at the Universität Hannover, Hannover, Federal Republic of Germany, where he is Professor of Management and Organization. He heads a program of research on the impacts of the new communication technologies in organizations. Picot earned his Ph.D. and Dr. Habil at the University of Munich, and has since become noted as one of the leading European scholars of office automation. During 1980–81 Picot was a visiting scholar in the Institute for Communication Research at Stanford University. During 1985, Picot will become professor at the Technical University of Munich.

Everett M. Rogers is Janet M. Peck Professor of International Communication at Stanford University. He is a former President of the International Communication Association. During 1981, Rogers was a Fulbright lecturer at the French Press Institute at the Université de Paris II, where the present book was planned. Rogers is best known for his work on the diffusion of innovations. His recent research on new communication technologies is represented by his 1984 book (with Judith K. Larsen), *Silicon Valley Fever*. During 1985, Rogers will join the Annenberg School of Communication at the University of Southern California.

Wilbur Schramm lives in active retirement in Hawaii, where he is associated with the East-West Communication Institute at the University of Hawaii. A former Director of the East-West Communication Institute, Schramm is Professor Emeritus (and the founder) of the Institute for Communication Research at Stanford University. He also founded the Institute of Communications Research at the University of Illinois. His personal career spans the history of communication research in the United States, and he is widely regarded as the most important influence on this field.

Karl Erik Rosengren holds the first Chair of Mass Communication Research in Sweden, at the University of Göteborg. Rosengren is known for his work on research methods, content analysis (his book on this topic was published by Sage in 1981), and the diffusion of news events. Previously, Rosengren was a professor of the sociology of mass communication at the University of Lund, Sweden.

Miguel Urabayen is Professor in the Facultad de las Ciencias de la Informacíon, at the Universidad de Navara, Pamploma, Spain, and also at the Universidad de Madrid, in Madrid. He has a special interest in the analysis of American films, and in comparisons of the mass media among European nations.

Osmo Wiio is Professor and Chairman of the Department of Communication at the University of Helsinki, Finland. Wiio is well-known for his theoretical interests in such basic concepts as information and communication. Wiio is a Fellow of the International Communication Association. His most recent book is *Information and Communication Systems: An Introduction to the Concepts of Information, Communication, and Communication Research*.

Introduction to Communication Research In Europe and America

Everett M. Rogers
Stanford University

Francis Balle
Université de Paris II

A necessary background to this book is a brief account of the rise of communication research in Europe and America. This introduction provides the historical context for the chapters that follow. Our field grew from quite different roots, and developed in contrasting ways, on the two sides of the Atlantic. Interchange between communication scholars in the two continents has been underway since (a) Robert Park, an early American sociologist of the press, completed his doctoral studies in Germany in about 1910 and returned to the University of Chicago, and (b) the influential writings of Gabriel Tarde, Auguste Comte, Georg Simmel, and Max Weber began to be incorporated in the thinking of American social scientists. Nevertheless, Euro-American exchange has continued at such a low level that communication research in the two continents developed historically in two separate intellectual streams.

We begin our introduction to this history with the origins of social science scholarship in Europe.

THE EARLY ROOTS OF SOCIAL SCIENCE RESEARCH IN EUROPE

Until about 1960, doctoral candidates in American universities were required to pass a language exam in both French and German. This requirement was based on the assumption that a competent scholar in any scientific field had to be able to read publications available in these two languages. Why German and French? Because the academic foundations of sociology, psychology, political science, anthropology, and the other disciplines from which communication research grew, had grown to strength in Germany and France (and England). In fact, until the beginnings of World War II, most American scholars felt that earning a Ph.D. degree from a European university was superior to studying at an American university. There were good reasons for this belief, as U.S.-style empirical social science grew directly out of the social philosophy of such European scholars as Comte, Tarde, Simmel, and Weber. Without the transplantation of their conceptions of the individual and society, U.S. communication research could not have gotten under way.

When European social theory was transferred to the United States in the first decades of the present century, it was often applied as a diagnostic tool to enable amelioration of social problems (Hinkle and Hinkle, 1954). America was then a society in transition from an agrarian to an industrial society. Crime, poverty, and other urban social problems were the object of study by early American social scientists. Understanding the severity and causes of such problems was considered to be of the highest priority. Empirical data-gathering and analysis were combined with the imported-from-Europe social theories in the 1920s and 1930s in order to form the basis for the distinctive empirical approach that has since come to be associated with American social science. When communication research began in the United States in the years just prior to World War II, it grew, naturally, out of this basis in empirical social science. As it grew in size and importance, it added increasingly-sophisticated research tools: survey sampling, measurement scales, projective techniques, statistical methods, and eventually, computer-based means of data-analysis. How was this technical advance in social science research methods reflected in the field of communication research?

THE RISE OF COMMUNICATION RESEARCH IN AMERICA[1]

About 25 years ago, Bernard Berelson reviewed the previous generation of communication research, and found disturbing trends:

> The innovators have left or are leaving the field, and no ideas of comparable scope and generating power are emerging. The expansion of the field to new centers has certainly slowed down and perhaps even stopped. . . . Some of the newer places are currently repeating what the pioneering places did years ago and are now disappointed with. (Berelson, 1959)

Coming as his presidential address to the then leading association of communication researchers, Berelson's "coroner's report" had the impact of an intellectual bombshell.

---

[1]The present section borrows from Rogers and Chaffee (1983), an account written on the twenty-fifth anniversary of the Bernard Berelson statement about the "death" of communication research.

Responses to Berelson's Pessimistic Assessment

By no means did most other communication scholars agree with Berelson at the time, and important events have occurred since in our field that show Berelson was far off base in his pessimistic assessment. In fact, it is entirely possible that Berelson "engineered" his negative assessment in order to shake up the field of communication scholarship, and that his private feelings were quite different from his stated pronouncement. In any event, Berelson (1959) felt the field had gone flat. He wrote:

> It seems to me that 'the great ideas' that gave the field of communication research so much vitality ten and twenty years ago have to a substantial extent worn out. No new ideas of comparable magnitude have appeared to take their place. We are on a plateau of research development, and have been for some time.

Presumably one of the "great ideas" that Berelson referred to was the linear model of communication effects originally proposed by Shannon and Weaver (1949). Their engineering model of information-transmission provided the basic paradigm around which the emerging field of the social science of communication could organize its intellectual interests. The Shannon-Weaver model of source-message-channel-receiver headed communication scholars, especially those concerned with the mass media, toward a concentration on investigating communication effects. This overwhelming focus on a common paradigm provided a certain unity of purpose to communication researchers for several decades, presumably causing Berelson to complain about a lack of new models for communication research. Finally, in the 1980s the overemphasis upon studying communication effects with a linear model begin to be questioned seriously (see, for example, Rogers and Kincaid, 1981).[2]

Modern mass communication research in the United States was launched by the work of Harold Lasswell, Paul Lazarsfeld, Kurt Lewin, and Carl Hovland; two were Europeans, and Lasswell and Hovland were strongly influenced by Continental scholarship. These four founders were teaching at elite U.S. universities, and they were at the centers of their

---

[2]An extreme form of the linear effects model, which was labeled "the hypodermic needle model," served in the 1960s and 1970s as a "dominant non-paradigm" for the field of communication research, which was thus intellectually organized around a model that communication scholars did *not* believe in (Paisley, 1984). Actually, a variety of alternative models of communication have been prepared by communication scholars; these models are not linear and do not focus on investigating media effects on the part of receivers.

discipline's "invisible colleges" (Paisley, 1984). Thus the founders were in a good position to launch the field of communication research, which must have been a somewhat radical innovation at the time. They helped legitimize its study. These founding fathers provided important points of departure for generations of mass communication researchers. But in the opinion of a contemporary European scholar who teaches in the U.S., "Their students and followers, as is often the case, were less successful in sustaining interest in those approaches with their particular methodologies and disciplinary frames of reference" (Hardt, 1979).

In his response to the Berelson dirge, published in an accompanying article in *Public Opinion Quarterly,* Wilbur Schramm (1959) stated that communication research "is one of the great crossroads where many pass but few tarry." That comment was basically accurate in America of the late 1950s, because communication research was at that time only beginning to be institutionalized in university departments, schools, and institutes of communication. Ph.D. programs in communication research were only beginning in 1959 at Illinois, Stanford, Minnesota, Wisconsin, and other U.S. universities. Previously, most communication research had been conducted by scholars in departments of sociology, psychology, political science, and other behavioral sciences, and in specialized university centers like the Bureau of Applied Social Research at Columbia University.

From Field to Discipline

So what Berelson and Schramm may have been observing 25 years ago in American mass communication research was the beginning of a transition from a field to a discipline. Prior to about 1960, the study of communication research was a matter of wide disciplinary concern, and one result, pointed to by Berelson and Schramm in 1959, was its lack of continuity in the careers of individual scholars. Men like Park, Lasswell, Lewin, Lazarsfeld, and Hovland gained an intellectual interest in studying communication as one of their variety of interests, and later might shift to other research concerns. Schramm (1959) stated: "Scholars came into it from their own disciplines, bringing valuable tools and insights, and later go back, like Lasswell, to the more central concerns of their disciplines." This in-and-out venturing in America was logical given the lack of an institutionalized structure for communication research. This typical career patterning of the American founders provided a rich diversity of intellectual backgrounds for communication research. But it did not contribute toward the integration of theories and methods for attacking communication research problems. That development had to await the 1960s and 1970s. Since about 1950, it had been the vision of Wilbur Schramm that communication research could become a field of scientific study

(Paisley, 1984). No other scholar did more to make this vision become a reality in the sense of its intellectual and institutional basis in U.S. universities.

The Institutionalization of Communication Science

During the past two decades, hundreds of university departments of communication were created in the United States. Some arose out of existing departments of speech, journalism, and other university units emphasizing a professional and/or humanistic kind of communication study. Other communication departments in U.S. universities were created new. All centered around a behavioral science approach to understanding human communication, in part because they employed new Ph.D.'s trained in this intellectual viewpoint, thus gaining academic respectability and an ability to attract large numbers of good students.[3] In fact, were any of the four founding fathers of communication research alive today, they would certainly be surprised by the multitude of university students attracted to studying communication. The major in communication, both by undergraduate and graduate students, has come in vogue in America, especially in the past dozen years or so. Likewise the volume of mass communication research is impressive; for example, about 115 Ph.D. dissertations in mass communications are completed each year, or about $\frac{1}{250}$ of all dissertations in the U.S. (Paisley, 1984).

As communication research in America moved from being a "field" toward becoming a "discipline,"[4] during the era of intellectual consoli-

---

[3] An insightful account of the academic institutionalization and growth of communication over the past decades is provided by Wilbur Schramm (in a later chapter in this volume), one of the key participants in this history.

[4] There is still considerable doubt about whether communication research is a discipline or not (a) in many European universities, and (b) in the older, well-established U.S. universities like Harvard, Chicago, Columbia, Yale, Princeton, and Berkeley, none of which have departments of communication. Yet by many indicators, communication research seems to be approaching the status of a discipline: It has attracted an estimated two thousand or so individuals in the U.S. alone who devote their full-time efforts to scholarly work, about which they share a common identity and a mutual sense of intellectual challenge. Certainly, however, communication research is not yet a discipline in the sense that sociology, psychology, and anthropology are. Communication research differs from these "level fields," which encompass a wide range of human behaviors at one level of analysis (for example, the individual, the group, and society); instead communication research is a "variable field," giving attention to one category of behavior (economics, political science, and cybernetics, for example) across many levels of analysis (Paisley, 1984). This useful classification of levels and variable fields implies that communication research is a discipline, or at least that it has carved out adequate conceptual space to become eventually a discipline.

dation and integration of the 1960s and 1970s, some of the diversity of intellectual inputs decreased. Communication research lost some of its strong academic connections to the other social sciences. Part of the old excitement of the early days of communication as a field inevitably disappeared, along with some of the diversity of viewpoints. It is now much easier for communication scholars to talk with each other and be understood, in light of the increased homogeneity of their concerns, their common backgrounds in a shared training experience, and the rise of scientific journals reporting their research. The gradual accumulation of theoretically oriented, empirically based research findings is thus facilitated.

This contemporary era of consolidation does not necessarily mean that a certain degree of diversity is now entirely missing in the scope of communication research. Our work still spans a very wide range of human behavior because communication is such a ubiquitous process. Our concerns still cut across most of the other social sciences. We are less able to place strict boundaries around our focus on communication than are such other behavior sciences as economics, psychology, and sociology with their concerns with the market, the individual, and the group, respectively. We have a wide area in which to maneuver, and we still have not located effectively just where the theoretical center of communication study should be. That is an important task for the future.

CONTEMPORARY COMMUNICATION RESEARCH IN EUROPE

Mass communication research in most European nations can be divided into four, more or less distinct periods; here we choose France's experience to illustrate these four stages. The first can be called the ''Age of the Founding Fathers''; communication research in France concentrated on legal studies of the press, while researchers closely followed the work of American social scientists such as Lazarsfeld. During the second period, which was a Golden Era for Lasswell's model, the little research that was done in France consisted primarily of studies of direct effects of the media or else of descriptive analyses of the mass media. The third period represents France's revenge on the previous two. It started around 1960 and might be called the Dispersion Age because of the many tendencies prevailing simultaneously in French communication research at that time. The fourth (current) period might be entitled ''Politics Return in Full Force'' because right-wing and left-wing intellectuals both question and criticize the influence of the mass media on society.

Age of the Founding Fathers
In 1938, only a few months before World War II was declared, Jean Stoezel founded the first French institute for the study of public opinion.

After having closed down during the war, the French Public Opinion Institute (IFOP) resumed its activities and introduced sample surveys in France, but not without having aroused certain negative reactions.

Neither the French radio-television agency (RTF) nor the German media organization during the occupation of France were equipped with research centers until well after the BBC (British Broadcasting Corporation) and the American commercial broadcasting networks had such research facilities. The specific orientation of French communication research immediately after World War II was to formulate new legal frameworks for the press. Between 1945 and 1949, no less than five bills for a press statute were laid on the table of the "Assemblée Nationale," none of which materialized. As early as 1937, an Institute for a Science of the Press was created within the University of Paris. After having closed down during the war, the Institute resumed its activities in 1947, and in 1951 became known as the "Institut Français de Presse" (the French Press Institute). The director, Fernand Terrou, defined the area to be covered as a new branch of law dealing with information. This special branch of law treated four basic issues: the press statute, the statute of media content, the statute of professions dealing with the media, and an international press statute.

Terrou, a legal scholar, followed a definition of information and media which oriented French research along a different path than that taken in America. By giving preference to the word "information" for a number of years, French researchers emphasized the content of what is transmitted by the mass media, especially by the mass-circulation press, with less emphasis upon radio and television broadcasting. The concept of information designated a specific element of knowledge or judgment, regardless of its form or degree of intelligibility for a given public. Information was regarded as news.

The approach adopted by French researchers was therefore from the start quite distinct from that of their American colleagues. In fact, the differences were primarily political, if not ideological. They were due to the differing conceptions of the role of information held in France and the U.S. The U.S. attached great importance to the First Amendment on freedom of the press and freedom of expression. This amendment was interpreted to mean that the State, by law, should restrain from any interference in the field of communication. Through the force of circumstances and ideas, France chose the opposite path in the name of the same principle of freedom of the press. Thus it was no accident that an article should be entitled *l'Information Clef de la Democracie* (that is *"Information as a Key to Democracy"*) in 1951 by Alfred Sauvy. This author placed his hopes in a democracy that would triumph because compete and objective information would be at the disposal of citizens.

Jean Stoezel (1947, 1963) enumerated the other functions of the press in addition to information. He believed the press was an instrument of social linkage, an object of recreation, and the preferred means of catharsis. Stoezel's ideas were not very well received at the time because they were too far removed from the prevailing ideas of the period; reference was still being made to the mass media in terms of information, rather than communication.

The Golden Era of Lasswell's Model

Up until the 1960s, Lasswell's four questions (of who says what to whom with what effect) dominated studies of the mass media in France. Not only did his simple expression define the different research areas for communication investigations, but also seemed to prescribe the appropriate concepts and methodological orientations to be followed. Thus Lasswell's paradigm served the entire scientific community of communication scholars. Few pointed out its limitations, and no one really challenged its relevance during this period. In France little research on the media was actually done during this time; the few researchers who studied the media were to stay within the Lasswell equation. Examples were studies of the direct effects of certain television and radio programs; these studies were mainly carried out by scholars working within the production and administration sectors of the mass media institutions.

Pertinent articles were published in *Les Études de Presse (Press Studies)* founded in 1946 by Fernand Terrou and in *Les Cahiers d'Études de Radio-Télévision,* edited by Bernard Blin from 1956 to 1960; other articles about communication research appeared in the periodical *Télévision et Education Populaire (TV and Popular Education)*, edited by Joseph Rovan.

Just as this period of the 1950s saw few media studies conducted by French researchers, the period following was literally inundated with media studies by all sorts of researchers.

The Dispersion Age

French researchers suddenly became fascinated with the media in 1960; since then, a great number of communication studies emanating from many different researchers represent various currents of thought. Three specific tendencies can be found within the seeming confusion engendered by this wide dispersion. The first is towards "massmediology," the second is "new horizons," while "the return of theoretical analysis" fittingly defines a third tendency. A few researchers continued to follow Lasswell's model of communication (such as Jacques Kayser's (1963) descriptive work, *Le Quotidien Français*), but most did not.

Several American sociologists wrote about the mass culture that was born with the advent of radio and television broadcasting; Leo Bogart

(1956) in his *The Age of Television* stressed the increasing standardization of industrial societies. In France, Edgar Morin (1962) published *L'Esprit du Temps,* in which he borrowed and applied the new ideas about mass-mediology coming from America, focusing on the norms and stereotypes communicated by radio, TV, and film. Massmediology was not well accepted by many French intellectuals; Pierre Bourdieu and C. Passeron questioned the very existence of a sociology of the mass media (which they displeasingly entitled "massmediology").

Within the social sciences and anthropology, the main event of the 1960s was the publication of the *Savage Mind* by Claude Levi-Strauss (1962). This work, which became the basis for structural anthropology, aimed at demonstrating that archaic societies have a universal mode of thought. Levi-Strauss argued that the mental keys to a particular society could be unveiled by studying the culture's myths through the methods of structural linguistics.

The works of Roland Barthes also opened a new horizon for media studies; he felt that linguistics is perhaps only the "advance post" of a general science of signs, semiology. Edgar Morin took into consideration the contributions made by both structural anthropology and semiology to espouse the cause of what he referred to as "linguistic-semiological structural" analysis. These studies, however, while interesting when applied to media research, were unsatisfactory because they were not considered very scientific or reliable.

New theoretical approaches elaborated during the early 1960s marked a decisive turning-point for media research. McLuhan argued that the same message could have very different effects depending on the media used to transmit it. His work had a tremendous impact on media research in general, and on French research in particular. The 1960s were also the decade of Jacques Ellul's *Propaganda: The Formation of Men's Attitudes* (1962), a critique of the empirical American studies of media communication. Ellul challenged the relevance of the "hypodermic needle" model as a representation of mass media effects. He considered this model to be the exact opposite of what actually happens in mass communication. The propagandist is not a "Sorcerer's apprentice" lying in wait to force information upon innocent victims. Ellul claims the "propaganda-receiver" existed long before the propagandist, as modern man has an unquenchable thirst for propaganda. Ellul's interpretation argued against the approach used by sociologists to study the effects of the media, and he disputed the results engendered by their empirical investigations.

Politics Return in Full Force

Major criticism of the media, principally of television, can be traced back to Spiro Agnew's violent indictment, made in 1969 when he was vice-president of the United States. Agnew's charges nourished debate on the media throughout the 1970s, not only in the U.S. but also in other countries. Furthermore, while the differences between the American television system and those of Europeans diminished, grievances against TV during this period became worldwide. Common criticisms pertained to the media's obsession with polls, conservatism and conventionalism in the media, and the show-business treatment of politics.

Political criticism of the mass media culminated in spring, 1979 with the convergence in Paris of (a) Regis Debray's analyses, and (b) those of what was then known as the "new right." Debray (1979) defined three cycles in the modern history of the French intelligentsia, the third being the media cycle (which he dated from 1968 onward). He believed there is a media monopoly in France which holds all the power and has the technological and political means to determine how the entire society thinks. Debray's diagnosis is akin to that of the new right of the 1970s, whose aim was to take the monopoly of political discourse away from the Marxist left. *La Politique du Vivant* states:

> The metapolitical universe is now monopolized by an anti-liberal intellectual minority. Some 200 intellectuals alone create ideological styles; veritable *coururiers* (tailors) of the spirit, they design "ready-to-think" products for an entire society."

Ten years after Agnew's speech, Alain de Benoist, the new right's main ideologist, praised the latest book of Regis Debray, who was closely connected to the extreme left movement of the 1960s. Such an occurrence is uncommon in France; it emphasized the fact that a wide range of intellectuals criticize the media (and those in control of the media) for the exact same reasons: the monopoly of a few and their power to influence the way society thinks.

This political criticism of the mass media oriented research studies along new routes. In France the main path taken by researchers was towards the study of media institutions. Those researchers who adopted the institutional approach are: Bernard Voyenne, Pierre Schaeffer, and Jean-Louis Servan-Schreiber. Voyenne's studies of the press follow for the most part the morphological tradition which was mainly represented by Jacques Kayser and later by Pierre Albert. The aim of this type of study was to describe the nature of newspapers, including their "upstream" and "downstream." Voyenne is especially known for his research on the profession of journalism. He traced the major steps of a profession seeking its identity, subject to suspicions and torn between specialization versus a generalist overview of all subjects.

Also interested in the role of journalists, Pierre Schaeffer explored the difficulties of being a professional communicator (or "mediator," the term he prefers). In any mass media system there are two triangular structures of relations: (a) a "visible" triangle of the author, the mediator, and the public, and (b) a "hidden" triangle, which places the mediator in an interface between the authorized experts who are supposed to legitimately monopolize knowledge in a given field, and the heads of the "communication machine." The mediator is at the center of gravity of a specific social system, condemned to perpetually reconcile interlocutors whose expectations and interests (economic and other) are often divergent.

Another researcher who followed the institutional approach, Jean-Louis Servan-Schreiber, examined the media's modes of operation in *The Power To Inform* (1972). He assumed the posture of an economist in discussing whether or not the press is capable of keeping up the same image as yesterday. Although it is still quite unique, information has definitely become an industry.

What can be said about the present state of mass communication research in France, and, more broadly in other European nations? Such investigation is booming. Researchers from various disciplines study the mass media on a larger and larger scale. Europeans are very interested in their media, if only to criticise them, and they demand that more studies of media systems be conducted. For example, L'Institut Français de Presse (French Press Institute) studies the media through communication research. More students are enrolled each year, and more pertinent theses are being written by the students here and at other such schools in Europe.

Studies of the media became more scientific. It was once quite common in France for so-called researchers to approach their work from an ideological point of view. Rather than attempting to be objective, these researchers studied the media in order to prove something they already believed because of their political affiliations. This approach is no longer generally accepted by the scientific community. Most present communication research in France (and elsewhere in Europe) is conducted by qualified researchers whose results are more objective, more methodologically sound, and therefore more precise and more reliable than ever before.

NEW COMMUNICATION TECHNOLOGIES AND THE INFORMATION SOCIETY

Western European nations and the United States are the most advanced information societies in the world (along with Japan), and hence they should be able to learn from each other about the problems and uncertainties that necessarily accompany the sudden change from industrial production, based on energy as the basic resource, to an economy centered on the gathering, processing, and outputting of information. More than half of the gross national product (GNP), and of the workforce in European nations and in the U.S. presently come from information industries and occupations. Particularly important in an information society is communication technology, including computers, telecommunication, and semiconductors (which rests on the more fundamental technology of semiconductor chips). Jerry Sanders, president of Advanced Micro Devices (AMD), a Silicon Valley microelectronics firm, says: "Semiconductors are the oil of the 1980's" (Rogers and Larsen, 1984). Production of communication technology is concentrated in the United States, Europe, and Japan. And it is this new communication technology that drives the Information Society.

The concern of communication scholars with the impacts of a new communication technology has a long history. Had there been communication researchers in the vicinity of Mainz, Germany shortly after 1450, undoubtedly we would have had investigations of the impacts of movable type. About 1930, a thorough set of studies of the impacts of motion pictures on children was commissioned by the Payne Fund (Lowery and De Fleur, 1983). Special attention was given to the possible negative influences of film, as indicated by the research question: "Are the emotions of children harmfully excited?" (Charters, 1933, p.v). Twenty years later, when television began to spread widely to U.S. and English households in the 1950s, influential investigations were mounted by leading communication scholars (Schramm, Lyle, and Parker, 1961; Himmelweit, Openheim, and Vince, 1958). These studies recognized that television had negative, as well as positive, influences on children.

Pioneers in investigating the new communication technologies of today were Ithiel de Sola Pool of MIT, Edwin B. Parker of Stanford, and Frederick Williams of the University of Southern California. Soon these scholars were joined by many, many others, and today the study of the new media has become very popular in both Europe and America.

THE REVOLUTION IN INTERACTIVITY

What is "revolutionary," at least potentially, about the new communication technologies is their interactive nature. Such interactivity of the new communication systems derives from the computer that they contain as one of their components. Examples of such interactive systems are Hi-OVIS in Japan, *Bildschirmtext* in the Federal Republic of Germany, Prestel in England, *Antiope* in France, Telidon in Canada, and QUBE in the U.S. These experimental systems, and there are hundreds of others in Europe and America, are technically and economically feasible due to the miniaturization of computers through recent advances in semiconductor development, especially dating from invention of the microprocessor in 1971 (Rogers and Larsen, 1984). The Information Revolution now under way is basically a microcomputer revolution. Thanks to microprocessor technology, computers are now everywhere. In 1946, there was one computer. In 1984, eight million. The number has doubled in the past couple of years. The interactivity made possible by computers is forcing communication scholars to revise their theories and research methods, leaving behind their prior focus on linear models of mass media effects. When each household has a home computer and can thus access information systems, the old distinction between "source" and audience becomes meaningless.

> A telephone conversation is an active bilateral thing, controlled by both parties, either of whom can hang up, and both of whom can direct the conversation by their remarks. Similarly, interacting with a remote computer is an active thing controlled by the user, not by the machine. (Pool, 1980)

Every node in a telephone system is an originating point as well as a receiver. Monitoring and censoring of an interactive communication system is much more difficult than that of controlling a one-way mass media system (such as the press or television in a nation), where the number of communication sources are usually relatively few. In this sense, the long-term trend during the last third of the present century is not only (a) from scarcity to abundance of communication resources, but also (b) toward the decentralization of control of mass communication systems. This decentralization is made possible by newer forms of communication technology. Nevertheless, the individual user of a new communication technology may still be constrained in important ways by the design of the technology. Other constraints are the cost of the technology and the skills needed to use it. But in general, the hallmarks of the new communication technologies are abundance and decentralization.

What Are The New Media?

Exactly what communication technologies are included in the "new media?" Although each of these technologies is becoming integrated with certain of the others, here is a list of the still-distinct technologies:

1. *Microcomputers* are stand-alone units, usually with provision for individual loading of software, and sometimes connected with other microcomputers in a network. The central processing unit (CPU) of a microcomputer, which reads and executes program instructions, is a single semiconductor chip (a microprocessor).

2. *Teletext* consists of text and graphic frames of information that are transmitted by television stations during the vertical blanking interval of the television signal. The lines of information are located above the picture seen on a television screen. Each of several hundred frames can be chosen by an individual via a keypad/decoder at the receiving set.

3. *Videotex* consists of text and graphic frames sent to a receiving set via telephone, cable, or some other non-broadcast channel. The number of frames is potentially unlimited, and millions of frames are already loaded in various videotex systems. Videotex requires a request channel (unlike teletext), so it is more interactive in nature. Sometimes videotex is spelled with a final "t", as "videotext."

4. *Interactive cable* provides for sending text and graphic frames, as well as full video pictures, to receiving sets via cable. The content is potentially unlimited. Cable serves also as the request channel. The source computer is usually capable of polling and tabulating responses, accepting orders for services or products, etc. QUBE is an example of an interactive cable system.

5. *Direct broadcast satellite (DBS)* consists of broadcasting television and other messages directly to small antennas located in households or other buildings. The satellite is usually placed in a stationary orbit around the equator, at about 22,300 miles from the earth's surface. Essentially, satellite transmission of television, telephone, and other information removes the effect of distance on the cost of communication. One reason for the recent quickening in the rate of adoption of cable TV in the U.S. is that satellite broadcasting to cable stations has greatly increased the number of cable channels available to the viewer.

6. *Video recorders* allow an individual to record off-the-air or to purchase videotapes from commercial sources, and then to view these recorded materials when time permits. Essentially, video recorders allow an individual to shift the time of watching televised programs.

7. *Fiber optic cable* is made of glass (silicon) and provides a network for carrying a very large number of telephone or television signals. The advantage of fiber optic cable over electrical wire is that it has greater fidelity; in addition, there is no interference with nearby electronic equipment like radios or television sets. The Hi-OVIS experiment in Japan is believed to be the first use of fiber optic cable in an interactive communication system; Hi-OVIS is completely interactive in that each participating household has a television camera as well as a TV receiving set.

These new technologies can be combined in various forms in communication systems. For example, an interactive cable television system may include a microcomputer at the headend to handle the incoming messages from households, and be connected to one or more satellites that transmit special channels (such as 24-hour news, for example) to the cable system. The new technologies not only are creating entirely new communication systems, but they are also changing the conventional media. For instance, computer based equipment has taken over the newsrooms of most major newspapers, so that writing, editing, and composition is done by, or with, a computer. Further, in many countries, experimental programs are under way in which subscribers can read their daily newspaper on a computer terminal instead of on a piece of paper; with this technology, the reader can request that only certain types of news be shown on his terminal.

Are the New Media Good or Bad?

By no means do we, or our co-authors in this book, mean to imply that we are necessarily pro-technology. Certainly the new media have important advantages for many individuals, households, and organizations. That is the basic reason for such widespread interest in these new technologies. But their future potential far outshines their present performance. New communication technologies like home computers, video recorders, interactive cable, teletext, and videotex have reached only a small share of households; the most widely-adopted medium is video recorders, which have reached up to 20 percent of all households in several nations. The other new media are presently at a lower rate of adoption.

Why do European governments in such nations as England, France, and Germany promote the development of new communication technologies like cable TV, videotex, teletext, fiber optics, and direct broadcast satellite?—in order to create jobs in the high-technology industries that design and manufacture these new media, both for sale within the country and internationally. Further, and more generally, these new communication technologies help a nation move forward into becoming an information society. Most governments feel this is a desirable direction. Many of the new teletext and videotex technologies recently began in European nations, often as a result of direct government action, while the new computer-related technologies (like microcomputers) arose in the United States, especially in Silicon Valley (California), without government involvement. Thus the growing interest in studying the social impacts of the new communication technologies is increasing the exchanges between European and American scholars.

This introduction has described the background of communication research in Europe and America. It is a history of mutual influence, with important intellectual ideas flowing from one side of the Atlantic to the other. Today, scholars in both the Continent and in the New World are becoming increasingly interested in the work of their counterparts. The chapters that follow seek to spell out some of the detailed understandings learned about human communication behavior from both sides of the Atlantic. Throughout, our emphasis will be upon the new media.

REFERENCES

Bernard Berelson (1959), "The State of Communication Research," *Public Opinion Quarterly*, 23, 1–6.

Leo Bogart (1956), *The Age of Television*, New York: Ungar.

W.W. Charters (1933), *Motion Pictures and Youth: A Summary*, New York: Macmillan.

Regis Debray (1979), *La Politique du Vivant (The Politics of Living)*, Paris: Remsey.

Jacques Ellul (1962), *Propagandes*, Paris: A. Colin; translated as *Propaganda: The Formation of Men's Attitudes*, New York: Knopf, 1965.

Hanno Hardt (1979), "Introduction to 'Social Theories of the Press,'" in G.Cleveland Wilhoit (ed.), *Mass Communications Review Yearbook, Volume 2*, Beverly Hills, CA: Sage.

Hilde T. Himmelweit, A.N. Openheim, and P. Vince (1958), *Television and the Child*, New York: Oxford University Press.

Roscoe E. Hinkle, Jr. and Gisela J. Hinkle (1954), *The Development of Modern Sociology: Its Nature and Growth in the United States*, New York: Random House.

Jacques Kayser (1963), *Le Quotidien Français*, Paris: A. Colin.

Claude Levi-Strauss (1962), *La Pensée Sauvage*, Paris: Plon; translated as *The Savage Mind*, Chicago, IL: University of Chicago Press, 1966.

Sheron Lowery and Melvin L. De Fleur (1983), *Milestones in Mass Communication Research: Media Effects*, New York: Longman.

Edgar Morin (1962), *L'Esprit du Temps (The Spirit of the Times)*, Paris: Grasset.

William Paisley (1984), "Communication in the Communication Sciences," in Brenda Dervin and Melvin J. Voigt (eds.), *Progress in Communication Sciences, Volume 5*, Norwood, NJ: Ablex.

Ithiel de Sola Pool (1980), "The Volume of Information Flow and Quantum Evaluation of Media," *Telecommunication Journal, 42*, 339–349.

Everett M. Rogers and Steven H. Chaffee (1983), "Communication as an Academic Discipline," *Journal of Communication, 33*, 18–30.

Everett M. Rogers and D. Lawrence Kincaid (1981), *Communication Networks: A New Paradigm for Research*, New York: Free Press.

Everett M. Rogers and Judith K. Larsen (1984), *Silicon Valley Fever*, New York: Basic Books.

Alfred Sauvy (1951), "L'Information, Clef de la Démocratie," *Revue Française de Science Politique, 1*, 26–39.

Wilbur Schramm (1959), "Comments on 'The State of Communication Research,'" *Public Opinion Quarterly, 23*, 6–9.

Wilbur Schramm, Jack Lyle, and Edwin B. Parker (1961), *Television in the Lives of Our Children*, Stanford, CA: Stanford University Press.

Jean-Louis Servan-Schreiber (1972), *Le Pouvoir d'Informer*, Paris: R. Laffont; translated as *The Power to Inform*, New York: McGraw Hill.

Claude E. Shannon and Warren Weaver (1949), *The Mathematical Theory of Communication*, Urbana, IL: University of Illinois Press.

Jean Stoezel (1947), *L'Opinion Publique et la Presse (Public Opinion and the Press)*, Paris: Institut d'Etudes Politique, Université de Paris.

Jean Stoezel (1963), *La Psychologie Sociale (Social Psychology)*, Paris: Flau-Marion.

Part I

The Changing Nature of the Mass Media in Europe and America

The first four chapters of this book describe the mass media of communication in the United States and in the Western European countries, in the early 1980s. What are the major characteristics of the press, radio, television, and cinema, as institutions? How are these mass media owned and organized? What do their audiences do with these media? What are the social impacts, in the U.S. and in Europe, of the new communication technologies that are causing revolutionary changes in the media, as American and European nations become information societies? Increased competition among the media, accompanied by specialization and diversification, are occurring.

We begin Part I with a description of the media in Europe and America, by Claude-Jean Bertrand/Miguel Urabayen and Bradley Greenberg, respectively. This is followed by Henry Breitrose's discussion of how the new communication technologies are changing the existing mass media, and the society that they serve. Finally, Francis Balle shows how the new media are forcing a redefinition of the concept of freedom of information.

Chapter 1

European Mass Media in the 1980s[1]

Claude-Jean Bertrand
Université de Paris X

Miguel Urabayen
*Universidad de Navarra, and
Universidad de Madrid*

INTRODUCTION

In comparison to their counterparts in America, the European mass media are highly varied, as a result of the heterogeneity of languages, national cultures, and disparities in per capital income among the 18 nations of Western Europe. Nevertheless, one can speak of the European mass media, and place them somewhat midway (but toward the American end) of a continuum with U.S.-style press freedom on one extreme and the high degree of government control of the rest of the world at the other end. On average, Europeans have somewhat less mass media exposure than do Americans. Advertising is a less important source of support for the European media, which rely in part on license fees and State subsidies. Generally, State influence on the mass media, particularly the broadcasting media of radio and TV, is much stronger in Europe than in America. The trend is toward the Europeanization of the mass media, as is exemplified by two newspapers: *The Financial Times* and the *International Herald Tribune.*   *E.M.R., F.B.*

Few will dispute that Europe was the cradle of the press: from the handwritten *Acta Diurna* in ancient Rome to Gutenberg's invention, to the periodical *avvisi* in Venice, to the first daily newspaper in Leipzig in 1660, or say the British *Daily Courant* in London in 1702. Europe was also the pioneer of modern journalism, from the first powerful independent newspaper, the early 19th-century *London Times,* to the first large circulation popular daily, *Le Petit Journal* in Paris in 1863 (20 years later it reached 1 million copies).

What of the European press now? If a European press could be pieced together using only the best elements in the media of each country, it would be clearly superior to the "least worst" on earth today, that of

---

[1]The co-authors of this chapter have for years taught courses on the mass media in Europe at the Université de Paris and the Universidad de Navarra, respectively. Certain data presented here were drawn from *World Media,* a book co-edited by Claude-Jean Bertrand and Miguel Urabayen, published in 1984 simultaneously in three languages, in English by Iowa State University, in Spanish by EUNSA, and in French by PUN.

the U.S. Conversely, if the European press consisted of the worst elements in each nation, it would be inferior even to that of America's rival in world hegemony, the Soviet Union.

Actually, even leaving out the communist countries (whose media have all been modeled on the Russian pattern), it is not easy to generalize about Europe, for it is not 1 but some 18 very diverse and very unequal nations. Europe is not a federated whole, like the U.S., though it is one-third smaller with a population 8 percent larger. Geography and climate, historical, economic, and political forces have made its nations clearly different. World War II, however, marked a turning point. At that time, Eastern Europe was cut off completely, and the countries in Western Europe started drawing closer to one another. As the major nations lost their empires and as, in Southern Europe, facism gradually vanished and industry developed, Europe has grown into a more homogeneous region, much more so than Southeast Asia or the Near East or Black Africa. And strong currents of Europeanization began to develop.

In order to define European media, a logical strategy is first to compare them to media systems they most resemble, U.S. media—and then to contrast them among themselves. So our general description of European mass media is detailed in several tables in this chapter.

European media occupy an intermediate position. Politically, they neither enjoy U.S.-style freedom, nor suffer anything like the high degree of government control normal in most of the rest of the world. While nowadays no country, even in southern Europe, has print media under an authoritarian regime, no country, even in northern Europe, has broadcast media under a liberal regime. Economically, European media stand somewhere between the high degree of wealth and development in the U.S. and the poverty and underdevelopment in most of the rest of the world—although generally nearer to the U.S. position.

Less restrictively, 18 or so nations of Western Europe, taken together, possess media whose quantity and diversity, whose quality and influence are matched in no other region of the globe. If at least the major European nations cooperated (as they seem more inclined to do) in the production of communication hardware or software, Europe could become the number one power both as far as the traditional and the new media are concerned (Tunstall, 1982). Let us take a few scattered examples: Among world electronics manufacturers, Dutch Philips is number 4 in total sales and Germany's Siemens is number 5; the color TV system used by the Soviet Union and its satellites is the French SECAM; the most credible international radio program is the BBC World Service; Belgium is the most cabled area in the world; the French Antiope and the British Oracle/Ceefax are two of the three major videotex systems; and of the most important newspapers in the world, several are European: The British *Times* and *Guardian*, the French *Le Monde*, and the German *Frankfurter Algemeine*.[2]

SIMILARITIES BETWEEN EUROPEAN AND AMERICAN MEDIA

Because some 90 percent of Americans have European forebears, because cultural and economic and technological exchanges never stopped across the Atlantic, and because industrial and scientific development is now much the same in the Old and New Worlds, the mass media on either side of the Atlantic Ocean show much similarity. Consumption is comparable, although it varies widely among the 18 European nations (Table 1). According to UNESCO, 243 dailies were sold per 1,000 inhabitants in Europe in 1976, and 281 in North America. Admittedly there are many more radio sets in the U.S. and more TV sets, but just about all European households are equipped with these electronic media, and their consumption is at least two-thirds of the American.[3]

Many media products of American origin are sold in Europe: among print media, the original news magazines; the *International Herald Tribune* and (since 1983) the *Wall Street Journal;* the translated and adapted editions of quite a few women's and men's magazines, and the *Reader's Digest*. American TV series and films are of course a staple all over Europe, especially in smaller countries. AP, UPI, feature syndicates, and news services of big dailies, find Europe one of their most lucrative markets, whereas their European rivals are to a large extent kept out of the U.S. market (with exceptions like Reuters or the Anglo-American UPITN). The mere presence of U.S. media in Europe is bound to have exerted an influence on the evolution of the mass media there.

European nations own the other of the two Big Four wire services, Reuters and Agence France Presse (AFP), and thus tend to extend their influence to media far away, mainly to the South (for example, France to North, West, and Central Africa). However, a basic similarity in the evolution, structure, and influence of the print media appears among European nations: a free enterprise sector where the hard-won principle of press freedom from government interference is respected. Every country has an elite press, interested in international and cultural news, that sells

---

[2]In 1963 a sample of U.S. professors answered a questionnaire sent by the University of Syracuse about the best 10 newspapers in the world. The result: 6 were European.

[3]UNESCO in 1976 counted 1,793 radio sets per 1,000 inhabitants for North America, as opposed to 334 for Europe (including Eastern Europe), and 554 TV sets against 237.

Table 1. Mass Media Consumption in 18 European Nations[a]

Country	Daily Newspaper Circulation per 1,000 Inhabitants	Radio Receivers per 1,000 Inhabitants	Television Sets per 1,000 Inhabitants
1. Austria	320	288	247
2. Belgium	239	384	252
3. Denmark	341	336	308
4. Finland	425	427	269
5. France	214	324	235
6. Germany (Federal Republic of)	312	337	305
7. Great Britain	388	750	315
8. Greece	107	279	106
9. Iceland	431	295	230
10. Ireland (Eire)	222	287	178
11. Italy	113	228	213
12. Luxembourg	447	515	257
13. Netherlands	315	284	259
14. Norway	412	320	256
15. Portugal	70	174	68
16. Spain	98	229	174[a]
17. Sweden	572	378	348
18. Switzerland	402	314	264
United States	287	1,895	571

[a] *Source:* UNESCO (1975), *UNESCO Statistical Yearbook: World Communications,* Paris.

nationwide; with exceptions, it has a politically conservative popular press; and a vast middle-brow regional press enjoying a local monopoly. Most European countries have news weeklies adapted from the U.S. model, and a multiplicity of specialized periodicals, with television guides always leading the pack in circulation, and with women's magazines coming next.

In Europe, as in the U.S., the number of titles has tended to decrease and ownership has become more concentrated as the press went more and more commercial (Toussaint-Desmoulins and Lateinturer, 1980). Much concern is being voiced: Although journalists have grown more competent and responsible, and newspaper contents have been made more attractive (with offset printing and color supplements), in Europe there is a growing indifference towards newspapers on the part of the public, and by young people especially. Competitors for advertising and for time and attention by the audience have appeared in the form of freesheets and of the rapidly multiplying radio stations.

DIFFERENCES BETWEEN EUROPEAN AND AMERICAN MEDIA

Differences between European and American mass media are certainly easier to list, than are the similarities. The central contrast regards the crucial role played by the State, a heritage of the Roman Empire and centuries of Catholic Church hegemony. The State is expected to provide the media with organization, discipline, protection, help, and innovations. This assistance is the most obvious in the field of broadcasting, especially as reorganized since World War II, often on the British model. Everywhere in Europe, radio and TV are considered not as a mere business, but primarily as a public service. Broadcasting is usually a monopoly owned and operated by the State.[4] Sometimes programming is entrusted to a separate non-profit corporation, but the transmitting network remains in the hands of the State. When a parallel commercial system exists, it is closely supervised by the State (with one exception in 1983, Italy). Where there are two systems (one being commercial), both are expected to provide not only entertainment but also information, education, and culture.[5] Audiences for the two systems turn out to be approximately equivalent, unlike those in the U.S. Competition between public and commercial broadcasting in Europe indisputably produces good results, like the renaissance of the BBC in the 1950s and that of the Italian RAI in the 1970s.

State control in Europe results in broadcasting usually being centralized in the national capital, although in a few cases it is regionalized.[6] European governments by far prefer the broadcast media to be national, rather than local or international. This preference accounts for the absence, or the very small number, of local broadcasting stations (at least until the late 1970s), and hence their relative lack of specialization. It also accounts for the very late (really only in 1982) awakening of Europe to cable TV. Another effect of State control of broadcasting is that, with few exceptions such as Spain, radio and TV broadcasting is financed by an advance fee paid by users (Table 2), although revenue may also come from strictly regulated advertising.[7]

---

[4]The State may even be a newspaper owner, directly in Spain (when Republican papers were seized by Dictator Franco in the Civil War of 1936–1939), and indirectly in Italy (when dailies owned by business firms were controlled by the State, like the oil giant ENI).

[5]An international survey has shown that whatever the nature of the television schedule (for example, cultural programs are 19.7 percent of TV program hours in France and 8.6 percent in Italy), consumption is about the same (6.4 percent in France and 4.4 percent in Italy) (UNESCO, 1981).

[6]For example, ARD in West Germany and commercial ITV in Great Britain.

[7]Advertising normally does not interrupt television programs. In Germany, advertising is only allowed between 6 and 8 p.m., and (as in Holland) never on Sundays and holidays.

Table 2. Incomes to the Mass Media in 16 European Nations

Country	Annual TV License Fee (in U.S. dollars)[a]		Advertising Expenditures as a Percentage of Gross National Product (in 1980)[c]	Percentage of Advertising Expenditures by Medium (in 1980)[d]		
	Monochrome	Color		Television	Radio	Newspapers & Magazines
1. Austria	103	103	1.04	34.5	15.0	50.5
2. Belgium	67	103	0.55	11.7	0.5	87.8
3. Denmark	76	129	1.31	0	0	100.0
4. Finland	51/62[b]	94/108[b]	1.75	16.3	0	83.7
5. France	51	76	0.80	22.3	14.5	63.2
6. Germany (Federal Republic of)	76	76	0.81	16.9	6.8	76.2
7. Great Britain	28	78	1.83	31.8	3.5	64.7
8. Greece	...	82	0.28	52.2	4.3	43.5
9. Ireland (Eire)	48	55	0.84	35.2	9.2	55.6
10. Italy	28	60	1.25	27.9	0.01	72.0
11. Netherlands	60	101	1.77	11.4	1.8	86.8
12. Norway	83	...	1.33	0	0	100.0
13. Portugal	...	...	0.23	45.4	25.1	29.5
14. Spain	...	...	0.79	36.7	16.3	47.0
15. Sweden	92	126	1.13	0	0	100.0
16. Switzerland	76	150	1.42	12.3	0	87.7

[a] *Source:* The British Broadcasting Corporation.

[b] In Finland, the lower license fee is charged in the one-network region of the country, and the higher fee in the two-network region.

[c] *Source:* Starch INRA Hooper (1981), *World Advertising Expenditures, 1980,* New York.

[d] *Source:* Stern *Magazine* (1981), *Consumer Magazines in Europe,* Hamburg, Gruner and Jahr.

Table 3. Size, Population, and Gross National Product Language Diversity in Eighteen European Nations

Country	Surface Area (in square kilometers)	Population	Density (in persons per square mile)	National Language(s)	Gross National Product (GNP) in U.S. Billions	GNP Per Capital in U.S. dollars
1. Austria	83,853	7,559,440	90	German	$ 76.5 B	$10,230
2. Belgium	30,519	9,863,374	324	French (36%) Flemish (44%)	$ 119.7 B	$12,180
3. Denmark	43,076	5,122,073	119	Danish	$ 66.3 B	$12,950
4. Finland	337,032	4,798,154	14	Finnish Swedish	$ 47.2 B	$ 9,720
5. France	547,026	53,838,000	98	French	$ 627.7 B	$11,730
6. Germany (Federal Republic of)	248,667	61,658,000	247	German	$ 827.7 B	$13,590
7. Great Britain	244,103	55,944,900	229	English	$ 442.8 B	$ 7,920
8. Greece	131,900	9,706,000	72	Greek	$ 42.1 B	$ 4,520
9. Iceland	102,846	229,187	2	Icelandic	$ 2.6 B	$11,330
10. Ireland (Eire)	70,300	3,368,217	49	English Gaelic	$ 16.1 B	$ 4,880
11. Italy	301,263	57,140,355	189	Italian	$ 368.8 B	$ 6,480
12. Luxembourg	2,586	365,100	141	French German Letzeburgish	$ 5.2 B	$14,510
13. Netherlands	33,940	14,208,586	417	Dutch	$ 161.4 B	$11,470
14. Norway	323,895	4,092,340	13	Norwegian	$ 51.6 B	$12,650
15. Portugal	88,941	9,933,000	91	Portuguese	$ 23.1 B	$ 2,350
16. Spain	504,744	37,682,355	74	Spanish	$ 199.7 B	$ 5,350
17. Sweden	448,661	8,317,937	18	Swedish	$ 111.9 B	$13,520
18. Switzerland	41,293	6,329,000	153	German, French, Italian	$ 106.3 B	$16,440
TOTALS	3,584,645	350,154,760	97		$2,902.0 B	...

Advertising, as a whole, is less developed than in the U.S., although the wealth in the two areas is approximately the same: The 1980 GNP of the U.S. was $2,626 billion, and in Western Europe, $2,902 billion (Table 3). In 1980, advertising represented 2.08 percent of the GNP in the U.S., but only 0.80 percent in France, 0.81 percent in Germany, and 1.25 percent in Italy. The lack of advertising is a major cause of the financial crisis that has plagued most European mass media for years, and especially since the mid-1970s, while the U.S. media on the whole maintained their extraordinary profitability.

Although most of the advertising goes to the press (Table 3), newspapers do not get enough income for their needs. This partly explains why, in quite a few cases, they cannot properly be looked upon as a business proposition. For example, in Great Britain most national newspapers are kept alive by group incomes from the provincial newspapers or by non-media resources like the North Sea oil. In Italy the press is subsidized by the textile and chemical industries, and in Norway and in other nations by the State. These newspapers consequently have clear ideological leanings, and may even have political attachments. Although this character is fading, or at least becoming less visible, the European press is clearly more politicized than its American counterpart.[8] This politicization, together with national fragmentation and press regionalism (rather than localism as in the U.S.) explains why syndicates are uncommon, and newspaper diversity is still great. And also relatively mediocre.

The mediocre character of European newspapers can be partly blamed on the press workers and journalists. Labor unions have blocked the introduction of new technology. Newspeople have both resisted formal and specialized education, and maintained an illjustified arrogance in the face of criticism. Hence the poor standing of the journalism profession. It is an old tradition in Europe to suspect journalists of corruption and submissiveness before authority (Rothman and Lichter, 1982). Generally speaking, journalism is not considered a respectable field of university training and research, especially in such countries as Great Britain and Switzerland.

WHAT THE EUROPEAN MASS MEDIA HAVE IN COMMON

The European media have to a large extent experienced the same problems in their evolution, starting with a long struggle against an excess of church and State control and a lack of technological facilities. In the

---

[8]This politicization of the European media is particularly obvious if one compares U.S. news magazines with *Der Spiegel, Oggi,* or *Le Nouvel Observateur.*

17th century, periodicals appeared everywhere in Europe, and dailies in the 18th century. The press gained its independence some time during the early 19th century. Towards the end of that century, the development of communication technology, of political democracy, and of mass advertising enabled the press to become a commercial and popular medium. Radio was launched everywhere in Europe during the early 1920s, and by 1930 had become a State monopoly. TV in most countries was not born until the 1950s.

A similar environment, and a certain degree of imitation,[9] have generated a similarity of organizational structures especially within regions (like Scandinavia) and among nations having experienced a similar upheaval (like fascism in Spain and Italy). This basic similarity is particularly striking in broadcasting. Everywhere in Europe you find public monopolies that produce three or four types of radio programs (pop music, varied entertainment, news and talk, and culture and classical music).

The European print media show a strikingly common feature in both the concentration that has been going on,[10] and its limitation factors: (a) public ownership of broadcasting (or at least of its technical facilities), which has restricted multi-media conglomerates, and (b) State intervention in the form of laws restricting concentration (as in Great Britain and Germany) or of rules benefiting smaller publications (as in France) through financial help (Smith, 1978, p. 53).

In only a few countries (such as Germany) do governments fail to use one or several of the following means of preserving media diversity:

- A low tax rate (the tax rate is zero on value-added earnings in Great Britain, Holland, and Norway).
- Low rates on telecommunications and mail (France, Holland, and Italy).
- Low tax rates on public transportation (for example trains).
- Low-interest loans (Holland, Norway, and Italy).
- Subsidized newsprint (Italy, Spain, France, and Sweden).
- Fiscal incentives to investment (France and Italy).
- Direct aid to newspaper enterprises (Sweden, Norway, and Spain).

In Italy, State assistance represents one-third of total newspaper revenues, and about one-fifth in Norway. Governments often protect tra-

---

[9]Cross-border inspiration is rather limited, however. France was slow to get the message from neighboring Belgium about its separation of government from broadcasting, its expansion of cable, and its tolerance of "free" radio stations and of CB radio.

[10]In the Flemish-speaking part of Belgium, 13 press groups published 19 newspapers 30 years ago, and now 7 groups publish only 12.

ditional media against new communication technologies. For instance, in France, Great Britain, Switzerland, and Holland small-scale experiments with cable TV and/or local-origination TV were set up in the 1970s, but always under such conditions as to ensure their failure. Their closeness to national governments partly accounts for the lack of aggressiveness by the European media. Another cause is simply that conservatives control the press and, in some countries, the government. Few leftist publications have managed to survive. Even in countries where social-democrats always obtain a little under or over half the vote (such as in Great Britain and Sweden), the socialist press reaches only a small minority of the population.[11] In England, only one national daily, the *Mirror,* sides with the Labour Party when it does express an opinion (which is not often).

The diversity of languages in Europe no doubt hampers intercommunication, as does national chauvinism. However, there are exchanges. On a business level, some media groups are multinational, like Bertelsman (Germany) or Del Duca (Italy). Consumers, when they know an appropriate language, make no bones about buying foreign newspapers in that language. The largest circulation magazines in Austria are local editions of German magazines. In Switzerland, German periodicals sell quite well. One of the best-selling women's magazines in France *(Femmes d'Aujourd'hui)* comes from Belgium, as does one of the most famous children's magazines *(Tintin).*

Broadcasting naturally ignores borders. Not only do small nations like highly cabled Belgium consume TV programs from France, Luxembourg, Germany, Holland, and Great Britain, but so also do larger nations like Italy, where special relays were built. People along all European borders get foreign broadcasts without special equipment. For example, Swedish TV reaches half of the Norwegians and half of the Danes. In the Tessin (the Italian-speaking part of Switzerland), Swiss, Italian, French, German, and Yugoslav TV can be watched. Exchanges are also organized, regionally as within Nordvision (in which the five Nordic nations cooperate) or within continent-wide Eurovision (launched in 1954). All nations, little ones particularly, need to buy from several large TV producers (in addition to the U.S.). England buys little and sells a lot; while Sweden buys from all major European nations. Finland is special in that it tries to balance its purchases from the West and East, and is the only country active in both international associations, the Western EBU (European Broadcasting Union) and the Eastern OIRT.

---

[11]In Switzerland, for example, where the Socialist Party gets more votes than any other, the socialist press has a circulation of only 50,000 out of 2.6 million.

EUROPEAN MEDIA DIVERSITY

Obvious differences exist between the extreme north and south of Europe, let us say between Norway and Italy, which are reflected in their mass media. Differences exist also between immediate neighbors like Belgium and Holland, and even within a country, such as between the major cities and the rural parts of Greece or Portugal. The wide diversity necessitates creativity. Solutions have been invented and tested in Europe to some basic problems of the media that are unknown in the U.S. or the Soviet block.

The wealthy, industrial, Protestant north (in Europe) owns media that are much more developed than those of the developing, warm, agricultural, Catholic (and religiously orthodox) south. The same can be said of the Piedmont in Northern Italy, as opposed to Sicily. Every 1,000 Scandinavians read about 500 dailies. In Italy, the consumption is only 200 dailies in the North, but 30 in the South (that is, less than the UNESCO threshold of 100). The six Italian dailies officially considered national together have a circulation equal to that of the British *Daily Telegraph* (about 1.4 million copies).

Whereas in Spain (with 37 million inhabitants) only six dailies sell more than 100,000 copies, in Great Britain (with 56 million inhabitants) six dailies sell over 1 million, and two over 3 million copies. About 83 percent of adult Germans regularly read a newspaper, whereas only 61 percent do in neighboring France. Newspaper consumption is up in Germany and down in France, up in Holland and down in Belgium.[12]

Diversity also manifests itself in another way: small nations (like Norway and Switzerland) import much or most of their TV fare, while larger nations produce most of their own material. Great Britain and France even prepare other countries' information, via news agencies like Reuters and AFP.

THE LEGAL AND POLITICAL ENVIRONMENT FOR THE MEDIA

Some European nations have no general press laws, like Great Britain and Norway. Some have only one, like the 1881 Press Act in France. Nations like Italy (in 1948), Sweden (in 1949) and Spain (in 1978) have integrated the basic principles of their press laws into their constitutions. In some federal countries, like Germany and Switzerland, legal respon-

---

[12]Between 1969 and 1975 the number of dailies sold per 1,000 inhabitants went up in Germany, and down (from 243 to 214) in France.

sibility for the media is held by the *länder* or *cantons,* respectively, not by the national government.

The existence of a press law in a given nation has little relationship to the degree of press freedom actually existing there, contrary to what Anglo-Saxons may think. In England, which has no general press law, freedom is sharply curtailed by the Official Secrets Act, the rules of contempt of court, and libel laws (Lloyd, 1968), whereas in Sweden, the general law excludes censorship *even* in time of war; it forbids anyone to seek a journalist's sources; it makes it a duty for civil servants to answer questions and give access to official archives; and it sets special safeguards in case the press goes on trial.

Certainly the legal obligations for Spanish journalists to have graduated from one of the three journalism schools in the nation was meant to control the size of the profession, just as is the obligation for Italian journalists to pass an exam and be admitted into the Order of Journalists. This Order, on the other hand, has provided exceptional protection for the 7,000 full-time and 13,000 part-time Italian newspeople (it is just about impossible to fire any of them). A French law of 1935 makes it possible for a journalist to quit a newspaper, and get severance pay if the publication clearly changes its line, or its owner. In Holland, the government predicates its financial aid to the signing of a covenant by management and staff that protects the newsroom from owner interference. Indeed, State intervention in press affairs can cut both ways. In Great Britain, local monopoly is the rule and extreme concentration has occurred (as in Denmark). In the rest of Scandinavia, State assistance has allowed the survival of an extraordinary diversity, even including a partisan press. In the late 1970s, 25 Norwegian towns had two dailies and four had three or more.

In order to avoid government intervention (for reasons other than economic), nations in the north of Europe have been pioneers in media accountability systems, Swedish media prople set up something like a press council back in 1916. The British press was threatened by Parliament into setting up a press council in 1953, and then into opening it to lay members in 1963; it thus became a model for many nations in the world, especially the Nordic nations plus (to a certain extent) Holland, Germany, and Austria (Levy, 1967; Bertrand, 1977). In 1969, the Swedish Press Council was provided with an ombudsman to screen public complaints, settle many of them, and initiate some of his own.

MEDIA STRUCTURES IN EUROPE

Differences among European nations are most striking in broadcasting, where these contrasts are mostly due to differences in degree and mode of State involvement. Normally, some public institutions (usually the Ministry of Posts and Telecommunications) owns and operates the distribution and transmitting facilities for broadcasting. The only exceptions outside of Italy (where private radio and TV stations have for some years done what they pleased) are: (a) the recently-tolerated or legalized "free" local radio stations (as in France); (b) some private radio networks (in Spain); (c) the commercial TV stations and long-range radio stations in the micro-nations of Luxembourg and Monaco; and (d) cable systems in Belgium, Holland, and Switzerland.

The State makes major technological decisions. All nations now use the UHF band and the 625-line standard for TV. But Great Britain and France, for instance, started in VHF, one with a 415-line standard, the other with a 819-line standard.[13] On the other hand, all European nations, except France, prefer the German PAL color TV process to the French SECAM. Also the State decides whether a second, third, or fourth radio or TV channel is to be launched, whether the channels will compete or will complement each other, how many hours will be broadcast, etc.

The State is also responsible for the development of cable TV. Originally the huge investment and the threat to existing media were only felt to be justified in mountainous countries (like Austria and Switzerland) and/or small nations surrounded by heavy TV producers. Big nations, presumably insecure about their unity, were apprehensive about the local and transnational capabilities of cable TV. In the early 1980s the penetration of cable was negligible in France, Great Britain, and Germany, and where it existed, it mainly functioned as mere CATV (community antenna TV). In late 1982, Belgium and Holland were the most cabled countries. In the former most systems were run by electric power companies, and in the latter about half were run by municipalities.

Basically, traditional broadcasting systems can be divided into three categories:

1. Nations that maintain a monopoly for public radio and TV, like Sweden or Greece. In some nations, all functions are assumed by a single company, as in Austria; or one company per language group, like RTB (French) and BRT (Flemish) in Belgium. In other nations, programming is entrusted to two or more companies, as in France (where seven share the work, with two central programming units and one that is regional), or in Germany (where the first company, ARD, is a cooperative of autonomous regional stations, and the second, ZFD, is a national network, while the third is a regional of the ARD stations).

---

[13]Which both of them began phasing out in the early 1980s.

2. Nations that allow the existence of a private broadcasting system parallel to the public one like Great Britain, where it is tightly-controlled, and Italy, where it is not. In the British ITV system, 15 regional companies provide programs (and commercials) that a public institution, IBA, checks and transmits. In Italy, although the Constitutional Court has only allowed private firms to broadcast locally, in 1982 even over-the-air commercial networks operated quite freely.

3. One nation, Holland, has a system all its own: 60 percent of the programming is entrusted to associations (supposedly ideological) which obtain air time in proportion to their membership, actually to the number of subscribers to their weekly guide.[14]

With the exception of the Dutch system, the national government always maintains the right to appoint all (Great Britain), most (France after 1982), or many (Sweden) of the members of the top broadcasting board. Sometimes the national parliament (Italy) or the regional legislatures (Germany) enjoy that prerogative. In some cases appointments are non-partisan (Great Britain), while in some the party in power appoints only its own people (France before 1982). In other nations, appointments are proportional to the strength of the majority party and its opposition. In Italy, for instance, the first channel of RAI-TV is supposedly dominated by the Christian-Democrat Party, while the second RAI-TV channel is Socialist-Communist. Then there is the special phenomenon of "peripheral" stations whose transmitters are situated just outside France: The French government tolerates the operation of four private commercial stations, two of which cover the nation (and two of which operate short-range TV stations), the reason being that the French State is the majority stockholder of three of these peripheral stations (via the SOFIRAD holding company).

The state also decides how broadcasting is to be financed. The norm is an annual user's fee supplemented by advertising, although there is no advertising in four of the five Nordic countries (the exception is Finland). In Great Britain, the BBC is funded by an audience users' fee, whereas ITV lives on advertising. In Germany, ARD gets the larger part of its income from the license fee, and ZDF from advertising. In Spain, funding for television comes from advertising revenues and from the State budget.

---

[14]In other European nations broadcasting guides normally hold the circulation record: *Hör Zu* (3,881,000 copies) in Germany; *Radio Times* (3,697,000, BBC) and *TV Times* (3,649,000 ITV) in Great Britain; *Télé 7 Jours* (2,563,000) in France, etc. These circulation figure are for 1980.

As regards the print media, on the contrary, the State has little influence, at least directly, with their variegated development and structures. Ownership is in private hands, from transnational conglomerates that own 85 percent of the British national press (with foreign-based giants owning one-third), to foundations, such as are entrusted with the control of 11 Danish newspapers accounting for 40 percent of total circulation. Some nations, like Greece, have a powerful national press. In Great Britain, the London-based newspapers enjoy nearly twice the circulation of the provincial press (15 to 8 million copies, respectively). In France, on the contrary (and contrary to the situation there before World War II), provincial papers sell three times as many copies as the Paris dailies.[15]

Some countries have a distinct national popular press: Sweden has two tabloids, and England has five. The only one in Germany, the *Bild Zeitung*, enjoys the European circulation record. The right-wingism and vulgarity of the *Bild* and the British *Sun* do seem somewhat archaic. But some of the less-developed European countries, on the other hand, seem incapable of generating a popular daily press, like Spain or Italy (where the popular press consists of illustrated weeklies, especially the sentimental *fumetti*, or photo-comics, of Italy). An interesting compromise is to be found in the Netherlands and Denmark where quality dailies publish popular versions of themselves. The Dutch *Telegraaf* puts out *Het Nieuws van der Tag,* and Copenhagen's *Berlingske Tidende* publishes *B.T.*

Differences are no less clear in the end-of-the-week press. The eight national Sunday papers in Great Britain sell 20 percent more than the nine dailies; in France, only one daily in five has a "seventh day" edition; and in Norway there are no Sunday editions. In Spain, strangely, the Monday papers (*Hojas del Lunes*) have long been required by law to be produced not by their owners, but by their journalists.[16]

Generally speaking, it is difficult to compare newspaper figures from various countries (although we try, in Table 4). One reason is that, while most countries divide circulation figures between dailies and weeklies, Scandinavians distinguish newspapers published more or less than three times a week. Another reason is that Great Britain, France, and Italy, for instance, have regional newspapers with zoned editions, whereas Belgium,

---

[15]Only the austere *Le Monde* can be called a national newspaper, although other newspapers are offered for sale in the provinces. In Italy, the major newspapers published in Milan, Turin, and Rome are influential, but cannot be called truly national.

[16]The monopoly conferred to journalist associations in Spain has been broken since 1980 with the publication on Mondays of the most important Spanish dailies. A consequence is the progressive disappearance of *Hojas del Lunes;* in 1980 there were 33, and three years later only 25.

Table 4. Mass Media Systems in 18 European Nations

Country	Number of Daily Newspapers	Total Newspaper Circulation (millions)	Broadcasting System	News Agency
1. Austria	30	2.6	Three radio and 2 TV systems, government-owned.	Austria Presse Agentur, owned by the media.
2. Belgium	38	2.2	Three radio and 2 TV channels in each of two languages (govt. financed); also many free radio stations.	Agence Belga and Agentschaap Belga.
3. Denmark	55	1.9	Three radio and 1 TV system, stateowned.	Ritzaus Bureau I/S.
4. Finland	94	2.6	Two radio and 2 TV systems, all govt.-owned (but one private company produces TV programs).	STT-FNB, owned by the media.
5. France	86	8.7	Three national radio channels and 3 TV programming companies, all govt.-controlled.	Agence France Presse.
6. Germany (Federal Republic of)	124	20.0	Two federally-funded radio stations, plus many others; ARD is an association of 9 German states that airs 3 radio channels plus 1 national TV channel.	Deutsche Presse Agentur.
7. Great Britain	110	24.0	BBC (government) provides 2 TV channels plus 5 national radio channels; 2 commercial TV channels and 39 local radio stations.	Reuters (international news) plus Press Association (domestic).

8. Greece	88	1.0	Public broadcasting (10 radio channels plus 2 TV channels).	—
9. Iceland	6	0.1	State broadcasting system for radio and TV.	—
10. Ireland (Eire)	7	0.5	State broadcasting system: 3 radio and 2 TV channels.	—
11. Italy	80	5.0	RAI (the state system) has 3 radio and 3 TV channels; 2,000 private radio and 300 TV stations.	ANSA and Italia.
12. Luxembourg	4	0.2	CIT is the broadcasting monopoly, with radio channels in 5 languages and TV in 2, directed to neighboring nations.	—
13. Netherlands	89	4.7	Four radio and 2 TV channels nationally, with most programs produced by consumers' associations.	ANP
14. Norway	156	2.1	NRK is a state monopoly largely independent of government.	Norsk Telegrambyná.
15. Portugal	21	0.5	Four nationalized radio channels plus one church channel; 2 state-owned TV channels.	—
16. Spain	118	3.3	Two state-owned radio networks, plus many private stations; 2 TV channels are a state monopoly.	EFE, others.
17. Sweden	161	4.4	Sveriges Radio is non-commercial, operating 2 national radio channels plus 2 TV channels.	TT
18. Switzerland	126	2.8	SSR is a non-profit corporation that operates 2 radio channels and 1 TV channel in each of 3 languages.	ATS

Holland, Germany, and Switzerland have editorial units producing many similar newspapers, all with different titles.

Obviously, in countries with a higher-than-average level of education, newspaper sales are higher.[17] The price of dailies plays a part too, as does the availability of newspapers.[18] Most important is whether newspapers are home-delivered: They are in the north of Europe, and in the north and east of France. In the south of Europe they rarely are. In Italy, newspapers can only be sold by news vendors.

EUROPEANIZATION OF THE MASS MEDIA IN EUROPE

The mass media in Western Europe are characterized by great variety and concentration. It is impossible to put them in homogeneous groupings. The diversity of Europe—of which the media are a reflection—defies any classification that does not keep in mind national borders or the geographical and historical differences of well-defined areas. National borders have been, and continue to be, the main obstacle, in addition to linguistic diversity, to the emergence of international European media that would embrace the entire continent or the part of the continent in which they are located. Although the most important daily newspapers of France, Great Britain, Germany, and Italy are sold in the capitals of all the Western countries, only one of them has made the effort necessary to enable its being read in foreign cities at the same time as in its city of origin. Paradoxically, the only daily newspaper that has a truly European circulation is North American. Let us look briefly at these two cases: *The Financial Times* and the *International Herald Tribune*.

The British daily newspaper, *The Financial Times* (specializing in economic themes but also covering current politics and culture) began publication simultaneously in London and Frankfurt (Germany) in 1979. Part of both editions is common copy, sent by facsimile from Great Britain with another portion prepared especially in Frankfurt. This German city lies less than four-hundred kilometers (250 miles) from such important political and industrial centers as Paris, Brussels, Amsterdam, Hamburg, Munich, and Zurich, to which it is linked by excellent highways and rail-

---

[17]The existence of daily newspapers exclusively devoted to sports seems to be a sign of relative underdevelopment: There is one in France, one in Great Britain, two in Greece, five in Italy, and five in Spain.

[18]In 1983 the price of daily newspapers was 40 to 52 (U.S.) cents in France, 10 to 15 cents in Great Britain (the *Financial Times* at 20 cents is an exception), 23 to 26 cents in Spain, and 15 to 33 cents in Germany.

ways. Consequently, daily copies of this newspaper rapidly reach throughout this wide area; in 1982, the European edition of the *Financial Times* accounted for 41,000 copies out of its total circulation of 204,000 copies. In addition, a Lufthansa cargo flight leaves Frankfurt every night, and due to the time difference, arrives in New York at 6:30 a.m., local time. The *Financial Times* is then sold in New York at 9:30 a.m., almost the same time of day as in London and Frankfurt.

The *International Herald Tribune*, founded in Paris in 1887 as the European edition of the *New York Herald*, today is an independently-staffed newspaper although among its proprietors are *The New York Times* and the *Washington Post*. This successful newspaper reaches its public, overcoming the barriers of international borders, thanks to (a) the English language's position as Europe's *lingua franca*, and (b) the current world interest in American points of view. To improve its speed of distribution, the *International Herald Tribune* began to publish simultaneous editions by facsimile in Paris and London in 1974, in Zurich in 1977 (and, via satellite transmission, an Asian edition in Hong Kong). At present its readers can be found in every country in Europe, making it an international journalistic accomplishment difficult to equal.

During 1980, the average daily circulation of the *International Herald Tribune* was 129,827 copies, of which 109,921 (85 percent) were sold in Europe (Table 5).

Table 5. Average Daily Circulation of the
International Herald Tribune in Europe

Country	Daily Circulation
1. Austria	1,780
2. Belgium/Luxembourg	5,592
3. Denmark	1,213
4. Finland	380
5. France	19,328
6. Germany	15,642
7. Great Britain	16,552
8. Greece	2,628
9. Netherlands	3,880
10. Italy	5,485
11. Portugal	930
12. Spain	4,014
13. Sweden	1,375
14. Switzerland	10,760
15. Other Europe	2,996
16. European-based airlines	17,366
Total	109,921

Table 6. International Circulation of Selected European Newspapers

Country/Newspaper	Total Daily Circulation	Circulation in Foreign Countries as a Percentage of Total Circulation
1. France		
Le Monde	431,536	16.7
France-Soir	712,491	5.3
Le Figaro	402,436	5.0
2. Germany (Federal Republic of)		
Frankfurter Allgemaine Zeitung	352,547	8.6
Die Welt	276,075	7.0
3. Great Britain		
The Times	315,873	10.6
Daily Telegram	1,315,061	3.0
Daily Express	2,750,614	3.0
4. Italy		
Corriere della Sera	517,000	6.0
La Stampa	420,892	4.1
5. Switzerland		
Neue Zurcher Zeitung	101,010	16.4

National and linguistic barriers pose difficult limits to international circulation of the great European dailies (Table 6), with the previously detailed exception of the *Financial Times*. Nevertheless, there have been efforts at cooperation that reveal the existence of an impulse toward European integration. Thus, in 1972 the dailies *The Times* (London), *Le Monde* (Paris), *Die Welt* (Bonn) and *La Stampa* (Turin) established a common editorial staff to produce a monthly supplement on a theme chosen by common agreement. Once edited, the supplement was published on several pages of each of the four collaborating newspapers, in their respective languages. This supplement was called *Europe* because its basic purpose was "to present to Europeans the elements of an explanation of the world in which they live, offering them a realistic vision from the European point of view."[19] The experiment ended in 1981, due in part to economic pressures and to the difficulties of cooperation among the four newspapers.

Nevertheless, the idea of a European daily newspaper continues to preoccupy the leaders of the press in a number of countries, as the director

---

[19]This statement was made by Jacqueline Grapin, editor-in-chief of *Europa* in its final stages of publication, to the monthly magazine *30 Jours d'Europe*.

of the International Press Institute, Peter Galliner, indicated before the Japanese Newspaper Publishers' and Editors' Association in 1981:

> It must be a paper which should be published in at least two if not three languages; Spanish must be one of the languages, English and French most likely the other two. Perhaps one should be less ambitious, perhaps one should start first of all to create such a paper in one language only. This may be a highly interesting and worthwhile journalistic experiment. I have comparatively little doubt that such a paper would be financially viable, because you could get a relatively large circulation together and at the same time you would need and get the business support from industry for such a publication.

Magazines, not subject to the demands of daily news reporting, can cross borders more easily than newspapers, especially if we remember that in five European countries there are important population centers that speak the language of bordering nations: Belgium, divided into two linguistic communities; Austria (where 98 percent of the population speak German); Ireland (where 94 percent speak English); Finland (7 percent speak Swedish); and Switzerland (where German, French, and Italian are the official languages). There is a considerable circulation in these countries for magazines published by one of the neighbors: France's *Paris-Match* has a total circulation of 621,537, with 29 percent of sales outside of France; *Burda Moden* has a circulation of 2,194,939, with 28 percent outside of Germany; and *Women's Weekly* has a circulation of 1,631,966, with 17 percent outside of Great Britain. *L'Express* (in its international edition) sells 60,800 copies in 15 European nations, compared to 545,000 copies in France; *The Economist* sells 31,100 copies in 15 European nations, compared to 68,600 in Great Britain. Impressive as these foreign sales in Europe are for *L'Express* and *The Economist*, they are far outdistanced by the American news magazine *Time*, which sells 400,000 copies in 16 European nations.

In the future, the internationalism of European media will increase, as the current technologies of facsimile and satellites make long-distance printing faster and easier. Publication by tele-facsimile, pioneered by the *Asahi Simbun* between Tokyo and Sapphoro in 1959, has been used by Parisian newspapers (in addition to the *International Herald Tribune*). Since 1976, printing centers have operated at some 400 kilometers (250 miles) from Paris in order to serve their circulation zones more quickly. Pioneering the use of satellites in newspaper publication was the North American *Wall Street Journal* with an Asian edition (of 25,000 copies) in 1976. *The Wall Street Journal*, after having achieved simultaneous publication throughout the United States through a series of coast-to-coast publishing centers that receive pages via satellite, began a European edition (of 10,000 copies) in 1983. Further important transformations in newspaper publishing are going to come with other new communication technologies, particularly combinations of cable and direct-transmission satellites.

The new media and their consequences are examined in other chapters of the present book. The panorama of the European air waves as described in this chapter will be modified considerably in the future. Control over radio and especially over TV transmission, dominated by European governments until now, will either cease or will change in form to maintain its nature.

When the decade of the 1980s reaches its end, the European mass media will have attained an interpenetration far greater than now. Perhaps in this manner Europe, without losing its basic diversity, can become closer to its desired unity.

REFERENCES

Claude-Jean Bertrand (1977), "Press Councils: An Evaluation," *Gazette, 23,* 217–229.

Philip H. Levy (1967), *The Press Council: History, Procedures, and Cases,* London: St. Martin's Press.

Herbert M. Lloyd (1968), *The Legal Limits of Journalism,* London: Pergamon.

F. Rothman and S. R. Lichter (1982), "Media and Business Elites: Two Classes in Conflict?" *The Public Interest, 69,* 117–125.

A. Smith (1978), "State Intervention and the Management of the Press," in James Curran (ed.), *The British Press: A Manifesto,* London: Macmillan.

Nadine Toussaint-Desmoulins and Ch. Lateinturier (1980), *Analyse Comparative de l'Evolution de la Concentration dans le Secteur de la Presse: Belgique, France, Grande-Bretagne, Italie, Pays Bas, Republique Federale d'Allemagne,* Brussels: Commission des Communautes Europeennes.

Jeremy Tunstall (1982), "West European Media Superpower?" *The Media Reporter,* 32–37.

UNESCO (1981), *Trois Semaines de Télévision: Une Comparaison Internationale,* Paris: Report.

Chapter 2

Mass Media in the United States in the 1980s[1]

Bradley S. Greenberg
Michigan State University, East Lansing

INTRODUCTION

The United States is a very mass media-saturated society, but the audience attention to such traditional media as newspapers, radio, and television is increasing. And cable television, along with certain other new media, is booming. New communication technologies like the computer and the satellite are also bringing about major changes in the nature of the existing media. For example, many of the additional channels recently added to cable television systems are provided by satellite transmission. While print and broadcasting media in the United States are predominantly commercial enterprises (and very profitable), a small but growing public radio and television also exists. Overall, the U.S. mass media are dynamic, commercially successful, and rapidly changing.   *E.M.R., F.B.*

Tom and Debbie Morrison and their two children live in a suburb of a middle-sized city (about 200,000 population) in the central part of the United States. Tom is a partner in an insurance agency and Debbie has been a part-time teacher at a local community college. Their daughter, Beth, is a high school freshman, and their son, Richard, a first-grader. Their home contains the inventory of mass media available in many if not most American homes. There are two television sets, at least one of them in color. The largest set is connected to the local cable television system, whose franchise to operate has been granted by the political entity that governs their suburb. The cable firm provides 33 channels for $9 a month, and offers three premium channels (two with movies recently shown in local theaters and one with films labeled as ''soft pornography'') each at an additional $9 per month. The Morrisons subscribe to one of the premium channels for films.

Tom still has his television aerial on his roof—just in case the cable system has problems. By rotating his antenna, he can pick up three nearby stations, one from each of the major commercial television networks, one public television station, and on clear nights, two or three more distant

[1]Suggestions and/or sources of information for this chapter were kindly provided by Carrie Jill Heeter, Kay Ingram, Barry Litman, Steve Meuche, Robert Page, and Stan Soffin, all at Michigan State University.

stations with essentially the same network programs. There are half a dozen radio sets scattered through the house; most of them receive both AM and FM signals. A dozen local radio stations within a 15-mile radius, and an equal number of more distant signals, provide alternative programming. Each of the two family cars offers radio to the driver and passengers. One auto has a tape/record stereo system that gives the family the option of selecting its own music. A second in the teenager's bedroom permits her to listen endlessly and privately to her collection of rock music, particularly if she uses the earphones available to her.

Two daily newspapers arrive on the doorstep, one in the morning and the other in the late afternoon. The former comes from a major city some 80 miles away and the latter from the suburb's adjacent city center. Each is about 40 pages, nearly two-thirds of which is advertising content. In most American homes, there would be but a single daily newspaper, but Tom wants to read a paper with his morning coffee, as well as when he returns home from work. In addition, the Thursday mail brings a weekly paper with strictly suburban news.

A total communication inventory of this household also would include the telephone and its two extensions, the movie and still cameras occasionally used, and certainly the receipt of several news, professional, teen, and fashion magazines that are mail-delivered. But we describe only the three major media in some detail, later in this chapter.

That is a composite of the media environment of the American family today. All data describe the majority of U.S. homes, except for the penetration of cable. What media will this household have in 1989? Even with the teenager likely away at college, there will be a significant upgrading of the family's media systems:

- Cable offerings may have expanded to a 54-channel system, including several pay services in addition to the premium channels. The cable company will have activated the return cable capacity from the home, making the system interactive. The Morrisons will subscribe to the security system for burglar and fire protection available through the cable system, and will access their checking account and thus pay bills on their bank's cable TV channel.
- The larger number of television offerings will induce the Morrisons to invest in a videotape recorder ($400 to $500). They can tape one show, watch another, borrow tapes from the local library, and share movie tapes they have recorded on their premium channel with the neighboring family that is taping movies on a different premium channel.

- Tom's passion for gadgets will convince him that an inexpensive home videocamera ($200 to $300) will be the ultimate in sound, motion, and picture for recording his family's trips, adventures, and holidays. Instant playback of these home movies will be a major selling point, as well as the ability to record over mistakes.
- Off comes the unsightly rooftop antenna. Up goes a more modest satellite dish ($200 to $300). In come additional television signals and numerous viewing options. The dish can pick up programs not available on the cable system, including foreign signals, and it can even pick up a premium channel that is subscribed to and descrambled in the home. All that makes direct reception of satellite signals worth the relatively small initial cost of the dish antenna.
- High quality radio signals fed through the cable and into the home's stereo system increase listening pleasure and choices.
- Sometime before the end of the decade, a small home computer ($200 to $2,000) will be integrated into this home's media system. The initial excuse may be that it is primarily for Richard to play video games, but Richard's in-school computer programming course and the proliferation of available software for the computer will soon make it a home utility for much more than entertainment functions. Schoolwork, the family budget, tax-form information and preparation, the social and professional calendar of family members, an inventory of home videotapes—all will find their way into computer storage. The home computer will interface with broadcast and cable signals for video games, videotex, the computer network of friends, and will provide access to several major computer data-banks.

It is likely their daughter's college dormitory will have a computer terminal in the lounge and an electronic mailbox for each resident; the problem of children never writing home may be thus diminished.

Wishful thinking? I doubt it. Current purchase trends and available information on technology development suggest this is a modest inventory of expected changes in the next 6 years. But let us now end both the current family portrait and our speculation about its future. The remainder of this chapter will describe three major segments of the U.S. media industry as they exist in the early 1980s: daily newspapers, radio, and television. For each, the institutional structure, ownership and organizational patterns, content emphases, and audiences, among other attributes, will be examined. Such a description is likely to be a bombardment of information and data. As such information tends to pile up, remind yourself occasionally of the Morrison family, their current and potential media environment, and how the composition of the industry may impact on them.

THE DAILY NEWSPAPER IN THE U.S.

Daily newspapers in small cities in the United States consist of 20 to 30 pages on weekdays, exclusive of special advertising sections. In larger communities, they are 40 to 50 pages, and in the largest cities, they are about 70 pages. A systematic analysis of the content of those papers, regardless of their size, indicates that about two-fifths of the pages are given to display advertising and another 20 percent to classified advertising. For your 15–25 cent purchase of the paper, one-third of the content will consist of news. "Soft" news (sports, leisure-time activities, feature columnists and entertainment, feature stories, social events, marriages, etc.) fills 24 percent of the pages. "Hard" news (politics, crime, disaster, and government) consists typically of 5 percent local news and 8 percent of national and foreign news.

Trends in the Number of Newspapers and Their Circulation

There are about 1,750 daily newspapers in the United States, and somewhat more than 700 Sunday papers. The overall number of daily papers has remained very stable since the end of World War II, preceded by a loss of about 300 daily newspapers between 1920 and 1945. A strong share of the losses came in major cities where the second or third daily paper folded. As of 1982, fewer than three dozen cities in the United States had competing daily newspapers; the great majority do not. In contrast, there has been a substantial growth in Sunday papers in the last decade.

Although there are three afternoon papers for each morning paper in the U.S., the overall circulation differences are small because most morning papers are located in major cities and most afternoon papers are in small communites. In 1981, total daily newspaper circulation was a little more than 62 million copies; of this total, 29.5 million copies came from the 400 morning papers and 32.8 million from the nearly 1,400 afternoon dailies. Further, since the mid-1970s, there has been a measurable increase in both the number and circulation of morning papers, primarily resulting from the conversion of afternoon papers. The daily circulation totals have not changed much in the last 10 years while Sunday circulation has increased by more than 10 million copies, reaching 55 million copies in 1980.

As one might infer, the vast majority of daily newspapers serve small communities and have a small circulation. They make available local news and local advertising. Whereas about 75 papers are published in communities of at least half a million population, more than 1,200 papers serve cities of 50,000 or fewer people. The former distribute 14.5 million copies each morning and an additional 7 million in the afternoon, or 280,000 per newspaper. The small dailies distribute 3 million morning copies and 12.5 million in the afternoon, or 13,000 per newspaper. Stated somewhat differently, the 35 largest newspapers in the country distribute 25 percent of all the daily newspapers.

As these figures intimate, the United States has no truly "national" newspaper, in contrast with several European nations. Perhaps those papers most often thought of as national in nature are *The Wall Street Journal* and *The New York Times*. The *Journal* is the largest daily newspaper in the United States, with a circulation slightly greater than 1.8 million daily. The *Times* circulation is about 900,000. In 1982, *US Today* was launched as a national paper by the Gannett Company, and has gotten off to a fast start in circulation. In 1983, only two other U.S. dailies exceed one million daily circulation: *The New York News* and the *Los Angeles Times*. Ten others maintain half a million or more sales each day.

Group ownership is and has been characteristic of the daily newspaper in the United States. About 150 different groups own 1,150 daily newspapers, or 65 percent of all the dailies. Although more than half the groups own but two or three papers, a few very large groups dominate the newspaper industry. Gannett owns nearly 100 daily newspapers with a total daily circulation nearing 4 million; Knight-Ridder has the same circulation with some three dozen papers; the Hearst chain has been reduced to 15 papers and 1.3 million daily readers. The other major circulation groups include Dow Jones (2.4 million), Newhouse (3.1 million), Scripps-Howard (1.5 million), Thomson (75 papers and 1.2 million), Times-Mirror (2.3 million), and the *Chicago Tribune* group (3 million). The 10 largest groups encompass over 35 percent of total U.S. circulation.

In 1980, advertising revenues for U.S. daily newspapers exceeded $8 billion; 5 years earlier, it had been $5 billion. Among medium-size newspapers (30,000–40,000 circulation), advertising receipts account for two-thirds of total revenues; among large city papers (250,000), advertising receipts account for three-fourths of revenues.

The Newspaper Audience

Who reads the daily newspaper? Numerous academic and industry studies have identified the principal characteristics of newspaper readers and non-readers. First, the weekday reader audience is just about two-thirds of the American population 18 years of age or older. Thus, a substantial portion of the adult population does not read a daily newspaper on a regular basis. The following differences in readership characteristics have also been found with considerable consistency.

1. Men and women read the daily paper with equal frequency.
2. Young adults (18–34) are less likely to read a daily paper.
3. Education is a strong correlate of newspaper readership; only half of those with a grammar school or less education read a daily paper, compared with three-fourths of college graduates.
4. Income correlates in a similar fashion to education; three-fourths of those with household incomes of $25,000 or more read a daily paper; only half of those under $10,000 do so.
5. Differences by occupation are not as large as for income or education, but the pattern is similar, with more reading by professionals, managers, and administrators than by any other occupational group.

In addition, smaller but consistent differences indicate that married persons are more likely to be readers of newspapers than are singles. Caucasians are more likely readers than other ethnic groups, and those living in the northeastern United States or in any metropolitan area read the daily newspaper more frequently.

The Changing Technology of Newspaper Production

Our general inspection of the daily newspaper in the United States in the early 1980s concludes with projections for the end of this decade. The video display terminals that are commonplace in large newsrooms and in journalism school teaching labs as replacements for typewriters, are likely to be only one of many technological innovations adopted by major newspapers. Here is a sampling:

- Transmitting newscopy electronically to remote printing facilities will create small out-of-state publishing plants with which major metropolitan newspapers will attempt to penetrate new markets. It is likely that computers will be linked to satellites in some cases, avoiding more costly land-leased telephone lines.
- Reporters will be equipped with remote computer/typing terminals, so that on-site reporting can be done in the same fashion as in-house story preparation, and (when edited) fed directly to the printing facility.
- Field photographers will experiment with cameras whose content can be transmitted electronically, thus avoiding the need to transport and process standard film.

- Advertising agencies will do far more with computer graphics and related technology in the preparation and updating of advertising copy. Computerized text and layout terminals should be in wide use.
- Video newspapers will be offered, using text broadcast on leased channels on local cable systems or more interactive systems whereby a reader can randomly access selected portions of a newspaper by means of a special decoding device linked to his home TV set or cable system.
- The newspaper will consist of a complex automated information system, wherein old stories, data, reference material, revenues, circulation, and subscription information will be easily retrievable. Storage needs will be a fraction of their current physical demands.
- In addition to the use of satellites by publishers to deliver news-copy to remote printing plants, satellites will also be used by commercial news services, e.g., the Associated Press and United Press International, to deliver news to clients. Satellites also will enable group-owned newspapers to share information bases and news-copy.
- The large-scale data-base maintained by a newspaper will find commercial uses such as the provision of services to customers; for example, newspapers will market information services from their data-base to small businesses, sales firms, government agencies, and individual subscribers. What initially was created to make the publishing of a newspaper more timely and cost-effective will itself become a diversified income-producing segment of the newspaper industry.

RADIO IN THE UNITED STATES

Home, office, car, beach, park, jogging, restaurant—radio is there, radio is everywhere. Sound like a commercial? Yes, but there would be truth in such advertising. It results from total public access to radio receivers and to an extraordinary abundance of radio station signals. Everyone has radios. They are in 99 percent of U.S. households, and 95 prcent of cars (not necessarily U.S.-made cars). There are 340 million radios in U.S. homes and 120 million elsewhere; there are 5.5 radios per U.S. household.

Commercial Radio
At the end of 1981, 9,092 radio stations were operating in the United States. These included 4,630 commercial AM stations, 3,346 commercial FM stations, and 1,116 noncommercial FM stations. Radio stations have

bred rapidly in the last 30 years. There were 2,351 AM stations in 1951, 3,667 in 1961, and 4,383 in 1971. In those same years, there were 676 commercial FM stations, then 815, then 2,196. Such large numbers do not necessarily mean stations that have announcers, news staffs, and disc jockeys. Fully 1,500 of these stations (about 16 percent of the total) were fully automated, using tapes or national distribution by satellite to program music, public affairs, and feature shows. Further, the number of automated stations is expected to double before the next decade begins.

Visit Boston, a city of 600,000 people, and you can choose from some 9 AM and 8 FM stations. If you prefer a southern city, like Atlanta, with a population of 400,000, you can hear 22 AM and 9 FM stations. Go west to San Diego, with 800,000 people, and you'll find 10 AM and 19 FM stations. Seattle, with only 500,000 people, has some 30 stations. If you're a big city enthusiast, Chicago, with more than 3 million people, has 15 AM and 17 FM stations to fill your ears. No medium has expanded in the United States as has radio.

The proliferation of stations has occurred in part because of the license allocation policy to provide local broadcast service throughout the nation. But all stations are not equal. There are four major classes of AM stations and three major classes of commercial FM stations, classes being a function of the power of the station to transmit. For AM, Class 1 stations (1 percent of the total) serve remote rural areas as well as large population centers; Class 2 stations (25 percent) serve a population center and an adjacent rural area; Class 3 stations (50 percent) share a regional channel with many similar stations to serve a population center and an adjacent rural area; Class 4 stations (24 percent) share a local channel with a very limited range. For FM, class A stations can provide good service for about 15 miles and are assigned throughout the country; Class B stations can serve a broadcasting distance of about 33 miles and are limited to 18 northeastern states and to southern California; Class C stations transmit for 64 miles throughout the rest of the country.

Radio stations are formatted; music is by far the dominant format. Stations develop identities on the basis of a single primary orientation to the type of music they play. Among AM stations, in the spring of 1982, the three most frequent formats were adult contemporary/pop music (25 percent of all stations), country music (21 percent), and standard/nostalgic music (13 percent). AM stations that were all-news formats comprised 8 percent of the total stations. Then came religious (7 percent) and black music (5 percent) stations.

Adult contemporary music was also the dominant format for FM stations (21 percent). Then came country music and "beautiful music" (each with 16 percent), album-oriented rock (13 percent), and other rock (12 percent); no other type was found among more than 4 percent of the stations. All-news FM stations were virtually nonexistent. "Music, news, and sports" may be the slogan used by stations priming their advertisers and their audience, but it would be more accurate to describe U.S. radio as "music, music, and music."

Audience preferences for radio formats correspond closely to the distribution of station formats; when audience preferences change, stations change their formats. National ratings for the largest 100 radio markets indicated that adult contemporary music drew a 20 percent share of the radio audience (a substantial drop), country music a 15 percent share, easy listening ("beautiful" music) 11 percent, album-oriented rock at 10 percent, and other rock at 8 percent. In that ratings period (of three months), standard nostalgic music had a 9 percent share, more than double the prior year's rating.

Four major networks provide national programming (primarily short newscasts and features) to somewhat to more than 60 percent of the commercial AM stations in the U.S. The largest of these has been the ABC radio network with more than 30 percent of the affiliated stations, the Mutual Broadcasting System with 17 percent, and the CBS and NBC radio networks, each with 5 to 6 percent. In 1977, the ABC radio network subdivided into four formatted networks: one each for entertainment, contemporary and information programming, and one for FM stations.

Prime-time radio is primarily drive-time radio. The commercial radio audience is largest between 6 and 10 a.m. It is smallest after 6 p.m., when television takes over as the country's principal media habit. In the early morning hours, more than 20 percent of all adults are listening to radio, for a little more than an hour during that time block. Overall radio listening averages about three hours a day per person in the United States, according to the Radio Advertising Bureau. Males listen more than 4 hours per day, with 18–24 year olds constituting the largest age–sex listening group by far. Least-frequent listening groups are men and women 50 and over, and teenagers. Certain "upscale" groups spend more time with radio than with television or print media: college graduates, professional/managerial men, full-time working women, and those with household incomes greater than $30,000.

Both radio and television operate within the principles established by the U.S. Congress in the Communications Act of 1934. That act established the Federal Communications Commission (FCC) as the regulatory agency which oversees broadcasting in the United States. The FCC has three principal regulatory activities: (a) the allocation of space on the frequency spectrum to broadcast services; (b) the assignment of station operators in each service to specific frequencies with technical and power requirements; and (c) the regulation of existing stations.

Presently, the FCC is proposing major changes in its regulatory stance toward radio, all designed to deregulate. The FCC asked Congress to abolish the Fairness Doctrine (which requires that reasonable opportunity be afforded for the presentation of opposing views), to withdraw the obligation to provide reasonable access to the public, and to repeal the provision that insists on equitable distribution of broadcast services nation-wide.

Several hundred "groups" own radio and television properties. There are several hundred, rather than a few, because FCC rules limit multiple ownership to 12 AM and 12 FM (up from 7 in 1984), and 7 TV stations. Monopolization of broadcasting signals cannot accrue from station ownership.

The total amount paid by advertisers to buy radio time in 1980 was slightly more than $4 billion, of which $3 billion was in local billings, $200 million in network ad sales, and the remainder spot advertising. Six years earlier, total audio advertising was only half that amount. All this accumulates from the sales of commercial advertising time. In major markets, ads may run $600 or more for a 30-second spot, down to a few dollars at the smallest radio stations. The top national radio advertisers include auto companies, food product companies, travel and shipping firms, and alcohol, each accounting for more than 10 percent of national radio expenditures. The top local advertisers are auto dealers, department stores, banks, and clothing stores, each accounting for more than 7.5 percent of all local radio advertising expenditures.

Public Radio

Among the 1,100 noncommercial FM radio stations licensed in 1981, 850 were very small, with less than a handful of employees, few broadcast hours, a very limited transmission range, and located largely in educational facilities. The remaining 250 were members of the National Public Radio (NPR) system, governed by the member stations. NPR provides an interconnection service and programs. NPR member stations were interconnected through a satellite distribution system in 1980; prior to that, interconnection occurred through land-leased telephone lines. With this new distribution system, the number of programs and program hours available from NPR doubled in 1981, and the distribution volume tripled in 2 years. In 1981, more than 16,000 program hours were made available to local stations. Original programming from NPR (3,000 hours) heavily emphasized news and information (57 percent) and culture and the performing arts (21 percent). It also included special programming (17 percent) for the 11 million Americans who are print-handicapped, such as the blind. NPR's largest source of revenue is the Corporation for Public Broadcasting, a private non-profit corporation whose primary income is from the Federal government. CPB provides grants to NPR for program development and production.

For the local public radio station, NPR programming fills about 25 percent of its 6,800 annual broadcast hours. Some 60 percent is locally produced, and the remainder originates with syndicators and other public radio sources. In content, the local public radio station is heavily music (60 percent), news and public affairs (20 percent), and combined music and news (9 percent). Two-thirds of the NPR stations are located at U.S. colleges and universities. Instructional broadcasts comprise only 2 percent of the schedule. On public stations, the dominant music is classical (39 percent) and jazz (15 percent), formats rarely represented on commercial radio.

Income of the local public radio station derives primarily from federal sources (34 percent in 1979), from state colleges (25 percent), and local and state governments (15 percent). As income from some of these sources has dwindled in recent years, stronger efforts have been made to enlist financial support from the listening public. These efforts have raised approximately 10 percent of station incomes, with the expectation that public support will and must increase substantially through the 1980s.

Who listens? Audience research data indicate that listening to public radio (at least weekly) has doubled since 1977, with somewhat more than seven million listeners weekly. However, that overall figure encompasses but 5 percent of the adult American public who listen to radio regularly each week. The public radio audience is heterogeneous, but is substantially more likely to include among its regular listeners those who have higher incomes, are college graduates, are employed full-time primarily as professionals or managers, are younger (18–34), male, and mobile.

Public radio provides alternative programming to commercial radio, but to a relatively small and distinct audience.

What's in store for radio during the remainder of the 1980s?

- Increasing dependence on syndicated programming.
- Higher quality audio as a result of cable transmission and digital recording.
- Deregulation, and thus less oversight of station services.
- Decreasing support of public radio by tax-based sources, and increased dependence on public subscription, foundation and business support.
- Increasing FM audience.
- Cable radio as a standard feature of cable television systems.
- Flux in station formats, with additional talk/news programming.

COMMERCIAL TELEVISION

The broadcasting system that created (and then distributed to most European nations) such long-running series as "Bonanza," "Dallas," "The Wonderful World of Disney," "All in the Family," "Gunsmoke," "M*A*S*H," and "I Love Lucy" is the commercial television system in the United States. It also is responsible for dozens of series that failed to last even half a season: for example, "Mr. T and Tina," "The Waverly Wonders," "Ball Four," "When Things Were Rotten." With dozens of winners and hundreds of losers in nearly 35 years of prime-time programming, the commercial television system dominates U.S. television programming and the nation's television audiences.

There are 82 million homes with TV sets, 98 percent of all U.S. homes. Each evening, between 8:30 and 9 p.m., two-thirds of the households in the U.S. with television sets are watching television. That is the peak viewing time, but television watching is a day-long (and for some a night-long) phenomenon. The average U.S. home tuned in television for 6 hours and 45 minutes each day during the 1981–1982 season, 45 minutes more per household than a decade earlier. One-fourth of the TV homes watched before noon and one-third watched in the afternoon, on a daily basis. They watched in color (88 percent of all homes) and half the homes watched on more than one TV set and received more than 10 different channels. Since 1964, both VHF (channels 2–13) and UHF (channels 14–69) signals have been built into the same receiver, and since 1974 all new sets have dials with fixed positions for both UHF and VHF channels.

Background of U.S. Television

Where did American television come from? It is about 32 years since the Federal Communications Commission (FCC) rescinded a freeze it had imposed on the awarding of television station licenses. In 1952, an additional 70 UHF (ultra high frequency) channel frequencies were created and added to 12 VHF (very high frequency) channels already established, and some 2,000 local channel assignments were made to 1,300 communities. At the end of 1981, there were 524 commercial VHF and 248 commercial UHF stations in operation.

Station-building across the country, the availability of increasingly inexpensive and multiple TV sets, improved reception, the development of television networks, free licenses, advertiser access to a mass audience at a single time, and the oportunity for large profits—all are key factors in making television the pervasive medium it is in the United States. Television households grew from 50 million in 1961, to 62 million in 1971, to 82 million in 1981.

Early licensing procedures and technical constraints made three sta-tins in or near a given community the typical number feasible to operate. The FCC's mixing of superior (VHF) and inferior (UHF) quality signals and the networks' access to the former for their affiliates, biased the de-velopment of three national commercial networks which continue to dom-inate television programming. Each of them—ABC, CBS, and NBC—has about 200 stations which "affiliate" with the network, giving them the opportunity to broadcast the network-scheduled programs, to share in network advertising revenues, and to sell local advertising in time adjacent to network shows. The networks do not generally own their affiliates, who sign two-year contracts giving them first rights to network programs. Exceptions are the networks' owned-and-operated stations (each network is limited to five). However, the 15 stations they own can be received by more than 20 percent of the households in the country. Non-network owners of television stations are limited to no more than 7 television sta-tions, with a maximum of 5 VHF stations, and no more than one in a single viewing area. Group owners have evolved and there are more than 100 groups controlling about 60 percent of all TV stations. In addition, there are about 200 independent, non-network stations.

Television Advertising
The television industry draws more than 20 percent of the total advertising revenues in the United States, half of all national advertising revenue, and about 15 percent of local advertising dollars.

In 1980, commercial television in the U.S. had revenues of $8.8 bil-lion; $1.6 billion of that was profits. About 30 percent of industry profits accrue to the networks, another 10 percent to the 15 stations owned and operated by the networks, and the remaining 60 percent to the other 760 local commercial stations. National network advertising billings were $4.8 billion in 1980, a 12 percent increase over the prior year; national non-network advertising amounted to $2.9 billion, a 14 percent increase; and local advertising billings were $2.5 billion, an 11 percent increase in one year. A 30-second commercial during prime time averaged $100,000 on the networks (from about $45,000 for low-rated shows to $175,000 to top-rated ones). In 1979, the top television advertiser was Procter and Gamble, which spent $289 million, followed by General Foods ($203 million), American Home Products ($123 million), and General Motors and Bristol-Meyers ($117 million each).

At a local station, the price range for a 30-second commercial is $10 to $10,000, depending on population and program audience share. Of commercials aired, 85 to 90 percent are 30 seconds long. Individual tel-evision stations had average pre-tax profits of about 20 percent; some 90 percent of their income was non-network, with about half of it derived from local advertising sales. Consistently, the profit percentage for local stations exceeds that of the networks; virtually all VHF stations show a profit and more than two-thirds of the UHF stations do also. In 1976, more than 200 network-affiliated stations ended their fiscal year with profits of $1 million or more, as did 18 independent stations.

Regulation: The FCC

The television industry is regulated by the FCC initially through its licensing process, with TV station license renewals every five years. Subsequent regulatory decisions by the FCC include the limitation of network programming to three of the four prime-time hous (8 to 11 p.m. Eastern Standard Time), with 7 to 8 p.m. reserved for local stations. Program syndication by the networks has been banned, and the networks are barred from cable TV ownership and from cross-media ownership of media in the same market. Current discussions focus on removing bans on network syndication, on network cable ownership, and on network commercial interest in programming produced by non-network firms. In addition to the requirement of the Fairness Doctrine, there are now stronger opportunities for minority licensing of new stations. On the other hand, license challenges are rare and successful challenges even rarer. In practice, the initial receipt of the license to operate a television station has been equivalent to a permanent award.

The Nature of Television Programs

The daily fare of U.S. television looked like this for the 1982–1983 television season. In early morning (6 to 8 a.m.), the networks offer news/interviews/talk. In mid-morning, the local stations air syndicated exercise, quiz, more talk/interview shows, and series reruns. From noon until about 4 p.m., the staple on network affiliates is the "soaps." No less than 13 of these soap operas were being aired in 1983, in both half-hour and hour versions. Some quiz shows are sprinkled among them. From 4 to 6 p.m. the local station again brings in syndicated offerings, usually reruns of popular defunct series and older episodes of still-running series. From 6 to 7 p.m., there is local news and then a network news broadcast. From 7 to 8 p.m., the local station again opts primarily for syndicated offerings. The next three hours are prime-time television, and almost exclusively network programs. At 11 p.m. (EST), there is usually local news and then back to the network schedule of late-night entertainment, including movies, reruns, variety/interviews, and public affairs. Recently some post-midnight news programming started as part of the regular network schedule, in response to 24-hour cable news channels.

During prime time,the staple television menu is situation comedies. Among some 70 weekly network series 30 were sit-coms in 1981–1982; they drew the bulk of the network audience share (45 percent). They were followed in popularity by general drama (10 series and 15 percent share), mystery and suspense series (10 series and 11 percent), and feature films (7 series and 8 percent). Although prime time makes up 13 percent of the broadcast schedule, it attracts 30 percent of the total television audience in the United States.

Audience content preferences have not been stable since the advent of television. There have been noticeable shifts away from westerns, quiz shows, action adventure, and variety shows, and shifts toward more feature films, crime/detective shows, and sports programming in prime-time. Program type preference cycles have been noted, usually lasting about five years. Network programming for children is now waning; in 1982, there was no regularly-scheduled weekday children's program on any commercial network after 8 a.m. Saturday morning is the children's program block on all three networks, as well as on independent stations.

Another noticeable shift has been in the number of series, the number of episodes per series, and the length of individual episodes. In 1956, there were 123 series on the network schedule, with about 36 new episodes per series in the season. Five of 6 were half-hour shows. Twenty years later in 1976, there were 67 series, each with about 26 original episodes. A majority were 60-minute shows. Today there are perhaps 55 series, about 22 new episodes a year, and an even larger majority are hour-long shows.

The Commercial Television Audience

Everyone is in the television audience, some more often than others. Women over 50 watch more television than any other age/sex group, and women 18–49 watch more than their male counterparts. Although teenagers watch the least television, the viewing by pre-teens is equivalent to that of adults in total hours per day, but it is done at different times. By households, Nielsen reports that viewing is greater among:

1. Larger households, for example, average viewing for all households is 50 hours a week, but it is 60 hours in households with three or more persons;
2. Households with any non-adult, also averaging 60 hours a week;
3. Households with cable TV plus some pay cable channel, averaging 58 hours per week; and
4. Households with black Americans, whose viewing is more extensive in every day and night-time period.

PUBLIC TELEVISION

For citizens in the United States, public (noncommercial) television has meant the availability of such regular series as "Sesame Street," "The Dick Cavett Show," "Wall Street Week," "Mister Roger's Neighborhood," "The MacNeil/Lehrer Report," "Evening at Pops," "Great Performances," and "Nova." It has given extended live coverage of national events like the Nixon–Watergate hearings. It has introduced significant European productions, particularly those from the BBC. It has meant television without commercials, save for repeated pleas to contribute money to support public television.

Support for Public Television

Among the 1,000-plus television stations in the United States, there are about 300 public television (PTV) stations, two-thirds of which operate on UHF channels. Colleges and universities, state governments, and non-profit community organizations each operate from 25 to 30 percent of the PTV stations, with the remainder operated by local school districts. Revenues for the public television system originate from the same operators, plus certain additional sources. Currently, federal and state governments each provide about 25 percent of the funding, individual viewers and businesses each provide 10 percent, and the remainder generates from state colleges, local authorities, and foundations. These national averages are more variable than constant; many PTV stations depend on contributions for more than half their income. Announced reductions in governmental support at both federal and state levels will increase reliance on corporate, foundation, and individual viewer revenues in the immediate future for most stations.

Federal support for public television in the U.S. is channeled through the Corporation for Public Broadcasting (CPB), a non-federal agency. Congressional funding to CPB in fiscal year 1982 was $172 million, but will decrease to $137 million and then to $130 million in the next 2 fiscal years. Of the 1982 funds, $81 million were awarded in the form of Community Service Grants to public television stations. These grants strengthen station operations and support the production and acquisition of programs. In turn about 300 PTV stations affiliate with the Public Broadcasting Service (PBS), which operates a satellite-connected system for program distribution. PBS is not a production house but rather a coordinating and distribution system; its prime purpose is to achieve economies in the production of quality programming that no single station acting alone would be able to do. Thus, there is a pooling of production resources by the member stations through PBS. PBS is also responsible for assessing which programs offered to it are suitable for national distribution and for creating a national program schedule.

Public television programs, as distributed by PBS, originate in three ways: (a) underwriting of a program's production by a foundation, corporation, etc.; (b) programs provided and made available free by member stations and other sources; and (c) member station support of program offerings by the Station Program Cooperative (SPC). The SPC works on the principle that if sufficient stations will financially support a new programming effort, its per station cost will be low enough to be affordable. An individual station's share of underwriting of SPC programs is based on its budget. In practice, the member stations vote annually as to which offered and projected programs they wish to finance. There may be 100 or more offerings from which to choose; those that emerge with sufficient station support are then produced or acquired. The SPC provides about one-third of the PBS program schedule.

The programming budget for PBS in 1982 was $140 million. Businesses provided 29 percent, PTV stations 25 percent, CPB 15 percent, other federal agencies 12 percent, independent producers 11 percent, educational institutions 5 percent, and foundations 4 percent. The top eight corporate funders were all oil companies.

A PBS survey reports that 48 percent of its schedule is news and public affairs, 30 percent is cultural programming (including pop and country music as well as classical, opera, and ballet); 15 percent educational services, and 7 percent sports. Overall, member stations produce more than 70 percent of the network program schedule. The daily schedule offerings of public television stations are divisible into three roughly equal segments—news and public affairs programming; children's programming; and "other," which encompasses dramatic, musical, cultural, and instructional programs.

Audience

The audience for public television is growing. During the first week of September, 1982, half the households in the United States watched something on public television, a week when the commercial networks were mostly showing reruns from the prior season. In those viewing households, there was just short of three hours of PTV viewing for the week. Across the 1981–1982 season, PTV viewers averaged 3.5 hours per week.

Who watches public television? Above-average viewing of PTV is found among households with children, college graduates, professionals/managers, incomes over $30,000, and among those 35–49 years old. However, these differences are relative, and PTV actually penetrates into all demographic groups. For example, 38 percent of U.S. households have incomes of less than $15,000; in the PTV audience, 30 percent are at that income level.

Overall, public television in 1982 claimed 5 percent of the television audience as its average share. This audience share compares with 83 percent for the commercial networks, and 11 percent for other sources, primarily available only on cable TV. It also compares with a 2.5 percent share for public television as recently as 1978 and 1979.

CABLE TELEVISION

The decade of the 1980s will be called the decade of cable television in the United States. It is estimated that by 1990, half the homes in the country will be receiving their primary television programming by cable. The growth rate—in systems and in subscribers—is so pervasive and changing that data for any single time period are likely to require radical revision 6 months later. In July, 1982, the two major television research companies in the United States—Arbitron and the A. C. Nielsen Co.—were 6 *million households apart* in their estimates of cable penetration! Nielsen estimated 27.9 million basic cable subscribers (34 percent of all TV households) and Arbitron estimated 21.8 million (27 percent). Splitting the difference, one might estimate that about 30 percent of U.S. households then had basic cable service. In 1980, according to Arbitron, it was 20 percent; it 1975, 14 percent; and 1970, 8 percent. The cable boom is a real phenomenon, with 40% of American homes cabled in 1984.

What is cable television? It is a means by which broadcast services are augmented; cable originates or picks up broadcast signals through a central receiving antenna, by microwave relay or satellite, and then retransmits them by cable to individual homes, apartments, businesses, schools, etc. The cable can carry dozens of broadcast signals at the same time. Originally developed to bring television to areas which could not receive broadcast signals, cable subsequently was introduced to areas wanting more stations and to areas wanting better and more consistent picture quality. Advances in satellite signal reception and changes in federal regulation of cable have led to the augmentation by cable systems of local and non-local television station signals, with a dozen or more specialized satellite network channels (news, sports, health, and children's programming) as part of the basic service, and several premium (pay) channels, particularly for feature films. Cable's entree to large population centers, the explosion of programming services, the demand for premium channels, and the modest subscription costs have pinpointed cable as *the* medium of the 1980s.

Cable television also is regulated by the Federal Communications Commission. It requires cable systems to carry local and nearby stations, to comply with the Fairness Doctrine, and to identify sponsors. It prohibits the commercial networks from owning cable systems, and television stations from owning cable systems within their coverage area (although some exceptions are now being made and others are being considered by the FCC). In contrast to commercial television stations, permission (a franchise) to operate a cable system is granted by the local or state governmental entity in which the system is located, and not by a federal authority. Currently, local governments initiate the cable process for their communities by issuing a "request for proposals," seeking offers from cable operators desiring the local cable franchise. Each potential cable system operator must file a franchise bid specifying the channels to be carried, other services offered, subscriber costs, the means of hooking homes to the system, and other specifics of the proposed cable system. In larger communities, there are usually several competing petitioners and the offers made to the community to receive the franchise are expansive, e.g., multiple channels set aside for government and educational use, production facilities and equipment for the public to use to produce their own shows, low fees for basic cable service, discounts or free service for community institutions, or two-way service. Cable television has become big business and highly competitive.

In late 1982, there were nearly 4,800 cable systems in the U.S., 700 more than the prior year. About 70 percent of them had 3,500 or fewer subscribers. But the growth is in large population centers; in 1980, there were 360 systems with 10,000 or more subscribers and this grew to 500 in 1981. A majority of all systems could still provide only 12 channels. However, the number of systems that could provide 30 or more channels grew from 358 in 1980 to 763 in 1981, a 113 percent increase. New systems are typically offering 36-, 54-, or 108-channel capacities, and many old systems are retrofitting their capabilities to provide increased channel offerings.

Home subscribers are being offered "tiers" of cable service. The basic cable service averages about $8 a month. In new systems, this provides the household with perhaps 24 or 36 channels. They include the offerings of all commercial networks with some network duplication from more distant locales; local and non-local public television stations; and a variety of special offerings; plus instructional, government, and access channels—all for a basic price. The next tier usually involves one pay channel, e.g., Home Box Office (a feature movie channel), for an average additional fee of $9 per month. In mid-1982, 900 systems were offering two or three pay channels. Additional pay channels at about the same cost are also available, with more movies or "adult" fare. At the end of

1980, 70 percent of cable systems had one or more premium/pay channels available and had penetrated half of the cabled households; by the end of 1981, 69 percent of all cabled homes were subscribing to a pay cable channel. The success of pay cable has paralleled or precipitated the burgeoning spread of cable television.

Aside from carrying the signals of commercial and non-commercial television stations available locally and nearby, cable systems in mid-1982 could choose from among 46 different basic satellite programming services and 13 pay services. The former are either advertiser-supported channels like ESPN (Entertainment and Sports Programming Network) and CNN (Cable News Network), or a small fee is paid by the cable operator, usually at no additional charge to the subscriber, for services like Nickelodeon (children's programming) or for "super-stations" like WTBS (Atlanta) and WGN (Chicago), independent broadcast stations whose signals are re-transmitted by satellite. All three of these charge ten cents per month per subscriber. Other services available include religious networks; weather channels; financial news; ethnic networks; other sports, news and public affairs networks; and a video music channel, some charging as little as one cent per subscriber.

In July, 1982, the top five satellite programmers offering basic service to cable systems in the U.S. are shown in Table 1.

The run-away winner in pay channel success has been Home Box Office, used in 3,600 cable systems with nearly 11 million subscribers. Two other premium services appear in the 1982 list of the top 25 cable program services: Showtime (also offering movies and some original specials) in 3.5 million households, and the Movie Channel, in 2.2 million households.

Table 1. The Five Major Progammers to U.S. Cable Television Systems

	Systems Served[a]	Subscribers (in millions)	Content
1. WTBS (Turner Broadcasting Service)	4,699	23.3	Movies, syndicated shows, sports
2. ESPN (Entertainment Sports Programming Network)	4,586	18.1	24-hour sports
3. CBN (Christian Broadcasting Network)	3,189	17.7	Religious programs
4. CNN (Cable News Network)	2,807	15.8	24-hour news
5. USA Cable Network	2,400	13.0	Sports

[a] Estimates made by the program services.

Many cable systems also offer local origination channels, where they program continuous weather channels, public affairs and local news programs, etc. In cable systems with 36 or more channels, certain channels are made available to various minority interest groups for programming, in addition to school, government, and general public access channels.

Cable system revenues from subscribers can be projected. If there were 24 million subscribers in 1982, paying about $100 annually for the basic service, and half of them paying another $100 for one pay channel, then revenues would be in the $3 billion dollar range. Figures released by the FCC for 1980 indicate more than half a billion dollars from pay cable revenues and a total of more than $2.25 billion in operating revenues for cable systems.

In such a context, the industry has seen an evolution of group owners, called multiple-system operators (MSOs). The top 25 MSOs service slightly more than 15 million subscribers, or about 60 percent of the total. Half a dozen of them have more than 1 million subscribers each.

What of viewing in cabled homes, given the multiple additional options from which to choose? Little sophisticated analysis of cable viewing has been reported to date. Homes with only basic cable services engage in less total television viewing than uncabled homes; 90 to 95 percent of what is watched are network programs. Homes with both basic and pay cable selections watch more total television, and the portion of network viewing is reduced to 70 to 80 percent. The remainder is shared by pay channels (15 to 20 percent) and basic service channels (5 to 10 percent). Thus the projection is for the commercial networks to receive an increasingly smaller share of the total television audience as more portions of the country receive and subscribe to cable and to pay channels. In fall, 1982, the three networks' share of prime-time viewing was about 83 percent for all TV households. The audience is likely to be further segmented, making it more difficult (and more expensive) for advertisers to reach massive audiences.

Cable advertising currently occurs at a national level on advertiser-supported satellite channels and on a local level. Efforts are being made to interconnect cable systems on a regional basis to offer advertisers a larger audience base.

NEW TELEVISION TECHNOLOGIES

What's next? Actually, most of the future has already begun, is beyond the initial research and development phase, and is actually being implemented or is in advanced stages of field testing. Our offering of what the future looks like for U.S. television is not a projection into the 21st century, but for the remaining two decades in this century.

Interactive Cable

Cable systems now being installed, and many already installed, have two-way capabilities, although that capability has been activated in only a handful of systems. When activated, the home user will be able to send immediate responses to information coming into the home, selecting a response on the channel selector box which is then sent back through the cable into the cable system's computer. Individuals can make product purchases, answer market surveys, participate in quiz games, or complete achievement tests. Citizens can vote, express opinions, or answer polls. Diagnostic testing can occur. Participants can receive immediate feedback as the information is compiled, analyzed, summarized, and otherwise treated by the headend computer. Cable systems will receive immediate feedback from viewers about program rating information, and can obtain more qualitative program evaluations if desired. Activating the interactive capability will require some fiscal basis; those being offered and tested include home security systems, e.g., fire and burglar alarms, and health monitoring. Those receiving primary consideration include banking and shopping transactions.

Optical Fiber

The coaxial cable, as a physical piece of equipment, may be short-lived, particularly in the placement and building of new cable systems. The potential of optical fiber as an alternative can be summarized by indicating that currently manufactured glass fibers can carry more than 100 TV signals in about the thickness of a human hair. What to do with all these potential signals remains unanswered. One scenario would have this single wire in the home carry telephone, television, computer, and high-fidelity audio information now serviced in multiple ways.

Satellites

The 1979 feature item in the Neiman-Marcus Christmas catalog was a backyard satellite receiver for $35,000. Few were bought. By the middle part of the 1980s, homeowners can expect to find a necessary converter and small receiving dish in their Sears catalog for perhaps $300. The antenna that comes off the roof when the coaxial cable comes into the home will be replaced by a small receiving dish. Direct broadcast reception by satellite will be abundantly available, with signals originating in Canada or Mexico or England, as well as New York and Los Angles.

Of equal import is the fact that programming can originate from anywhere in the U.S. Uplinks from stations to the satellites could provide the basis for additional programming to broadcast across the country. Non-local programming could become attractive to local stations if they believed that it would be more profitable. And the satellites can be used to inter-connect stations, networks, cable systems, and other components of the telecommunication industry to feed a massive variety of messages into American homes.

Videocassette/Disc Units

Videocassette recorders are now in about 3 million American homes, with the current price of $400 to $800 an inhibitor to more rapid expansion. They are now used largely to record off-air broadcasts for delayed play-back. Two competitive and incompatible cassette formats (Beta and VHS) have also inhibited exchanges of recorded material. However, the price of these videorecording systems is falling. More and more programs, pri-marily films, are being offered for rent and sale to complement home re-cordings. Further, the increasing availability of inexpensive color video cameras for "home movies" is a measurable threat to the more traditional camera manufacturers. Movies made with video cameras can be watched concurrently with their production, and the tape itself is reusable.

Videodisc systems are more problematic. They are now being mar-keted for about $300, but with playback capabilities only. The disc looks like a phonograph record and yields high quality video and audio. Its in-ability to record marks it as a supplemental piece of media equipment. Nevertheless, it is inexpensive, and should a sophisticated exchange sys-tem for software be developed, e.g., through libraries or schools or mail, it may diffuse more readily.

Electronic Text

Text of books, bus schedules, menus, news, sports scores, diction-aries, community calendars, etc. can be transmitted onto home television receivers using several different methods. In its most primitive one-way format, an entire channel is dedicated to text which proceeds page-by-page through the stored information, and the viewers wait for what they desire to reappear. In a less primitive, but still noninteractive format, text information is encoded and transmitted along with an over-air or broadcast signal. The viewer can use a special tuner to access different pages of text being transmitted. Electronic text is also being developed on two-way cable systems and, using telephone lines linked directly to computers, providing interactive access to a large collection of stored material. In this way, the viewer can select pages, sections, or categories of stored information to be provided on request. Little waiting, no fuss. This searching capability for material now found in the phone directory, its business pages, any large catalog, newspaper or magazine collection, or even encyclopedias, may be judged a reasonable investment by families as well as business and government agencies. And what is stored on one computer can be linked by satellite or phone lines to other computers, thus expanding the collection of available text.

Electronic text is more than a television industry development. Some large newspaper organizations have been among the first field testers of this technology. They conceive of providing electronically tailored newspapers to those who would as soon avoid some newspaper sections in favor of more content in other news interests areas. The text system can provide far more stories per topic category than one daily newshole makes available, with continuous updating possible.

Competition for Cable

Cable television will receive increasing competition from several new technologies in the next decade. Single and multiple channel pay services featuring movies, sports, news, and other fare will be offered in a variety of distribution modes. Direct Broadcast Satellite (DBS) services are high-powered satellite transmissions which can be received on a small home receiving dish. Television signals are scrambled for transmission, so that the potential viewer must subscribe to the service and receive a special decoding device to unscramble the code. Offering the most popular types of content found on cable, perhaps only 3 to 5 channels may satisfy many viewers' reasons for subscribing to cable. Subscription television (STV) offers similar services, broadcasting scrambled signals on unused UHF or VHF channels. Low power television (LPTV), operating in a very limited area on unused channels, can also be opeated on a subscription basis with a scrambled signal. These competing technologies may reduce the current dominance and growth of cable television.

Our final projection for mass media in the 1980s, insofar as the American family is concerned, is that this assemblage of hardware and software will be melded into an integrated home communication center. Integral to such a center will be the personal computer. Now available in a wide range of prices and for as low as $100, the initial impetus may well be for video games, word processing, and some basic home information storage. Subsequently, as an information-retrieval device and/or as a word processor, the microprocessor will move from toy status to that of home information utility, much the same as may be expected from some cable TV offerings and electronic text menus. Combined with advances antic-ipated for other media, the roster of social implications of these new media for individuals and for families remains to be more fully defined and re-searched. Issues of control, of privacy, of choice, of accessibility, of iso-lation and interaction—all demand attention from communication re-searchers.

The media world is changing and we are likely to change with it. But how?

REFERENCES

Leo Bogart (1977), "How the Public Gets Its News," Address at the Associated Press Managing Editor's Conference, New Orleans, LA.

Broadcasting Publications (1982), *Broadcasting/Cablecasting Yearbook 1982*, Washington, DC.

Tim Brooks and Earle Marsh (1979), *The Complete Directory to Prime Time Network TV Shows*, New York: Ballantine Books.

Michael Burgoon and Judee K. Burgoon (1980), *Predictions of Newspaper Readership and Nonreadership*, Rochester, NY: Gannett Company, Gannett Research Report.

Corporation for Public Broadcasting (1981), *Status Report of Public Broadcasting 1980*, Washington, DC.

Corporation for Public Broadcasting (1982), *Annual Report 1981*, Washington, DC.

Editor and Publisher (October 3, 1981), "Special Report", *44*, 12–14.

Editor and Publisher (1982), *Editor and Publisher International Yearbook*, New York.

David Giovanni, Effie Metropoulos, and Evelyn Jones (1982), *The NPR Audience, 1981*, Washington, DC: National Public Radio.

John Haring (1975), *Competition, Regulation, and Performance in the Commercial Radio Broadcasting Industry*, Ph. D. Dissertation, New Haven, CT, Yale University.

Neil Hickey (September 4, 1982), "Television in Transition", *TV Guide*.

Inside Radio, Ratings Report and Directory (1982), New York.

Don R. LeDuc (1982), "Deregulation and the Dream of Diversity," *Journal of Communication, 32*, (4): 164–178.

National Cable Television Association (1982), "Cable Television Developments", Washington, DC.

National Public Radio (1982), *Annual Report 1981*, Washington, DC.

Neilson Media Research (1982), *'82 Neilson Television*, New York, A.C. Neilson Company.

Public Broadcasting Service (1982), *PBS Corporate Information Book*, Washington, DC.

Radio Advertising Bureau (1983), *Radio Facts 1983*, New York.

Dale Rhodes and J. Fuller (1982), "National Audience Estimates, August 30–September 5, 1982," Washington, DC: Public Broadcasting Service, PBS Research.

Don Richards, Mike Hobbs, and Ed Pfister (1975), "Public Broadcasting in the United States: A White Paper," Washington, DC: Public Broadcasting Service.

Joseph Rowe (1979), "Newspapers and Technology", Melbourne, FL: Harris Corporation.

Simmons Market Research Bureau (1981), *1981 Daily Newspaper Readership Demographic Tables for Total United States and Top 100 Metros*, New York: Newspaper Advertising Bureau.

Cobbett Steinberg (1980), *TV Facts*, New York, Facts on File, Inc.

Christopher H. Sterling and John M. Kittross (1978), *Stay Tuned: A Concise History of American Broadcasting*, Belmont, CA: Wadsworth.

Television/Radio Age (September 6, 1982), "Radio Station Analysis".

Titsch Publishing Company (1982), *Cablefile/82*, Denver, CO.

Arthur Unger (October 20, 1982), "Public Television: Big Business Stays Tuned," *Christian Science Monitor*.

Chapter 3

The New Communication Technologies and the New Distribution of Roles[1]

Henry Breitrose
Stanford University

INTRODUCTION

A basic shift in the locus of power is occurring in society, as the new communication technologies are empowering the audience with an active control over the flows of information. This shift is a Communication Revolution. The old media of mass communication, like television, radio, and print, are means by which a relatively few creative individuals prepare and transmit various kinds of expensive messages to a large audience through a relatively few scarce channels. These old technologies will continue, but are increasingly being supplemented with a set of new communication technologies that center around the semiconductor chip, which provides a communication system with low-cost, high-speed memory. As a result, the new technologies have a higher degree of *interactivity*, the ability to engage in a "conversation" with a human participant who is using the technology. An example is the newer cable television systems, especially their interactive channels through which individuals can make information requests, go "teleshopping", etc. Such a television of abundance (a) carries the idea of paying for information (which runs counter to the prevailing custom of the past), and (b) raises policy issues concerning privacy.   *E.M.R., F.B.*

A COMMUNICATION REVOLUTION?

To state that we are approaching the threshold of, or are at the beginning of, or in the midst of, a Communication Revolution is banal, but like many other banalities, it is worth some contemplation. I think that the term "revolution" makes a certain amount of sense in this context, because the history of revolutions makes it clear that the outcomes of revolutions tend often, if not always, to be rather different from the intentions of the revolutionaries. Revolutions seem to take on a life of their own, and despite the sincerest and most profound aspirations of the rev-

---

[1]This chapter was originally presented in a somewhat different form at the 1982 National Media Educator's Conference in Adelaide, Australia.

olutionists, the results are all too often disappointing to them. This is not to say that, historically speaking, revolutions have not on the whole been positive forces. However, there is no guarantee that change is universally for the better, or that the results of rapid change are predictable or that they can be attained without a great deal of dislocation.

The term "revolution" implies a basic shift in the locus of power, and I would argue that the current technological revolution in communication has at least the potential for shifting power, assuming that we agree that information is a kind of power. The more thoughtful computer scientists, especially those who work with microcomputers, often describe the work that they do as "empowering." One might think about it in much the same sense that literacy or numeracy "empowers" people to operate in society. Let us press the analogy a bit further and distinguish the difference between a "revolution" and a *coup d'état*. A revolution implies a basic shift in the locus of power within a society; a coup implies a lateral transfer of power from one part of the existing structure to another. I leave it for you to decide whether we make the mistake of confusing "Communication Revolution" with "Communication Coup."

Within the past few years we have seen the development of technically sophisticated cable and fiber-optic video and data distribution systems, home videocassette recorders (in at least three noncompatible formats), three major systems of videodisc, direct-to-home satellite broadcasting, teletext, videotex, and the burgeoning growth of microcomputers. Each of these technologies, in turn, has been heralded as "revolutionary" in its own way. Ultimately, the extent to which any of them is truly revolutionary must await the verdict of history.

THE OLD TECHNOLOGIES

In order to understand the meaning of the new technologies, one must begin with a description of the old technologies. The new technologies are fundamentally different in their structure and implications from the old technologies. The old technologies of communication are what we spend most of our time teaching about in our schools or departments of communication or cinema or journalism and in our institutes of the press or audiovisual studies. The old technologies are mainly film and television and print. These technologies are what we tend to describe as "the media." We teach students how to produce them, how to analyze them, how to criticize them, how to speculate about their social impacts, and how to measure the social, psychological, political, and cultural aspects of their makers and their audiences. We are at once fascinated at their potential and enthralled by their sensory attributes. The feel of handling film or the excitement of directing television or the smell of ink or the heft of a fine book are all immensely attractive to us.

Often quite separate from their formal attributes, the media's content alternately, sometimes simultaneously, appalls and attracts us. Most of us, I believe, have become involved with various aspects of media education because we love or respect or are fascinated with the mass media of communication. We begin with an *a priori* assumption about the power and potential of the mass media, and we try to help our students understand how the media work and what their impacts might be on society and the individual.

The old technologies are technologies for those few who may believe that they have something to say to the many. Documentary film or hard-hitting current affairs television or investigative reporting or elegantly crafted fiction films use old technologies. The nature of these technologies gives the creators or producers an opportunity to give the audience what they want to give them. Their purpose may be crassly commercial or ideological or educational or paternalistic. The audience, in turn, may accept or reject, interpret and criticize, selectively attend and perceive, and be moved or bored or entertained or enlightened or dumbfounded by the closed-ended linear message that is sent to them.

We may broadly but usefully characterize the old communication technology as a *producer-driven* technology, a one-way technology, a technology in which the creators of complex messages offer the audience what they want to give the audience or what they think the audience wants.

The characteristics of the older technologies derive from several factors. First is scarcity. There are a limited number of over-the-air television channels, and whether for commercial or political reasons the programs broadcast on these channels tend most of the time to be directed toward the largest possible audience. From the point of view of the commercial broadcaster, the reasons are obvious. In the words of the American television critic Les Brown, what commercial television sells is not products to people, but rather eyeballs to advertisers. The more sets of eyeballs, the higher the price that can be charged to the advertiser.

In a state system, in which television is supported either wholly or in part by government subvention or by a license fee, as is most often the case in Europe, there is inevitable pressure that television should provide the greatest good for the greatest number. After all, it is argued, there are few channels, and television supported by the people's money should be used to serve the broadest possible constituency.

In much of the recent discussions of communication policy, the argument has been used that the market creates a kind of cultural democracy, rather than the traditional argument of centralization and paternalism that had hitherto prevailed.

A closely related characteristic of the old technologies is their economic dimension. Television or films or newspapers and magazines require very large investments in capital equipment and sustain substantial operating costs. Again, the pressures are all in the direction of maximizing audience size. The old media technologies are technologies of *mass* media, of *mass* communication.

Mass communication at its core consists of a few people speaking to many. The flow is in one direction: from the producers of the communication message, to what they conceive of as their audience. The audience is inevitably thought of as a mass, an aggregate, a collectivity of individuals, and seldom as an individual watching television or sitting in a cinema seat or reading a newspaper. Mass communicators tend to think about the audience as something large and rather amorphous. The audience of the old media is thought of as essentially passive, as reactive.

We can think of the old communication technologies as mass technologies, in which (a) *relatively few* creative individuals (b) prepare and transmit various kinds of *expensive* messages (c) to a *large audience* (d) through a *relatively few scarce channels*.

This sort of schematization is inevitably brutal in its generality. It should be quickly noted that these old technologies have produced great works of art like the films of Jean Renoir, intellectual syntheses of the highest order like the BBC (British Broadcasting Corporation) series "The Ascent of Man," and have made available to vast numbers of people information about the events of the world in which we live that would have been inconceivable a century ago. These old technologies of mass communication have also created a world in which drama is represented by "Dallas" and intercultural understanding by the "Eurovision Song Contest" or "Je sans frontieres."

For better or for worse, the old technologies of mass communication are still with us and will remain with us in one form or another for a very long time. It is probably for the best. Wouldn't it be inappropriate to sacrifice the opportunity for the most creative and gifted individuals to communicate with the society at large? After all, Shakespeare and Molière did rather well with the old technologies.

THE NEW TECHNOLOGIES

Let us now turn to the new communication technologies. If one penetrates to the core of the new technology one finds a very small piece of silicon bearing the tiniest amount of metal. It is the semiconductor chip. These tiny chips are cheap to produce and immensely versatile, but they excel in one function: they remember a great deal. They can retain vast amounts of information and instructions about what to do with this information. The art of supplying chips with instructions is called programming. In essence what is "new" about the new information technology derives from the microcircuit and its ability to store and retrieve large amounts of information with great speed and at very low cost.

Lenin once defined communism as "socialism with electricity;" one is tempted to paraphrase him by describing the new technology as the old technology with memory.

Cable television is a good example of a transition point from the old technology to the new technology. Much of what cable television is about is in fact old technology, but much of its revolutionary potential lies in the domain of the new technology.

Cable television is a method of transmitting electronic impulses through a glorified wire. One can send through the wire any information that can be converted to electricity: sound, pictures, data, whatever. When we first think of cable television, we quite naturally think of the *television* first and not the *cable*. The first promise of cable television is *more* television, which is very different from *better* television.

Because the electronic signal is contained in the cable, the availability of over-the-air spectrum space is not a limitation for cable television, and depending on the size of the cable and the number of cables, the number of channels is virtually unlimited. In the United States today, all of the systems currently under construction have no fewer than 54 channels. Some can carry 104 channels. So much for the problem of scarcity. Replace the common coaxial cable now in use with fiber-optic bundles and the channel capacity becomes virtually infinite.

The recent application of a major cable television company for the franchise to install and operate a system in the city of Milwaukee, Wisconsin, is a useful case in point. The application proposes to carry 14 over-the-air channels, including all of the Milwaukee local transmissions, and stations in the nearby cities of Chicago and Madison as well as stations in New York and Atlanta, and an array of special cable channels: a local arts channel; a consumer information channel; four public access channels; a community bulletin board; a multi-cultural channel; a senior citizens channel; three local educational channels; a health and safety channel; the Reuters newswire; a woman's channel; a museum and library channel; a local religious access channel; a channel for Catholic programming (Milwaukee being a largely Catholic city); two local sports channels; a channel showing nothing but the local weather radar and time; an entertainment and sports channel; a French and Italian channel; a channel devoted to televising the proceedings of the U.S. House of Representatives; a channel of imported programs from the United Kingdom (known, of course, as

"The English Channel"); a Spanish channel; two ethnic community channels; three 24-hour news channels; two arts and culture channels; two children's channels; 10 channels of recent films; 22 radio stations; and 9 special music services. In addition, the system capacity provides for 36 megaHertz, the equivalent of 6 channels for videotex and the equivalent of 8 channels for signals travelling from the home (about which more shortly).

THE PROMISE OF A TELEVISION OF ABUNDANCE

What's new about the new technology? At first glance the differences are largely quantitative. There's just a lot more television. But quantity, at some point and under certain circumstances, may be transformed to quality, and one of the most interesting and as yet untested areas of what one critic has called "the television of abundance" is the availability of community access channels. Here, for the first time, television is available to ordinary citizens and community groups who have something to say.

Our traditional notions of broadcasting are challenged by a system of transmitting television that at least enables the possibility of transmitting material to a small audience without ignoring the interests of the majority. In a sense, and conceptually at least, the phenomenon of cable television begins to resemble that of magazines. In most of the world small circulation magazines for specialized audiences exist side-by-side with mass circulation general magazines. But this analogy loses some of its usefulness when one examines the economics of making television as compared with the economics of printing. We are quite comfortable with an assortment of printing methods, from silkscreen to simple offset to color printing. On the other hand, our experience with television is not the same.

Virtually all television tends to look alike. The established visual grammar of television tends to be much the same, regardless of content or intended audience. The tools of television that most people see are pretty much the same, regardless of the program or, for that matter, the culture. China and Tunisia use their studio cameras and special effects generators and lighting in much the same way as does France or Japan. When we have a television that is the equivalent of cheap printing (the single-tube camera and the portable recorder) somehow it tends to look amateurish, like a kind of "8-millimeter" television. The intent of the advocates of local access channels is to produce programs with simple equipment, so that ordinary citizens can have easy access to the technical means of production. Granted that such access may be good for society, our very limited experience in America indicates that unless they have a very strong interest in the subject matter of the television program, the audiences for whom these programs are intended opt for more conventional entertainment television (or as one viewer put it, "television that looks like television").

Considerable research in the United States indicates that there are two television audiences; (a) those who watch *television,* and (b) those who watch *programs.* By those who watch television, I mean the majority of people who turn to their television sets regardless of what happens to be broadcast. They watch television for its own sake, much as others would go for a walk. No destination in mind, just a desire for diversion and the gentlest of exercise.

The minority of the television audience watch specific programs. In effect, they make a mental appointment with their television sets to see a program of specific interest. One can easily imagine that the immense potential of the television of abundance, the possibility of truly democratizing television, may founder on the established habits of watching television, and that local access pograms may become little more than a means for talking to oneself electronically.

THE PRICE TAG OF ABUNDANCE

The immense array of program possibilities available on cable television comes with a price tag. In the United States, as in Canada (which is perhaps the most cabled nation in the world), cable television is, with few exceptions, operated by entrepreneurs whose ultimate concern, quite understandably, is profits. The investment in capital equipment is very heavy indeed. Current cost estimates run at about $20,000 per mile of cable if hung from telephone or power poles, and $30,000 per mile if installed underground. Add to this equipment for a headend, satellite dishes for program distribution and local studio equipment and electronics. It all adds up to a fair sum. Sacramento (California), a city of about 300,000 population, is now in the process of deciding which company will be awarded the cable television franchise. The companies' best estimate is that the plant will cost $100 million to install.

Let me lead you through some gentle arithmetic. A city of 300,000 has some 80,000 or so households. Let's assume that only 40 percent of the households decide to subscribe to cable television. That's 32,000 households. A modern cable system will have various levels of service available, arrayed into what are called "tiers." The first tier, or basic service, will have all of the local and imported over-the-air channels, all of the local access channels, and a number of other services that are relatively popular (and that are inexpensive to provide at $5 to $10 per viewer), or that carry advertising. The basic tier costs the subscriber approximately $10 per month, or $120 per year.

Income to the cable franchisee from providing the basic service will be about $3,840,000 per year, but that's just a beginning. Let's assume that about half the subscribers would like a second tier, one containing services that transmit first-run movies. That means 16,000 subscribers for the second tier, at $20 additional per month, or $240 per household per year. The income from the second tier, then, is $240 times 16,000 subscribers or another $3,840,000. Add this to our first-tier income and we have $7,680,000. The numbers are beginning to look rather interesting.

Now let's look at another possibility. In a modern cable television system, it is possible to control, from a central place, who sees what. The jargon for this capability is that the programming is "addressable." Let's assume that the World Cup Final, or the World Series of baseball, is available *only* to those who have cable and are willing to pay for the specific event. This mode of service is called "pay-per-view" and it is where the economics become truly breathtaking. Let us assume that only one pay-per-view event is available monthly, at a cost of $10, and that only half of our subscribers want it. That's $120 per year for pay-per-view times 16,000 families, or $1,920,000.

We now have a total of $9,600,000 per year gross revenue, from 32,000 subscribers, or $300 per household per year, on the average. These are exceedingly conservative estimates, and come not from Stanford's ivory towers but from the worst-case assumptions of businessmen. Perhaps we now understand why cable television can be such an attractive possibility for profit-seekers.

INTERACTIVITY; WHAT MAKES THE MEDIA NEW

Having recognized the awesome magnitude of potential revenue services that may be derived from the *television* part of cable television, let's now look at the attributes of the *cable* part. Simply stated, electricity flows through a cable. With the introduction of some microchip technology, electricity can be made to flow both ways: from the central facility to the viewer ("downstream"), of course, but *also* from the viewer back to the central facility ("upstream"). This capability of utilizing a normal forward channel and a so-called "back channel" finally gives us the possibility of talking back to the television set with some real results. The jargon word for this capability is "interactivity". One interacts with the cable television and thus it becomes a two-way communication system.

Interactivity differentiates the new technology from the old. The old technology can tell, but it cannot answer. A good analogy can be found in historical antecedents. What's the difference between a phonograph record and a telephone? The phonograph is a one-way mass medium. The telephone is an interactive system. But the telephone, a most useful interactive device, is limited insofar as we usually call only those people who we know, and who know about as much as we do. Such a social limitation constrains the diversity of information that we can receive from the telephone. But it is an interactive technology of communication.

Imagine the possibilities if one could connect a common and relatively inexpensive and accessible technology, like a television set, to a memory of virtually infinite size, by means of a cable and a so-called "black box." Here we meet the microchips again, which we find arrayed *en masse* in a computer. This system of interactivity between the viewer at the set and the memory of a computer is called "videotex."

What would we like to know? The current temperature in Marseilles or San Francisco, today's sports results, or the week's program at the symphony? Let's stop there. We call up the symphony program. We see a concert that we'd like to attend. We ask for a seating plan for the hall and inquire about which seats are still available and their prices. Two in the balcony center. We request that these seats be booked in our name. The screen asks us for the name of our credit card company and the card number. Done.

Perhaps we'd like the Air Inter schedule to Le Mans, or the number of standby seats still available on the San Francisco to London flight? Or a restaurant guide written by our most reliable knowledgeable local gourmet? What's at the local cinema? A series of lessons in the intricacies of chemin de fer? Perhaps someone is advertising a 1978 Volvo at a price that I can afford?

All of these illustrations are true examples. They are drawn from videotex systems currently up and running, either commercially in the United Kingdom where a hybrid system using telephone lines is in commercial use, or in the U.S., where these systems are being used on an experimental basis with real cable television subscribers. There is no doubt that between the time this chapter was written and the time it appears in print, substantial advances will have been made. Were it to have appeared in videotex form, the changes could have been immediately entered and the chapter would be up-to-date. And it could be continuously so.

SOME ECONOMIC ASPECTS OF THE NEW TECHNOLOGIES

A crucial part of the American experiments with the new technologies is economic, and the main question being asked is "How much are people willing to pay for various kinds of information?" The price of information, and the idea of actually paying for *information*, is at once the ultimate economic rationale and the basic problematic of interactive television. Paying for information in and of itself is a novel concept, although when we buy newspapers or magazines or books we are, in effect, purchasing information. The difference is that when we acquire information in print we regard the medium, the book, or the newspaper as a tangible commodity. It has weight and physical dimension. It may be carried and set down. It is visible. The information, of course, is intangible. Information carried by the new technologies is equally intangible, but it is transient and exists for the moment as light on a screen and not on a carrying medium with physical dimensions. There is a considerable question as to the proclivity of people to purchase information that, quite literally, is intangible and has virtually no physical existence.

The idea of paying for information runs very much counter to the tradition of the American public library, which has been dispensing free information since the mid-19th century. There is a strong correlation between income and education in the United States, and children of higher-income families typically get more education that children of lower-income families (this despite the universality of free public education). Education and income both correlate strongly with information-seeking activity, so we already live in a world that can be characterized by two classes of people: the information-rich and the information-poor. The commercialization of information may exacerbate the gap between those who can afford to pay for information, and those who cannot. If we are to believe that knowledge empowers, then we face some very serious policy problems concerning the new technologies, and the complex interrelationships between technology, economics, and social concerns (such as equality).

One final economic note about interactive television. In the long term, the entrepreneurs who are investing in cable television in the United States are quite interested in what are called "transaction" uses. To illustrate, in a previous example we booked symphony tickets. That was a transaction. The operators of the cable system would then bill the symphony management, say, 25 cents per ticket for this service. Transactions become very big business when one considers the possibility of electronic funds transfers, bill-paying by transferring funds from one's own bank account to the account of the electricity or gas supplier or the local department store or to a credit card company. Paper checks are messy to handle and labor-intensive. Branch banks require considerable investment in real estate, construction, maintenance, and personnel. Banks seem to be willing to pay a considerable sum to cable television operators in order to make banking transactions possible on interactive cable, once a sufficient base of subscribers has been established.

ISSUES OF PRIVACY

One does not have to be paranoid to get a bit queasy about issues of the invasion of privacy. Once something is inserted into a memory, it can be retrieved by anyone having the appropriate means of access. I find the comments of Gustave Hauser, one of the leading exponents of transaction services, when he was President and Chairman of Warner-Amex, a bit chilling. Hauser told *The New York Times:* "People who buy the service will simply have to accept that they give up a bit of privacy for it. Beyond that, we'll try to protect their privacy all we can." That, and similar assurances from commercial organizations, is less than completely reassuring advice. Issues of personal privacy and the not-unrelated issue of national information integrity focusing on transborder data flow, will occupy much of the policy agenda for a significant period in the future.

CONCLUSIONS AND DISCUSSION

Interactivity, the ability for a user to drive a communication system, is also an attribute of other new technologies than interactive cable TV. The video-disc, when appropriately organized and driven by a microcomputer, is a powerful interactive device. It allows the user to access a vast amount of information, still pictures, motion pictures, sound, and frames of text, in a variety of ways, at his or her discretion. So far, only one of the videodisc systems on the market allows for fully interactive programming, the laser-disc system developed by Philips and Pioneer. The other systems have limited interactive potential, but the inherent technologies make them rather more suitable for displaying film. I've tried to characterize the new technologies as being fundamentally different from the old technologies in two ways:

1. The old technologies empower a few to communicate with the many, and to give the many what the few think the many want or need. The new technologies empower the many to seek the information that they think they want or need.
2. The old technologies are producer-driven and provide the same communication content for all in the audience; the new technologies are user-driven and provide a diversity of ways to access information stored in machine memory.

Somewhere between the old and the wholly new technologies are technologies that, while qualitatively similar to the old technologies, are quantitatively different. These are the technologies that transform television, for example, from a medium of scarcity to a medium of abundance. Cable television, direct satellite broadcasting to the home, videocassettes, and videodiscs are examples.

The nature and ramifications of these technological developments present communication researchers, educators, and professionals with some very perplexing problems. The love or respect or fascination with the media that led many of us into teaching, research, or practice about mass communication seems at odds with certain implications of the new technologies. Concerns about film as art or journalism as craft or television as a tool for social change are centered on a hierarchical model of communication in which information flows in one direction: from transmitter to receiver, from the knowledgeable professional to the malleable audience. The interactive nature of the new technologies leads us inexorably to a primary concern with the user. We need to deal with the social, cognitive, and economic considerations of communication side-by-side with our traditional media-oriented concerns. We must look closely at fields such as cognitive psychology and modern linguistics for information about how people seek, use, and understand communication.

We must closely attend to issues of economics and the social dimensions of communication technology. Ameliorating the gap between the information-rich and the information-poor is one very important issue. Another troubling social issue is the seeming contradiction between (a) the traditional use of the mass media as a means for building social consensus and for holding society together, and (b) the fragmentation of the audience into many discrete and separate divisions. One person's cultural pluralism is another's social divisiveness.

In a democracy, is it most appropriate to give people only the information they desire, or should they be exposed to the information necessary for them to make thoughtful decisions about their nation and their lives?

The new technology affects our way of looking at the audience. To use the technology is, by its very nature, to be active and not passive. The semantic difference between a *viewer* and a *user* is worth contemplating. An audience *views* the old technology; an individual *uses* the new technology.

Finally, a cautionary note. Advertisers often describe products as "new and improved." The caution is that *new* doesn't necessarily mean *improved*. There have been a great many claims made for the promise of the new technologies, some by the entrepreneurs who have a vested interest in their promotion, and some by academics who tend to be enthralled and bedazzled by the new and the shiny.

Until a human intelligence makes a decision about what to put in a memory, it remains only a very cheap piece of impure silicon, or a lump of plastic or a plastic ribbon covered with rust. Until a human intelligence uses a new technology, it remains a technology and not a true medium of communication.

Chapter 4

The Communication Revolution and Freedom of Expression Redefined

Francis Balle
Université de Paris

INTRODUCTION

The central issue of mass communication policy throughout the world has been the freedom of expression. On one hand, communicators should have complete independence to write and say what they wish, without having to consider what the State wishes. In reality, the State often constrains such complete freedom of expression, so as to ensure that the mass media act in a way that is socially responsible. In this chapter, the historical background of the freedom of expression is traced, both in America and in Europe, leading up to the current concern with the new media (that represent the Communication Revolution). These new technologies, because they represent a basic change in who can communicate with whom (and what content is transmitted), force a basic reexamination of the conditions for the freedom of expression.   *E.M.R., F.B.*

The press, radio, and television are techniques of communication. In every country, in every region, the media are also both a reflection of, and an element of, the political system. The media constitute a means for the expression of forces which crisscross, and which mold, society.

The history of mass communication is thus mixed together with a double adventure: (a) the industrial revolution, and (b) the freedom of thought. The impressive possibilities of print technologies led to the distribution by the thousands of book copies, and thus defied the dogma of personal interpretation of intellectual thought. In the 19th century, the first daily newspapers with millions of copies in circulation made possible the development of public opinion in the modern sense of the term. This advent of public opinion coincided with industrial civilization and with disputed elections. For the past two centuries, the progressive quest for freedom of speech, of writing and printing, and of the freedom to communicate one's thoughts or opinions, has worked against the monopoly of the State over speech. The American First Amendment concerning freedom of speech and of the press, suppression of the authorization act concerning the publication of French newspapers in 1881, and the formal abolition of the state monopoly over radio and television in 1982 in France, all are symbols of the march toward greater freedom of expression.

The simultaneous arrival of cable, cassettes, and satellites in the 1980s, creates a challenge for liberal democracies: these new communication technologies influence the freedom of thought; the conditions for exercising the freedom of informing, or of communicating, one's opinion; creating audiovisual works, and making them accessible to the public. Above all, the new media invite different thinking about the freedom of expression: the possibility of having access, without discrimination and through individual command, to information of one's choice. Our theme in this chapter is that the new communication technologies, far from repudiating the freedom of expression, can provide for a return to the precept of freedom of the press. Thus, contrary to some popular thinking (as expressed in books like Orwell's *1984*), the new media *can* be liberating, rather than conformist.

THE QUEST FOR FREEDOM OF EXPRESSION

We owe an early plea in favor of the freedom of thought to an English poet, John Milton. In his pamphlet entitled *"Areopagitica"* (published in 1644), arguing for the liberty of unlicensed printing, Milton declares for the first time that the quest for truth by everyone is sacred; he implies that no one has the right, in the name of truth, to forbid anyone else to express his/her opinion.

By declaring "that the freedom of the press is one of the bulwarks of liberty, and can never be restrained but by despotic governments", the Virginia Bill of Rights of June 12, 1776, followed the inspiration of Milton, arguing for the end of legal monopoly over speech by the State. The First Amendment to the Constitution of the United States confirms the freedom principle: "Congress shall make no law restraining the freedom of speech or of the press".

Two years previously, in 1789, the French Assembly had inscribed the freedom of opinion in the marble of the Declaration of Human Rights and the Rights of the Citizen in assuredly universal terms:

"No one shall be harassed for his/her opinion."

The following article (Number 11) affirmed the principle of the freedom of publication, and stated its necessary corollary:

The free communication of his thoughts and his opinions is one of the most precious rights for a human being: Every citizen can therefore speak, write, print freely, under the condition that he/she assumes the responsibility of the abuses of that freedom in the instances determined by law.

The First Amendment to the American Constitution and Article 11 of the French Declaration, show a difference of formulation that is not very significant: The former poses the principle of preventing limitations on exercise of complete freedom of expression by legislatures; the latter poses the principle of freedom of the press, an essential means for the expression of opinion.

The rise of capitalism and the development of political democracy, and the advent of a big-business press in the 19th century, took place under different auspices in North America than in most European countries. Faithful to its First Amendment, the United States took no actions which would limit the free expression of thoughts and opinions. They extended to the other media, such as broadcasting, the freedom which authors of the First Amendment had reserved only for the written press, especially newspapers. But in Emile de Gerardin's country, freedom of the press was only established by a July 29, 1881 law, after a long history of alternating authoritarianism and liberalism by the French government.

French law on the "freedom of the press" therefore concretized an ideal of freedom growing out of three centuries of philosophy and political struggle. Its two main elements constitute, for European liberals, necessary conditions for the exercise of freedom of the press: (a) the freedom to create, to set up, and organize a press enterprise, whether a news agency or a newspaper; and (b) on the other hand, legal limitations to the complete freedom to publish, which rest upon respect for other public liberties guaranteed by law, such as the safeguard of public order and respect for the freedom of others. Elements of the freedom of information derive logically from the concept of freedom inherited from the Century of Enlightenment and from Anglo-American liberalism: free access to journalism, free circulation of information, and freedom of reception of that information.

PROBLEMATICS OF FREEDOM AFTER 1945

Three American communication scholars, Fred S. Siebert, Theodore B. Peterson, and Wilbur Schramm (1956) formulated a new doctrine for the press called social responsibility. In 1963, the Papal encyclical *Pacem in Terris* designated "the right of every human being to an objective information." Inevitably different in their formulations, these two problematics derived their inspiration from the same obsession against totalitarian propaganda. While seeking to subordinate the media to public regulation, both statements are heir to the liberal ideas of the 18th century. Detractors retort that the two statements betray the precepts of such liberalism.

Freedom of Expression in the U.S.

The American doctrine of social responsibility of the media sprung out of certain concerns with the American press, radio, and television just after the Second World War: the declining number of information agencies, and an increase in advertisements in the press and on the air. The press in America was attacked for its subordination to big business, its conformism, its attacks on public morality and private life, and its submission to the pressures of advertisers. Broadcasting was accused for the preponderance of the networks, for being too readily conservative, or even too demagogic. Television produced too many mediocre programs, and those featuring sex and crime.

The Hutchins Commission on the Freedom of the Press in 1947 stated:

> The press must know that its errors and passions have ceased to belong to the private domain, and have now become public hazards. If it makes a mistake, it misleads public opinion. It is no longer possible to allow it to err like every individual has the right to error or even to be half-right . . . . We are facing a real dilemma: The press must remain a free and private activity, hence human and fallible; yet, it does not have the right to err, because it fulfills a public services.

Further, media critics in America questioned the virtues of the market and of competition. The sound idea that the media must have a sense of social responsibility, sometimes led to support for public regulations, and even for public appropriation of the means of expression, rather than support for the competition, private initiative, and free market forces.

Freedom of Expression in Europe

In Europe, facts and ideas mixed to create the problematic of the public's right to information, symmetrical to the American-originated doctrine of the social responsibility of the media. This European evolution of ideas challenged, at about the same time, the notion of freedom of expression and the democratic ideal. Freedom is a sterile prerogative so long as people do not exercise it. What good does it do for an individual to be free to be well-informed, if materially he/she does not have the vital minimum to live on? Of what value is the freedom of leisure for someone whose entire time is absorbed by his/her work? As the French scholar Raymond Aron remarked, the Marxist protest against formal liberties in the name of the realities of existence, like the complacence of the privileged, has not lost its novelty today. However, protest should not make us forget that the authority of the State extends so as to dangerously limit individual autonomy and freedom.

The evolution of ideas has imposed a new interpretation of freedom. Progressively, a shift occurred from a conception of individual freedom as resistance to power, toward one which no longer conceives the State as a Leviathan from which citizens must protect themselves, but rather as the ultimate guarantee of all freedoms. Thus, the same liberal inspiration which nowadays forces governments to action, were not long ago imposing upon them inactivity. People no longer talk so much of liberties to be preserved, as of the State becoming the obliged proxy for citizens.

THE RECENT TREND TOWARD PRIVATE BROADCASTING IN EUROPE

After 1945, European governments worked at removing radio and television from competition and from private interests. While important differences existed from one European country to another, all instituted a State monopoly over the character of broadcasting programs. Such State control is in sharp contrast to the role of government in U.S. broadcasting.

Thus, European radio and television systems differed from their North American forerunners in how they approached two problems: (a) financing, and (b) State intervention in the production and dissemination of broadcasting programs.

In Europe, the qualities and flaws attributed respectively to "public" and "private" radio and television appear to be symmetrical. Public television was recognized as superior for cultural programs. At the same time, however, it was feared that public broadcasting could be a formidable instrument in the hands of government. In contrast, the image of private television was that it could be quicker at guaranteeing a complete, objective information, but that such private systems might use commercial demagoguery to better conquer the public mind.

Although still deeply rooted in public opinion, these two images of private and public broadcasting correspond less and less to reality. Other elements must be considered in order to understand the complex relationship between radio/television, and society. European television systems and their American forerunners have changed more since 1970 than since their inception,and neither are today what they were in 1970.

After having justified the public monopoly for many years, European nations are discovering, one after another, the virtues of competition in their broadcasting systems: competition, decentralization, and a greater capacity for initiative (vis-a-vis the tutelary authority). Private broadcasting systems in Europe reflect a renewed confidence in the mechanisms of the market: free choice for the public, competition among producers, and a plurality of information sources. The recent history of European television systems illustrates a progressive commitment toward (a) a widening pluralism, and (b) more intense competition among broadening programs.

During the period of the 1980s, the United States appears anxious to restrain the excesses of competition in its broadcasting systems. Through the 1960s, the three major networks had won the battle of commercial television. However, at the end of 1967, the Carnegie Commission reported severe charges against commercial television, and called for the creation of a new television system to be supported with federal funds. The U.S. Congress then adopted a law creating the Public Broadcasting System. On November 5, 1967, for the first time in the United States, a news program was aired for more than two hours without commercial interruption. Since that date, while the "fourth network" has had only questionable success, the FCC's control over private television stations has tightened. Very recently, however, one notes a trend to deregulation.

So it seems that European television systems and their North American counterparts followed the same path, only in opposite directions. These systems are seeking to combine the advantages of both systems, while avoiding the flaws. The goal is to imbue television institutions with equality, neutrality, and subordination to public interest. Without doubt, this convergence between broadcasting situations in the two continents that were formerly opposed (and are still often perceived as such), constitutes a major evolution of radio and television systems in the Western world.

However, by and large, certain important differences between American and European television systems still prevail, and will undoubtedly do so for many years to come. But the emerging convergence of the two types of television systems represents a reconciliation between private competition and public control.

CHANGES IN THE FRENCH BROADCASTING SYSTEM

The successive reforms of French radio and television help illustrate the challenge to European broadcasting monopolies, monopolies that have alternated between authoritarianism and liberalism. In 1968, modifications were made in the 1964 legal statutes of the *Office de la Radio-Télévision Française* (ORTF), amounting to a reduction of state tutelage. However, the most important reforms came in 1969 under the ministry of Jacques Chapan-Delmas with the creation of two autonomous media units. Then in 1974, President Valery Giscard d'Estaing's government created seven distinct agencies to replace ORTF. This August 7, 1974 law set up four "programming companies" with the government as the sole stockholder: *Radio France,* the national radio broadcasting corporation; and three for television: *Télévision Française 1* (TF1), *Antenne 2* (A2), and *France Region 3* (FR3). Three other public agencies were also created by the 1974 law: (a) *Télédiffusion de France* (TDF), in charge of installing and maintaining the hertzian waves network; (b) the *Société Française de Production et Création Audiovisuells* (SFP), in charge of producing TV programs; and (c) the *Institut National de l'Audiovisuel* (INA), in charge of archives, research on audiovisual materials production, and of professional training.

Thus, the 1974 law clearly circumscribed the State monopoly. It included programming, broadcasting, and archives, but excluded TV prodduction, research, professional training, and (above all) reception. The monopoly is not extended to reception because peripheral stations with their headquarters in countries bordering France, broadcast French-language programs to the French public. These stations are Radio-Luxembourg, Radio Monte-Carlo, Europe 1, Radio Andorre, and Sud Radio for radio; and Télé Monte-Carlo and Tele Luxembourg for television. Their existence is tolerated by France. Indeed the programs are produced in studios located in Paris, and then sent by cable to the transmitters across the frontiers! Sometimes, these transmitters are even located in French territory (for example, in Monte-Carlo). The cost of such tolerance is the control exerted by the State through the *Société Française de Radiodiffusion* (SOFIRAD), a joint stock-company created in 1942, in which the French Government controls 98 percent of the stock. SOFIRAD, in turn, holds 35 percent of Europe 1's stock, 83 percent of Radio Monte-Carlo's, and 97 percent of Sud Radio's.

The next development in France was the law of July 29, 1982 ("the law on broadcast communication") which erased at last every explicit reference to monopoly. Certainly the State remains owner of the transmitters and the airwaves. But the word "monopoly" is no longer part of the official vocabulary. Instead, "concessions" are now given by the State for national radio and television agencies, and licenses are given to local radio stations and cable television stations. These words translate as a boldly liberal inspiration for French broadcasting.

At the center of the broadcasting apparatus, as the instrument of the announced liberalization, is an institution something like the Federal Communications Commission in the U.S., the Canadian High Council for Radio and Television, or, to a lesser extent, the Independent Broadcasting Authority (a counterpart to the venerated BBC in England), or the federal agency which links the radio and television systems of West Germany's ARD. None of these institutions, however, concentrates so much power as the French high command established in 1982. It issues licenses to local radio stations, to cable TV stations, and to videotex agencies. It rules by injunctions concerning the right of reply, the right of rejoinder to the government, the protection of children and teenagers, and over political campaigns. The high command mitigates conflicts between producers (except journalists) and radio and television agencies of the public sector. Finally, it nominates the administrators of radio and television organizations, including the senior executive directors of the programming corporations.

French radio and television are relatively limited: only three television channels in 1982, one public radio agency, and a few peripheral radio stations, only two of which (Europe 1 and RTL) come close to covering the national territory. The ban on commercials on independent local radio stations was only lifted in 1982. Today, however, these stations refuse to accept commercials (which in fact jeopardize their chance to grow). Since 1979 extremely promising experiments have been carried out with teletext (the ANTIOPE service, under the auspices of TDF) and interactive videotex (by the *Délégation Générale aux Télécommunications*). These experiments have led to the export of the ANTIOPE method of screen visualization, and the international use of the French word *"télématique"* (which designates the combined application of telephone, television, and computer technologies).

HERE COME THE NEW MEDIA

In the early 1980s, new communication technologies appeared: cable, videocassettes, computers, and satellites. These new media have an influence upon the freedom of thought, upon the conditions of exercising the freedom to communicate one's opinion, upon the creation of written and broadcast works, and upon their diffusion to the public. At the same time, the new media force us to think differently about the freedom of expression, without necessarily destroying the precepts of 18th century European and American liberalism.

For the sake of convenience, the new media can be divided into two categories: (a) tools (in the sense used by Henri Bergson), or (b) networks for the transmission of signals carrying written, sound, or visual messages from one location to another. Because these media extend the functions of the eye and the ear (like Bergson's tool extends the hand), three of the new media are classified in this first category: videograms (usually called "videotapes" in the United States), videography systems (also commonly called "teletext" and "videotex"), and the equipment for individually accessible coded programs. The prototype videotape was transmitted in France in 1964, a few weeks after the first broadcast of the Olympic Games via satellite. The videotape makes possible the distribution of animated pictures in cassette or disc forms (since 1970), constituting for the television picture what the phonograph record was for sound.

Videography experiments underway in the 1980s include (a) teletext, which uses radio and television networks; and (b) videotex, which uses telephone voice channels for transmission of frames of information. The first teletext system in France became operational in 1977. The transmitted program information is transmitted in response to viewers' demand. A simple decoder is hooked to a television set, so that news, weather, stock markets, administrative records, and information concerning training and professions, can be received.

The first French videotex experiment began in 1981 in Velizy, near Versailles, on the outskirts of Paris. Videotex offers a wider variety of services than French teletext because it makes possible a dialogue (at a distance) between two or more people or two groups of people. Thus videotex is like the telephone (it actually uses telephone lines for transmission). It allows its user (an individual or enterprise) to consult, search, or to process data that is stored in a computer. Videotex is also a transaction instrument that can be used for theater seat reservations, magazine subscriptions, banking transactions, or casting votes at a distance. Finally, videotex is an instrument for entertainment since it offers a variety of games to the user.

A third new medium has appeared recently in France which also belongs to the category of tools: Pay-TV in the form of a device for accessing television programs through a decoder sold to users (who are either private individuals or enterprises). When the device is adapted to a giant screen for group viewing, it is called "video-transmission."

The second category of the new media includes direct transmission satellites, teledistribution cables, and telecomputer cables; all act as communication networks. Planetary television started in 1964 with the American satellite Telstar. Direct broadcasting policy was made in 1977 in Geneva by the International Telecommunication Union, when its members assigned channels to countries so that each covered their own territories while limiting overlap on neighboring nations. Another policy decision made by France and West Germany anticipates the launching of two satellites in 1985 which will offer five television channels and many sound channels.

Teledistribution (or cable television) consists of the transmission of television signals through coaxial cables or optic fibers in a community. Such teledistribution has been used in Canada, the United States, and Belgium for more than 10 years. In France, after a few limited experiments in 1973 and 1975, teledistribution in 1982 could become available to a community once a government license was obtained. Presently, the French city of Biarritz is pioneering a fiber optic cable system that is two-way (interactive) in nature.

Finally a new medium, which the French call *télématique,* or preferably *téléinformatique,* combines capabilities of the computer and of telecommunications in the form of a telecomputer network which, at a distance and upon individual command, displays data on a television screen that have been stored in a computer. The signals are carried through a regular telephone line. This new medium illustrates the unexpected and exceptionally promising rapprochement between the "old" technologies of communication which have previously ignored one another.

WHAT DOES THE FUTURE HOLD?

What is common between these tools and networks, together called the new media? All are electronic and their recent interlinkages encourage us to consider them together, as a single wave of new communication technologies.

Telecommunication engineers, now acting as fortune-tellers, made these new media as the instruments and symbols of our new civilization. The policy advisors of our Princes, through extrapolations and experiments, depict tomorrow's society as rosy (or somber). The engineers' scenarios and the functionaries' forecasts, equally imaginary, are all part of our present reality. Engineers were the first in Europe and in the United States to develop technico-industrial scenarios for the future information society. They think that technical innovations will affect the circulation of messages in two ways.

1. New frequency bands and new networks via cable and satellites will considerably increase communication capabilities.
2. The new media will also make it possible to reach particular and limited audiences whose members, although dispersed, share the same interests. This capability of the new technologies will lead to an ever-increasing diversification and specialization of messages available to the public.

Radio and television will be geared down by cables and cassettes, and the new media will suppress the frontiers between the old and new media. Humanity will be precipitated at the same time toward the infinitely large and the infinitely small. These simultaneous evolutions inspire the promise of universal communication, the advent of Marshall McLuhan's "global village", and of a humanity at last reconciled with itself, thanks to the multiplication of the means to communicate. Other observers, on the contrary, think that the proliferation of media indicates the end of private life and individual liberty, an absolute transparency of society, and the unlimited possibility for a few to watch over (and to subjugate) the many.

McLuhan became famous in 1964 because he prophesized the end of written and abstract thought, and the "retribalization" of humanity through television, allowing men to at last dialogue with one another. Now the Toronto professor's followers, encouraged by the satellites in space, and the first tests of certain prototypes on the ground, see the new media as a first step toward a society where everybody communicates with everyone, where everyone at last has access to anyone. The Canadian prophet of communication technology, writing more than a decade ago, could not foresee the providential liberation of the television viewer from authoritarian programming, thanks to cable, videotape, and individual-access devices.

For those who find their inspiration in George Orwell rather than Marshall McLuhan, the new media promise a somber future in which cultural indentity will be swept away by the rising of a standardized culture. They refuse the subservience of man to machine, and they relegate the new media to serving as suspicious accessories to power against right. Certain social observers, borrowing vocabulary from both Marx and economics, speak of cultural consumption, and condemn the industrialization of culture and the domination of the world of information by multinational corporations. Their inspiration comes from the works of the Frankfurt philosophers. They condemn the new media.

What are the implications of the increasing fragmentation of media audiences? Will a lack of common identity be created as a consequence of the diversity of messages and the multiplicity of media? The answers are not yet clear.

REEXAMINATION OF THE CONDITIONS OF FREEDOM

What fate do the new media hold for the freedom of expression? Will they open new perspectives for such freedom?

The simultaneous arrival of cable, cassettes, and satellites today invites us to examine the power of the mass media in the past. When radio appeared in the 1920s, it was considered as an incredible instrument for democratization; it seemed that the time had come for the end of privilege regarding information. In the 1950s, observers expounded indefinitely on the powers of television. Today, some dream of a universal communication, while others dread an electronic Gulag. We think that the new media are neither as neutral nor as tyrannic as some say.

The new media invite us to examine the new conditions of exercising freedom of expression. For a long time, the freedom of information was only identified with the freedom of the written press. Today the press has lost its monopoly over information. The public monopolies of radio and television in Europe forced a different formulation of the problem of freedom of expression. Why should anything good for the written press, such as competition and private initiative, necessarily be bad for radio and television? The broadcasting monopolies erected by European States seem to be fading. The new media invite us to think differently about the freedom of expression: the possibility to access indiscriminately, and upon individual command, information, is a counterpoint to the freedom to create public opinion. In other words, the freedom of expression must now be redefined both as the freedom to transmit *and to receive* communication messages.

The inception of the new media forces reexamination of the relationship between the State and the means of expression. Pluralist democracies generally comply with the laws of the market, and with the reciprocal adjustments of supply and demand. Throughout the years, these democracies invoked explicitly the social responsibility of the media. But the potential power of the media upon society commands the State to enact regulations in the name of public interest. The seeming contradiction here derives from two different conceptions of public liberties: (a) that which sprung from a 19th century notion of liberty as resistance to power (a notion which limited the intervention of governments solely to keeping the rules of the game), and (b) a contrasting view, born after the Second World War, which considers the State as the ultimate guardian of freedoms.

Today we await the policy directions in which our governments will redefine freedom of expression, as they are faced with the new media.

REFERENCES

Fred S. Siebert, Theodore B. Peterson, and Wilbur Schramm (1956), *Four Theories of the Press,* Urbana, IL: University of Illinois Press.

Part II

The New Worlds of the Mass Media

The mass media are faced today with several crucial challenges. What does Jacques Ellul think of mass communication in the information society, some 20 years after publishing his famous book, *Propaganda?* What are the social impacts of the new communication technologies? How do they force us to change our epistemology of communication research? The developing countries of the Third World consider the new media as a possible way to overcome their underdevelopment, and as a means to the new world communication order which they demand. But will it be so? In recent years, the greater specialization and decentralization of the new media pose yet another challenge to the Establishment through participatory media. Finally, we consider the challenge to a national language policy that television can represent, allowing for a bicultural situation instead of the homogenization that one might have expected. Each of the challenges in Part II, each so different, aim at a new concept for the freedom of speech.

Chapter 5

Preconceived Ideas About Mediated Information

Jacques Ellul
Université de Bordeaux

INTRODUCTION

The author of this chapter is a highly original European communication scholar, noted for questioning ideas that most of the rest of us rather blindly accept. Here Jacques Ellul discusses nine "preconceived ideas" that are commonly accepted by most media professionals and other intellectuals. The author comes down harshly against the new communication technologies, arguing in a humanistic vein that the resulting information overload is often dysfunctional for the individual and for society. Ellul has grave doubts about the high claims often made for computer-based information systems. Instead, he feels that the nature of human relationships, which cannot be transmitted effectively through mass media content, is the essential element in communication. Thus the world is *not* a global village nor can it become so through the new media. Instead, a deeper wedge is driven between the information-aristocrats and their plebeian masses. Everyone may not agree with the arguments that Professor Ellul presents here, but they will profit from considering them.   *E.M.R., F.B.*

What are preconceived ideas about information and communication? This terminology does not imply a value judgment that these ideas are false or stupid. Some of them are false and stupid, but others are perfectly exact and sensible.

Preconceived ideas are rather different from what we generally call "common knowledge"; it usually is the result of a slow process, a gradual conviction, as it spreads among the public. Common knowledge is an expression of a sort of popular wisdom which says a lot about those who share it. On the contrary, preconceived ideas are not accepted by the general public (although they will probably be exposed to them gradually through repetitive advertising and the omnipresence of the mass media), but rather in intellectual circles, by people who think and by individuals who act, like media professionals.

WHERE DO PRECONCEIVED IDEAS COME FROM?

Preconceived ideas are not the result of political ideology; instead they come from sociological, political, and economic research studies, and therefore, are the result of scientific elaboration. When a political slogan succeeds in becoming a popular idea, we understand very well the process of irrational motivation which led to this mutation. But an opinion which appears to be the result of scientific research can impose itself among intellectuals, who accept it almost without questioning.

This phenomenon of forming preconceived ideas deserves special attention by communication scholars. Why are preconceived ideas constructed? The universe of communication and information is an incredibly fluid, uncertain world which is difficult to grasp and in which the human intelligence seems disoriented. Many communication scholars do not agree that such a high degree of uncertainty exists, and remind us of "theorems" about communication. But the rigor of these scientific theorems obtains only through a drastic simplification of reality, as often must be the case in the social sciences. I am convinced that our understanding about human communication is a blurred one in which we are somewhat lost and usually ready to accept formulae which represent a fixed point from which we can understand part of communication behavior.

"Information is Power"

This preconceived idea, of course, is related to the unchallenged idea that knowledge and power are perfectly reciprocal. It is not wrong to say that the possession of knowledge confers power today, or that power can only be exercised when based on knowledge, and through knowledge. I think, however, that knowledge and power do not coincide exactly. The acquiring, and the withholding, of information equally confer power. Such power is often based on information unknown to the general public. And, inversely, the diffusion of information seems to coincide with "democracy."

But it is impossible to proceed with a global formula. Information gathered and used by public authorities is often false (or at least incomplete), because those in power do not have the time to digest the necessary quantity of information to properly exert their power. However, in some specific situations, the acquisition of an item of information not available to others can indeed help to exercise power for a while, such as in a military operation or on the stock market. Obviously, individuals who possess great knowledge in a certain field, acquire a certain superiority and exert an unquestionable power. Such expertise is characteristic of the bureaucrat, the technician or consultant appointed to a political council, or professors vis-a-vis students. It is unquestionable. But at the other end of the spectrum is a general public more and more saturated with information and yet increasingly unable to exercise power, to formulate a sensible opinion, or to exert pressure upon the political environment.

Yet another example of the incompatibility of information and power was France's Algerian War. In that case, the more informed one was, the more unable one was to side with either protagonist (that is to make a decision). During the Algerian War, one had to begin by choosing one's position, and then carefully filter out all information about this conflict, keeping such news as was congruent with one's position. This selective behavior amounts to rigorously transforming every element of news into propaganda (the same alchemy that every political adherent does without being told to). All other information was blacked out. Anybody who tried to get as much accurate information about the F.L.N.[1] as about the French in Algeria, about the way Algerians were treated before the war, and about the way the French Army acted, anybody who tried to look impartially at the two opponents and to know the truth, became more and more unable to take a position for one or the other (that is to say, to exercise power).

Today, the same observation can be made of the war in Lebanon. If we want to consider the Israeli viewpoint, or, on the other hand, only the war, with as much information as possible, we become totally unable to side with one party or the other. We become upset witnesses, tossed around in a chaotic universe which information makes us more and more aware of.

We cannot overlook one other relationship between information and power: Individuals in power either control the means of information, or at least try to use the mass media for their own benefit, so we must inevitably deal with the nature of propaganda. On one hand, information overload is a necessary condition for the development and success of propaganda in affecting opinion. On the other hand, propaganda can only be used when based on true information and through normal communication channels. Here we do see the transfer of information to the domain of power.

I tried to show here that the formula "Information is power," accepted as an obvious truth, covers complex, contradictory, and confusing realities.

"The Flow of Information Replaces the Flow of Goods"

Today we live in a new type of society, one where information is very important, where nothing can be done without information, and where communication networks function constantly. But from this viewpoint, we jump to a confused and inconsistent conclusion. Yesterday's society was characterized by the production of material goods, and its functioning

---

[1]*Translators' note:* The F.L.N. was the Front de Liberation Nationale (National Liberation Front), the Algerian freedom fighters' movement during their war of independence 25 years ago.

was based on the transfer of those goods, or their exchange. Marx founded his theory, in part, on the very exact idea that social injustices come from the transition from a stage of use value of goods to a stage of the exchange value of goods, from the transformation of the good produced by a worker into a commodity (a transferable element of capital). Marx perfectly analyzed the flow of goods and capital.

Now that our world is interconnected through a dense web of communication networks, the essential exchanges are flows of information. The indispensable element for every action is now information. Machines obey people who feed them information.

But the trend toward our becoming an information society does not mean that the flow of information is replacing the flow of goods. What does this preconceived idea really mean? Communication networks indeed cover the world. But the modern world remains based upon material goods. Information is produced, transmitted, gathered, and manipulated by technologies which are material goods. Information is most interesting when it refers to the flow of goods directly (as in advertising commercials) or indirectly (as in political campaigns). This exchange of goods still dominates even in socialist countries. We see how important commodities are when we realize that information itself becomes a commodity. Yes, the world is covered by information flows, but they are necessarily secondary. They convey information *about* something, information which produces effects which affect the world, but which is not an information world. The content of the information necessarily refers to something, to material commodities. This secondary nature of information is obliterated in our preconceived idea, as if information ends up being an object per se, independent from what it refers to.

Our preconceived idea becomes absurd when it is pushed to the limit, as in the all-too-famous book of Servan-Schreiber (1980), where he says that we can develop the Third World through the diffusion of microcomputers. The politician ignores completely the possibilities of real help that the microcomputers can provide. The computer is only a management tool, and that is all. To use a computerized system implies that there is something to be managed: industrial plants, big cities, intensive agriculture, harbor traffic, etc. But the tragedy of the Third World is precisely that there is no useful economic production. There is nothing to be managed with a computer. Using many microcomputers will not resolve any of the problems of the Third World: hunger, domination by the great powers, ferocious dictators, financial deadends. The Servan-Schreiber argument shows the absurdity of the idea of substituting the flow of information for the flow of material goods: Information does not feed a hungry man. It is a supplementary luxury for rich nations.

"An Excess of Information Informs"

I helped spread this preconceived idea (Ellul, 1972). It is obvious that we are often overwhelmed by too much information which is too intense and too invading: commercials, political ads, comics, traffic signs, and instantaneous information, much of which we have to memorize if we are to know the world in which we live. But it is impossible to do so. A qualitative difference in information exists because of the quantitative excess.

Even in a traditional, closed society, without any media other than direct speech, drums, or visual "telegraphs", information was not scarce. I am always surprised by the extreme rapidity with which really essential information spread in ancient times. For example, during the popular uprising against the King of France in November, 1314, the unrest started in Burgundy on November 6 and spread very fast, from province to province, from Lyon to Normandy, from Artois to Dauphine. On November 24, the Federation of the Revolutionary Leagues was created! It could not happen so fast today. Another example: In Spain, a pogrom against the Jews started in Seville on January 6, 1391, and within a few days spread to all the cities in the province: Alcala, Carmina, Olalla. Twenty cities revolted in 10 days! The social unrest spread in less than 1 month, first to all the cities of Northeast Spain, and then it reached Valencia and Salamanca on the one side of Spain, and Barcelona on the other, in less than 4 months.

So information about very important matters circulates very rapidly, and action immediately follows that information. But that was true in a society not yet overloaded with information. Information was therefore memorizable, as evidenced by the many diaries kept in the 16th century. In such an information-poor environment, really decisive news took on an extraordinary importance. For example, the launching of a crusade or of a heresy led to immediate action.

We live now in a completely different universe, with instantaneous information available to everybody (whether they are concerned or not). Most information is generally not very interesting nor very useful, but it is incredibly numerous. We are exposed to a huge mass of information, but we discard most of it soon after; human memory is totally unable to sort out useful information from useless information. Among the crowd of advertisements which left me indifferent, one of them could have interested me. This torpor is a fortunate phenomenon because if I could memorize everything, I would become crazy. Since I have no reference which would enable me to sort out what should be forgotten, I do so randomly; I memorize an absurd detail of no avail, and I discard decisive information that I should have memorized.

Information-blocking is a refusal to recognize the reality of our information society, an unconscious protest against information overload. The overexposure to information destroys our critical and imaginative reactions. It is impossible to critically examine the thousands of bits of information we are exposed to daily. The multiplicity of different media invades our communication capacities, surrounding us with a world of purely fictional information. Our experience of the real world disappears almost completely in a flood of information. The aspects of life which become most important are those transmitted through the magic of the screen. The rest is of little consequence.

But there is a basic ignorance under the cover of the abundance of information bits. Through the media, *everything* can be said, shown, broadcast about China, Russia, war, hunger. Everything, but without any guarantee of proof or coherence. It is fantasy. We know of numerous examples of newsmen who spread thousands of essentially false facts. They are not liars. They obeyed (although not consciously) that fundamental law stated by Einstein: "Theory determines what *must* be observed." At present, in the midst of numerous news reports, I claim we do not know anything about the war in Lebanon. We may know in about ten years, but at that moment, we will be overwhelmed by thousands of news reports about another world tragedy. Because of the proliferation of the media, and its immediateness, there is no trustworthy news. We can state it as a principle.

So, information which invades our defenses and remains in our minds, and which appears as trustworthy, is actually manipulated and scientifically organized to strike our attention (for example, through propaganda techniques), or else it is shocking.

"Modern Information Systems Endlessly Spread Bad News, While Reducing the Depth of the News Through Transparency"

The more crowded our intellectual universe, the more striking we find information that is dangerous. Shocking and upsetting information becomes more striking. It has been repeated a thousand times (and it has become a popular idea) that only bad news is "news." Although we recognize the obvious truth of this assertion, we do not always comprehend how it is inherent in all media. The media only transmit "transparency," evidence. It is only possible to grasp the surface of an event and to give the audience a film that has been exposed to a transparent picture. The transparency of tragedy, war, death, and sickness is sufficient in a mass communication medium.

But it is impossible to transmit a deeper dimension, even in a long newspaper article (which the reader will not finish reading) or a lengthy speech on TV. Such messages are targeted to an anonymous audience and consequently cannot go beyond the surface events. It is impossible for a journalist, even if he is very clever and honest, to make his audience see what is complex. But everything really human is also inevitably discreet, slow, and spiraling. Information in the media can only be linear, and hence tragically simplified. Because a mass medium transmits instantaneously, by its very nature it can only transmit immediate evidence. The mass media may try to transmit other kinds of news, but they are reduced by the inevitable law of transparecy. Thus the picture of the world possessed by the modern human should not be taken as real (Ellul, 1962).

In other words, the modern human lives in a fictional universe of tragedies which he is completely powerless to prevent, and which ignores the positive environment in which he lives.

"Everything Is Possible With the Computer"

We mystify computer systems. The solution to information overload, we are told, is the computer. Obviously, I cannot memorize and use all the mass of information gathered and transmitted throughout the world. I am limited. Fortunately, I can keep this information in the memory of a computer. I feel reassured.

Unfortunately, the computer cannot memorize everything. Computers follow a binary logic, they can only memorize data that are translated and reduced to binary form. Qualitative, moral, spiritual, and cultural information, or that about human or divine relationships, cannot be so translated. Of course, one can enter data concerning the history of religions, or the formulating of dogmas, but it is impossible to enter data concerning the motive and the motor of faith, and of what leads religion from a state of objective knowledge to a subjective experience.

Information traditionally had both a qualitative and a quantitative aspect which were linked. I transmit information, via a computer, in such a way that you change your behavior accordingly. Your new behavior is not the result of some kind of quantitative calculation, but the result of the human relationship between you and me. If Jesus had been a teacher of dogma, nothing would have happened. The calculations of Einstein have been accepted not because they were correct, but because they were Einstein's calculations. It is useless to separate information from the way in which it is transmitted, the person who transmits it, the place where it originates, and the qualities it evokes to the audience. Try to reduce Hitler's speeches into binary language and you get nothing. But these same speeches made by Hitler changed the world.

The way that knowledge is transmitted depends entirely on the personality of the teacher. If a teacher is enthusiastic, strong, and eager to develop intellectual ability, students follow and learn. Pedagogy is much more than the untiring patience and the constant repetition of a computer.

Conversely, the teacher must have something to teach. But students are beginning to believe that all learning is useless, since it is already in the computer, and that many basic intellectual operations are now unnecessary since they can be done by a small machine. If the knowledge of the teacher is undermined by the infinite knowledge of the computer, teaching abilities are not useful anymore.

"One becomes a good blacksmith only by forging" is still true even in this time of universal electronic memory. It is impossible to train the mind if there is no formalized content to exercise that mind. Therefore, the handy formula that "It is all in the computer" should not lead us to rely only on the computer. The quantitative and the qualitative in the human being are absolutely inseparable. When we use a data-bank, if the user does not know anything about the subject matter, he is unable to consult the computer. He simply does not know what question to ask. To know completely what to ask the machine, we have to know as much as its memory does. We have to have analyzed the problem, we have to have planned the operation, and we have to know at what point we need more information. To have learned electronics, computer science, how to use a computer is not enough. You could know how to drive a car, but if you didn't know where you wanted to go, if there are no roads to get there, and if you have no motivation to get started, then your knowledge is useless.

There is yet another difficulty. It is incorrect to say that "Once all the information is entered in the computer, I don't have to worry." Data-banks are organized by human beings. So it is impossible for everything to be recorded. Only data which seem important to one individual (or to a group) are entered in the data-bank. Thus a whole category of facts are necessarily obliterated and discarded as unimportant and irrelevant. If Marx had relied on what a computer could have told him about the economic system of his time, he would never have done the analyses of the economic system, as he did. He used facts that he considered important, but which were disregarded by the (then) dominant paradigm (Kuhn, 1970). Only recognized and accepted knowledge is entered in a computer data-bank. So a data-bank only gets information that has been filtered by specialists.

Once I did an experiment with a very good research assistant. Since I was falling behind in reading my journals and magazines, I hired her to update my files. It was a disaster. She gathered much data in which I was not at all interested, and she discarded details, objectively insignificant, which nonetheless for me had a lot of meaning. Similarly, individuals in charge of entering data in a computer do not have a "keen nose" for our interests. They cannot. So the computer data-bank is almost useless to help us cope with the information overload.

"The World Is a Global Village"

Another preconceived idea which is very popular but very questionable, concerns McLuhan's famous concept of the global village. He argued that communication technologies would shrink the entire world, so that we will no longer be isolated from one another. Formerly, in a village of two hundred individuals, everybody knew each other. When something happened, it was known immediately; the information system was almost perfect. When we were introduced to the larger universe through exploration and journeys, we became very poorly informed. At first the individual learned about events years later, then months later, and finally only weeks later. Today, thanks to the Marconi galaxy, we immediately know everything happening everywhere in the world. So we come back to the village situation.

What characterized the traditional village was that everyone knew everyone else. It was global person-to-person knowledge. Information was transmitted by an individual and was accepted as more or less serious and important, depending on the way that the individual was perceived. The story of the shepherd boy who pretended to be attacked by a wolf is significant in that respect. There is no global village today because I do not personally know the personality, the nature, and the ideology of the individual who transmits the information to me. In this sense, I know far less today about China than at the time when I was reading Marco Polo's stories. The infinite communication networks do not bring me closer to anything or anyone. Although the telephone allows such personal contact, the human relationship is greatly altered when information is transmitted through that technology.

Information transmitted by a human is not the same as that transmitted by bees or ants, although a risk of the worldwide communication networks is that it is to be reduced to that. We can now separate the code from the language, the information from the spoken words, or reduce information to bytes. We are making the same mistake as economists did in their classical theory, when they created a human model (the homo-economicus) through reductionism, so that it fit their model of economic behavior. Communication scholars should not forget that words cannot be separated from the person who uttered them. The words have the content, the importance, and the pertinence of the person who formulated them. Such was the situation in the original village, but it is not in the world village!

The same sentence uttered by the president of France and by me is not really the same sentence. We dissociate words from the individual who says them in modern communication systems. It is impossible to do otherwise. When I listen to a TV news report, I don't know whether or not the news organization is connected to the political power being described, nor can I establish if the advertising sponsors influenced the way the facts are presented. I have an immediate source, but does that person act independently or not? In the United States and in Europe there is no censorship (in the usual sense of this word). Censorship also exists as the interposition between the source and the receiver of an invisible third party who gives the real meaning of what is said. That tendency is increased with the capacity of the media to instantaneously transmit a multitude of varied, contradictory, and ever-changing news, in a way that rules out control and verification. Try reading a newspaper one month after its publication and you will notice that about 25 percent of its content was not worth reading.

In the real village, information transmitted from one individual to other inhabitants was relevant to their lives (even when the information was a joke, gossip, or slander). Such information caused a change (for example in the relationship between families), and it almost always led to action. On the contrary, the information I receive today through the media is usually not related to my life. I cannot change my behavior because of this information. What can I do against the advance of the desert in the Sahel, against worldwide hunger, against the Pol Pot regime, against the condition of Cambodians in the camps in Thailand, against the invasion of Afghanistan or of Lebanon?

Information may be instantaneous, and bring about a new mode of thinking, but it has not changed our world into a global village. At most, it caused the disappearance of real villages!

"Dialogue Is Possible"

Another preconceived idea is that dialogue is still possible. On the contrary, we argue that dialogue via the media is impossible; a listener cannot instantaneously respond to whomever is on radio or TV. Moreover a response to a newspaper article, often published a month later, no longer makes sense because the first article has already been forgotten. Furthermore, if the audience already made up their mind as the result of the first article, the response is inconsequential. A dialogue implies a continuing exchange, and a reciprocal adaptation.

We do not dialogue anymore in our society, we "communicate." The role assigned to information-communication in our society is that of lubricant or correlator. Information never concerns individuals as such, but the members of a social corps which must function correctly, consequently excluding the possibility of dialogue. There is futility in advocating exchange between an administration and those who it administers, or in seeking to suppress organizational secrecy through the disclosure of administrative files. Because mass communication is a flow, it excludes the possibility of feedback or dialogue. People are not supposed to provide information *to* the system.

Once everything becomes communication the goal is to receive without distortion, to accumulate as much information as possible about everything. When the effort is to create an international order through information and communication, then we have a new conception of the world. It is completely different from that in which we have lived heretofore. When information facilitates everything, every opinion, what confrontation can still exist? The over-abundance of information creates a kind of transparency, in that everything is known (everything becomes transparent).

Mass-communicated information alerts the process of thinking, but suppresses dialogue.

"Dialogue Is Impossible"

Our previous preconceived idea has two contradictory aspects; we just looked at the pessimistic side. Now we argue that modern means of communication make everything possible, including the exchanges of information ("dialogues"). Since the media have become less and less expensive, an incredible potential capacity to communicate is offered to everyone. Since we can now communicate with everybody, an endless and universal dialogue is created.

In the two contradictory aspects of "dialogue," the word does not have exactly the same meaning. On one hand, everything can be said, communicated, or exchanged at every level of society. But let us consider what really happens in three cases of increased communication. The French telecommunication services complain that the French do not use their telephones enough. Less than two telephone calls are made per customer per day. The French do not try to communicate, to dialogue through this wonderful tool. Consider Teletel. The French who have it, do not use it; only one-fourth ever use it.

Or take the phenomenon of CB radios in recent years. Here we have enthusiastic, fanatical people. We remember their angry demonstrations when it appeared that the French government might not authorize this marvelous means of "dialogue." But we also notice the worthlessness of the CB conversations, the stupidity of these dialogues, and the nonexistence of a real relationship. The conversation is limited to such exchanges as "How are you buddy?" or "The weather looks great today." There is not one worthwhile dialogue out of a thousand. What can we talk about with a total stranger, about whom we know nothing, and whom we do not even see? The same worthlessness appears with the multiplicity of Free Radios (*Radios Libres*) in France. Now is the time to reconsider Beranos' question: "Freedom to do what?"

It is fascinating that we find nothing to say with these wonderful means of communication. We cannot find a way to provide new and original information. So we give out cooking recipes, advice to housekeepers, answers for worried parents, horseracing prognostications, restaurant locations, and other fascinating trivia. We have nothing to transmit. When we talk to someone we know, the conversation is enhanced by common experience. Conversation with a stranger is reduced to nonexistence. When we say proudly that "everything" is possible with modern media, we talk only about the possibility of the material transference of information. But for everything to really be possible, the human being should be capable of doing "everything." For example, think of the mediocre films or slide shows put together by thousands of amateur photographers after returning from their vacations. The means of communication outweigh the ability of the communicator to use the medium. The result is emptiness.

The proliferation of communication technologies today demonstrates that these tools are only gadgets; they only serve to transmit the absurd.

"The Mass Media Foster Democracy"

Contrast the worthlessness of the information that is transmitted versus the weight, the importance, the immediacy, and the seriousness of the same information when transmitted by the State or by big companies. A division still exists between those who transmit, those who have every possible means to gather, sort out, manipulate, and pass on information, versus the receivers who cannot use these means. "Everything is possible" is not true. There is an aristocracy of transmitters and a plebeian mass of receivers, audiences, and spectators. Great specialists have huge power and cannot be controlled. The division between the information-rich and the information-poor more profoundly divides society than the former social classes. You cannot do anything against individuals who have information power. A writer unfairly treated by important newspapers cannot do anything. If he tries he will simply become a non-person. Nobody will publish his books. He will be thrown into oblivion, as in feudal times.

The plurality of information does not help close the inequality. Nowadays, everything depends on public opinion. And public opinion depends very much on its opinion-makers' roles. Those who use the mass media are technicians, as aristocratic as other, great technicians; it is out-of-the-question to penetrate their domain. The amateur has but his hobby. He is more eager to accept the great information, because he thinks he is taking part in the big game. The proliferation and sophistication of the media make it impossible for the common person to have information worth transmitting through such media. Thus the division between the two classes of the informer and the informed becomes wider.

The belief that anyone can send information is only a wish and a myth; not reality. Thus our traditional conception of democracy is forced to change. So the proliferation of the media seems to be fundamentally anti-democratic.

CONCLUSIONS

After having questioned nine preconceived ideas about modern mass communication, I conclude that everything, and its opposite, is said about these communication media. We know everything about microcomputers but we do not know anything about their social impacts and human possibilities. We are in complete doubt about the consequences of the new media. I have examined important studies about the potential of computers, office automation (*bureautique*), artificial intelligence (*robotique*). We are now very uncertain because of the new communications.

I think the first step into wisdom (and also perhaps to knowledge) is to admit that we do not know where we are. We cannot use the research methods of experimentation, analysis, reduction, and deduction heretofore used. We need a different epistemology because of the novelty of the research topic.

My second conclusion is that the incredibly complex and diversified systems of communication technology have the effect of inflating information. We cannot avoid it; so news items have to be produced every hour. You will not pay much attention to your empty television screen. Such inflation is inevitably induced through the existence of communication networks. The famous formula about "The right to be informed" is stupid. Information growth is not the result of a human right, but the industrial product of an apparatus which must transmit it. This highly technical, sophisticated mechanism inevitably produces completely insignificant information. The technological apparatus erases the existence of a significant referent.

The media refer only to themselves.

REFERENCES

Jacques Ellul (1962), *Propagandes*, Paris: A. Colin; translated as *Propaganda: The Formation of Men's Attitudes*, New York: Knopf, 1965.

Jacques Ellul (1964), *L'illusion Politique, Essai*, Paris: R.Laffont; translated as *The Political Illusion*, New York: Knopf, 1967.

Jacques Ellul (1972), "La Deinformation par Exces d'Information," *Economie et Humanisme*.

Thomas Kuhn (1970), *The Structure of Scientific Revolutions*, Chicago, IL: University of Chicago Press.

Jean-Jacques Servan-Schreiber (1980) *Le Défi Mondial*, Paris: Fayard: translated as *The World Challenge*, New York: Simon and Schuster, 1980.

Chapter 6

The Impact of New Communication Technologies[1]

Everett M. Rogers
Stanford University

Arnold Picot
Universität Hannover

INTRODUCTION

The computer is the heart of the new communication technologies that are now beginning to have important social impacts in the home, the office, the school, and the factory. Here an American and a European scholar who have pioneered in communication research on the new technologies combine to synthesize some lessons learned about the acceptance and use of these new media, their positive and negative consequences, and the basic changes in the nature of communication research that are demanded. In many countries, communication scholars are turning to study new communication technologies; a theme of the present chapter is that very major reorientations will be forced in the predominantly linear effects-oriented studies of mass communication researchers in the past. More attention must be given, for example, to convergence models of communication because of the interactivity of the new media. Thus, it is argued: "The Information Revolution may cause a Communication Research Revolution."   *E.M.R., F.B.*

We live in a society that is well into the early stages of experiencing an "Information Revolution" in which the *nature* of the individual household, the work organization, and society itself is undergoing a very major transformation (Forester, 1980; Warnecke and others, 1981).

1. Many countries (for example, Japan, the United States, Canada, and most of Western Europe) are becoming "information societies" (Nora and Minc, 1978; Schmoranz, 1980; Machlup and Kronwinkler, 1975; Picot, 1979), in which (a) more than half of the work force is engaged in occupations that mainly entail the processing of information (examples are a teacher, manager, secretary, computer programmer, or journalist), and (b) more than half of the GNP (gross national product) is from such in-

[1]The present chapter originated during 1980–1981, when Professor Picot was a Visiting Scholar at Stanford University, where he collaborated with Professor Rogers in research on the impacts of electronic messaging systems. This chapter was then developed further during Rogers's visit to the Federal Republic of Germany, where he consulted on Picot's research projects on the impacts of office automation. Certain of the ideas in this chapter are also reported in Rice and Rogers (1983).

formation-processing work. Information is about to replace energy as the basic resource on which an economy runs. Microelectronic innovations of information-processing and transmission are the powerful forces driving the development of the information society (Rogers and Larsen, 1984).

2. At the organizational level, the very nature of work life may be changing, due to the impact of such new communication technologies as video- and computer conferencing, electronic messaging, word processing, telecopying, and electronic filing and retrieval. These technologies are presently at a very early stage of diffusion and adoption, but their potential impact may be considerable (Rogers, 1983b).

3. At the household level, new communication technologies like interactive television systems (representing a unique combination of computers, satellites, and cable television), videotex, home computers, and videotape recorders are being introduced. These innovations too are at a very early stage of acceptance, and some (like interactive television systems) are only at the stage of relatively small-scale experimentation by national governments and by private companies. In fact, the reality of use of these new technologies as disclosed by surveys of users, provides a sobering contrast with well-publicized accounts of their future potential. For example:

- The PRESTEL system has been available for 5 or 6 years in England, but has only about 10,000 subscribers today, many fewer than originally expected.
- The QUBE system in Columbus, Ohio, U.S., is used interactively only rarely by participating households (Chen, 1981); a similar experience has been reported with interactive TV systems in several other nations.
- Home videotape recorders are only used an average of about 12 minutes per day, and that mostly to record TV broadcasts for delayed viewing (these are results from a recent survey in Sweden). In the United States, Levy (1980) reported an average of about half an hour of video recorder watching per day.

At the heart of the new communication technologies being applied to society, work organizations, and the home, is the computer. And what is new about these computer applications is their small size and low cost, an advantage made possible by putting increased amounts of computer memory and computer control, on a semiconductor chip. The Information Revolution, is fundamentally, a Microcomputer Revolution. Together with other technical innovations, microelectronics technology increases the capacity of both crucial components of communication technology (Picot and Anders, 1983a and 1983b): (a) the technical network, which allows for the telecommunication of signals, and (b) adequate end-user equipment, which allows for comfortable handling of complex telecommunication processes. Chips, digital data transport, fiber optic cable, and other new technical means enhance the quality, quantity, and speed of information traffic in technical communication networks. Microcomputer innovations enrich the end-users' terminals by facilitating access and handling, as well as by integrating this equipment with other functions of information processing (storage, retrieval, computing, printing, etc.).

SOCIAL IMPACTS OF NEW COMMUNICATION TECHNOLOGIES

As we face the potential, yet unfulfilled, of the new communication technologies, one might expect that social scientists in general and those specializing in communication behavior in particular, would play an important role in conducting policy-relevant investigations. But this has not occurred to date. As an eminent Finnish scholar stated:

> The communication scholars could have been in the forefront of not only studies of new communication technologies but also in planning their applications. However, research has been both late and inadequate; many fine research opportunities have been lost forever. Research data have been replaced with personal opinions and normative value judgements. (Wiio, 1981)

But in very recent years, a small number of useful researches have been carried out that deal with certain aspects of the new communication technologies. There are an estimated 83 field experiments underway on videotex around the world, but many, especially in the U.S., are being conducted by private companies that will not allow scholars to gain access to their research results. Based on the authors' participation in several investigations, and our literature review of others, plus personal discussions with some of the researchers and practitioners involved, we wish to draw certain general lessons about the nature of the impacts of the new communication technologies. We will concentrate heavily, but not exclusively, on the new communication technologies being applied in the work organization.

Our discussion of impacts takes the form (a) of important research results or perspectives, and (b) of methodological problems and their partial and/or possible solution.

Channel Versus Content Studies

The general research question addressed by a very great deal of behavioral research on new communication technologies in the work organization is: "What are the effects of the new communication technologies?'' This question is similar to the main direction of mass communication research in the United States and (less so) in Europe for the past 40 years, but with some very important differences. One such contrast is that the contemporary research concern is with the impact of a new type of communication *channels*. Although computer-based communication technologies are much more than just another communication channel—very often they are, at the same time, a tool for information-composition, searching, filing, and retrieval—many studies deal only with the channel effect, rather than with a particular type of message content (Short, Williams, and Christie, 1976; Johansen, Vallee, and Spangler, 1979; Christie, 1981). For example, we now study the effect of electronic messaging systems in the office, while various mass media researchers have studied the effect of TV violence on children. Both are effects studies, but they are quite different in the details of their research design and in their degree of specificity.

But clearly there are parallels in the general research designs used in past media effects studies, and in contemporary researches on the impact of new office (and home) technologies. This similarity is entirely understandable, but we are concerned that a too-close following of the intellectual paradigm of the past will limit the policy payoff of present research. Nevertheless, we begin by listing some of the important effects now being investigated in studies of new office technologies, and then suggest some additional possibilities.

Channel Use in Organizations

How does the introduction of new communication technologies in a work organization change the existing patterns of organizational communication?

A general issue here, of great importance, is to determine the magnitude of the consequences of the new technologies. Do they indeed cause a "revolution" in communication behavior? The early evidence on this point seems to be negative. The impacts are incremental, rather than revolutionary. For example Picot, Klingenberg, and Kränzle (1982) conclude from studies of the impact of new office automation technology in German organizations that new electronic text media (such as computer mail, telefax, and computer conferencing) will mainly replace such older text media as mail and telex, which—in terms of number of contacts—play a minor role in organizational communication. These new media will replace oral channels only to the extent that oral communication is used for transmission of relatively simple information content. However, the proportion of that kind of oral channel use is not very high in organizations. The explanation for this finding is that much face-to-face communication is still considered necessary by organizational participants, mainly (a) for

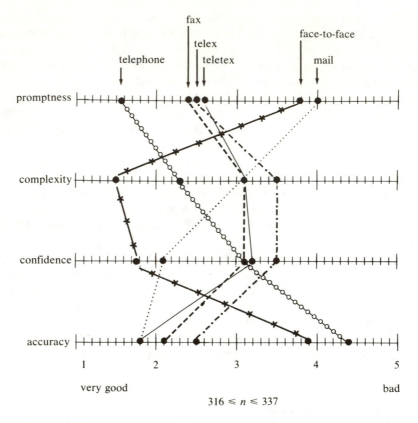

Figure 1. Task-Oriented Evaluation of Communication Channels in Organizations

its social relationship content, and (b) for the complex task-oriented, non-programmable information that it conveys.

Organizational hierarchies emerge because they are more economical for carrying out difficult information-exchanges associated with certain types of divisions of labor (Williamson, 1975 and 1980). This information-exchange demands a high symbolic and material communication capacity typically provided by oral (especially face-to-face) channels (Watzlawick, Beavin, and Jackson, 1967). The new media cannot serve as an equivalent substitute for the "social presence" that is crucial for the functioning of social relations and of unstructured information-exchange (Short, Williams, and Christie, 1976; Picot, Klingenberg, and Kränzle, 1982). Thus, new communication technology will facilitate various intraorganizational communication processes, but it will not wipe out the principal problems of information-exchange characteristic of organizations. On the other hand,

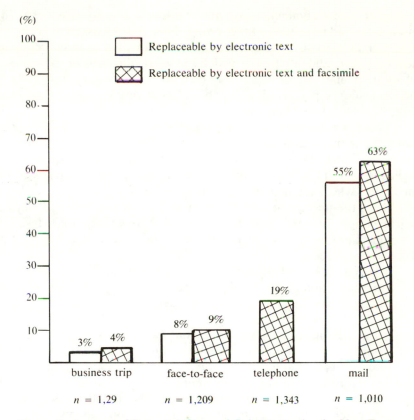

Figure 2. Amount of Potential Channel Substitution by the New Text-Oriented Technologies

the structure of external organizational communication, which to a greater part consists of standardized information-exchange, will be more greatly affected by the new text media.

The German research found four key problems to be overcome by organizational communication:

1. Managerial promptness,
2. Semantic complexity,
3. Interpersonal confidence, and
4. Administrative accuracy.

The suitability of six organizational communication channels for resolving these communication problems is shown in Figure 1. In terms of number of contacts and in terms of time consumed, the first three problems prevail in organizational communication and the fourth is also of eminent importance for administrative functioning. This general assessment of the new communication technologies' suitability for organizational communication is reflected in Figure 2, which shows, on the basis of an empirical substitution analysis, the degree to which the new electronic text and facsimile media are perceived as capable of replacing business trips, face-to-face contact, telephone, and mail.

These conclusions are also generally supported by our findings from investigating the "Terminals for Managers" (TFM) electronic office messaging system at Stanford University (Rogers, Heath, and Moore, 1981). Highest use of TFM was by the accounting and finance officials of the university, who were mainly exchanging budgetary-type data; academic officials of the university used TFM much less, in part because more of their message content involved social relationships or complex task-oriented questions for which they preferred face-to-face (or telephone) channels.

The general issue here is what existing communication behavior the new communication technologies substitute for. Also important are such topics as expressed in the two research questions that follow.

Structural Changes and Organizational Communication

To what extent do the new office technologies support or subvert the organizational structure as it channels communication flows?

One of the anxieties expressed about the introduction of certain new technologies, such as electronic messaging, is that it will break down the constraining effect of the organization's structure on communicating behavior. Will a top executive be swamped with messages when all of the organization's employees are directly connected to the official by an electronic messaging system? Will the relative ease of sending "carbons" of messages lead to problems of information overload? Does removing the constraining effect of physical distance (and the effort required to communicate across it) between two individuals in an organization greatly increase the volume of messages that they exchange? Or will the new technologies, by enabling employees to work at home, increase physical barriers to face-to-face interaction among colleagues? To what extent will the role of "bosses" and secretaries be reversed by the new office technologies (as has been reported in some organizations, with the "boss" now doing his own typing/composing and the secretary moving into new office managing tasks)?

One of the general issues here is who communicates with whom, via what channels of communication, before and after the introduction of the new office technologies. This question is made to order for communication network analysis to answer (Rogers and Kincaid, 1981). But we know of no such investigation that has been conducted to date. We ought to measure the impact of new communication technologies on the users' interpersonal networks, through a "pre-post" research design.

We stress the optional character of the new technologies: They offer a potential which can be used in either direction. New communication technology in organizations can provide individuals with more, better, and more relevant information, and thus enable them to become more autonomous decisionmakers. Thereby the organization's hierarchy can be flattened. On the other hand, these technologies can be used in a way that isolates people from each other and that tightens control by managers over office workers by demanding instantaneous feedback about current work progress. Thus, technology itself is neither good nor bad. Rather the way technology is used in a certain situation tells us much about an organization's climate, ideology, or problems.

As far as the geographical decentralization of work is concerned, we feel that the new technologies will allow homogeneous work groups and rather independent job-holders to locate their activities in remote places, perhaps far away from their mother organizations. Thereby organizational coordination shifts from a hierarchical pattern to a more decentralized mode involving a tendency towards office workers' compensation on the basis of measurable outputs. However, such teleworking will not represent a majority of office workers, as most office tasks are not programmable on a clear input/output-basis. Thus, most office jobs cannot be scattered, and have to remain concentrated in order to guarantee the unstructured interpersonal information-exchange which is necessary for most organizational problem-solving and control. A requisite for the successful build-up of social relationships and complex information-exchange, social presence cannot be satisfactorily replaced by telecommunications (Short, Williams, and Christie, 1976; Klingenberg and Kränzle, 1983; Brandt, 1983).

Office Productivity

How will the new technologies affect office productivity? Will the greatly-increased capital costs be offset by reduced labor costs gained through increased labor productivity? What problems (including management relationships with clerical unions) will accompany the reduction in the total office labor force that is likely to occur? To what degree will the quality of work life be improved through the reduction of repetitive, monotonous tasks like typing? Will employee stress of certain types be increased, such as by working on display terminals? Will the organization's capability of adaptation to change be improved?

A comprehensive economic evaluation of new communication technology is a most difficult task (1) because many of the assumed effects are difficult to quantify, although they seem to be very important (for example, an improved information supply and increased flexibility), and (2) because the effects occur at different levels of observation (the individual, group, organization, and society). In order to overcome these difficulties, a multi-level framework has been developed which should guide evaluation discussions. Interestingly enough, that concept was independently and almost simultaneously proposed in Europe (Picot and others, 1979; Picot and Reichwald, 1979; Picot, 1979) and in the U.S. (Bair, 1979a and 1979b). It discerns costs and benefits at four levels of evaluation which have to be explored and taken into account before a proper decision can be made:

1. Isolated equipment efficiency;
2. Efficiency of a subsystem's throughput;
3. Efficiency of the organization; and
4. Social efficiency.

These concepts have served as a basis for empirical evaluation research (Picot and others, 1979; Bodem and others, 1983). Results show that the payoffs from new communication technology lie mainly in non-quantifiable performance, rather than in monetary cost calculations.

The difficulties in measuring the impacts of office automation on productivity may be one reason why the rate of adoption of the new office technologies seems to have slowed somewhat in very recent years. Organization leaders have to decide to adopt on faith, rather than hard evidence.

Equality
Do the new office technologies have greater effects (a) on certain individuals in an organization than on others, and (b) on certain organizations? Here we are looking at whether the technologies are information gap-widening or gap-narrowing. At issue is the degree of equality in the consequences of the new communication technologies.

One basic, and often implicit, assumption in this discussion is that technology-richness would trigger information-richness, i.e., that access to new information technology would provide a higher quality level of information. Although this assumption can be contested under certain circumstances, it seems acceptable in many others. The issue of equality is of central importance in the case of new communication technology in the household, where policymakers are concerned about whether this relatively expensive technology will widen the knowledge gap between the information-rich and the information-poor. Certain types of knowledge (that only certain individuals will possess) can be converted to political power, in some cases. For example, a U.S. data-bank that can be accessed with a home computer and a telephone modem connection now provides daily voting records of national legislators, as well as the U.S. president's daily schedule. Such information might be useful to the politically-active citizen. Access to the German *Bildschirmtext* system grants a much higher level of market transparency in the banking, travel, or insurance industry than consumers can dispose of otherwise.

In the case of such past communication technologies as television, it seems that the new technology, in its process of diffusion, first widened knowledge gaps in society, but eventually closed them, when everyone adopted the innovation (Katzman, 1974). This first-widening/then-closing sequence occurs if the technology is widely adopted, and the temporary inequalities are less serious when the rate of diffusion is rapid (as with television in the U.S.). But what about an expensive communication technology like home computers that may never become a consumer item in all households (Figure 3)?

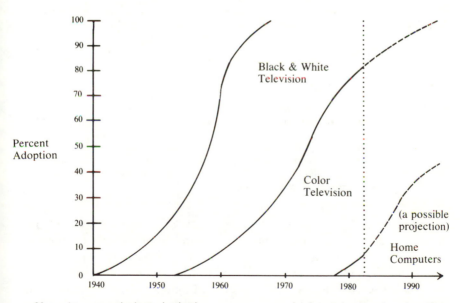

Note: At any particular point in time, a new communication technology has the effect of widening the knowledge gaps in society, because the first to adopt are the socioeconomic elites who are already the information-rich. But later, when everyone has adopted the technology, it again has an equalizing effect between the information-rich and the information-poor. But what about a technology like home computers that may not reach 100 per cent adoption?

Figure 3. Diffusion Curves for the Adoption of Three Household Communication Technologies

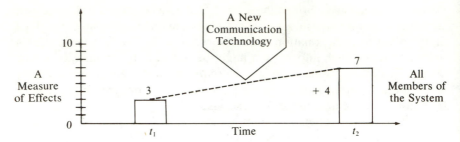

Figure 4a: The First Dimension of Communication Effects (for all members of the system) as an Average Increase of 4 Units, Measured as the Difference from t_1 to t_2

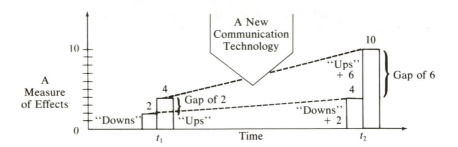

Note that the "Downs" are *absolutely* better off as a result of the new communication technology (+2), but they are *relatively* worse off (as the "Ups" gained +6). So the rich get richer (informationally) and the poor get less poor. (*Source:* Rogers, 1983a.)

Figure 4b. The Second Dimension of Communication Effects (which analyzes effects separately for "Downs" and "Ups") Indicates that the Effects Gap is Widened by the Introduction of a New Communication Technology

Is there a close parallel to the case of new office technologies? Figures 4a and 4b depict two dimensions of communication effects: (a) the first dimension, where we ask "What average or aggregate effect does a new communication technology have?" and (b) the second dimension, where the main research question is "Do certain individuals or systems experience a relatively greater effect of the new communication technology than do others?" Policy-makers are usually very interested in the equality dimension of new communication technology; they are concerned with the new technology's potential for creating a wider gap between the information-rich and the information-poor.

Such gap-widening often occurs (unless strategies are explicitly followed to prevent it) because:

1. The new communication technologies of home computers, teletext and videotex systems, videotape recorders, etc. in the home, and teleconferencing and electronic messaging in the office, are expensive. So only the socioeconomic elites can afford them. They adopt them first, and others can only follow slowly, if at all.
2. Because these new technologies are computer-based information tools, an individual must be a motivated information-searcher to use them (at least effectively). The information-rich are most likely to be the first adopters.
3. Those new communication technologies that support inter-individual communication require that potential communicators are equipped with compatible devices (electronic mail, picture phone, teletext, telecopy, computer conferencing, etc.) so that a relevant network can emerge. Such networks are much more rapidly created among the early adopting information-rich socioeconomic class than among other potential users. Thus, the information-rich get richer by networking. This argument can be applied to international, national, and organizational levels of investigation, as well as the individual.
4. The information-rich particularly want specialized information, which the new communication technologies are uniquely able to provide. Thus, they can increase their information advantage. An example of this point comes from an evaluation of *Bildschirmtext,* an interactive information system (videotex) now undergoing experimentation in Düsseldorf and Berlin. The several thousand accepters of this technology use the *Bildschirmtext* system to obtain specialized information about news, travel, banking, and to purchase catalog products.

ACCEPTANCE AND USE

A second major issue in research on new communication technologies is how they are accepted and used. In fact, this issue obviously precedes the issue of effects, in that effects only occur after acceptance. The acceptance issue has generally received less research attention than have the effects questions, at least to date, in the case of new office technologies.

Networks and the Critical Mass Problem
How does the networking nature of the new office technologies affect their acceptance and use? A general research paradigm of the diffusion of innovations (Rogers, 1983a) is directly applicable to studying acceptance

of new communication technologies, but of course with some very special twists. One particular aspect of many of the new office technologies is that they provide an improved means for connecting with other individuals (or organizations); thus these technologies essentially are "networking," not one-way "broadcasting" nor "stand-alone" technologies. This distinctive aspect affects the acceptance and use of the new interactive technologies. At one extreme consider the only individual in an organization who has an electronic messaging system; it is worthless to him as a means of communicating with his co-workers. As each additional individual gains access to this technology, its usefulness increases to each of the individuals already on the system. Another example: Consider the employee whose boss sends him a message via the new technology. Here the networking nature of the technology strongly encourages the individual to use the technology to respond.

More precisely the real diffusion take-off of a new communication technology heavily depends on a "critical mass" of individuals (or organizations) which must have adopted previously. Only if one can be sure that a majority of current addressees can be reached by a specific communication tool will one be willing to use it on a habitual basis. Thus the net benefit to an end-user of equipment for individual communication is influenced by the number of installations within his/her relevant group of reference. There is no exact formula available for calculation of the minimum level of the critical mass that is necessary for adoption to occur. However, a critical mass for a new communication technology must be higher, if:

- The relevant communication contacts to be carried out by the new technology are perceived as less important.
- The group of potential addressees who must be reached by the new technology is large and varied.
- The proportion of communication messages to be carried by the interactive technology is low compared to the total communication volume of a typical user.
- The new technology's use is not compatible with other information services that can serve as a substitute or a complement for that type of communication.
- The new interactive technology demands installation of a new physical network.

By thorough analysis and, if possible, influencing of these (above) determinants, the level of the critical mass can be roughly assessed and, perhaps, lowered. Reaching a critical mass, once it is assessed, can be accelerated by:

- Careful market segmentation and initial concentration on the relatively closed networks of potential user groups.
- A low price-strategy during market introduction.
- Decentralized installation of end-user equipment.

Such steps will facilitate purchases and terminal access; they will increase communication traffic and help create new experiences with the technology which in turn may trigger new adoptions. The history of the diffusion of the telephone illustrates these points.

During the first phases of diffusion, potential users and decision-makers might better adopt a wide, rather than a narrow, view of the adoption decision. Usually people interpret investment decisions as choices for or against adopting a stand-alone unit. The decision calculus asks, for instance, whether the cost per unit is lower when using the new machine compared to existing procedures.

If this decision rule is applied to interactive communication technology, the result may be unintended (Picot 1982). Figure 5 shows a network of information flows between four points (for example, departments in an organization) with the figures representing the average number of communication contacts per day suitable for electronic text communication. A cost analysis on the basis of investment costs and operating costs of the old and new equipment may show that production and mailing of 10 or more messages per day is necessary for an economically advantageous application of the new communication technology. Thus, according to traditional stand-alone decision-making, Departments A, C and D would purchase new equipment. However, A and C would not be able to secure these expected economic benefits, as part of their mail goes to B who decided not to adopt. Thus A and C can only achieve their return on investment in the new technology if B also adopts the new technology.

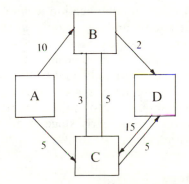

Figure 5. Information Flows in a Network (number of contacts per day suitable for electronic text communication)

Hence, B's adopting will create the critical mass for adoption by the others. This acceptance can be achieved through: (a) lowering the costs of the technology, (b) subsidies, or (c) shifting the responsibility of the adoption decision to a higher level such as an association of these organizations or the government.

The foregoing discussion suggests that *how* a new office technology is introduced may be at least as important as *what* the technology is.

Redesign and Implementation

How can the new office technologies be redesigned so as to become more acceptable and more useful?

This research question puts the behavioral scientist in the position of designer/redesigner of the communication technologies, along with the more familiar role (in the past) of evaluator of effects. In fact, the two roles seldom can be kept completely distinct in research on the new communication technologies (as we show later in this chapter).

Here a specific issue to be studied may be: What are the factors preventing acceptance/use of the new office technologies (such as computer fear, lack of typing ability, and concerns about the invasion of privacy)? The interface between the individual and the technology is crucial here, an issue that is far from completely understood in the case of the new office technologies.

Perhaps people have a basic desire to use the new technologies in their own unique ways, to be active shapers of the tools rather than just passive "acceptors." We feel this issue needs more attention than it has received to date; investigators often have overlooked the creative and individualized ways in which people use technological innovations (Rice and Rogers, 1980). Five individuals may adopt the same make and model of an office word-processor, but modify this tool to do five different tasks.

Redesign of technology also involves its organizational embedding. Implementation of new office communication technology may affect job characteristics, work relations, and organizational structure, often in a beneficial way. However, in order (a) to reduce fears and resistances from employees, (b) to mobilize motivation, redesign capabilities, and relevant knowledge about communication needs, and (c) in order to ensure later acceptance and cooperative use, a transparent, participatory planning and implementation strategy should be followed. Involvement of affected managers and office workers at an early stage in the discussion and implementation process is important for long-term success with office automation.

Naming The Technology

How important is the name of a new communication technology as a factor in its acceptance?

Market research on new products consistently shows that what an innovation is called has an influence on its acceptance. Obviously it is the potential users' perceptions of a new communication technology, including its name, that determines its rate of adoption. New communication technologies ought to be given names that are meaningful and understandable to the users. Instead, names are often given in a way that, while technically correct, may confuse potential users and turn them off. We ought to devote much more care than in the past to the name for a new communication technology.

"Bildschirmtext" is composed of three German words: *"Bild"* or picture, *"Schirm"* or screen, and *"Text."* An official in the Ministry of Posts and Telecommunication chose this name to stress that *Bildschirmtext* uses a TV set only as a screen, and not for broadcasting (as the frame-images are conveyed to the home by telephone line). This non-broadcasting aspect of *Bildschirmtext* is important to the Ministry for Posts and Telecommunication, which has responsibility for telephone services but not for TV broadcasting. This non-broadcasting nature of *Bildschirmtext* is also conveyed by its logo: a prominent symbol of a telephone, on a blue TV screen, with the name *"Bildschirmtext"* written underneath the telephone in computer text. Whether this name and symbol are appropriated for the system's users is not known, as the new service is still in the process of being introduced. One may doubt that the political distinction between a TV broadcasting and a telephone-channel technology is very important to the users, and in fact the system offers much more than just text on a screen.

The same emphasis on the telephone is found in the German Ministry of Posts and Telecommunication's most recent experiment with "BIGFON" (pronounced "big phone"), *Breitbandiges Integriertes Glasfaser-FernmeldeOrtsNetz*. This broadband fiber optical experiment is now getting underway in six German cities. The acronym does not reveal the real nature of this new network technology, at least as it is likely to be perceived by users.

The "Green Thumb" system was originally named "Extele" by U.S. government officials, indicating the technology's role in providing extension service information at a distance (to farmers). But a U.S. senator's secretary began calling the system "Green Thumb," a name that stuck (to the dismay of the technologists who designed the system). Kentucky farmers (the users), however, reacted favorably to the name "Green Thumb." So, by accident instead of design, this new technology was given a name that seemed to help its acceptance. At least the name is unforgettable.

The French teletext system, officially called "ANTIOPE" (for *"L'Acquisition Numerique et Televisualisation d'Images"*) after Antiope, daughter of the king of Thebes in Greek mythology, is widely confused by the public with the French (and English) word "antelope."

The naming of new communication technologies is often done rather haphazardly, or, worse, by technologists without the benefit of formative evaluation to guide their choice of words that would be meaningful to the public. Understandably, such names then hinder acceptance of the new technologies by the public.

METHODOLOGICAL LESSONS

Figure 6 diagrams a somewhat typical research design for studying the impacts of a new communication technology. The main elements in the design are a sample of users of the new technology (perhaps at least 100 to 200) from whom data are gathered, often by means of personal interviews, both before (at t_1) and after (at t_2) the introduction of a new communication technology. So far, the design is the usual one for a field experiment, based on the kind of experimental design that behavioral scientists have taken from the classical physics of some years ago.

The distinctive aspect here is the possibility of obtaining "use-data" from the technology system itself, such as from computer records of an electronic messaging system or from an interactive television system (Rice and Rogers, 1983). The use-data indicate who uses the technology, how frequently, and for what purpose. Sometimes data are also gathered from

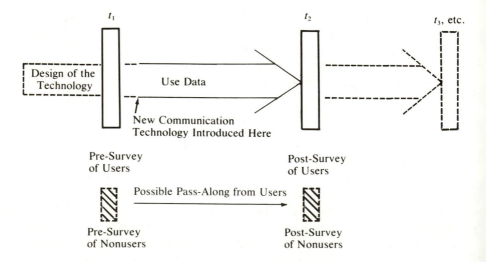

Figure 6. Diagram of a Usual Research Design for Studying the Impacts of a New Communication Technology.

a sample of non-users of the communication technology, who may have received pass-along information from users.

A number of methodological questions and problems accompany the usual experience with using this type of research design.

The evaluation researchers usually enter the research process too late to make their maximum contribution. Very seldom do the behavioral science researchers participate in designing the communication technology, where engineers and technologists usually dominate. Sometimes, there is no t_1 survey of future users (as in the 1981 Green Thumb Project by Stanford University). Then, the researchers must depend mainly on the users' perceived and remembered impacts of the communication technology (a rather unsatisfactory methodology for data-gathering).

But sometimes behavioral scientists are involved very early in the technology design process, as occurred in the *Bildschirmtext* Project in the Federal Republic of Germany (Figure 7). Here the evaluation researchers conducted an "acceptability" study of potential users of *Bildschirmtext*, and of the actual users in a short test phase of this interactive TV technology. The purpose of this formative evaluation research was to gain understandings of the future acceptance of *Bildschirmtext*, by

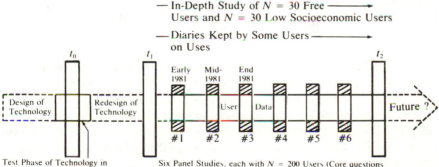

Note: Not shown here is a survey of the 800–900 private information-providers, who are mainly studied by the Kammerer Research Group (in Munich) at the Berlin location. The Düsseldorf users studies are mainly conducted by Infratest Media-Forschung (in Munich) under the direction of consultant Prof. Dr. Heiner Treinen of the Ruhr-University Bochum.

Figure 7. Diagram of the Evaluation Research Design for the *Bildschirmtext* System of the German Ministry of Posts and Telecommunications in Düsseldorf and Berlin

dealing with such questions as how many (and which) households would purchase the *Bildschirmtext* services, at what price, and how the technology should be designed/redesigned for user acceptance. A somewhat similar strategy was chosen for the planning, design, and implementation of the new office automation service in Germany (Picot and Reichwald, 1979).

Such acceptability studies of a new communication technology face many difficulties, stemming from the basic inadequacies of most available social science methods to predict future behavior. Nevertheless, acceptability studies represent one type of formative evaluation that at least involves behavioral scientists along with the technologists early in the process of designing the communication technology.

The computer-recorded use-data often cannot be matched with the pre/post survey data. There are many possible reasons for this problem, such as that each unit of the technology (such as a computer terminal) may be used by various individuals other than the individual that it is officially assigned to (such as the secretaries of the official users of the TFM system in the Stanford University study). There are also confidentiality problems of an ethical nature, which may prohibit analysis of the use-data because it cannot be matched with individual users. And there is the problem that the computer recording of use-data may be intrusive (and thus affect use of the system) if the users know that their use is being recorded.

Logistical and timing problems often interfere with execution of an ideal research design. Perhaps all of the intended users do not get their equipment at t_1 (Figure 6), or perhaps they are not trained to begin using the new technology at t_1. Sometimes the technology is changed/modified/improved from t_1 to t_2, perhaps due to feedback from an early evaluation research. Then exactly what technology system is being evaluated as to its impacts?

There is often no control group for comparison with the users, so it is impossible to remove the effects of other variables on use of the communication technology (Figure 7). The lack of a control group often occurs in studying a communication technology, such as when it is introduced in an entire organizational unit at the same time. It is difficult to do otherwise, given the network nature of interactive technologies (this is the critical mass). Perhaps another unit could be selected as a control group, if it matched fairly well. But even then, the random assignment of respondents to treatment and control groups is usually impossible. There are just so many problems involved in having a true control group in field experimentation (Picot, 1975), that they are almost never utilized in evaluations of a new communication technology. As a consequence, such evaluations consistently overestimate a new technology's effects, because any extraneous effects that may exist are included as a disguised residual in the measured effect. This problem should not be forgotten when we analyze and report the research results of these studies.

Other means of control can be (and are) utilized in evaluating new communication technologies, such as multivariate statistical control. But such an evaluation design is weaker than an experiment because all of the variables to be controlled on must be measured; in an experimental design, all variables are controlled, whether measured or not.

Users of the new communication technology often are not representative of the population of future users, so the research results cannot be generalized. The issue of the generalizability of an experiment's results are illustrated by our respondents in the 1980–1981 TFM study, who were the top 110 administrators at Stanford University. Are they typical of the next 110 users of TFM at Stanford? Hardly. And how representative is Stanford University of other organizations that are expected to adopt TFM in the near future? Probably not very.

Another example of the generalizability problem while evaluating the impact of new communication technologies comes from the *Bildschirmtext* Project in Germany. The 1,455 household users of this interactive TV system in Düsseldorf were recruited through two campaigns aimed at recent purchasers of color TV sets (Figure 7). The 1,455 users probably tend to be socioeconomic elites, like the early adopters of most other innovations (the individuals in the left-hand tail of the S-shaped diffusion curves shown in Figure 3). One indication that the households volunteering to be participants in the *Bildschirmtext* Project were already information-rich is shown by the fact that about 25 per cent of these volunteers had home videotape recorders, compared to only 3 per cent of all German households at the time. The evaluation studies carried out in order to assess the impacts of office automation in Germany show similar biases; after intensive search, two large organizations were found for field experimental studies (they surely were among the pioneer adopters of any new office technology).

The general lesson that we are learning here is that individuals, families, and organizations that voluntarily participate in a communication technology experiment are very untypical of the population of potential users. Instead, the users in an experiment are usually typical of the early adopters of an innovation: information-rich and socioeconomically advantaged.

It is very difficult to avoid this threat to generalizability, even when one tries. For example, in the Green Thumb Project in Kentucky, the 200 users of this free system (in 1981) were chosen by a local committee from the approximately 400–500 farmers who applied for a Green Thumb Box (in response to a mailed announcement from the local county extension agent to about 2,600 farmers in the two counties of study). The committee chose the 200 users so they were approximately representative of three categories of farm size (small, medium, and large-sized farmers). This selection procedure guaranteed a range of socioeconomic status among the 200 users, but it introduced another bias: The small-sized farmers who volunteered to participate tended to be untypical of all small farmers in the two counties in that they had a high degree of prior contact with their county extension agent (most small farmers do not have much extension contact). So the Green Thumb selection procedure guaranteed that small farmers were included in our study, but also tended to make these small farmer-users untypical of all small farmers. And a further problem: The Green Thumb system was free to the user in 1981 (thanks to the U.S. Department of Agriculture), but a fee was charged later for the Green Thumb service. Not many small farmers will use Green Thumb in the future. So again our small farmer-users in the 1981 study are a sample whose research results cannot be generalized to any future users.

The *Bildschirmtext* Project went to special pains to include lower socioeconomic status households in the Düsseldorf evaluation study. As Figure 7 shows, 30 users were recruited by offering free service (all other households paid a monthly fee of 5 *Deutschmarks,* or about $2.50 (U.S.), plus any frame charges; many of the 150,000 frames are available at no charge, but others may cost from .001 to .99 *Deutschmarks* per viewing), and another small sample of 30 users were identified from among the lowest socioeconomic households to apply for the *Bildschirmtext* system. Both of these small samples were investigated via unstructured personal interviews, group interviews, and by telephone, and (according to the evaluation research group) these research results from the extremely information-poor were useful in redesigning the *Bildschirmtext* system.

The research strategy suggested by the *Bildschirmtext* Project is to concentrate certain data-gathering activities on "extreme groups": households very low in socioeconomic status, for example, or the information-poor (and/or perhaps for contrast, a small sample of the information-rich, the socioeconomic elites, or the highest users). The strategy amounts to oversampling sub-audiences that are usually underrepresented by volunteer participants in the trial of a new communication technology. But with this oversampling strategy, the researcher does not have a random sample from a population of future users (and thus cannot utilize statistical inference as a basis for generalizability of the evaluation research results).

Quantitative research approaches, based on a notion of "variance research," seldom can provide a satisfactory understanding of the behavioral change process through which a new communication technology has effects. Almost all research designs for evaluating the acceptance and effects of new communication technologies (a) are highly quantitative, and (b) follow a variance research approach (Figure 6). Usually these researches (a) measure a large number of variables, (b) with data gathered from a large sample of users, at least several hundred and perhaps several thousand (as in the *Bildschirmtext* evaluation, where German politicians in the national parliament influenced the Ministry of Posts and Telecommunications to design an evaluation of the technology with several thousand users in two locations). The assumption here is that a large sample of users will provide more precise research results about acceptance and impacts (as well as helping the communication technology pilot project move rapidly toward becoming a national program).

Variance research is a type of data-gathering and analysis that consists of determining the co-variances among a set of variables but not their time-order (Mohr, 1982). A pre/post design (Figure 6) heads an investigation toward using (a) "difference" statistics (like the t-test between means or analysis of variance) in his/her data-analysis, or (b) "correlational" statistics (like zero-order correlation, multiple correlation and regression, or partial correlation techniques) in which the researcher seeks to determine the correlates of a dependent variable, which often is either acceptance or use of the new communication technology.

Variance research alone usually cannot tell us much about the time-order of our variables of study, other than rather crudely (through the t_1 to t_2 differences in a variable), and seldom can provide a very complete understanding of the over-time process nature of the behavior change effects that are caused by the new communication technology. In this situation, a process research approach may be more appropriate.

Process research is a type of data-gathering and analysis that seeks to determine the time-ordered sequence of a set of events. Data-gathering methods for process research are often more qualitative in nature (like participant observation, the case study, and unstructured interviewing). A special advantage of such qualitative methods is that they allow the investigator (a) to identify unexpected variables, and (b) to study the wider context of the user system and of the new communication technology. For example, the *Bildschirmtext* evaluation involves qualitative data-gathering (a) via user diaries, and (b) from an in-depth study of 30 low-income users.

Process research is not necessarily qualitative. For instance, the *Bildschirmtext* evaluation includes quantitative data-gathering from the six-stage panel of 200 users, in which a set of core variables are measured every four months or so (Figure 7). This panel strategy allows tracing user behavior changes over a number of time periods (this approach is highly intrusive in that the repeated data-gathering undoubtedly conditions the responses that are gathered, although with the large sample of *Bildschirmtext* users that are available, this intrusion may not be too serious).

Variance and process research are not necessarily in competition; a research design can include both approaches, with each providing a unique type of data. Most research designs for evaluating the impacts of new communication technology consist solely (or at least mainly) of quantitative data-gathering for variance research. That is certainly a mistake, in our opinion.

Evaluation researchers who study a new communication technology are presumably separate from the managers of the new technology system, but in practice they are usually almost co-designers (or co-redesigners) of the new communication technology. Conventional wisdom about evaluation research holds that the evaluators should be independent and separate from the system or program that they are evaluating. Politicians and other policy-makers often require such separation, so as to minimize possible pro-technology biases of the evaluation. For instance, U.S. Department of Agriculture officials required that the Green Thumb system be evaluated by other than the University of Kentucky (who operated the 1980–1981 Green Thumb Project in two Kentucky counties). And German government officials and politicians required that the Ministry of Posts and Telecommunications contract with external research groups for evaluation of the *Bildschirmtext* system. The independence of the evaluation researchers from the technologists who design and operate the technology system is thought to raise the credibility with which the research results are perceived. In many cases, such independence and separation may indeed create a healthy tension between the evaluators and the technologists, and lead to more reliable research findings about the technology's effects.

But the reality of the situation is usually that the evaluators and technologists must collaborate closely if an evaluation is to be conducted in an effective manner, and if the research findings are to be utilized to improve the communication technology through its redesign. Often this redesign occurs during the time period (t_1 to t_2 in Figure 6) in which the communication technology is being evaluated; the evaluators suggest needed improvements to the technologists, which may then be implemented. This sequence of events was partly the case in the German office automation studies.

Further, it does not seem so certain that the independence of evaluators and technologists is ideal, even in principle. It may be crucial for both technologists and behavioral scientists to be involved jointly in a new communication technology; each has an important type of expertise to contribute to the new communication technology project. Perhaps it is realistic and advantageous for the technologists and behavioral scientists to be organized as one team of equals, rather than always insisting on their separate independence.

CONCLUSIONS AND DISCUSSIONS

At this crucial time, communication research can play a useful role in determining the impacts of the new technologies, so that government and private policies can be more soundly based upon empirical evidence. In order to play this crucial role, the nature of communication research must be quite different from past studies of the effects of the mass media; many of the new technologies are interactive, hence linear models of the communication process, based on the single act of communication, are inappropriate. Perhaps convergence models of communication, which conceive of human communication as the exchange of information among participants, are more valuable in investigating the new interactive communication systems (Rogers and Kincaid, 1981). Finally, due to the computer element that is part of the interactive technologies, a variety of new types of data can be utilized in impact studies. Investigations of the new communication technologies will thus change the methods and theories of communication research.

Thus the Information Revolution may cause a Communication Research Revolution.

REFERENCES

James H. Bair (1979a), "Communication in the Office of the Future: Where the Real Pay-Off May Be," *Business Communication Review, 1–2,* 3–12.

James H. Bair (1979b), "A Communications Perspective for Identifying Office Automation Payoffs," Paper presented at the Symposium on Automated Office System, New York University.

Helmut Bodem, Peter Hauke, Bernd Lange, and Hans Zangl (1983), *Kommunikationstechnik und Wirtschaftlichkeit: Eine Analyse am Beispiel Teletex und Telefax,* Munich, Germany: CW-Publikationen.

Stefan Brandt (1983), *Kommunikation und Räumliche Struktur von Bürotätigkeiten,* Dissertation, Hannover, Germany, Universität Hannover.

Milton Chen (1981), *Site Visits to New Communication Technologies Used by Children: Videotext, Teletext, Interactive Cable, Personal Computers,* Stanford University, Stanford, CA: Institute for Communication Research, Report.

Bruce Christie (1981), *Face to Face Communication,* New York: Wiley.

Tom Forester (1980), *The Microelectronics Revolution*, New York: Oxford University Press, and Basil Blackwell.

Robert Johansen, Jaques Vallee, and Kathleen Spangler (1979), *Electronic Meetings: Technical Alternatives and Social Choices*, Reading, MA: Addison-Wesley.

Natan Katzman (1974), "The Impact of Communication Technology: Promises and Prospects," *Journal of Communication, 24*, 47–58.

Heide Klingenberg and Hans-Peter Kränzle (1983), *Kommunikationstechnik und Nutzerverhalten: Die Wahl Zwischen Kommunikationsmitteln in Organisationen*, Munich, Germany: CW-Publikationen.

Mark R. Levy (1980), "Home Video Recorders: A User Survey," *Journal of Communication, 30*, 23–27.

Fritz Machlup and Trude Kronwinkler (1975), "Workers Who Produce Knowledge: A Steady Increase, 1900 to 1970," *Weltwirtschaftliches Archiv, 111*, 752–759.

Lawrence B. Mohr (1982), *Explaining Organizational Behavior: The Limits and Possibilities of Theory and Research*, San Francisco: Jossey-Bass.

Simon Nora and Alain Minc (1978), *L'informatization de la Société*, Paris, La Documentation Francaise, et Editions du Seuil; published as *The Computerization of Society: A Report to the President of France*. Cambridge, MA: MIT Press.

Arnold Picot (1975), *Experimentelle Organisationsforschung: Methodische und Wissenschaftstheoretische Grundlagen*, Wiesbaden, Germany: Gabler.

Arnold Picot (1979), "Rationalisierung im Verwaltungsbereich als Betriebswirtschaftliches Problem," *Zeitschrift für Betriebswirtschaft, 49*, 1145–1165.

Arnold Picot (1982), "Neue Techniken der Bürokommunikation in Wirtschaftlicher und Organisatorischer Sicht," in *Europäischer Kongreβ über Bürosysteme und Informations-Management: Proceedings*, Munich, Germany: CW-Publikationen.

Arnold Picot and Wolfgang Anders (1983a), "Telekommunikationsnetze als Infrastruktur Neuerer Entwicklungen der Geschäftlichen Kommunikation," *Wirtschaftswissenschaftliches Studium, 12*, 183–189.

Arnold Picot and Wolfgang Anders (1983b), "Telekommunikationsdienste für den Geschäftsbereich," *Wirtschaftswissenschaftliches Studium, 12*.

Arnold Picot and Ralf Reichwald (1979), *Untersuchungen der Auswirkungen Neuer Kommunikationstechnologien im Büro auf Organisationsstruktur und Arbeitsinhalte, Phase 1: Entwicklung einer Untersuchungskonzeption*, Eggenstein-Leopoldshafen, Germany: Fachinformationszentrum Energie, Physik, Mathematik.

Arnold Picot, Heide Klingenberg, and Hans-Peter Kränzle (1982), "Office Technology: A Report on Attitudes and Channel Selection from Field Studies in Germany," in Michael Burgoon (ed.), *Communication Yearbook 6*, Beverly Hills, CA: Sage.

Arnold Picot, Ralf Reichwald, Hans Bodem, Peter Ramsauer, Roland Stolz, and Johann Zangl (1979), *Untersuchung zur Wirtschaftlichkeit der Schreibdienste in Obersten Bundesbehörden*, Munich. (To be published at Fachinformationszentrum Energie, Physik, Mathematik in Eggenstein-Leopoldshafen, Germany).

Ronald E. Rice and Everett M. Rogers (1980), "Reinvention in the Innovation Process," *Knowledge: Creation; Diffusion; Utilization, 1*, 499–514.

Ronald E. Rice and Everett M. Rogers (1983), "New Methods and New Data for the Study of New Media," Paper presented at the International Communication Association, Dallas, TX.

Everett M. Rogers (1983a), *Diffusion of Innovations*, New York: Free Press.

Everett M. Rogers (1983b), "The Impact of Information Systems on Organizations," Paper presented at the Harvard Colloquium on Information Systems, Boston, MA.

Everett M. Rogers and D. Lawrence Kincaid (1981), *Communication Networks*, New York: Free Press.

Everett M. Rogers and Judith K. Larsen (1984), *Silicon Valley Fever*, New York: Basic Books.

Everett M. Rogers, S. Brice Heath, Jeffrey H. Moore, Carson Agnew, Arnold Picot, Ann Porteus, Donald Case, Jane Kingston, Jane Marcus, and Ronald E. Rice (1981), *Evaluation of the Terminals for Managers (TFM) Program*, Stanford University, Stanford, CA: Center for Information Technology.

Ingo Schmoranz (1980), *Makroökonomische Analyse des Informationssektors*, Munich, Germany: Oldenbourg.

John Short, Ederyn Williams, and Bruce Christie (1976), *The Social Psychology of Telecommunications*, London: Wiley.

Hans-Jürgen Warnecke and others (1981), "Change of Technical, Organizational, and Social Structures brought about by Microelectronics," Paper presented at the Sixth International Conference on Production Research, Novi Sad, Jugoslavia.

Paul Watzlawick, Janet H. Beavin, and Donald D. Jackson (1967), *Pragmatics of Human Communication*, New York: Norton.

Osmo A. Wiio (1981), "Information Society and Communication Research," Paper presented at the Nordic Conference on Mass Communication Research, Reykjavik, Iceland.

Oliver E. Williamson (1975), *Markets and Hierarchies: Analysis and Antitrust Implications*, New York: Free Press.

Oliver E. Williamson (1980), "The Organization of Work," *Journal of Economic Behavior and Organization*, *1*, 5–38.

Chapter 7

First World Communication Technologies in Third World Contexts[1]

Bella Mody
San Francisco State University

INTRODUCTION

Scholarly attention to the role of communication technology in the process of socio-economic development in the Third World was launched by Wilbur Schramm's (1964) book *Mass Media and National Development: The Role of Information in the Developing Nations*. At that time, the transistor radio revolution promised to help solve the problems of poverty, hunger, poor health, overpopulation, etc. in the Third World. The 1960s were tremendously upbeat about development communication, in part because of the recent success of the post–World War II Marshall Plan in Europe, and due to the fact that many nations in Latin America, Africa, and Asia had recently gained their independence. Unfortunately, we now understand that the role of mass communication (like radio and television) in development is much less important than what was once imagined. Recent technologies like broadcasting satellites, cable, and microcomputers are causing renewed optimism about opportunities for development in the Third World. Certainly, we are wiser today in assessing these contemporary possibilities, as a result of the past 20 years of communication research. The present essay deals with the contexts of Third World nations that affect the relative success of new communication technologies imported from information societies in the First World. Professor Mody concludes that communication scholars need to consider the specific environmental contexts of communication for a realistic appraisal of the power of the "old" and "new" communication technologies.   *E.M.R., F.B.*

> The technological choices open to Third World countries are ultimately choices within an all-foreign range of hardware designed for different time and place conditions. (Stewart, 1977)

This chapter deals with the impact of the extra-communication context on national configurations of communication technology in terms of organization structure, equipment, programming, and professional norms. Our particular focus is on communication technologies that have been

---

[1]The present chapter draws its theme and many of its examples from a forthcoming book by Mody (in process).

researched, designed, and manufactured in First World countries (in response to their own needs) which are then configured in distinct Third World contexts. The term *context* is defined to include the groups, institutions, laws, and sets of social relations that constitute the specific environment or surroundings within which a communication technology is introduced, modified, or allowed to die over time.

Communication technology is the techniques and institutions by which information is produced, packaged, and disseminated to geographically-dispersed receivers. This definition is not limited to communication equipment, machinery, or hardware. Nor is it limited (a) to information production and processing via cameras, sound recorders, printing presses, and computers, or (b) to information reception through radio, TV, and the press.

First World countries, following common usage in economics and political science, refer to the industrialized market economies of North America, Western Europe, and Japan; the *Second World* is the non-market industrial economies of the Soviet Union and Eastern Europe. The term "Third World" was coined by French authors, the most famous being Alfred Sanvy, as an analogy with "Third Estate," a pre-French Revolution term that negatively defined all those individuals who did not belong to the privileged estates of the nobility or the clergy. *Third World* designates all nations that were not privileged to become industrialized and wealthy during the establishment of the present world order, and refers to most countries in Asia, Africa, Latin America, and the Caribbean.

In the 1960s, the then "new media" of radio and TV were recommended as high-quality low-cost remote-area information delivery channels for the developing nations of Asia, Africa, Latin America, and the Caribbean (Schramm and others, 1967). Today, it is not the availability of a *single* "new" technology that is impressive: What is unique is the *combination* of information processors (e.g., computers) and producers (e.g., TV stations) coupled with delivery systems such as cables or satellites that together represent the technical possibility of decentralizing and individualizing information selection, processing, and transmission capability. How realizable is this technical potential in the present-day organizational structure of specific societies? Given the skewed distribution of the benefits of the mass media in the 1960s and 1970s, what factors should be borne in mind when predicting social realization of the technical potential of the telematics technologies of the 1980s?

In 1982, a well-intentioned international aid agency gifted a Caribbean country with radiotelephones. The objective was to base a radio station's agriculture programming on suggestions from extension workers at the grass roots level. Immediately after the radiotelephones were distributed, the director of the rural development project forbade his extension staff from using them to contact the radio station (or any other outside agency directly). Instead, "proper channels" in government hierarchies would have to be followed: All information to be sent to any outside agency by an extension worker would first have to be cleared by his/her immediate superior, the director of agriculture extension, who would then send it to the project director. The project director would decide to whom to send the information, if he approved its content. The logic of decentralization and an efficient distortion-free, bottom-up communication technology clearly clashed with the "social" logic of the prevailing bureaucratic power system in the country, making the technology ineffective.

Such contextual incompatibility with a communication technology is not an isolated phenomenon. Examples in Third World countries range from gifts of donated audiovisual vans without adequate clearance for the deep ruts in village roads, to film projectors that are cannibalized for spare parts, to donations of educational TV systems too expensive to operate.

COMMUNICATION TECHNOLOGY IN CONTEXT

Technology-centered assessments of the national transformational power of technical apparatus that ignore contextual surroundings are not restricted to communication applications. Historic events such as the rise of the world's first cities in ancient Sameria are explained primarily in terms of the agricultural technologies that enabled high farm yields with less labor (so that everyone did not have to live on farms). The emergence of the United States as a world power after the Second World War has been frequently attributed to the role of assembly-line industrial technology, just as the development of Europe has been frequently attributed to the Industrial Revolution. Neglected in such analyses are the political, economic, and cultural conditions that made these technological changes possible. What is further forgotten is that the utilization of these technologies was influenced by the filter of the prevailing economic and social order, and thus became "refracted" (like light), sometimes increasing rather than decreasing the disparities within and between communities (Morehouse, 1979).

Human civilization has advanced, in part, due to the increasing sophistication of its technologies. However, one cannot deduce from this general societal transformation due to technology that it is the best solution in *particular* cases. Such a deductively invalid generalization from one level of analysis (e.g., institutions) to another (e.g., individuals) is as dangerous as generalizing from particular cases of successful technological application to the belief that these particular technologies are capable of transforming whole societies single-handedly.

Communication researchers and policy-makers, like specialists in every other field, often assume that the introduction of *their* technologies would have powerful, beneficial, and immediate impacts in Third World countries. Continuing to ignore the context surrounding and qualifying the technology, present-day idealists perceive the combination of satellite and cable systems with interactive computers as necessary and sufficient conditions for national development.

True, communication equipment is one very major *part* of the communication structure of society. It is reasonable to expect technological solutions to solve technological parts of problems. Social, economic, and political problems require social, economic, and political solutions. Better crime detection hardware has not eradicated crime, better agricultural machinery has not put food in the mouths of the poor, and the fact that the United States and the Soviet Union build two or three nuclear weapons every day has not reduced the likelihood of a world war. Perhaps a part of the solution is confused with the whole solution. An accurate assessment of the situation requires analysis of the communication parts along with the interrelationships among the many extra-communication parts that make up the larger context.

While it seems a platitude to say that communication hardware, communication programs, and communication institutions take distinct forms in distinct economic, legal, political, and ideological conditions, the fact of the matter is that communication research, practice, and policy-making have only recently started to take this factor into account. Pleas for contextual conceptualization in communication research go back a long way, at least to the sociological model of communication advocated by Matilda Riley and John W. Riley, Jr. (1951), and include the more recent plea by Golding and Murdoch (1980). Contextually-situated work is less likely by psychologists studying communication and more likely by sociologically oriented scholars (e.g., Melvin De Fleur, Herbert Gans, Paul Hirsch, Gaye Tuchman, and Muriel Cantor in the United States).

How and whether we see the world around us determines how and whether we study it. The 17th-century Cartesian framework (that continues to be the framework for much behavioral science) did not recognize the world very fully. Researchers studied organisms living within the universe but saw the universe itself as an empty container that had no impact on the organism living within it. Until very recently, the process of communication has been similarly conceptualized without context, as if it occurred "out of this world." The focus was rather strictly placed upon studying its component parts (Rogers and Kincaid, 1981). Scholars looked within the communication process in order to understand it, and ignored its context. Only a few investigations looked at selective adaptations to environmental contexts that might account for differences in the form, functioning, and benefit structures of communication technologies in different time and place settings. The scientific study of communication continues to disregard situational patterns, stressing the development of universal laws of communication across settings. Even though physicists have shifted away from analyses-of-the-parts and universally-applicable mechanistic Newtonian cause-effect laws, when social scientists want to appear respectably "scientific," they often turn to this analysis-of-the-parts approach, assuming that the parts are the same across all settings (Capra, 1982). Pending a holistic approach to the study of development communication, differential adaptations in different Third World environments tend to be perceived as distortions and substandard adoptions of a Western norm, rather than the natural product of a local interaction.[2]

As in the case of the early days of other fields, the infant communication field, in search of academic legitimacy and a distinct identity, gave precedence to affirmative studies of the power of communication as an independent variable in leading to behavior change. Thus, in the optimistic 1960s, promises made on behalf of communication technology were not qualified by considerations of their interactions with different international, national, and subnational contexts. The popular retrospective myth called the "magic bullet theory" or the "hypodermic needle model" was presented as if media messages were all-powerful. Thus, the specific time-and-country context of the source of this model (the U.S. as a site for early mass communication research in the 1940s) was not expected to make a difference in spite of Lazarsfeld and Merton's warning (1971) that the social effects of the media would vary with the nature of media ownership and the control system prevailing in each society.[3] Here we seek to understand reasons for the existence of different information-communication systems in different societies, a topic that has lacked systematic investigation to date.

The preconceptions of the academic field of mass communication were heavily influenced by the engineering model of Shannon and Weaver (1949): Communication was conceived as a linear act of transmission of a message from a source to a receiver via a signal-producing transmitter.

---

[2]The point here is that although the political, economic, and cultural context and the communication system vary between societies, the relation of the environmental context to the communication structure that functions within it, is fundamental and constant *across* societies.

[3]Lazarsfeld and Merton (1971) say: "To consider the social effects of American mass media is to deal only with the effects of these media as privately-owned enterprises under profit-oriented management. . . . The structure of control is altogether different in this country. . . . Since the mass media are supported by great business concerns geared into the current social and economic *system,* the media contribute to the maintenance of that system. . . . Organized business does approach a virtual psychological monopoly of the mass media."

A component called "noise" acknowledged the presence of context in the electrical engineering model, but noise was difficult to operationalize in studies of human communication.

After the Second World War, the United Nations Educational, Scientific and Cultural Organization (UNESCO) called for advice from mass communication scholars (especially from the U.S.) who were supposed to have successfully learned about media power from applications to commercial and political propaganda. Their challenge was to now harness the "magic multiplier" capacity of the media for the new applications to development problems that UNESCO was responsible for: literacy, health education, nutrition, agriculture, and nation-building in Latin America and in the newly independent countries of Asia, Africa, and the Caribbean. Wilbur Schramm's (1964) book, *Mass Media and National Development*, was one result. The foreign aid packets of governments in Western Europe and North America, and the UN agencies, began to include printing presses and broadcasting equipment, along with technical assistance and evaluation expertise from communication departments at U.S. universities such as Michigan State, Florida State, and Stanford.[4] The fact that the communication equipment being transferred had evolved as a historical and social response to distinct First World country needs did not inhibit the idealistic policy-makers for the Third World. The uncritical transfer to Third World settings of broadcasting hardware, along with First World financial and organizational systems, resulted in locally inappropriate professional norms such as mass-audience programming and non-stop transmission (Katz and Wedell, 1979).[5] The fact that communication researchers were finding that the power of the mass media was limited (this since Lazarsfeld and others' [1948] election study) did not inhibit UNESCO's enthusiasm for mass communication. The assumption was that the broadcasting media could promote freedom of information and national development.

Two misconceptions need to be highlighted. One misconception was that communication technology had actually performed rather miraculous feats in the U.S. (Gitlin, 1981). The second misconception was that societies were basically identical systems consisting of various parts, to which new parts like communication technologies could be transferred,

---

[4]For instance, the Institute for Communication Research at Stanford University has been contracted by international and national agencies to help design and evaluate mass media impacts in Colombia, Costa Rica, El Salvador, Egypt, Guatemala, Honduras, Jordan, Mexico, Nicaragua, American Samoa, Tanzania, Senegal, Ivory Coast, Niger, Liberia, the Gambia, India, Pakistan, Thailand, Jamaica, and South Korea.

[5]The social, economic and cultural conditions in U.S. society impacted on the form that the mass media took in American society (De Fleur and Ball-Rokeach, 1982).

each addition being expected to perform identically across societies. This chapter primarily deals with the second misconception.

THE CONTEXTS OF THIRD WORLD COUNTRIES

What are the contextual differences between Third World contexts and First World settings that impact on communication technology?

Third World countries are more or less poor, while industrialized First and Second World countries are more or less rich. Third World nations are mostly dependent on the centers of decision-making in the capitalistic First World, and the socialist Second World, economies. Stunted by decades of colonization (with a few exceptions), the Third World is externally dependent on foreign technologies and capital, on the one hand, and internally dominated by a small domestic elite of industrialists, landowners, civilian bureaucrats, military leaders, and a single national political party, on the other.

Given that in the year 1,000 A.D. Western Europe was technologically and culturally less developed than the Middle East, China, and India, and given that its level of living was no higher and was probably lower, how did this corner of the world move from a position of inferiority to colonize Asia, Africa, and Latin America, leaving behind economies that are handicapped and dependent to this day?

In the 14th and 15th centuries, increases in agricultural output in Western Europe led to two major changes in social structure: The emergence of rich peasants, artisans, and merchant traders on the one hand, and on the other hand, the displacement of poorer peasants who had to move to recently established towns in search of jobs. Instead of putting their money into pyramids as in ancient Sumer and Egypt, or into cathedrals as in medieval Europe, the new-rich merchants put their capital to work in ship-building and related armament technologies. Portuguese and Spanish traders financed the first European expeditions in search of a trading route to India in the early 15th century, closely followed by the Dutch and the English. Soon, Western Europe became master of the world's sea routes, eliminating the Arabs, monopolizing Asian trade in luxury goods (spices, tea, coffee, sugar, silk, and cotton), seizing gold and silver from Latin America, and trading in slaves captured in Africa. Thus, the wealth and power of the new merchant class increased, and the dominance of European feudal landowners declined.

Enriched by foreign trade, the wealthy merchants in Europe invested in factories. The need to ensure raw material for manufacturing, and food for labor in the new industrial towns, led to the forceful acquisition of colonies, satellites, and dependent territories. Thus, the State intervened to protect the interests of its merchant class. To obtain the wealth of Latin America, Asia, and Africa, European nations forced down the prices of mineral and plantation products that they purchased, and created a demand for the manufactured goods they were selling. European traders allied themselves with survival-oriented members of the national elites in the colonialized lands so as to preserve local political stability, extract raw materials, and to sell their machine-made imports. In many cases, roads and railways had to be built, a postal system organized, and indigenous landed and trading classes encouraged to establish slavery, bonded labor, and private enterprise systems to insure uninterrupted supplies of raw materials to run European factories and to feed European labor. These beginnings of the world business system depleted the natural and human resources of Asia, Africa, and Latin America, distorted their social structures, and thus created underdevelopment (Rodney, 1974).

The period following the Great Depression and the Second World War ushered in several changes in the world economy: politically independent countries in Asia, Africa, and the Caribbean, a middle class in the Third World unable to take the economic initiatives that its European counterparts took in the 15th century because of its long dormancy during colonization, a state that therefore had to take the responsibility to promote local employment and to generate economic growth, and the expansion of U.S.-based transnational corporations.

What are the external and internal characteristics of Third World countries?

EXTERNAL CHARACTERISTICS OF THIRD WORLD CONTEXTS

The Periphery of the Transnational Economy

Transnational corporations are orchestrators of a transnational world economy, in effect making assignments in the specialization and division of labor between nations. Along with continued raw material extraction (when price advantages continue), transnational corporations consign labor-intensive activities and the older manufacturing to the low-wage Third World periphery of the world economy. Thus, semiconductor chips, transistor radios, cassette recorders, TV sets, watches, and computers, products that often require the eye-straining assembly of microscopic parts, are produced by docile (usually female) labor in Southeast Asia and Latin America. Price and profit considerations win over such matters as citizenship, color, class, and creed at corporate headquarters in Western Europe, North America, or Japan, where major decisions are made.

Such dispersed transnational enterprise needs a massive management information network that can move data and funds efficiently and accurately. Texas Instruments is typical of many manufacturers and banks: It uses a satellite to link its computer terminals in 19 countries at 50 plants to its central computer in Dallas, Texas, so that production planning, cost accounting, financing, marketing, customer service, and personnel management can be coordinated (Schiller, 1982).

Unequal Trade Relationships

The typical Third World trade scenario is characterized by the sale of raw materials to First World and Second World buyers at prices that the Third World nation does not control, and the purchase of foreign manufactured goods through foreign bank loans that the nation finds very difficult to repay. The non-oil-producing Third World's debts are presently over U.S. $500 billion. Unfortunately, financing from the International Monetary Fund (IMF) to stabilize balance-of-trade deficits is only short-term, while development tasks and hence development-caused deficits are long-term. Such IMF financing carries demands for national austerity that often include cutbacks in social welfare and wage freezes that cause hardship for the masses in most countries, and in one case (Peru) even led to the imposition of martial law. The unequal trade relationship is often accompanied by heavy dependence on single-commodity exports (e.g., Chile's copper and Cuba's sugar) and trade relations concentrated on a single buyer in some cases (such as Cuba's trade with the Soviet Union).

Aid Dependence

A recession in the world economy, a cutback in orders for Third World products, or an increase in interest rates on commercial loans, increase the need for official development assistance from First World and Second World countries. Such aid is crucial for the survival of Third World populations and for the continued purchase of First World products. Financially strapped economies such as Bangladesh and Ethiopia cannot make the long-term investments in education and health necessary for national development, without foreign financial assistance on concessionary terms. Even their day-to-day short-term survival is jeopardized by the lack of food.

But the proportion of aid to total financial flows including commercial financing has been decreasing; the Brandt Commission reported that in 1977, only 32 percent of total financial flows to Third World countries came from aid as against 60 percent in 1960 (Brandt and others, 1980). This figure varied between 30 percent and 40 percent in the last five years of the 1970s (OECD, 1981). About 66 percent of aid was disbursed on a country-to-country bilateral basis in 1980 by organizations such as the United States Agency for International Development (USAID), which is the largest aid donor, the Canadian International Development Agency (CIDA), and DANIDA, the Danish International Development Agency (OECD, 1981).[6] The remainder is disbursed through multilateral agencies such as UNICEF (the United Nations Children's Fund), UNESCO, the World Bank, and regional development banks such as the Asian, African, and Inter-American Development Banks.

Major contributors of aid, and policy-makers in crucial multilateral agencies such as the World Bank and its soft-money affiliate, the International Development Association, are the same powers that once colonized the Third World, and who presently control their economies through their transnational corporations. Thus, the actual distribution of economic power in the world has not changed in favor of Third World countries.

International Power Politics and the Military

The expansion and containment attempts by the United States and the USSR power blocs have been the causes of major international tensions: Soviet domination of Eastern Europe and the creation of the Warsaw Pact, the struggle over Germany leading to its division, creation of NATO, and the struggle for dominance in Korea and Vietnam. The two superpowers agree that imperialism is the greatest ambition of the other. Third World countries are frequently used as proxies in their conflicts (e.g., Angola). Although the split between the Soviet Union and China, the emergence of the Third World "Group of 77" (now numbering over 125), and oil power (represented by the Organization of Oil Producing and Exporting Countries) occasionally creates exceptions, the Third World nations show solidarity only occasionally.

A major instrument of power between nations is the military; the two superpowers spend approximately $450 billion (U.S.) a year on weapons as against $20 billion on foreign aid (Brandt and others, 1980). In addition, each of the superpowers sold approximately $10 billion worth of weapons to the Third World in 1979 (*The New York Times, 1981*). Onetime colonies have proved themselves excellent markets for modern weapons; their military expenditure is several times higher than their combined health and education expenditures (Sivard, 1981).

---

[6]As in the case of trade, aid dependence is heightened when the donor is a single country. This dependence is further aggravated by the lack of clarity on national needs in the aid-recipient country. The net result is that the aid-giving nations often have considerable influence in a Third World country.

INTERNAL CHARACTERISTICS OF THIRD WORLD CONTEXTS

The external dependence of Third World countries is exacerbated by an internal power structure consisting of a tiny national "core" group, a small semiperipheral population, and a massive peripheral majority.

Cultural Characteristics

Many political scientists and idealistic Third World leaders like Sekou Toure of Guinea and Jawaharlal Nehru of India assumed that race, tribe, religion, language, and other inherited characteristics of Third World populations would become less dominant after national independence was achieved. It was hoped that modern associational groupings based on professional and political party affiliations would emerge. But the old and new dimensions have combined to form distinct local power patterns. To illustrate this point: In independent Jamaica, where over 95 percent of the population is of African descent, racial differences have been internalized over 500 years of white rule so that the black maid today insists that she will never work for a black family, the black doctor has to pull rank to be served in stores in the capital city, and a young black woman destroys a photograph of herself because it is printed too dark (Nettleford, 1970). Mexico provides an example of the establishment of an internal "colony" after liberation from the external colonizer. Today Latinos (a Creole mixture of Spanish and the local populations) dominate the native Indian Mexicans who constitute almost 25 percent of the country (Gonzalez-Casanova, 1965).

African politics is frequently explained in terms of tribes; the term itself was a result of European colonizers' attempts to make sense of a system of empires and nations based on shared dimensions such as physical type, occupation, political structure, and inheritance systems with which the foreigners were unfamiliar. The increasing importance of tribal affiliations today in economic and political matters shows that these colonial characteristics have taken on a new significance. Ibohood as identity in Nigeria only came to a head in the 20th century as a result of social and political competition that threatened the existence of the Ibo. Religion is not only a personal identity; it also has potential for political suppression and political mobilization in Africa, the Middle East, and in certain Asian nations.

For several generations, Christianity was interpreted by colonialists to promote the acceptance of exploitation by landlords and industrialists in return for the reward of eternal life in the next world. Only in the last 20 years did Latin American Christians in poverty areas formulate a "theology of liberation" that goes beyond spiritual well-being to leadership against all forms of injustice. The Catholic Church in the Philippines has taken an equally outspoken stance.

The extended family (and its several variants) is far more common in agrarian Third World societies than is the nuclear family. While women are more or less discriminated against in all contemporary societies, the difference in Third World contexts is that the discrimination is more frequently considered legitimate.

Economic Characteristics

Ownership of productive resources like land and equipment, and the relationships between owners and labor, are particularly crucial in Third World countries where the World Bank estimates 600 million people will be living below poverty levels at the end of this century. Present estimates of the proportions of a national population living below poverty levels (a per capita income below U.S. $1,000 at the official exchange rate) include: Ethiopia, 68 percent; Bangladesh, 64 percent; Burma, 65 percent; Indonesia, 59 percent; Uganda, 55 percent; Kenya, 55 percent; Sudan, 54 percent; Zaire, 53 percent; Tanzania, 51 percent; India, 46 percent; Pakistan, 43 percent; Nigeria and Senegal, 35 percent; the Philippines, 33 percent; and Thailand, 32 percent (Ahluwalia and others, 1979).

What are the modes of production in Third World countries that lead to poverty for such large numbers of people? About two-thirds of Third World populations still live on a semi-feudal style agriculture or small farming, while two-thirds of the national wealth is generated by the industry and service sectors. Slicing a shrinking pie into so many tiny pieces would not yield decent-sized bites even if the pie were divided equally. When the shrinking agricultural pie is divided between a few large landowners, and very many small-holders, tenant farmers, and landless laborers, the few rich get richer and the ranks of the poor swell.

Unfortunately, the distribution of property in the more dynamic faster-growing industrial sector of Third World countries is no better. The chief economist of the government of Pakistan revealed that 20 privileged families owned 66 percent of Pakistan's industry, 79 percent of its insurance business, and 80 percent of its banking; the rest was owned by foreign corporations for the most part (Alavi, 1972). In Jamaica, power and control of the corporate economy is mainly concentrated in 21 families who originally became wealthy from owning sugar plantations (Reid, 1977). These illustrations are typical of the structure of property ownership and poverty in Third World countries.

What does this economic inequality imply for communication infrastructure? With the rise of certain nations as information societies, centering around the production and distribution of information on the basis of the ability to pay, are individuals and nations, who cannot pay, to go without computer applications in education, entertainment, finance, and postal services? What is the prognosis for equity in the distribution of the new communication technologies? With rural installation costs for telephones five times urban costs, only the current "telephone haves" will be able to access computer networks (Schuringa, 1983). India illustrates this problem: Its 70 percent rural population accounts for only 7 percent of the country's telephones. While it is technically possible to link all the urban and rural telegraph offices in India by satellite, even the State-run Indian National Satellite (INSAT-1B) will primarily connect the telephone systems of only the revenue-generating metropolitan area.

There is now talk of the "barefoot chip" bringing about an information revolution in the Third World; Servan-Schreiber (1980) foresees village computer terminals linked to regional and national networks of data on agriculture, health, and industrial training. This dream is theoretically and technically possible, but the question is whether, why, when, and under which conditions the capital-owners and political powers will invest in such pro-social applications as telemedicine, computer-aided learning, and educational broadcasting.

Political Characteristics

The political systems in Third World countries are characterized by a one-party system, a military and bureaucratic State, and the high involvement of the national government in initiating economic growth. Leftover from the colonial period is a strong State with a law-and-order orientation and a nationalistic political party that arose to fight for independence (like the Institutional Revolutionary Party of Mexico and the Congress Party of India).

The typical Third World state supports the interests of such dominant groups as large farmers, industrialists, traders, and foreign investors. When the interests of these categories compete, the State attempts to mediate among them, deciding in favor of one or the other depending on what line of action will advance its own economic and political interests.

THIRD WORLD CONTEXTS AND COMMUNICATION TECHNOLOGY

To summarize, the distinct economic, social, and political contexts of Third World societies help us understand differences in the configuration of their communication technology systems: ownership, institutional, organizational, and professional operating conditions, and their primary beneficiaries. In First World societies, the mass media (like television) grew by selling consumer audiences to product manufacturers for advertising purposes. In Third World economies where there are a limited number of buyers (for goods other than essentials), it is difficult for the media to be completely financed from advertising incomes. The political context of Third World countries is one of young nations very vulnerable to superpower rivalries. The social fabric of Third World countries is characterized by major national and sub-national differences in race, tribe, religion, language, and the like. There is a lack of homogenizing influences like universal schooling that make single-language, single-audience, "mass" programming possible in most First and Second World countries.

The average individual in a Third World country lives at a completely different level of need-fulfillment on Maslow's hierarchy of needs, from the average individual in North America or Europe (Maslow, 1962). In general, the peoples of Third World nations are motivated by deficiencies in meeting their basic needs, while people of First World countries have gratified these basic needs and are preoccupied with developing their idiosyncratic potentials. The psychological life of those at different levels of need gratification are clearly different (Cantril, 1965).

This chapter has described some macro-level contextual dimensions that condition the configuration of First World communication technologies in Third World contexts. Important distinctions also exist within the Third World, between newly industrializing countries, oil-exporting nations, raw materials-rich countries, nations with large pools of skilled labor and domestic markets, and the least developed countries. Thus, Singapore is planning a future in designing computer software for the new information industries; Brazil is nurturing a domestic microcomputer industry, having taken the lead in regulating transborder data flow in the interests of its national sovereignty. Senegal, Pakistan, Chad, and Colombia are conducting experimental microcomputer projects in education and health with the French government's World Center for Computers and Human Resources. The multi-island University of the West Indies is sharing classes and conferences via satellite (through United States government aid). India, Indonesia, and Saudi Arabia are implementing national satellite television systems, while Tanzania is valiantly resisting the introduction of any kind of television.

Why were low-cost media such as audio cassettes so effective in the 1979 Iranian Revolution against the Shah's big media system? Why has the Ivory Coast recently closed its instructional TV system? Why did the British media corporation Lonrho terminate the editor of their Kenyan newspaper, the *Standard,* for protesting the Arap Moi government's detention laws? Why are some countries actively importing foreign media programs and imitating foreign programming norms, while other nations are totally opposed? The answers to these questions can only make sense in terms of an understanding of specific contextual conditions.

Past communication research on national development in Third World contexts has been based on historically-incorrect economic theories of underdevelopment. For example, it is frequently assumed that all countries were equally poor initially. The debilitating colonial experience has no place in hypothetical scenarios like Rostow's (1971) *Stages of Economic Growth,* which claim that all countries started off as traditional, and through a series of steps, all arrive at the same final goal of high mass consumption.

We maintain that it was a social engineering perspective on human problem-solving that caused the well-intentioned to ignore contextual differences between First World and Third World countries, and to make a fetish out of communication technology as an apparently powerful new Messiah for development. Thus, it was hoped that "classical" technologies such as radio and television in the 1960s and 1970s, and the "nonclassical" technologies such as satellites, cable, and computers in the 1980s, could facilitate growth in the gross national product and, more recently, provide redistribution of the benefits of growth.

The general lesson that can be drawn from experience with communication technology in the Third World is that *the different contexts of communication technology have a causal texture that is tremendously important in determining the different effect of this technology from one situation to the next.* This lesson should not be lost on those in the field of development communication. Nor on those concerned with any other kind of communication research.

REFERENCES

M. Ahluwalia and others (1979), "Growth and Poverty in Developing Countries," Washington, DC, World Bank, Staff Working Paper 309 Revised.

Hamza Alavi (1972), "The State in Post-Colonial Societies: Pakistan and Bangladesh," *New Left Review, 74,* 69.

Willy Brandt and others (1980), *North-South: A Programme for Survival,* London: Pan Books.

Hadley Cantril (1965), *The Patterns of Human Concern,* New Brunswick, NJ: Rutgers University Press.

Fritjof Capra (1982), *The Turning Point: Science, Society and the Rising of Culture,* New York: Simon and Schuster.

Melvin L. De Fleur and Sandra Ball-Rokeach (1982), *Theories of Mass Communication,* New York: Longman.

Todd Gitlin (1981), "Media Sociology: The Dominant Paradigm," in G. Cleveland Wilhoit (ed.), *Mass Communication Review Yearbook, 2,* Beverly Hills, CA: Sage.

Peter Golding and G. Murdock (1980), "Theories of Communication and Theories of Society," in G. Cleveland Wilhoit (ed.), *Mass Communication Review Yearbook, 1,* Beverly Hills, CA: Sage.

Pablo Gonzalez-Casanova (1965), "Internal Colonialism and National Development," *Studies in Comparative International Development, 1,* 4.

Elihu Katz and George Wedell (1979), *Broadcasting in the Third World: Promise and Potential,* Cambridge, MA: Harvard University Press.

Paul F. Lazarsfeld and Robert K. Merton (1971), "Mass Communication, Popular Taste, and Organized Social Action," in Wilbur Schramm and Donald F. Roberts (eds.), *The Process and Effects of Mass Communication,* Urbana, IL: University of Illinois Press.

Paul F. Lazarsfeld and others (1948), *The People's Choice,* New York: Columbia University Press.

Abraham H. Maslow (1962), *Toward a Psychology of Being,* New York: Van Nostrand.

Bella Mody (in press), *Communication Technology in Third World Contexts.*

Ward Morehouse (1979), *Science, Technology and the Social Order,* New Brunswick, NJ: Transaction.

Rex Nettleford (1970), *Mirror, Mirror,* London: Collins and Sangster.

The New York Times (June 23, 1981), "Weapons Sales to the Third World."

OECD (1981), *Development Cooperation: Efforts and Policies of the Development Assistance Committee,* Paris: Organization for Economic Cooperation and Development.

Stanley Reid (1977), "An Introductory Approach to the Concentration of Power in the Jamaican Corporate Economy and Notes on its Origins," in Carl Stone and A. Brown (eds.), *Essays in Power and Change in Jamaica,* Kingston, Jamaica: Jamaica Publishing House.

Matilda Riley and John W. Riley, Jr. (1951), "A Sociological Approach to Communication Research," *Public Opinion Quarterly, 15.*

Walter Rodney (1974), *How Europe Underdeveloped Africa,* Washington, DC: Howard University Press.

Everett M. Rogers and D. Lawrence Kincaid (1981), *Communication Networks,* New York: Free Press.

Walter W. Rostow (1971), *Stages of Economic Growth,* New York: Cambridge University Press.

Dan Schiller (1982), "Business Users and the Telecommunication Network," *Journal of Communication, 32* (4), 84–96.

Wilbur Schramm (1964), *Mass Media and National Development: The Role of Information in the Developing Nations.* Stanford, CA: Stanford University Press.

Wilbur Schramm and others (1967), *The New Media: Memo to Educational Planners,* Paris: UNESCO/IIEP.

T. M. Schuringa (1983), "The Impact of Information Technologies on the Development of Rural Areas," Paper presented at the Development Forum, Paris.

Jean-Jacques Servan-Schreiber (1980), *The World Challenge,* New York: Simon and Schuster.

Claude Shannon and Warren Weaver (1949), *The Mathematical Theory of Communication,* Urbana, IL: University of Illinois Press.

Ruth Lever Sivard (1981), *World Military and Social Indicators, 1981,* Leesburg, VA: World Priorities.

Frances Stewart (1977), *Technology and Underdevelopment,* London: Macmillan.

Chapter 8

International Communication: A New Order?

Elie Abel
Stanford University

INTRODUCTION

Undoubtedly the most important issue in international communication over the past decade has been the demand by Third World nations for a New World Communication Order. They criticize the imbalance of international news flows, blaming the Big Four news agencies for a Western bias. After an extensive debate in UNESCO conferences, the 16-nation MacBride Commission was appointed and, in 1980, published its recommendations. Here, a member of the MacBride Commission reviews the nature of the news flow issue, synthesizes relevant communication research bearing on the news flow debate, and summarizes the Commission's major recommendations for action. In the several years since the MacBride Report appeared, only rather limited achievements have been made toward a New World Information Order. New communication technologies, especially satellites, may eventually lead toward a more balanced flow of news in the world.   *E.M.R., F.B.*

News is perverse. It will not flow evenly. A great deal more news, for example, flows from Paris to Ouagadougou than from Ouagadougou to Paris. This regrettable lack of symmetry can and must be put right, some Third World spokesman suggest, by proclaiming a new world information order. What about the lack of symmetry in news flow between one region and another within the same country? Why does so much more news flow from New Delhi to Poona than flows from Poona to New Delhi? Or from Pine Ridge, Arkansas, to New York? These are not wholly frivolous questions. According to one scholar (Merrill, 1981, p. 156):

> Unevenness of flow is a basic characteristic of news—and not only of news but of water flow, oil flow, money flow, population flow, and food flow. . . . News, like oil, flows mainly from where the supply is greatest; also it flows from where there are more workers "drilling" for it; and finally it flows mainly to places where consumers seem to demand it.

THIRD WORLD DEMANDS FOR A BALANCED NEWS FLOW

To demand a perfectly even news flow between nations large and small, say, between the Soviet Union and Cape Verde (population,

300,000), or between metropolis and hinterland, would be plainly absurd. Third World spokesmen nevertheless suggest that news flows ought somehow to be metered on the basis of proportional representation. It is, they say, a case of flagrant imbalance that the major transnational news agencies should devote only 20 to 30 percent of their coverage to the developing countries when the aggregate population of those countries accounts for "almost three quarters of mankind" (Masmoudi, 1978, p. 10). The notion that news coverage ought to be allocated on a per-capita basis, without regard to salience or intrinsic interest, has not been broadly accepted by journalists anywhere.

Newsmen are charged with paying more attention to "bad news" than to good, with stressing crime and corruption rather than wholesome achievement, with exploiting disasters (whether natural or man-made), and focusing on conflict rather than peaceful accommodation. Yet it would be hard to demonstrate that news agencies reserve this treatment exclusively, or predominantly, for happenings in the Third World. Richard Nixon, speaking of the American scene, has complained: "For the press, progress is not news—trouble is." There is also the chronic complaint that Third World news is ignored when it is not distorted. Niger, for example, gets little press attention. So also do Norway and New Zealand.

THE UNESCO DEBATE

Since 1978, UNESCO has been committed to the goal of a free and balanced news flow, or more precisely, to "a free flow and a wider and better-balanced dissemination of information" throughout the world (UNESCO, 1978). That formulation, painfully negotiated at the UNESCO General Conference, necessarily leaves uncalibrated the concept of "better-balanced" and, perhaps out of political prudence, it does not attempt to define the slippery word "free." But for all the heated rhetoric of UNESCO debates over the past decade, there is little evidence that the news flow issue sets the blood of ordinary citizens racing, whether in the Third World, the Second, or the First. The passion is generated chiefly among journalists, social scientists, other assorted intellectuals, and, in some developing countries, by ambitious politicians. Certainly the mass of Americans, elected officials included, are at best only subliminally aware that such an issue exists. European opinion is probably better-informed, if only because the European media have paid more consistent attention to the news out of the UNESCO debate, but news flow is hardly a popular issue even in Europe. In Third World countries, however, the UNESCO debate received widespread media attention.

The Call for a New World Information Order

Flows of news and other information across national frontiers have been investigated intermittently over the past three decades.[1] The first post-war study to examine one-way flows was completed in 1953 by the International Press Institute. Not until the 1970s, however, did news flow become an obligatory agenda item at international conferences and at United Nations sessions. This issue surfaced in 1973 at a nonaligned summit conference in Algiers. It was a modest beginning. The nonaligned leaders decided that the mass media of their respective countries should start to exchange information "concerning their mutual achievements in all fields" and that they should work together to reorganize existing communication channels, which they saw as "a legacy of the colonial past." The more ambitious goal of a new information order began to be discussed in the following year or two, in parallel with the Third World nations' demand for a new economic order. The timing of this demand for a radical restructuring of world trade in terms more favorable to the raw-material-producing countries of the Southern Hemisphere may have been prompted by the success of OPEC in forcing up the price of petroleum so dramatically after the Arab oil embargo of 1973–1974. Both the news flow and the economic demands can be described as attempts to apply on a global scale the principle of distributive justice, developed by John Rawls. From the beginning of the debate, the attack on existing information structures and systems has been explicitly linked with the call for a new economic order.

The slowness of Western governments to respond with economic concessions may explain the rising intensity of attacks on the Western news agencies, other Western media, and their cultural influence upon developing societies. Rosemary Righter (1980, p. 56) of *The London Sunday Times* has written:

> It may be a slightly naive assumption that, if only the publics of the West were fully and properly informed of the implications of a new international economic order, they would rush to lobby their governments in its favor. But there is some force in the accusation by Third World governments that the international press is failing to explain the reasons behind the pressures for change and to put across Third World arguments.

Changing Voting Patterns in UNESCO

UNESCO, the first of the specialized agencies of the United Nations to concern itself with international news flow, has become the main arena

---

[1] It may be worth recalling that news is a species of information, but that information is not necessarily news. To qualify as news, the information must be timely, it should interest large numbers of people, and it ought to tell them something that has not come to their attention earlier. Andre Gide drew the line at "everything that will be less interesting tomorrow."

of controversy. Those who criticize UNESCO for meddling in matters of mass communication would do well to recall, however, that its constitution binds the organization to promote the "free flow of ideas by word and image." This mandate was written soon after World War II, when the United States, its West European allies, and Latin American neighbors were in full voting control of UNESCO.

The West's "mechanical majority" within the UN system, so frequently denounced at the height of the Cold War by Andrei Vishinsky and other Soviet delegates, has long since dwindled to a minority as a long procession of former colonial territories attained full sovereignty. The new majority is made up of developing countries of the Third World, many ruled by authoritarian regimes. Whether these regimes lean to the left or the right, they are for the most part equally unsympathetic to the free flow doctrine. Some see it as a smokescreen, designed to perpetuate the favored market position of Western news agencies, publishers, exporters of television programs and of motion pictures, all denounced as vehicles of "cultural imperialism." Free flow, moreover, is an essentially Western doctrine that does not sanction the internal press restrictions imposed by many Third World regimes.

Since the turnabout in the political arithmetic of the United Nations, the four Western news agencies which together account for some 80 percent of world traffic have become prime targets. They are the Associated Press and United Press International, based in New York; Agence France Presse, based in Paris; and Reuters, based in London. Tass, the telegraphic agency of the Soviet Union, is seldom mentioned in Third World polemics, perhaps because it is not widely regarded as a genuine news agency. Not even the Russians pretend that Tass reports are balanced or free. The Soviet Union, moreover, appears to have bought a degree of immunity from criticism by its support of Third World demands against the West.

The UNESCO Draft Declaration

The polarization within UNESCO can be traced more precisely to a Soviet initiative in 1974. The Russians, who make no secret of their opposition to press freedom, introduced at the General Conference of UNESCO a draft declaration "on fundamental principles governing the use of the mass media in strengthening peace and international understanding and in combating war propaganda, racism, and apartheid." It was a remarkable document, shrewdly designed to impress the several Third World constituencies. There was, to begin with, the notion that mass media are to be *used* by governments. This appeal to authoritarians was reinforced by an article setting out a quasi-juridical basis for state control of all news media: "States are responsible for the activities in the international sphere of all mass media under their jurisdiction." The reference to apartheid made it certain that no African delegation would abstain or vote against the Soviet proposition. Then, at a special drafting conference in 1975, the Russians added a denunciation of Zionism. This item assured them of Arab votes, although the delegations of the United States and 14 other Western countries walked out in protest. The Soviet draft, with some revisions, was placed on the agenda of UNESCO's 1976 General Conference in Nairobi, Kenya.

The fact that the draft declaration was never approved in that form owes much to the political skills of Amadou Mahtar M'Bow, UNESCO's director general, who worked long and hard behind the scenes to avoid a confrontation between the United States and the Soviet Union. The first African to head a UN agency, M'Bow persuaded a sufficient number of Third World governments to sidetrack the Soviet draft by postponing further consideration until the General Conference of 1978. To buy time, M'Bow promised to appoint a commission of "wise men" that would study "the totality of communication problems in the modern world."[2] Such was the origin of the International Commission for the Study of Communication Problems, better known as the MacBride Commission, after its chairman, Sean MacBride of Ireland. While the Commission went about its work—its final report was not published until 1980—M'Bow arranged to water down the Soviet draft. A new statement was drafted in close consultation between Western delegations and a group of the non-aligned nations. The Soviets were kept out of the negotiations until a compromise text had been worked out. Faced with the choice of accepting the compromise or having no declaration at all, the Soviet delegation settled for a half-loaf. Explicit references to state control of the media were eliminated. Press freedom was endorsed, including freedom of access by journalists to all news sources within a country, that is, to political opposition as well as to government sources. The explicit denunciation of Zionism had been dropped earlier.

REACTIONS TO THE MACBRIDE REPORT

The MacBride Report, when published, came in for considerable criticism. Like the draft declaration, it was a negotiated document containing something for everybody. Sergei Losev, the Soviet member, filed a dissent, objecting that the text was "a little bit too Westernized in its terminology and its approaches." Not enough attention had been paid,

---

[2]The original list of 16 commissioners appointed by M'Bow did not include a woman. When Marshall McLuhan withdrew from participation, he was replaced by Betty Zimmerman, another Canadian.

he said, to the achievements and experiences of "socialist and developing countries." He also protested the final report's recommendation that censorship or arbitrary control of information should be abolished. The Latin American commissioners, Juan Somavia and the novelist Gabriel Garcia Marquez, found in the report a tendency to "glorify" technological solutions to communication problems, which they joined in deploring.

Western critics were more vehement. *The New York Times* (October 24, 1980), in an editorial following the acceptance of the MacBride Report by the UNESCO General Conference of 1980, denounced not only UNESCO, but the United States delegation as well:

> The undemocratic governments that pine for order in what their people read, hear, and think have won yet another "compromise" to advance the cause of censorship. So it needs to be said again, and less temperately than before, that no American negotiator speaks in these matters for the free press of the United States. Let there be no doubt in [UNESCO], which aims to become the arbiter of "responsible" communication, that American journalism values its freedom from official scrutiny and control more than it values UNESCO, or even the United Nations.

The positive gains negotiated by Western commissioners—such recommendations as the call for abolition of political censorship, for the removal of internal barriers to the flow of information, for the provision of "diversity and choice" in the content of mass media, and for free access to news sources by journalists everywhere, including access to dissident as well as official sources—received only fleeting attention or none at all in many Western newspapers. There were relatively few practical recommendations in the report, but two deserve notice here. One proposed a major international research and development effort to expand the world supply of newsprint by exploiting new sources of feedstock, including a woody shrub known as *kenaf* which grows wild in many regions of the Third World. Enough has been learned from initial experiments with the cultivation of *kenaf* in Arizona to warrant pilot production on a larger scale. By providing a cheap and abundant alternative to pulpwood, it may become possible to expand the production of newspapers in Third World countries, thus reducing their dependence on hard-currency imports. The follow-up to this recommendation has been tardy.

A second concrete recommendation of potential benefit to the developing countries called for the systematic reduction of telecommunication tariffs to favor the poorest countries. Here again the follow-up has been slow, although the issue has not been allowed to die, thanks to the persistent lobbying of the London-based International Press Telecommunications Council.

COMMUNICATION RESEARCH ON NEWS FLOWS

The report would have benefited from fresh research, but budget and time constraints forced the MacBride Commission to limit itself to the published literature, some of it outdated or of questionable validity. The Commission had to debate a number of untested assumptions, some rooted in myth, others in a lack of rigorous research that invited criticism. However, a number of synthesis papers were prepared by communication researchers for the MacBride Commission.

One Third World assumption was that the major Western news agencies are immensely profitable enterprises and should, as one commissioner argued, pay a special tax on their operations for the benefit of developing countries. Although this notion did not find favor with the MacBride Commission's majority, it keeps cropping up from time to time in defiance of the demonstrable fact that not one of the Big Four agencies shows a profit on its news operations. Associated Press is a not-for-profit cooperative. United Press International, privately owned, has been running a deficit for several years, leading to a recent transfer of ownership. Agence France Presse, it is fair to say, owes its survival to French government subsidies. Reuters, in turn, depends heavily upon the earnings of its data services, designed to serve not the news media but trading companies, banks, brokerages, and other financial institutions.

News Agencies and News Flows

A second stubborn myth has it that the transnational news agencies subject the peoples of the developing countries to a tidal wave of unwanted, irrelevant, and frequently distorted news that does violence to their cultural values. The clear implication is that foreign news agencies have direct access to the minds of readers and listeners in developing countries.[3] The fact, carefully documented in one study (Pinch, 1977), is that outside of Latin America, with its mainly for-profit media, only a handful of Third World governments allow their newspapers to subscribe directly to any international news service. In roughly three-fourths of the countries surveyed, the subscriber is the government itself or a government-controlled agency which filters out any information that is judged to be unduly critical, lacking in balance, or socially harmful. Much of the information not considered appropriate for circulation to the general public through national media is reserved for official use only. It is then distributed to an elite layer of bureaucrats and politicians, who are presumed to have a greater

---

[3]And that the news media in developing nations have direct, measurable effects on their audience, a proposition that is not supported by most communication research.

need than the public at large to know what is happening in the rest of the world.

The Content of News Flows

A further study by communication researchers at the University of North Carolina provides support for the findings of several scholars that the Western news agencies, for all their acknowledged shortcomings, are neither as dominant nor as cavalier in ignoring positive Third World news as is frequently charged (Stevenson and others, 1980). Upon close examination, these researchers found that far from fixing their obsessive gaze upon disasters, accidents, and failures in the Third World, the media gave these negative topics very little attention in any country studied. The researchers noted that much foreign news published around the world seems to be of, or about, politics, and that the newsmakers appear to be mostly political leaders. Regional proximity is clearly the dominant characteristic of foreign news:

> African media report more about Africa than any other part of the world; Asian media print and broadcast more about Asia, and so on . . . Western Europe and North America are considerably less visible in the media and, in most areas, North America is less visible than Western Europe. (Stevenson and others, 1980)

Schramm and Atwood (1981) tested the assumption that the major news agencies are preoccupied with disasters, coups, and corruption (bad news) in the Third World to the exclusion of (good) news of economic and social progress in Asia. These scholars monitored the output of the four major agencies as delivered to client newspapers during a single week of December, 1977. They also measured the news content of 18 Asian newspapers, two from each of nine countries, for the same week. Their findings contradict certain of the complaints raised in the UNESCO debate. Development news, they found, tends to get short shrift in many Asian newspapers, but much of the blame ought fairly to be assigned to Asian gatekeepers: The international news agencies deliver far more development news than Asian editors print. The notion that Third World editors will, as a matter of duty or solidarity, print a great deal of news from other developing countries turned out to be a fallacy. Like gatekeepers elsewhere, Asian editors pick and choose. Schramm and Atwood (1981) found that almost half of the items transmitted to Asia by the news agencies in an average day dealt with news from the Third World. But the average Asian daily printed approximately 9 percent of the Third World news on the wires.

The high cost of newsprint, of course, enforces selectivity. But proximity was again the decisive element. Thus East Asian editors were not greatly interested in news from India and Pakistan, even less in news from Africa, the Middle East, or Latin America.

Two major news developments took place in Asia during the test week: the retrial of a former Philippine senator, Benigno S. Aquino, before a military court on charges of murder and subversion; and the denial of Zulfikar Ali Bhutto's appeal to the Pakistan Supreme Court against a murder charge. The Bhutto story was, of course, big news in West Asia. Every one of the Southeast Asian newspapers ignored it, although one found space to report that a wildcat in Pakistan had "made off with a man's ear." The Aquino story was big news in Hong Kong, Singapore, and Malaysia, but the Indian and Indonesian newspapers did not print it.

Harris (1977), in a study commissioned by UNESCO that is critical of the existing world communication order, investigated the process by which national news agencies in the Third World correct for what they perceive as Western bias in the news that flows to them from transnational agencies. For instance, one set of political labels was substituted for another at the Ghana News Agency:

> All that was really involved was changing the adjective. One of the most common examples cited in this context was the substitution in stories about Rhodesia, South Africa, Angola, etc. of "nationalists" or "freedom fighters" for "guerrillas" or "terrorists." another example was that stories about Ian Smith would generally be rephrased to describe him as the "racist Ian Smith." A few foreign editors objected to changing "terrorist" to "nationalist" or to "freedom fighter," unless the editor believed that the "cause for which they are fighting is just"—that is, in the African interest. In practice, most stories were amended.

Ideological labeling of this sort in U.S. agency reports on the Vietnam fighting a decade ago was sharply criticized at the time. It seems far less common today in copy supplied by the Western agencies. But substitutions of the kind cited by Harris in the case of Ghana continue to be penciled in by editors of national news agencies. Stevenson and others (1980), for example, found repeated references in the Zambian media to the "racist puppet Ian Smith" and his "sham, bogus election," as late as 1979. It is hard to believe that these epithets were in the original copy from AP or Reuters.

The Big Four News Agencies

The Big Four are unquestionably the news agencies of choice in most Third World countries, though not for lack of alternatives. A tabulation by Freedom House in 1980 identified no fewer than 104 government news agencies. UNESCO's survey of world communication, 1975 edition, identified 90 national news agencies. Many of these agencies are primarily concerned with internal distribution of news, but a considerable number participate directly in the global news flow by receiving—and exchanging—news files with other agencies. Typically, they are tied in with larger agencies of the Second and Third World, in addition to one or more of the Big Four. For example, MENA, the Egyptian agency, receives news from Reuters and Agence France Presse. According to the UNESCO tabulation, MENA also receives news from DPA, the West German agency; ADN, the East German agency; Agerpress of Romania, CTK of Czechoslovakia, PAP of Poland, Tanjug of Yugoslavia, and Tass.[4]

In 1977, when the Harris study was completed, the Ghana News Agency was receiving newsfiles from 12 agencies, "six of them regularly." Five were agencies based in the West, five in Eastern Europe, and two in Northern Africa. The Ghana News Agency managed to distribute something like 10 percent of the news it received in its daily domestic files, although atmospheric difficulties and mechanical breakdowns frequently disrupted the incoming flow.

This picture generally suggests a flood of available news from a diversity of sources. Subscribers who lack confidence in the Western output obviously have the choice of substituting news from Tass, which many Third World nations receive free of charge, or from the New China News Agency, the Non-Aligned News Pool, and any number of regional services. No Third World editor or publisher, in fact, is compelled to use UPI or AFP. Why then do so many of these editors prefer the Western agencies?

Their reach is more nearly global. Their newsfiles are delivered at high speed. Their reporting and writing tend to be more professional, that is, less partisan and therefore more credible than many alternative services. Above all, Third World editors tend to agree that news supplied by the Western agencies requires less editing to conform to local needs and sensitivities (which is not to say that the Western product is without fault or flaw).

IMPROVING THE NEWS MEDIA

Ethnocentricity in reporting remains a legitimate concern. There is a dilemma here that cannot be readily resolved. Heads of the Western news agencies acknowledge a responsibility to work at overcoming national or Western biases in order that their product better conform to the interests of overseas subscribers. The fact remains, however, that their most im-

---

[4]This list is not up-to-date, as UNESCO's figures are at least 10 years old, but the range of news agencies is illustrative.

portant markets are in the Western industrialized nations. "They cannot help but speak to the developing world with an alien voice," as Rosemary Righter (1979) has observed. "An international language that describes [a] rise in coffee prices as a 'coffee crisis' is patently a fraud." In coffee-growing countries that sort of language can only be read as an expression of hostility.

The Third World news problem is not, in most cases, a lack of quantity or even of diversity in available news flow. It has more to do with the quality of information supplied at both ends of the transaction. Just as the developing countries may be poorly, or at least indifferently, served by existing news channels, so also national audiences in Western countries could be better informed by more consistent, less event-oriented coverage of an increasingly complicated world. American news media, in particular, suffer from what James Reston has called the "dailiness" of their approach to news, whether foreign or domestic.

The MacBride Report (1980, pp. 262–263) recognized that many obvious shortcomings of contemporary journalism, far from being unique to developing societies, are shared by the media of advanced industrial countries:

> Conventional standards of news selection and reporting, and many accepted news values, need to be reassessed if readers and listeners around the world are to receive a more faithful and comprehensive account of events, movements, and trends in both developing and developed countries.

The Report states that reporters and editors should not be blind to the hazards of narrow ethnocentric thinking:

> The first step toward overcoming this bias is to acknowledge that it colors the thinking of all human beings, journalists included, for the most part without deliberate intent. The act of selecting certain news for publication, while rejecting others, produces in the minds of the audience a picture of the world that may well be incomplete or distorted.

Higher standards and greater media accountability could not, the MacBride Report conceded, be imposed by governmental decree; nor, I would add, by engineering a consensus resolution at UNESCO. The proposed remedies—freedom of access for journalists to foreign countries, more systematic preparation for reporters assigned to foreign posts, more newspaper space and broadcast time for international news, and enhanced standing for journalists as members of an acknowledged profession—would require "long-term evolutionary action towards improving the exchange of news around the world." Here was the MacBride Commission's acknowledgment that the new world information order, as yet undefined, would be a long time building.

TOWARD THE NEW WORLD INFORMATION ORDER

The new order, whether perceived as concept, process, goal, or slogan, means different things to different people. One communication scholar, Kaarle Nordenstreng (1979), described it as "a radical program to change the world," pointing toward "a global structure not far from Lenin's theory of imperialism."

There can be little comfort in such descriptions for those who are not devout Leninists. Others see the new order as the hoped-for outcome of a long-term process of building and development that, if carried out over a period of decades with good will and good sense, can reduce and eventually abolish the present-day gap between rich and poor countries in the field of mass communication. Some Third World advocates concede that the process will call for massive investments of human effort and material resources, demanding radically different investment and budgetary priorities *within* most developing countries, in addition to whatever assistance may be offered by advanced industrial countries. The long-term goal, if it is to receive the broad international support its advocates hope for, must be the creation of a global system in which many new voices will be heard, voices speaking not only from South to North but also South-to-South, North-to-South, East-to-West and West-to-West. It will, moreover, demand vigorous efforts to tear down internal barriers that impede or block communication among regions and language groups, and also between urban and rural populations. This change necessarily means a small-media approach—local newspapers, low-power local radio, and video, at least in regions remote from the center.

There is, however, a troubling ambiguity about the underlying purposes of the new-order campaign. To many Third World leaders, the new order suggests restrictive measures against existing transnational suppliers of news, motion pictures, television programs, computers, and software. The implicit rationale appears to be defensive, that is, to assert and maintain state control over the flow of information for reasons not markedly different from those of the medieval church and the crowned heads of 16th century Europe, who sought to license the printing press because it seemed to them a natural instrument of subversion. Fear of dissenting views is complicated in contemporary circumstances by official anxiety that new communication technologies, with their global reach, are even more difficult to control. Radio waves defy border controls, annihilate distance, and, along with the printed media, carry ideas that could disrupt internal order.

NEW COMMUNICATION TECHNOLOGIES AND THE THIRD WORLD

Arthur C. Clarke, the master of science fiction who in 1945 published his now-historic article setting out the principles of the communication satellite, considers the anxiety self-defeating. In a 1981 lecture at UNESCO, Clarke sought to answer the question, "What have satellites to do with the problems of the Third World?":

In highly developed regions like the United States and much of Europe, communication satellites are a great convenience, but not absolutely vital. These countries already have excellent cable and microwave links.

Clarke continues:

To many developing countries, however, satellites are *essential;* they will make it unnecessary to build the elaborate and expensive ground systems required in the past. Indeed, to such countries, satellites could be a matter of life and death. To put it as dramatically as possible, unless major investments are made in space, millions are going to die, or eke out brief and miserable lives. And most of those millions will be in the Third World. . . .

Clarke is not saying that satellites will do everything.

In heavily populated areas, fiber optics and short-range radio or infra-red broadcasts will often be preferable. But even these local systems will, of course be linked to the global network through satellites. And *only* satellites can provide every conceivable type of communication cheaply and efficiently over entire continents, and to all moving vehicles on land, sea, or in the air.

The news flow argument is far from being settled. Advancing technology is likely, however, to prevail over ideology in shaping a new multi-directional world system. Wisely applied, the new technologies can create an abundance of new communication channels beyond the imaginings of science fiction writers. Greater and more diversified message flows, and broader citizen participation, are within our grasp. With each passing year, the productivity of communication technology rises—and its costs keep dropping (even in inflationary times). The crucial point is that the information technologies, unlike coal or oil or other non-renewable materials, are inexhaustible. With the passage of time they have become ever more productive, hence cheaper, and universally available, the key to increasing self-reliance.

Television program flows provide an interesting case in point. An investigation by Nordenstreng and Varis (1974) traced a pattern of heavy dependence for TV programming upon the United States and other Western exporters. Various nations in Latin America, for example, imported from 10 to 84 percent of their total hours of programming. Nine years later, Antola and Rogers (1982) found an important counter-trend at work. Brazil went from importing almost 60 percent of its TV programs in 1974 to 28 percent in 1982; Venezuela cut back from 50 percent to 35 percent. The pessimism of a decade past over prospects of reducing dependence on imported TV programs has given way in several leading countries to an aggressive optimism. Radio Caracas increased its local production, using the motto, "Television must be made, not imported," from 30 to 70 percent. The competing channel in Venezuela, Venevision, produced about 55 percent of its programs in 1982. Both television channels have prospered thanks to the wide audience appeal of domestic television production. Brazil and Mexico meanwhile have become major exporters of TV programs, an outcome that was not broadly predicted a decade ago.

The lesson implicit in these findings about television flows in Latin America may have relevance for news flow in the years to come.

REFERENCES

Livia Antola and Everett M. Rogers (1982), "Television Flows in Latin America," Paper presented at the Conference on Flow of Messages, Flow of Media in the Americas, Stanford University, CA.

Phil Harris (1977), *News Dependence: The Case for a New World Information Order,* Leicester, England: University of Leicester Press.

MacBride Commission (1980), *Many Voices, One World: Report by the International Commission for the Study of Communication Problems,* Paris: UNESCO and Kogan Page.

Mustapha Masmoudi (1978), *The New World Information Order,* A document prepared for the MacBride Commission at UNESCO, Paris.

John C. Merrill (1981), "A Growing Controversy: The 'Free Flow' of News among Nations," in James Richstad and Michael Anderson (eds.), *Crisis in International News: Policies and Prospects,* New York: Columbia University Press.

The New York Times (October 24, 1980), "UNESCO as Censor."

Kaarle Nordenstreng (October, 1979), *The Communicator,* New Delhi.

Kaarle Nordenstreng and Tapio Varis (1974), *Television Traffic: A One-Way Street?* Paris: UNESCO, Reports and Papers on Mass Communication 70.

Edward T. Pinch (1977), "The Third World and the Fourth Estate," cited in Elie Abel (1979), *Communication for an Interdependent Pluralistic World,* Paris: UNESCO, MacBride Commission, Report Serie Mauve 33.

Rosemary Righter (1979), "Battle of the Bias," *Foreign Policy, 34,* 123.

Rosemary Righter (1980), "World Communication Issues," in James Richstad and Michael Anderson (eds.), *Crisis in International News: Policies and Prospects,* New York, Columbia University Press; this essay first appeared in a somewhat different version in 1979, "Newsflow International," *The Political Quarterly, 50,* 302–315.

Wilbur Schramm and Erwin Atwood (1981), *Circulation of News in the Third World: A Study in Asia,* Hong Kong, China: Chinese University Press.

Robert L. Stevenson, Richard R. Cole, and Donald Lewis Shaw (1980), *Patterns of World News Coverage: A Look at the UNESCO Debate on the New World Information Order,* Paper presented at the Association for Education in Journalism, Boston, MA.

UNESCO (1978), *The Mass Media Declaration, Article I,* Paris: UNESCO.

Chapter 9

Active Audiences in Europe: Public Participation in the Media

Alex Gryspeerdt
Université Catholique de Louvain

INTRODUCTION

One of the important surprises in European mass communication, starting in the early 1970s but growing to strength in the early 1980s, is an active audience that demands a greater degree of participation in creating media messages. One expression of this movement was the increased audience access to the establishment media by non-professionals. Even more important as a route to greater participation has been the creation of a variety of new forms of the media: parallel newspapers, videotape and video press production, television à la carte, communal television, and, most important, independent radio. For example, "free radio" (that is, non-governmental FM stations) in France provides an unprecedented variety of channels; in Paris alone, 156 free radio stations were operating in 1983. Independent radio may be reaching 30 to 50 percent of the European audience today. These alternative media have not always been financially successful, and sometimes their program/message quality is poor. In some cases, as in the U.S. underground press of the 1960s, the alternative media have gradually joined the establishment. Perhaps their greatest impact is the changes they have forced on the establishment media, especially the State broadcasting organizations in Europe. *E.M.R., F.B.*

The mass media, since their origin, apply meaning to a large audience that is anonymous and passive in nature. The relationship of the source to the reader/listener had almost always been the same until about the end of the 1960s. Mass media communicators focus on particular audiences, and create messages for them. Producers and transmitters are comprised of information and entertainment specialists, while listeners/readers form a very large audience that do not produce mass media messages. They are just passive consumers.

With only a few exceptions, the idea of mass media conceived not only *for* their audience but also *by* their audiences, began only in the early 1970s. This change is radical in that it represents a shift in the relationships between the media and their audiences. The public is now asked to *participate* in the construction of certain messages, and in the conception and management of the media. This change happened only in the Western world and comes from certain historical events, such as the student protests in the 1960s, and, more recently, from the technical invention of the

165

means of producing and issuing messages with a much smaller purchase and management cost.

THE CHALLENGE TO THE ESTABLISHED MEDIA

The 1970s marked a major challenge to the centralized, national media in Europe which filter the news, and feature only message content likely to interest a very large audience. The press and broadcasting media are particularly criticized for not diversifying their news sources. In spite of the diversity of newspapers (the audience notices their diminishing number because of economic factors), there is often a lack of pluralism in descriptions of a news event. The same sources are always consulted: official spokesmen and the public information officers of agencies, and generally, even for local events, people who have the power of giving opinions. Denise Bombardier (1975) says about the former French television system: "The voice of France is the voice of notables." If we believed only what we see on the screen, everybody in France is either a director, a president, or a general-secretary. Only people having extensive responsibility can talk on TV. Hence only one kind of information is given, and only one category of people has the right to speak. There is a kind of sameness about the mass media in Europe.

This lack of diversity is one reason for the rejection of the broadcasting monopolies in Europe, and, more generally, for the rejection of all media by some individuals. The media only talk about humble people when they become the heroes, victims, or delinquents of news events. Moreover, many subjects are still considered taboo by the press, at the very moment when the youth in France, the U.S., Italy, Belgium, Holland, West Germany, and Scandinavia criticize established authorities and the society in which they live, especially concerning war, nuclear energy, the conditions of young people, students, women, and immigrants. These youth speak out against the established cultural mode of taboos, about sex, violence, drugs, etc. With an explosion of protests against society, and with a desire to know and to talk, comes a desire for self-determination and self-management by an entire social group in Western Europe.

The protest comes from students, feminists, anti-nuclear groups, ecology action associations, radical groups, and other movements. The consciousness of the public is raised about the mass media content and other issues. Educational, religious, and political groups want to use the media themselves. The result is a critical reading of the media, and an attempt to control mass media effects. This critical reaction appeared in the 1970s, and grew stronger during the 1980s. The critical reaction is against every kind of media message, especially commercials. A strong boomerang effect opposes many messages and the underlying practices of the media. Edgar Morin (1975) called this phenomenon a long wave which follows more revolutionary shock waves.

THE NEW, "LIGHT" COMMUNICATION MEDIA

From a technical point of view, new communication media make possible, at a smaller cost, a new kind of small media. These so-called "light" media require only a relatively small investment, and only a short training period to be able to use them. Such light media include offset printing, portable video cameras, videotape recorders, several cheap transmission tools, and, more generally, electronics in miniature. People use every possible gap between established law and tolerated practice to get the necessary mass media to reach the public. Decentralization and regionalization of the media are occurring in Europe. For example, the same transmitter may send different messages to different regions with the help of local crews.

EVOLUTION OF THE ACTIVE MEDIA

During the 1960s, the existing mass media in Europe redefined themselves first as competitors of television, and then, in terms of their specific audience. Cinema, then the written press, and soon radio experienced a sharp drop in audience size. Because of rising production costs (due to equipment depreciation and the salary demands of workers), only large concentrations could make media institutions profitable. The revival appears in the form of a change of ideas and practices in the media around the years 1968–1970. Then a slow evolution occurred toward a more active participation of the audience. Such activity was in reaction to the existing mass media, and is yet far from being a majority phenomenon, even in the 1980s. The active audience is still an exception in the Western world, and in spite of its recent rapid growth, it remains marginal and an alternative. The great majority of mass media are managed and controlled by their owners, as before.

Audience participation in the year 1984 occurs in three ways:

1. The mass media involve their audience in their editorial and production work.
2. Unhappy with existing media, the audience creates new ones like film production and distribution companies, parallel (or underground) newspapers, and independent radio and television.

3. In order to improve or modify an existing medium, the audience creates media control structures like press boards, readers' and listeners' committees, etc.

These different forms can coexist. They can even create media that are absolutely not participative, and which are not any different from the media they criticized and set out to reform. Further, there is much diversity in national situations; for example, independent radio is not the same in Italy, Holland, Belgium, France, or the U.S. Very often, audience participation remains at an experimental level, whether it concerns free speech programs, new broadcasting stations, new newspapers, or the involvement of audiences in editorial work. Later in this chapter, we will evaluate different forms of public participation.

ACCESS TO EXISTING MEDIA BY NON-PROFESSIONALS

The Press

Apart from commercials (which are generally subject to precise rules), a newspaper's contents are normally left up to the decision of the editors. Even if editors or reporters report any testimony in their articles, the people whose testimonies are published will necessarily be people who are implicated in the event as witnesses, experts, victims, or stars. Rarely will ordinary members of the audience be able to express themselves in a newspaper. Important or extraordinary people are always preferred.[1] However, exceptions seem more frequent since 1975, than during the preceding decades.

Letters to the Editor. Traditionally, a newspaper's readers express themselves under the heading "Letters to the Editor" (when there is such a section). In most cases, it is the only section where readers have access to a newspaper and where their writing might be read. Most of the daily newspapers in Europe do not have "Letters to the Editor." However, some newspapers are exceptions, and they make special efforts to publish readers' opinions. A few newspapers have an ombudsman who interprets the readers' complaints against the administration of the newspaper, and may publish an article on the complaint. This journalistic approach, used particularly today in the Scandinavian countries and in Belgium, does not require that every audience member have writing ability.

---

[1]The ordinary people who are talked about in local newspapers are in fact the "stars" of such newspapers (Ringet, 1981).

Open Tribunes. The second traditional means of audience participation is the open tribune, which is only reserved for a few well-known personalities. When, occasionally, someone who is not well-known uses this rubric to express his point of view, he will almost always do so as a representative of a function like student or consumer. In most of the cases, the writer is solicited by the newspaper staff. The open tribune is different from an editorial only because it provides access to people who do not necessarily have the same point of view as the newspaper editors.

Pages Written by Readers. Even less frequent is the practice of asking readers to write an entire page. For example, some newspapers allow children, occasionally or on a regular basis, to make a special edition or to contribute articles. In France, the daily newspaper *Sud Ouest* in 1979 published several hundred articles written by children under the rubric *"Enfants, dites . . ."* ("Say Kids").[2] In 1975–1976, the Belgian newspaper *La Wallonie* carried out an experiment called *"La Parole aux Jeunes"* ("The Youth Speak Up"), which gave the young people (15 to 25 years old) of Liege the opportunity to talk about different aspects of their daily life: work, love, sex, family, etc. Technical and editorial help was provided to these one-time journalists (Lambert, 1976).

Cases where readers write an entire page of a newspaper may exist but the present author could not find any such experience in Western Europe, except where readers buy (at the regular advertising rate) space in a newspaper where they can express their point of view. Even at a high cost, such instances are very rare because many newspapers will not accept such advertising.

Newspapers Written by their Readers. A new type of newspaper exists which delegates to readers not the editorial work, but also a part of management. For example, the newspaper may be constituted as a cooperative (we will describe such newspapers later in this chapter).

Classified Ads. Some papers, especially in France, allow readers to insert an advertising text of their choice in the newspaper at low cost; not to sell or buy goods or services, but to exchange tips, advice, hitchhiking, sexual or love experiences, etc. Such is the case of *Le Nouvel Observateur,* among the more traditional French newspaper, and the French daily *Liberation.* Free classified ads in weekly newspapers sold in newsstands or via subscription have been attempted in Italy and Belgium.

---

[2]Jean-Pierre Spirlet (1981) discusses this experiment in his book.

Games. Games-related sections of newspapers have increased during the 1970s in Europe. Reader participation has been sought in suggesting ideas for new games (for example, crossword puzzles sent in by readers).

Broadcasting by Non-Professionals

Participation in Shows Produced by Professionals. The trend is for TV and radio stations to ask for participation by their audiences. Such participation on shows represents about 20 to 30 percent of the air time for most European stations, although on some free radio and decentralized radio and television stations it is much more. Participation can be achieved through attendance by the public in the studios when the show is being prerecorded, or through telephone calls to game, debate, commentary (such as movie reviews), or various entertainment shows, peer consulting, musical hit-parades, psychological counseling, experience-sharing shows, or talk shows. Other participation techniques include CB radio, which allows people to communicate road and traffic conditions to certain radio stations, which in turn, report them on the air. In a program like *Les Routiers sont Sympas* there is live communication between the on-air host and truckdrivers.

Participation in the Production of Shows. In some countries, for example, Great Britain and Holland, members of the audience are involved in the production of a broadcast, perhaps with professional directors and journalists operating the cameras and producing the show. Such audience participation is not very frequent. In the Netherlands, VARA *(Vereniging Atbeiders Radio Amateurs)* produced shows called *"Van Onderen."* A VARA official explains that this series of shows dealt with unskilled workers. After showing a movie about people doing boring tasks in factories, and describing their feelings about their work, viewers who might have recognized themselves in the pictures reacted. The next show dealt with these reactions; the third show with the further reactions of the public, etc. No supervisor, political personality, or union leader was allowed to take part in the broadcast. After the first show, 800 letters were received, some of which were poems. Only a small part of the reactions could be used in the TV series, so a radio show was produced every other week, a cheap newspaper was printed, and two inexpensive books and a miscellany of poems were published (Groombridge, 1974).

The Belgian experimental series *"Inedits"* was broadcast on the RTBF network *(Radio-Télévision Belge de la Communauté Française)*, featuring movies and pictures produced by anybody. These movies came from personal family collections, and showed how people spent their holidays, worked, etc.

Station-Originated Programs Accessible to the Public. Totally new since 1970, public-access shows (somewhat like cable TV in the U.S.) now are broadcast on some radio and television stations in Great Britain and Belgium. A fixed air-time is given over to non-professionals who want to communicate their ideas on radio or television. Technical assistance and equipment are provided by the station, which does not intervene in the proposed content or style of the show. The programs are not very successful in attracting an audience. Further, the number of individuals and groups willing to produce a show decreased rapidly because of the amount of effort required, in comparison with expectations.[3] However, diversified groups have received an opportunity to speak on the air, such as housemaids, conscientious objectors, retired people, homosexuals, and immigrants (Groombridge, 1974).

Finnish television also has audience-access shows, although they are more fully under the control of a professional. For example, in an isolated village, farmers meet and choose the questions they will ask officials who make decisions for them. Similar programs are also produced in factories.

CREATION OF NEW MEDIA BY NON-PROFESSIONALS

The Parallel Press

The "parallel," "underground," or "marginal" press is an attempt to return the newspaper to its readers. This parallel press in Europe is served by the News Agency "Liberation" since 1971, which retransmits information about minorities, oppressed people, and victims of the abuse of political, economic, and social power. A small number of non-professional collaborators typically produce a parallel newspaper by sharing the editorial work and such other chores as accounting, printing, and distribution of the newspaper. Reader participation is much more important than in the usual newspaper.

To be able to understand the alternative press in Europe, a comparison is made with the usual characteristics of the establishment press.

- It depends on financial groups or important institutions.
- It is organized as a business enterprise, with a division of occupational tasks, and it employs paid professionals.
- It subscribes to news agencies.

---

[3]The magazine *Etudes de Radio-Télévision* (1977a; 1977b) evaluated some of the free-access programs of the RTFB (Radio Open Doors and Free Access TV).

- It produces a newspaper which is distributed through commercial channels (such as postal services and newsstands) or via mail subscriptions.
- "Official" information is collected from notable people in positions of responsibility.
- Participation of the readers is almost nonexistent.
- The press content is neutral, objective, or closely related to an official political opinion.
- Advertising provides an important source of income.

In comparison, the characteristics of the parallel press are quite different (Gryspeerdt, 1979).

- It is independent and does not receive financial support from bankers or other established sources.
- In many instances, the editorial work as well as the management, production, and distribution of the paper is given to volunteers (who are often militants). In other instances, hired journalists are satisfied with a minimum salary or are not paid when the newspaper is unprofitable.
- Because of a lack of money, or for other reasons, such as to be close to the readers, the newspaper does not subscribe to news agencies.
- Distribution channels can take different forms, such as at the gates of factories, at the location of a conflict, or during celebrations.
- Unofficial information that originates from nonauthorized sources is predominant. The information often concerns minorities like strikers, prisoners, and homosexuals, and situations of conflict, such as repression, struggles, strikes, and demonstrations.
- The participation of readers is encouraged in that the newspaper may be produced by its readers, and it may contain many spontaneous articles.
- The tools of reproduction used are easy to handle, cheap, and generally rudimentary: dittoing, collating, stapling, offsetting, etc.
- The use of advertisements is limited.

There are differences between the American underground press and the European parallel press. The latter is more concerned with minorities, the questioning of taboos, and the communication of local news. The American underground press evokes an avant-garde graphic approach, the psychedelic, and themes related to the hippie phenomenon, drugs, new religions, and communal and collective life. However, at the level of student newspapers, anarchistic movements, and ecological or feminist movements, the European parallel press and the American underground press are similar.

The parallel press in Europe grew very rapidly from 1970 to 1980, but is now declining (a) because of the economic crisis manifested in inflation, unemployment, etc., and (b) because some needs are now satisfied through the influence of the parallel press on other media. Issues neglected by the established media, such as ecological problems, have been at the forefront of the underground press.

The alternative press, even if its goals are very general and not precisely stated, represents the will to do something collectively (Dietsch, 1972). The contents are of an expressive nature and much less instrumental than the establishment press. Rather than praising the work system, for example, the alternative media praise the individual who is a responsible militant (Spates and Levin, 1972).

An unusual experiment with a parallel newspaper which "belonged to its readers" happened in Belgium from 1974 to 1977. The idea was to produce a newspaper of good quality, using as a model the French daily newspaper *Le Monde*. *Notre Temps* was a weekly newspaper in which every cooperator was a collaborator, and every collaborator was a cooperator. *Notre Temps* published 140 weekly issues in which readers were allowed to express themselves. Many of the collaborators were political, social, cultural, and intellectual French-speaking Belgian officials. Very often, these collaborators gave comments, and sometimes it happened that contradictory opinions about the same subject were published in an issue. Articles about such social problems as nuclear arms, the humanization of hospitals, and help for prisoners, were featured. *Notre Temps* received almost no ads, and after three years it went bankrupt with a debt of several million Belgian francs.

New Forms of Broadcasting

Production of Videotapes and Video-Press. We distinguish between groups who produce videotapes from those who broadcast on cable TV or on television. However, their production methods are similar, and several groups who produced videotapes in Europe also are involved in communal television stations. Robert Wangermee, Director-General of the Institute of French-Speaking Belgian Radio-Television Broadcasting, stated:

Light video is the most important tool of participative television. At the beginning, we cannot really call it television. . . . Video is useful to confront groups with their own image, and to make them change. It works like an "electronic mirror" which reflects the situation of a community so that the situation is better perceived by its members who are consequently invited to react. (Wangermee and Lhoest, 1973)

In France, the Netherlands, Great Britain, Belgium, Germany, and Italy, many groups produce "video-press" programs for members of their community. Attempts at video-piracy (the injection of a videotape on the air on a cable system without permission) have occurred, especially in Belgium and the Netherlands.

Channels Accessible to the Public. Publicly-accessible TV channels are more American than European.

> In the U.S.A., the participative television came from the underground. The video had gone underground to lead cultural guerilla warfare: Its pioneers did not instigate political revolution nor violence. They only wanted to get for all minorities the right to freely express themselves. . . . American commercial television was essentially made by white men, for the bourgeois. Alternative television is done for racial and social minorities. An important place is given to women. (Wangermee and Lhoest, 1973)

In Europe, the pattern is to produce programs for the public inside a broadcasting station, or to create a communal television (which broadcasts locally on existing channels when they are not in use).

Television "à la Carte". One other form of audience participation is television "à la carte": Programs are chosen by members of the audience, although they are not involved in producing the programs. Some commercial television stations (like Radio-Television Luxembourg) invite their audience to choose between two or three movies by calling on the telephone; then the movie is selected on the basis of the number of calls it received.

Communal Television. In 1976, the French-speaking Belgian community authorized, on an experimental basis, and with certain conditions (for example, no advertising), about 10 experiments with communal and local television. Some have become permanent (for example, Gembloux, Tournai, and Liege). One, *Canal Emploi,* is concerned with the problem of unemployment, and produces television shows on adult education, news reports, and services for the unemployed.

Most cable television stations in Great Britain have tried to produce television programs that are accessible to the public. A major difficulty is the necessity to find audience members who know how to correctly present the news. For communal television, audience participation is important. "Swindow Viewpoint," the only English communal television today, is managed and directed by a committee of seven elected members. In Italy, communal television involves a few hundred groups producing and transmitting their own programs (from games to political debates). In

Holland, local television is tolerated but not officially authorized. Programs are broadcast after the transmission of accredited television on local stations.

Independent Radio. In Europe, independent radio was born in 1975, in Italy. By 1978–1979, several other countries began to follow the movement: Belgium, France, Holland, and Switzerland. At the beginning, independent radio was alternative and forbidden (for example, Radio Populare in Milan, dio Citta Futra in Rome, Radio Alice in Bologne, and Radio Eau Noire in Couvin, Belgium). By the end of the 1970s in some countries (Italy, French-speaking Belgium, and France), legislation which authorized and regulated independent radio was passed. A thousand independent radio stations had sprung up in Italy, and more than 100 in Belgium and in France. Their existence created an obvious breach in the State monopolies of radio and television. Some independent radio stations are commercial, created by local businessmen or local newspapers. Others are supported by political movements, and "manned" by amateurs or by music fanatics.

The first Belgian independent radio was launched in 1978 with an ideology very close to alternative newspapers: Ecology (Radio Eau Noire, in Couvin) opposed the construction of a dam in La Roche), about light drugs (Radio Noire in Huy), about the anti-nuclear struggle (Radio Noire, Radio Irradiee and Radio Activité in Andenne; Radio Tam-Tam in Brussels), and about social struggles (Radio Siderurgie in Charleroi).

DISCUSSION

The phenomenon of an active audience comes from the individual's right to freedom of expression. Such participatory activity is a relatively recent phenomenon which takes many different forms in Europe. Most experiences to date show that, far from using their right to communicate, most people hesitate to use it. One reason for low use, especially in the visual media, is the poor quality programs that have been produced in large quantity. In recent years, the participation of readers and viewers has increased, but now may be decreasing. Radio and television stations are trying to decentralize in several European countries where the alternative media have been strong. Prior to 1980, the parallel press had never reached more than 5 percent of the total audience in Europe, but independent radio stations today reach 30 to 50 percent of the total audience. Besides, the alternative media are politically and socially important. They made a breach in the State broadcasting monopolies. Because of the impact they leave behind them, the experiments with audience participation in Europe have changed the way the media operate.

It is difficult to forecast the nature of mass communication in the 1990s. But certainly the audiences will have become more participative and more active than in the years before 1980.

REFERENCES

Denise Bombardier (1975), *La Voix de la France,* Paris: Robert Laffont.

Jean-Claude Dietsch (1972), "Aujourd'hui, une Autre Presses," *Etudes,* 380–382.

Etudes de Radio-Television (1977a), "Les Televisions Ouvertes", 21.

Etudes de Radio-Television (1977b), "Radio Local et Communautaire," 23.

B. Groombridge (1974), *Television and Participation,* Strasbourg, France: Council of Europe, Comité de l'Education Extrascolaire et du Développement Culturel, Report.

Axel Gryspeerdt (1979), "Les Nouveaux Courants de la Presse Francophone en Belgigue après Mai, 1968: La Contre-Information Régionale, Locale, et Sectorielle," *Courrier Hebdomadaire du CRISP,* 845–846.

Michel Lambert (1976), "La Parole aux Jeunes," *Cahiers JEB,* 6.

Edgar Morin (1975), *L'Esprit du Temps-Z-Necrose,* Paris, Grasset.

Gabriel Ringet (1981), *La Mythe au Milieu du Village: Comprendre et Analyser la Presse Locale,* Brussels: Editions Via Ouvriere.

James L. Spates and Jack Levin (1972), "Les Beatniks, les Hippies, la Hip Generation et al Classe Moyenne Americaine: Une Analyse de Valeurs," *Revue Internationale des Sciences Sociales, 26,* 346–375.

Jean-Pierre Spirlet (1981), *L'Enfant et la Presse,* Paris: Casternan, Collection 3.

Robert Wangermee and H. Lhoest (1973), *L'Apres-Télévision: Une Anti-Mythologie de l'Audiovisuel,* Paris: Hachette.

Chapter 10

Television as Instrument of Cultural Identi
The Case of Quebec

Denise Bombardier
Radio-Canada

INTRODUCTION

In many nations the mass media of communication, especially television, tend to diminish or to destroy the distinctiveness of ethnic, racial, and linguistic subcultures. Thus, the mass media help to create a kind of culturally standardized mass society. But in Quebec the opposite happened, as French-language television contributed directly to greater cultural integration of the Quebeçois. Today, about 2.2 million Canadians (out of a total population of 24 million) have French as a mother tongue, and another one million from English-speaking backgrounds can also speak French. *E.M.R., F.B.*

Of all Western societies, without doubt, Quebec was the most affected by the new medium of television at the beginning of the 1950s. Television altered the monolithic image with which Quebec had been projected by its political and religious leaders. From the beginning, the political and religious institutions reacted with circumspection, prudence, uneasiness, and even mistrust vis-à-vis this picture box controlled by the nation's Parliament in Ottawa. During the early months of its existence in 1952, Canadian television offered its audience both English and French-speaking programs, with one channel alternating between programs using one or the other language; sometimes programs in both languages were offered at the same time. This formula was quickly abandoned as soon as adequate numbers of personnel were recruited. Then Radio-Canada and the Canadian Broadcasting Corporation became two autonomous networks with a centralized management, essentially a replica of the public radio service in existence since the 1930s.

LANGUAGE POLICIES OF CANADIAN TELEVISION

Those responsible for the new public service of television could not have predicted the consequences of their decision. They laid down the bases for one of the institutions which contributed most to the emergence of a new nationalism in Quebec. In the 1960s television became a fundamental instrument for social change, and was termed by some a "quiet revolution." For television officials in the 1950s however, the issue was only to bring Quebec into the era of the new television technology then becoming prevalent on the North American continent. That technology quickly became an infatuation for the Quebec population, which grew to be heavy television watchers. Television had a much greater influence than radio, which had begun broadcasting in 1932. One reason is because radio faced competition from private stations, while the impact of the "tube" was total for about the first 10 years. Only in 1961 was its monopoly in Quebec challenged by a French-language private channel.

From the beginning, the language barrier obliged Quebec to produce its own TV programs, different from those produced elsewhere on the North American continent. One of the greatest challenges for English-speaking Canada has been to create a television different in style and content from American television. The difficulty of being "Canadian" is expressed in this dilemma. In the case of Quebec, whose identity-quest lies elsewhere, this search was painfully felt at the beginning of the 1950s, and television became a fundamental instrument for the definition of Quebec's collective image. A relatively small number of people living on a territory 3.5 times as large as France, the 5 million Francophones, in a continent with 250 million Anglophones, discovered through the picture tube that they no longer existed just as individuals or as parishioners, but collectively. The view provided of such traditional structures as the family, the street or the country road, and the church, revealed Quebec to itself.

Those with creative ability were prompt in putting their talent to the service of the new medium of expression. The best writers created television serials, and the best actors portrayed characters with which the public identified. In entertainment programs, comic actors ridiculed the politicians and clergy of Quebec. This public demystification of traditional elites, through a medium whose impact was barely controlled because its consequences were not known, provoked a rapid erosion of official morals. Quebec songwriters and poets celebrated the country to build, the humiliation to overcome, and the liberty to conquer. Such diverse artistic expressions, conveyed through the extraordinary medium of television, quickly shaped a collective ego. Television in the 1950s contributed to the emergence of a new nationalism which inspired the *"Parti Quebeçois,"* the political party which has led Quebec since 1976. Contrary to what happened in other developed societies where television became a window open to the world, in Quebec, television has been first and foremost a window opened onto the distinctive culture of Quebec.

THE QUIET REVOLUTION OF TELEVISION IN QUEBEC

Before this quiet revolution of the 1960s was started by a liberal government, Quebec was a monolithic society. Schools, hospitals, and social services were entirely controlled by the clergy. For example, there was no ministry of education, but a Council of Public Instruction whose only members were the bishops of Quebec. They had the entire responsibility for the structure and the content of education. Creation of the Ministry of Education in 1964 aroused a passionate reaction among the conservative milieu which saw in it a "communist maneuver." More than 90 percent of the people were church-going Catholics. For the people then in power, progressive ideas, even expressed by Catholics, were perceived as seditious. From the start, television attracted the most dynamic and the most challenging elements within Quebec society. De facto, Radio-Canada became one of the strongholds of the intelligentsia and an exceptional stepping-stone for future political personalities. Rene Lavesque was then the star of news programs, and Pierre-Elliot Trudeau one of the most brilliant and provocative commentators.

This particular role of television, of bringing change agents together, can be explained in part by a structural paradox. The provincial government was headed, since the beginning of the 1940s, by Maurice Duplessis, a sort of local potentate. However, the institution of radio and television, Radio-Canada, was beyond his control. Broadcasting comes under federal jurisdiction and the prevailing philosophy in the institution is an advanced liberalism. The law covering this public service is inspired by the British model for the BBC; it ensures real independence vis-à-vis political power. In its public affairs programs Radio-Canada tried to present varied, different, and even controversial viewpoints and opinions. For example, when the private and public school system was in the hands of the clergy, the creation of non-religious schools was debated on television. In conservative Quebec, which many described as being a kind of Spain and Portugal in North America, and which Prime Minister Duplessis liked to say was like alcohol, in that some people could not tolerate it, Radio-Canada's small screen, present in most households, played the role of a symbol. The French-language television network, in French Canadian hands but under federal control, could not be censored by the provincial government and hence represented freedom.

The age of television brought about not only a new nationalism free of conservative values (particularly religious values), but, paradoxically, also helped create a new self-assurance among the Francophone elite whose objective became the control of power at the national level. The traditional nationalism of French Canada is based on two unshakable pillars: (a) language, and (b) religious faith. The expression "French Canadian pure wool" means a French-speaking Canadian who adheres without reservation to the Roman Catholic church. Everyone else is labeled a renegade or traitor to his/her "race." Such neo-nationalism is presented by spokespersons invited to participate on Radio-Canada's television programs.

Radio-Canada's supporters talk of modernism, of secularization, and of progressivism. They are young, more educated than the average, and professionally they belong to areas close to the social sciences. However, for Trudeau and for many of his contemporaries, the Radio-Canada experience (that of radio and even more so for television) demonstrated that freedom can only come from the national capital in Ottawa and only from Anglophones. Many intellectuals in Quebec suffer from the oppressive climate of socially reactionary Quebec. Some go into exile; others are barred from university teaching because of their opinions. Indeed, at the University of Montreal, when it was a pontifical university, every professor had to prove his/her belief in God and in the Church. These intellectuals therefore abhorred clerical nationalism, which they considered conservative and closed.

POLITICIZATION EFFECTS OF TELEVISION

In the 1950s and until the mid-1960s, television brought about two kinds of national identity among the Quebeçois: (a) a bilingual and bicultural identity superseding a Canadian identity, and (b) a Quebeçois identity based on the cultural and political autonomy of Quebec. The elite expressed this newly formed identity in political parties.

Furthermore, the obligation to create from scratch a television system different from what existed elsewhere in North America constituted another proof of the collective Francophone difference from Anglophone society. The image portrayed of Quebec differed from that portrayed by English-speaking Canadians in their television programs. Generally, Quebec television viewers preferred their local *feuilletons* to the dubbed American soap operas, and this is still the case in the 1980s. Even though the *feuilletons* do not present separatist or federalist characters (the playwrights avoid doing so), they induce a collective identification with Quebec. Some people assert that if Quebec could create its own *feuilletons*, it could build a country as well.

Through the television medium, a politicization of Quebec got under way. Television functions not only as an object of social change, but is itself an agent of social change. Its role and function are unusual in a society which is democratic in most other respects. When the new power of television was inaugurated in Quebec in 1960, it created institutions which by their very existence slowly diminished the influence of television upon Quebec society.

THE VOCABULARY OF IDENTITY

In the 1950s, when French-language television began, its role was different. Public affairs programs reported on liberation movements in Africa, and gradually a new vocabulary emerged of imperialism, colonialism, and the right to self-determination. The younger generation was particularly receptive to the content of such programs. It chose its social ideas from the Left, symbolized by both Trudeau and Levesque, and its nationalistic ideas from outside, particularly from the Third World (present thanks to television). Extensive coverage of the Algerian independence struggle, for example, affected the intellectual and ideological orientations of many young people. They established a parallel between their own nationalism and that of countries in the process of decolonialization, even including the use of terrorism to further their cause. Lacking historical reference, the slogan "Algeria-Quebec same struggle" does not sound ridiculous to them. The new, imported vocabulary conveyed through television news programs was also adopted by the new nationalists in Quebec.

In the 1960s this transformation of vocabulary reflected the reality they wanted to impose. While grandparents defined themselves as "French Canadians" (as opposed to "English"), the next generation defined themselves as "French Canadians," and the "English" became "English Canadians." In 1960, the "French Canadians" identified themselves as "Quebeçois." The entire political evolution of Quebec can be found in this vocabulary modification. The geographical down-scaling indicated the historical redefinition that was occurring. Television channels created a revolutionary vocabulary for Quebec by describing the struggles of oppressed peoples. But TV journalists had problems with the local vocabulary used to refer to Quebec. In news bulletins and political interviews, should they talk of "Quebec" or "French Canada"? Of the State of Quebec or of the Province of Quebec? At all costs, journalists wanted to keep their credibility, acquired through maintaining the apparent neutrality defined as important by the Anglo-Saxon philosophy of the press. TV journalists therefore had to avoid using words with obvious political connotations. Although there was then no particular directive at Radio-Canada covering the issue, journalists felt they were caught in a trap of words.

TELEVISION AND THE SEPARATIST MOVEMENT

Traditionally at Radio-Canada, there have been attempts to co-produce bilingual programs with the English network. The goal was to present an image of a unified Canada. But in Quebec, a small yet very active group started to advocate the separation of Quebec from the rest of the country. For the majority of Quebeçois, the consequences of the attempts to produce bilingual programs actually confirmed the cultural differences between the two communities. Television reflected an image of difference rather than that of similarity.

However, television did not convert the people of Quebec to the idea of independence. Nonetheless, TV may have convinced a number of people of the soundness of this option, if only by allowing its promoters to express themselves on television, where many showed an image of seriousness and moderation. Nevertheless, the television medium certainly helped the majority of Quebeçois to perceive themselves as being fundamentally different from English-speaking Canadians. Politically, this perception can be translated as an argument for two different nations and two different peoples. However, Prime Minister Trudeau only talked of one people, the Canadian people.

Not surprisingly therefore, some federal politicians consider the French language network of Radio-Canada as a nest of separatists. Actually, it is less separatist in news programs than in other programs. By its very existence and by the different cultural content which it channels, the French language network appears to many as a subversive institution.

The two parallel television networks—English and French—copy the sociological reality. The temptation for many is to transform this reality at the political level by severing Quebec from the rest of Canada. At present, the separatist movement exists outside of television, which only reports this ideological confrontation of separatist versus non-separatist. Despite the sharper differentiation in television programming, the Quebeçois, first and foremost, tune to the French-language public, private, and educational networks. More than 60 percent of the Quebec people do not speak English, and a Radio-Canada survey conducted in 1981 showed that 75 percent of Quebeçois television-watchers never switched to the English language channels. The highest audience ratings go to locally produced television programs, either *feuilletons* or other entertainment shows.

We conclude that television has been since its origin a powerful medium for the social integration of Quebec. But it is very difficult to establish its political influence clearly and concretely.

Part III

European and American Approaches to Communication Research

Not only are the mass media marked by important European-American differences (and it could not be otherwise), but the history of communication research on the two continents is also quite different. European research has parted from the U.S. variety more often than it has come near, even if the main concepts of information and communication have the same meanings. But the empirical school of communication research is not forever an American one, nor is the critical school entirely European. These two schools and Euro-American approaches to communication research are discussed in the following chapters, written by both European and American authors.

Chapter 11

European–American Differences in Communication Research[1]

Jay Blumler
University of Leeds

INTRODUCTION

The different historical contexts in which they developed are a fundamental reason for European-American differences in communication research. U.S. inquiry emerged within a commercial media system, while its counterpart on the continent developed at a time when public service television was the predominant medium. These contrasting origins help explain the greater European interest (a) in critical research, and (b) in addressing policy issues. The adversary relationship between different sets of European communication scholars, who are seeking to attain greater integration of the field, is missing in America. While U.S. scholars need to give more attention to the context of mass media communication, European critical scholars should focus more on weighing empirical evidence as it bears on their ideological positions. *E.M.R., F.B.*

In recent years communication research has gradually come of age in many countries of Western Europe, often exploring new directions thought to have been neglected in the United States. It is somewhat surprising therefore that so few attempts have been made to identify the resulting differences of approach, to understand their sources, and to draw appropriate lessons from them.[2]

Admittedly, generalizing about such developments and distinctions can be perilous. Although much of the field of communication research is firmly polarized into rival camps, it is becoming increasingly difficult to equate the underlying philosophical differences with a geographic basis. It is still true, for example, that, "Europe is providing a congenial proving

---

[1]The present chapter follows in a series of publications about Euro-American contrasts in communication research (Blumler, 1978, 1980, 1981, 1982), and builds upon this previous work.

[2]This is not to claim that European-American differences in approaching communication research have gone unnoticed or unanalyzed. Illustrative of writings that have discussed such differences are Lazarsfeld (1941), Carey (1979), Lang (1979), Hardt (1979 and 1981), and Rogers (1981a and 1981b).

ground for . . . much critically-grounded mass communication enquiry" (Blumler, 1978). Yet some major European figures in communication research do not regard themselves as critical scholars, and inside the critical school some quite exciting disputes of analytical standpoint and approach to evidence are coming ever more insistently to the fore. Moreover, as work cumulates in individual countries in Europe, certain distinctive areas of national concern are emerging. Much Scandinavian media research reflects egalitarian commitments (Thunberg and others, 1982); the value of communication diversity plays a similar part in research in the Netherlands (McQuail and van Cuilenberg, 1982); many German investigators are preoccupied with media relations to their country's political elites and party structures; and much of the British literature focuses on communication roles in upholding or undermining social order and its legitimating underpinnings (Cohen and Young, 1981; Hall and others, 1978).

Nevertheless, there are still vast differences between European and North American approaches to communication research. In this chapter we raise two questions about these distinctions: (a) What features of historical time and societal space help to explain the emergence of certain outstanding features of communication scholarship in Western Europe, in contrast to certain equivalent characteristics of American work? and (b) What constructive steps might adherents of the divergent research traditions take to overcome some of the more glaring "blind spots" uncovered by this comparison and hence come, if not into closer working relationships, then at least onto easier speaking terms, with one another?

CHARACTERISTICS OF EUROPEAN MASS COMMUNICATION RESEARCH

The fact that Europe began to find its mass communication research feet in approximately the mid-1960s is doubly significant. For one thing, the European research surge originated shortly after the publication of Joseph Klapper's then seemingly authoritative account of the American state-of-the-art outlined in his *The Effects of Mass Communication* (Klapper, 1960). Europeans formed the dominant impression that Americans had mainly concentrated on audience-level inquiries, effects research, and questions open to quantitative treatment by survey or experimental designs; and that as a result they had marched up a blind alley out of which there was no clearly signposted exit. Some Europeans attracted to communication study for the first time found little appeal in continuing to plough that furrow, and began to suspect that they might be out on their own having to define the field afresh. For another thing, as Karl Erik Rosengren (1980a) pointed out, the middle 1960s was a transitional period for European social science generally. In the early postwar years, American social science had "made an unprecedented incursion into European intellectual life, [bearing a] dominant strain . . . that can be labeled with catch phrases such as behaviorist, positivist, empiricist, and, to a lesser extent, pragmatist" (Carey, 1979). But when, two decades later, communication research was getting under way in Europe, social science there was hit by a wave of revived interest in Marxism, as well as hosting certain other more or less specialized schools of thought, such as semiotics, structuralism, interactionism, sociolinguistics, contemporary cultural studies, and others.

Temporal Influences

This conjunction of temporal influences helps to explain three prominent features of European work.

1. The characteristically "holistic approach of European communication science" (Nordenstreng, 1976), or the conviction that mass communication institutions and processes must be studied not only on their own terms, but also especially in their linkages to surrounding social orders. Of course such a broadly societal perspective is grist to a Marxist's mill. As Golding and Murdock (1978) urged in this vein, "We do not need a theory of mass communications but a theory of society to generate guiding propositions and research in the areas in which we are interested." But in Europe, Marxists hold no monopoly over holism. A similarly comprehensive thrust can be found as well, for example, in Elisabeth Noelle-Neumann's (1980a) spiral of silence theory, which postulates that journalists, when emphasizing certain societal trends at the expense of others, manage to convey impressions of standpoints that are winning and losing ground to audience members, to create climates in which people feeling in the ascendant are more prepared to voice their views to others, and so to enlist the powerful engine of interpersonal communication in the molding of public opinion. Holism also can be seen in the efforts of Rosengren (1980b) and his colleagues to interrelate media content data and extramedia trend data so as to chart sources of change over the postwar period in the symbolic environment of Swedish society. And holism can be found in Gurevitch and Blumler's (1977) and Blumler and Gurevitch's (1982) identification of diverse entry points into the analysis of political communication systems. So in contrast to an American tendency virtually to equate communication science with microscopic, individual-level investigation, in Europe macroscopic levels of inquiry are decidedly favored.

2. A second European trait is to tackle research questions by mixed methods. Noelle-Neumann's work (1980b), for example, relies on a combination of content analysis, panel research, and synchronized investigation of the opinions and perceptions held on certain matters by stra-

tegically placed communicators, such as journalists and members of the public. Another example is a cross-national project of research into the role of television in the 1979 elections to the European Parliament, which was designed by political communication scholars in each of the nine member states of the European Community. This research combined interviews with political party publicists; interviews with broadcasting executives and journalists; a content analysis of the themes of campaign programs; post-election surveys of audience response; and, in some countries, before-and-after electoral panels as well (Blumler and Gurevitch, 1979; Blumler and Fox, 1982; Blumler, 1983).

3. Except perhaps for a few specialized subfields, such as research on election campaigns, the uses and gratifications approach, studies of children's responses to television, and research into the structure of adult viewing patterns (Blumler and others, 1978; Blumler and Katz, 1974; von Feilitzen and others, 1979; Goodhart and others, 1975), there are relatively few coherently cumulative traditions of audience-level inquiry in Europe. It is as if, among critical researchers especially, the systematic attempt, empirically and quantitatively, to measure the impact on audience members' ideas of the flow of mass-communicated messages has been given a "bad name." Effects research in particular is virtually treated in some quarters as the brothel of media studies: the "madam" rather than the "queen" of our science.

Spatial Influences

The *spatial* origins of European mass communication research are particularly important in understanding European-American differences:

1. In contrast to the United States, where mass communication research grew up alongside a commercially dominated media system, including the privately financed newspaper, radio, records, and movie industries, in Europe, the predominant medium at the time when researchers were cutting their teeth was television (organized in all the countries concerned along public service lines). This meant that television programs would be provided by public service corporations, which were enjoined to serve all social interests impartially and were to some extent divorced from direct political control, although they were ultimately accountable for their performance to organs of the State. Such a system inevitably propels broadcasting right into the heart of the political arena, even in a country like Britain, where many safeguards of media autonomy have been carefully devised. Broadcasters are necessarily dependent on governments of the day for decisions vital to their continuing survival and welfare—to raise the level of its license fee, say, as in the case of the BBC, or for authorization to open an additional television channel, as in the case of ITV (Independent Television) in Britain. Public service broad-

casting organizations are also singularly lacking in self-sufficiency. They badly need outside support, much of it political, to keep afloat in turbulent societal seas. As Sir Charles Curran, late Director-General of the BBC, once said: "The broadcaster's life has to be one of continuous political ingenuity" (Curran, 1979).

Three further features of the work of many European mass communication researchers trace from the centrality of public service television in the communication systems of their societies. One is their preoccupation with the role of the mass media (especially broadcasting) in politics and, more specifically, with the tensions that arise between the supposed neutrality and independence of television on the one hand and its many ties to prevailing political structures, values, and interests on the other. Another is a frequent tendency to analyze mass media functioning through the concept of "constraints", i.e., institutionalized practices and patterned relationships, internal or external, to media organizations, which serve to narrow, limit, or closely circumscribe their ability to realize their professed social purposes. Yet another European characteristic which springs in part from the importance of public service television is a keenness to address issues of media policy (Nordenstreng, 1976). Europeans often strive to express the policy relevance of their work—for example, in concluding chapters to the books they write, in giving evidence to public bodies with media responsibilities, and in contributions to conferences often convened on policy issues with joint broadcaster/academic participation.

2. Another major contrast of societal space may explain why Europeans and Americans tend to focus on different relationships between mass communication systems and social and political structures. It was historically true that in many European societies, fundamentally opposed ideological and political options were not only conceivable in principle but were translated into organized partisan cleavages, including radical challenges to prevailing distributions of wealth and power, as in the case of Socialist and Communist movements. Yet, over the postwar period, the reality of socio-political advance towards greater equality has seemed to be negligible, leaving as if unmodified the traditionally unyielding patterns of social stratification. In contrast, the United States is a country where the clash of fundamentally opposed ideological options has seemed inconceivable and overridden by the American dream of equality of opportunity for all. Yet marked patterns of *within*-system conflict, often quite intense and long-drawn-out, have regularly buffeted the American body politic. These reflect its exceptional heterogeneity (geographical, ethnic, religious, etc.), its fragmented political system (including weak party structures and disciplines, as well as the constitutional separation of powers between the president and Congress); and its highly populist political culture.

Quite different formulations of the social and political role of mass communication seem to arise from such contrasts. In Europe, academics of a Marxist and critical bent typically regard the mass media as agencies of social control, shutting off pathways of radical social change and helping to promote the *status quo*. Golding and Murdock (1978) manifest such a stance when specifying their basic departure point as a "recognition that social relations within and between modern societies are radically, though variably, inegalitarian." This viewpoint causes them to focus in turn, they say, on "the relations between the unequal distribution of control over systems of communication and wider patterns of inequality in the distribution of wealth and power" as well as on "relations between the mass media and the central axis of stratification—the class structure."

In the United States, such formulations are found in the literature much less often. Instead, the mass media are more often seen (a) as partial cause agents in social change, as in the burgeoning literature on communication campaigns (Paisley and Rice, 1981), (b) as authoritative information sources, on which people have become more dependent as the complexities of social differentiation and the pressures of a rapidly changing world threaten to become too much for them (De Fleur and Ball-Rokeach, 1975), and (c) especially as counters in the power game, tools wielded by politicians in an intense competition to mobilize popular support for their own candidacies, priorities, and policies (Patterson, 1980).

COMING TO TERMS WITH THE DIFFERENCES

It would be naive to expect such deep-seated differences of outlook between rival approaches ever to be completely overcome. Take, for example, these ways of writing about mass media effects on audiences. On the one side, we have Gaye Tuchman's (1978) reference to media-constructed news "as a 'frame' organizing 'strips' of everyday reality and imposing order on it"; as well as Gerbner and Gross's view (1976) of television as a "medium of the socialization of most people into standardized roles and behaviors," the chief function of which "is to spread and stabilize social patterns." On the other side, we have Jack McLeod and Byron Reeves' (1980) opinion that, "It is from the unravelling of conditional and interactive relationships that the most interesting communication theory will come and not from simple assertions that the media set public agendas or that children learn from television." In one case, the mass media are regarded as imposing categories through which reality is perceived, by-passing potential neutralizing factors, and engulfing the audience in a new symbolic environment (Katz, 1979). In the other case, mass media influence is conceived as *essentially differentiated,* filtered through and refracted by the diverse backgrounds, cultures, affiliations, and lifestyles of audience members. Ultimately, this division reflects a conflict of political philosophy between those who see society as governed by a more or less unified economic or power elite and those who still adhere to a pluralist vision of society (Blumler, 1979). It is not merely unrealistic to expect either side to abandon its own philosophic platform: "Such a move if it happened would . . . dilute what is one of the most exciting sources of significant debate in the field at the present time" (Blumler and Gurevitch, 1982).

Nevertheless, it is unfortunate how the main combatants often appear to restrict their appeal to already convinced devotees by arbitrarily narrowing the range of phenomena they study or by turning a blind eye to their own philosophic soft spots. Cross-camp debate could become more mutually rewarding if attempts were made to break down some of these unnecessary barriers. How might such a prescription be followed on each side of the Atlantic?

Ways Forward for American Research?

A brisk diagnosis of the American field might start by noting how it compares with the European scene, where, despite a wide scatter of work, much of it seems to get pulled towards a few focal points of theoretical and policy gravity by the presence of scholars who in their different ways are each trying "to get it together." In contrast, the American scene appears nowadays (as distinct from its pioneering era) to lack such a synthetic and binding quality, resembling more a boxing gym, in which each individual is doing his own thing, so that some people are skipping rope, some are punching bags, some lifting weights, some sparring, some taking showers, and some are just having a rest! Perhaps this wide variety also explains why, to European ears at least, the spirit of scholarly debate between rival traditions in the United States seems curiously muted. It animates some book reviews and overview essays, but otherwise it is as if a stultifying spirit of live-and-let-live encourages each scholar to follow his own star. He may report how his research findings diverge from those of his fellows, and he will expect a searching scrutiny of the technical merits of his work. But he is often sheltered from a philosophically directed probing of his presuppositions.

Three ways forward from this state of affairs are proposed. First, there should be more attempts to push already vigorous traditions of audience-level inquiry back, not only to analyses of recurring patterns of media content, but also to those features of media organization that help to generate such systematically structured forms of output. Agenda-setting research is a striking case in point. As Steve Chaffee (1978) remarked,

"Agenda-setting is one of the two or three best research ideas this field has seen in recent years." So far it has been pursued mainly in a truncated version, however, dealing over and over again with just the media content/audience reception interface. Yet you cannot properly talk about agenda-*setting* without also considering who or what managed to lay out the agenda in a certain way, so that the issue agendas which audiences may take over are then seen to have derived from weights and meanings given to news events, that arise in turn from certain abiding features of news-media gatekeeping and story construction. This approach is not just a matter of looking at media organizations as processors of issue material, however; it is also one of expanding the range of actors whom we are prepared regularly to take into account when conducting such research, including not only journalists and audiences, but also all those political and other interest groups that strive to reach audiences by developing strategies for influencing them. So a more full and rounded version of agenda-setting still waits in the wings to be called onto the research stages.[3] But without such a step, there is a danger that investigators of agenda-setting will uncritically assign "the media an autonomous function in society," simply because inputs from external power centers were excluded from the research design (see Tichenor's [1982] review of Weaver and others [1981]).

Second, American researchers urgently need to remove some of their cultural blinkers. Far too often they write as if American circumstances were the most natural in the world. Although probably productive of more communication findings and data than are generated by national communities of scholars elsewhere, it is disturbing that the resulting propositions (say, on media impacts and role) are often unreflectingly couched in universal terms. Yet some of the findings reflect the numerous peculiarities of the specifically American social and media scene. The task of sifting what is culture-bound in American evidence from what is more widely applicable, however, must await the arousal of curiosity among American scholars themselves about the nature of their communication system—and especially about how the role of communication in American society is shaped by features of its political system, economic system, and political culture.

Third, American communication research should address the challenge of its virtual impotence to influence mass media policy. In a detailed review of "The Historical Relationship of Communication Research to Mass Media Regulation" in the United States, Reeves and Baughman (1983) concluded that: "The crucial political decisions have largely ignored

---

[3]See McCombs (1981) for recognition of the need for agenda-setting research to take such a tack.

mass communication scholarship," and that "Government has been more likely to influence research than research to shape policy." This record must ultimately be traceable to the failure of the scholarly community to evolve a considered philosophy of policy research allied to a considered strategy for injecting academic insights into the policy debate—and for legitimizing that contribution.

Ways Forward for European Research?

An equivalent diagnosis of European critical research would start by noting its ambivalence toward "the facts." Convinced that facts cannot speak for themselves but must be interpreted by sound theory, critical thinkers often seem reluctant to follow wherever the facts may lead. As T.W. Adorno, a pioneer analyst of mass communication from a critical standpoint, once put it, "No continuum exists between critical theorems and the empirical procedures of natural science" (Adorno, 1969). Yet he also acknowledged the legitimacy, even the necessity, for empirical inquiry. This paradox is soluble by critical scholars only by assigning to empirical work a firmly subordinate and guided role. The foundations of critical theory are rooted in self-evident truths about the nature of the social system and its connections with the communication system. The task of empirical inquiry, then, is largely to expose those links concretely and to show how the known social patterns impose themselves on, and operate within, the communication sphere in practice.

Viewed from an American angle, however, such an approach suffers from the lack of a falsification strategy. In the critical system, there are seemingly no methodological procedures whereby theoretically derived assertions can be countermanded by independently collected data. The outcomes of critical research are then frequently in danger of being compromised for "nonbelievers," who may suspect that the evidence is being used, not to test a problematic proposition, but to prove a favored point.

Nevertheless, there may be ways out of this closed circle, and it is to be hoped that critical scholars will increasingly explore and follow these routes. Such prospects can be envisaged, because certain tensions and rifts have recently appeared within the critical paradigm itself, raising certain issues on which there could be meaningful scope for empirically collected evidence to arbitrate. At this stage the outcome of the resulting tussle between doctrine and a more open-minded spirit cannot be predicted, but it may depend on what happens in two quite central problem areas.

One concerns the presumed role of ideology in sustaining the social and political powers that be. This topic has been fully discussed by Stuart Hall (1982) in an essay which depicts the recent history of mass media research as a "movement from essentially a behavioral to an ideological perspective." A prime point of departure for the ideological perspective in its more doctrinaire version is that liberal-capitalist society rests on a huge "confidence trick," by which the views of the majority have been aligned with the interests of the powerful. This trick has been accomplished, it is alleged, not by the exertion of force, nor by the free winning of consent, but through the ideological bias of much mass media content. This media bias gives a privileged airing to viewpoints that encourage the acceptance of dominant social and political values and that accord legitimacy to the socio-political and economic *status quo*.

The news viewed as coherently ideological, however, may involve too large a claim to be supported by other than a selective presentation of evidence, running the risk, then, of smudging the dividing line between scholarship and propaganda. It is difficult to see how the Glasgow University Media Group (1976), for example, could have judiciously substantiated its claim that, "the attentive and addictive viewer of the TV [news] bulletin would have found nothing in the period of our example . . . which did other than confirm this belief system" (namely, that strike action by organized labor was inimical to the national interest).

The temptation for critical researchers to assume what they cannot demonstrate is illustrated by the leading questions they ask about ideology. According to Hall (1982), for example, the critical paradigm raises two questions about ideology:

1. How does it work, and what are its mechanisms?
2. How is "the ideology" to be conceived in relation to other practices within a social formation?

Conspicuously absent, however, are questions of the form: How far (to what extent? how often?) do the mass media project certain ideological views of the world as distinct from others?

That is why in so many of the critical school's writings, supposedly *empirical* phenomena tend to be established *conceptually* and then *illustrated* rather than *weighed*.

Intriguingly, however, Hall (1982) also pointed the way toward a more problematic approach. "Ideology," he proclaims at a crucial point, "has . . . become a site of struggle between competing definitions," the outcome of which depends "on the balance of forces in a particular national conjuncture." Such intimations of a more open and ideologically diverse society and communication system raise the possibility that, through an analysis of media content, investigators could aim to gauge the relative weights of the conflicting tendencies. Hall does not pursue this prospect to its logical conclusion, however, because of "the risks of losing altogether the notion of 'dominance' " in ideological analysis. "Dominance is critical," he goes on, "if the propositions of pluralism are to be put into question." But if "dominance" is really to be validated in the face of pluralist claims, some methodology for independently measuring (instead of taking for granted) its prevalence will have to be devised. Such is the plunge which critical researchers, poised anxiously on the edge of the empirical pool at present, may eventually be obliged to take.

A similar tension affects the other main problem area of critical research: its neglect of audience responses to mass communication. Indeed, it is a striking indictment of the state of the field in Europe that it has so few cumulative traditions of effects research that can stand comparison with American work on, for example, agenda-setting, trust in government, and the social construction of reality.

An unfortunate consequence of such neglect is an occasional tendency to draw dubious inferences from flimsy evidence about supposed audience effects—in line with predictions of critical doctrine. A recent example may be found in *Images of Welfare,* in which Golding and Middleton (1982) claim to show how a wave of stories about fraudulent and excessive social welfare claims, which appeared in the British press in 1976, had helped rightwing forces to argue for a clamp-down on social service spending, while a more generous provision lacked a champion. Drawing on data from two local samples, the authors demonstrate that in the late 1970s many members of the British public perceived welfare "scrounging" as widespread and needing to be curbed. But Golding and Middleton present this finding as if it demonstrated an "agenda-setting effect" of the press, without providing any of the supporting evidence that would be needed to establish it. For example, whereas agenda-setting usually occurs when certain issues are given heavy and prominent media billing, in the period studied by Golding and Middleton social welfare stories actually appeared rather infrequently. Moreover, these scholars make no attempt to show that those individuals who were most concerned about and hostile to "scroungers" were also more exposed to, or dependent on, welfare news in the media. On the contrary, it transpires that in the sample of study, those who were convinced that "scrounging" was a serious problem actually cited personal experience and the evidence of their own eyes more often than they mentioned media reports.

Despite such temptations to perceive the audience as doctrine demands, a concern has also surfaced recently within Marxist communication analyses to get more directly to grips with audience members' actual "readings" of media messages. The intention here is less to measure communication effects than to study audience interpretations of media materials, aiming to discover, as Murdock (1980) put it, how "consumers negotiate meanings and . . . the limits to these negotiations." This last phrase reflects an assumption that media fare tends to incorporate and project certain "dominant" or "preferred" meanings, which correspond to ruling class interests, and set boundaries outside which few audience members would really be free to stray. Nevertheless, there is scope for a diversity of response *within* those limits, the mapping of which should be plotted against the varying social backgrounds of audience members. And indeed one British investigator, David Morley (1980), has been elaborating a methodology for this purpose. His approach involves the examination of free-ranging discussions of selected passages of media material, engaged in by socially homogeneous groups of people, whose acceptance, modification, or rejection of the dominant meanings therein can then be noted by an investigator. Like Stuart Hall, however, Morley is also hesitant to let the empirical world challenge or refute doctrinal expectation. The designation of certain meanings in program content and audience comment as "dominant" remains arbitrary. For example, Morley sets out no criteria in advance by which the resonance of the audience to hegemonically dominant ideas can be discerned—and tested as if, in principle, problematic. The pressure to resolve this tension is urgent, however, for the study of mass communication as a social process without a well-founded investigation of audience response is like a sexology that ignores the orgasm.

Thus it is our theme in the present chapter that American and European communication researchers can each learn from the other. Americans need to broaden their scope of inquiry (a) so as to take into account the institutional context of mass media communication, (b) to become more fully aware of the degree to which they are culture-bound, and (c) to direct their work toward greater policy relevance. European critical scholars should become more respectful of how empirical evidence bears on their theories, particularly when such data do not support an ideological position.

REFERENCES

T.W. Adorno (1969), "Scientific Experiences of a European Scholar in America," in Donald Fleming and Bernard Bailyn (eds.), *The Intellectual Migration,* Cambridge, MA: Harvard University Press.

Jay G. Blumler (1978), "Purposes of Mass Communications Research: A Transnational Perspective," *Journalism Quarterly, 55,* 219–130.

Jay G. Blumler (1979), "Communication in the European Elections: The Case of British Broadcasting," *Government and Opposition, 14,* 508–530.

Jay G. Blumler (1980), "Mass Communication Research in Europe: Some Origins and Prospects," *Media, Culture and Society, 2,* 367–376.

Jay G. Blumler (1981), "Mass Communication Research in Europe: Some Origins and Prospects," in G. Cleveland Wilhoit (ed.), *Mass Communication Review Yearbook, Volume
2*, Beverly Hills, CA: Sage.

Jay G. Blumler (1982), "Mass Communication Research in Europe: Some Origins and Prospects," in Michael Burgoon (ed.), *Communication Yearbook 5*, New Brunswick, NJ:
Transaction Books.

Jay G. Blumler (ed.) (1983), *Communicating to Voters: The Role of Television in the 1979
European Parliamentary Elections*, Beverly Hills, CA: Sage.

Jay G. Blumler, R. Cayrol, and G. Thoveron (1978), *La Télévision: Faite-elle l'Election?*
Paris: Presses de la Fondation Nationale des Sciences Politiques.

Jay G. Blumler and Anthony D. Fox (1982), *The European Voter: Popular Responses to
the First Community Elections*, Beverly Hills, CA: Sage.

Jay G. Blumler and Michael Gurevitch (1979), "The Reform of Election Broadcasting: A
Reply to Nicholas Garnham," *Media, Culture and Society, 1*, 211–219.

Jay G. Blumler and Michael Gurevitch (1982), "The Political Effects of Mass Communication," in Michael Gurevitch and others (eds.) *Culture, Society and the Media*,
London: Methuen.

Jay G. Blumler and Elihu Katz (1974), *The Uses of Mass Communications*, Beverly Hills
CA: Sage.

James W. Carey (1979), "Mass Communication Research and Cultural Studies: An American
View," in James Curran and others (eds.), *Mass Communication and Society*, Beverly
Hills, CA: Sage.

Steven H. Chaffee (1978), *Political Communication Review, 3*, 25–28.

Stanley Cohen and Jock Young (eds.) (1981), *The Manufacture of News: Social Problems.
Deviance and the Mass Media*, Beverly Hills, CA: Sage.

Charles Curran (1979), *Broadcasting: A Seamless Robe*, London: Collins.

Melvin L. De Fleur and Sandra Ball-Rokeach (1975), *Theories of Mass Communication*,
London: Longman.

George Gerbner and Larry Gross (1976), "Living with Television: The Violence Profile,"
Journal of Communication, 26, 173–199.

Glasgow University Media Group (1976), *Bad News*, London: Routledge and Kegan Paul.

Peter Golding and G. Murdock (1978), "Theories of Communication and Theories of Society,"
Communication Research, 5, 339–356.

Peter Golding and Sue Middleton (1982), *Images of Welfare: Press and Public Attitudes to
Poverty*, Oxford, England: Martin Robertson.

G.J. Goodhart, A.S.C. Ehrenberg, and M.A. Collins (1975), *The Television Audience: Patterns
of Viewing*, Farnborough, England: Saxon House.

Michael Gurevitch and Jay G. Blumler (1977), "Mass Media and Political Institutions: The
Systems Approach," in George Gerbner (ed.), *Mass Media Policies in Changing
Structures*, New York: Wiley.

Stuart Hall (1982), "The Re-Discovery of 'Ideology': Return of the Repressed in Media
Studies," in Michael Gurevitch and others (eds.), *Culture, Society and the Media*,
London: Methuen.

Stuart Hall, C. Critcher, T. Jefferson, J. Clarke, and B. Roberts (1978), *Policing the Crisis:
Mugging, The State and Law and Order*, London: Macmillan.

Hanno Hardt (1979), "Introduction," in *Social Theories of the Press: Early German and
American Perspectives*, Beverly Hills, CA: Sage.

Hanno Hardt (1981), "Introduction to *Social Theories of the Press*," in G. Cleveland Wilhoit (ed.), *Mass Communication Review Yearbook, Volume 4*, Beverly Hills, CA:
Sage.

Elihu Katz (1979), "On Conceptualizing Media Effects," in *25 Jaar Televisie in Vlandaaren*, The Netherlands: Centrum voor Communicatiewetenschappen, Catholic University of Leuven.

Joseph Klapper (1960), *The Effects of Mass Communications*, Glencoe, IL: Free Press.

Kurt Lang (1979), "The Critical Functions of Empirical Communication Research," *Media, Culture and Society, 1*, 83–96.

Paul F. Lazarsfeld (1941), "Administrative and Critical Communication Research," *Studies in Philosophy and Social Sciences, 9*, 2–16.

Maxwell E. McCombs (1981), "The Agenda-Setting Approach," in Dan D. Nimmo and Keith R. Sanders (eds.), *Handbook of Political Communication*, Beverly Hills, CA: Sage.

Jack M. McLeod and Byron Reeves (1980), "On the Nature of Mass Media Effects," in Steven B. Whitney and R. Abales (eds.), *Television and Social Behavior: Beyond Violence and Children*, Hillsdale, NJ: Lawrence Erlbrum and Associates.

Denis McQuail and J. J. van Cuilenberg (1982), "Diversity as a Media Policy Goal: A Strategy for Evaluative Research and a Netherlands Case Study," Paper presented to the Conference of the International Association for Mass Communication Research, Paris, 1982.

David Morley (1980), *The "Nationwide" Audience*, London: British Film Institute.

Graeme Murdock (1980), "Misrepresenting Media Sociology: A Reply to Anderson and Sharrock," *Sociology*, 17.

Elisabeth Noelle-Neumann (1980a), *Die Schwiege-Spirale: Offentliche Meinung unsere Soziale Haut*, Munich: Piper.

Elisabeth Noelle-Neumann (1980b), "Mass Media and Social Change in Developed Societies," in G.C. Wilhoit and H. de Bock (eds.), *Mass Communication Review Year Book, Volume I*, Beverly Hills, CA: Sage.

Kaarle Nordenstreng (1976), "Recent Developments in European Communication Theory," in H.D. Fischer, and J.C. Merrill (eds.), *International and Intercultural Communications*, New York: Hastings House.

William Paisley and Ronald Rice (1981), *Public Communication Campaigns*, Beverly Hills, CA: Sage.

Thomas E. Patterson (1980), *The Mass Media Election: How Americans Choose Their President*, New York: Praeger.

Byron Reeves and James L. Baughman (1983), "The Historical Relationship of Communication Research to Mass Media Regulation," in Oscar H. Gandy and others (eds.), *Proceedings from the 10th Annual Telecommunications Policy Research Conference*, Norwood, NJ: Ablex.

Everett M. Rogers (1981a), "The Empirical and the Critical Schools of Communication Research," in Michael Burgoon (ed.), *Communication Yearbook 5*, New Brunswick, NJ: Transaction.

Everett M. Rogers (1981b), "L'Ecole Empirique et l'Ecole Critique de Recherche en Communication," *Les Cahiers de la Communication, 1*, 311–326.

Karl Erik Rosengren (1980a), *Scandinavian Studies in Content Analysis*, Beverly Hills, CA: Sage.

Karl Erik Rosengren (1980b), "Cultural Indicators: Sweden, 1945–1975," Paper presented at the International Communication Association, Acapulco, Mexico.

Anne-Marie Thunberg, Kjell Nowak, Karl Erik Rosengren and Bengt Sigurd (1982), *Communication and Equality: A Swedish Perspective*, Stockholm: Almqvist and Wiskell International.

Phillip Tichenor (1982), "Agenda-Setting: Media as Political Kingmakers?", *Journalism Quarterly, 59*, 488–490.

Gaye Tuchman (1978), "Myth and the Consciousness Industry," Paper presented to the International Sociology Association.

C. Von Feilitzen, L. Filipson, and I. Schyller (1979), *Open Your Eyes to Children's Viewing,* Stockholm, Sweden: Sveriges Radio.

David H. Weaver, Doris Graber, Maxwell McCombs, and Chaim Eyal (1981), *Media Agenda-Setting in a Presidential Election: Issues, Images, Interest,* New York: Praeger.

Chapter 12

The Beginnings of Communication Study in the United States[1]

Wilbur Schramm
East-West Communication Institute

INTRODUCTION

Communication research is a relatively new field, and, perhaps as a result, very little has been written about the history of communication theory. Wilbur Schramm is in an especially advantageous position to write about the early days of U.S. communication research. He had the vision for creating the field, and founded early institutes for communication research at the University of Illinois and at Stanford University. In addition, one analyst of the communication research literature, William Paisley, recently reported that Schramm is the most widely-cited scholar in the field. Here Schramm describes (on the basis of his personally knowing them) the four main founding fathers of communication research: Lewin, Lasswell, Lazarsfeld, and Hovland. Many observers feel that Schramm should be considered a fifth. Certainly he played the major role in getting communication research launched in U.S. universities, a process that he describes (without mentioning his own name) in the final part of this essay. *E.M.R., F.B.*

The Smithsonian Institution in Washington has recently installed two remarkable window-panoramas of a Bronze Age village called Bab Elh-Dhra, that flourished 5,000 years ago just east of the Dead Sea. For many centuries, Bab Elh-Dhra was a stopping place for caravans and travelers in the Jordanian desert, because it was famous for its water. Then, shortly before 3,000 B.C., when farmers began to replace nomads in the area, some families moved into Bab Elh-Dhra and established a village. That settlement existed a thousand years and passed out of human history. But it left its marks on walls and artifacts and tombs; archaeologists dug them up, and the Smithsonian recreated what the village had been.

I have begun with that exhibit because it appealed to me as a metaphor for the early history of communication study in the United States and numerous other places. For centuries, scholars have stopped to look

---

[1]An earlier version of this chapter was presented at the 1980 International Communication Association, Acapulco, and published by Schramm (1980). The present chapter is a reorganization and expansion of this previous paper, and carries the founding of communication research further into its institutionalization in U.S. universities.

at communication problems, as travelers stopped to refresh themselves at the oasis of Bab Elh-Dhra, and them moved on. Only recently (for 25 years or so) have scholars moved into communication country to stay. But anyone who has studied community has had to pay some attention to communication. Scholars ever since Confucius, Plato, and Aristotle have stopped to look at it and think about it.

In the United States communication was a subject of interest to philosophers and political theorists for at least 200 years before Charles Cooley wrote the first modern-sounding analysis of social communication in his 1909 book, *Social Organization*. Cooley approached communication as a sociologist; Walter Lippmann (in his classic *Public Opinion,* 1922) as a journalist specializing in public opinion; Sapir as an anthropologist; Whorf as a linguist; Pierce, Wiener, Von Neumann, and Shannon because it was basic to cybernetics; Ryan, Gross, Bohlen, and Beal because it was a part of rural sociology; Cantril, Newcomb, Bauer, Osgood, Cartwright, Festinger, and many others because it was basic to psychology; Pool and Deutsch because it belonged in political science; Boulding because a socially minded economist needed to know about it; Mott, Casey, Bush, Nafziger, and others because it was the theoretical essence of journalism.

For the most part, scholars like these merely stopped by to visit. Some of them, however, made it a career. For example, both Ithiel de Sola Pool and Elihu Katz are rather more likely now to be identified as communication scholars than as political scientist or sociologist, respectively. So also is Everett Rogers who was trained as a rural sociologist. The point is, however, that many of the most productive of recent communication scholars have come into the field as "visitors," asked their own disciplinary questions, and gone back, many of them, to problems in their own fields. Only recently, as in Bab Elh-Dhra, have visitors begun to move in and establish permanent settlements in communication.

THE AGE OF THE FATHERS

Four men, however, came from their own disciplines into communication studies and made such enormous impacts that they have every right to be known as the fathers of this field in the United States. I refer to Harold Lasswell, the political scientist; Kurt Lewin, the social psychologist; Paul Lazarsfeld, the sociologist; and Carl Hovland, the experimental psychologist.

These "fathers" of our field had strikingly similar careers. All of them had rich early backgrounds, went to excellent universities, came into contact with great minds. All of them were broadly interdisciplinary by inclination. All of them went through abrupt career changes in midlife, and turned from their own discipline to communication through the experience of confronting "real world" problems. All of them gathered around them younger scholars who came to be leaders in the field, and all except one founded a research institute which attracted bright young people and able scholars. All four were enormously productive.

The Founders' Formal Training

Lasswell went to the University of Chicago in the great years when he could study with Anton Carlson, Robert E. Park, and Charles Merriam, and as a graduate student could share an office with Robert Redfield the anthropologist and Louis Wirth the sociologist. He spent most of two years in Europe where, among other activities, he helped Bertrand Russell campaign for Parliament (Russell lost so badly that he also lost his deposit), sat in seminars with John Maynard Keynes, and studied psychoanalysis with Theodor Reik.

Lewin studied at the University of Berlin when Wilhelm Wundt was head of the psychological laboratory there, and the Gestaltists Koffka, Kohler, and Wertheimer were on the faculty. Needless to say, the last three appealed more to Lewin than did Wundt.

Lazarsfeld studied at the University of Vienna during the years of Freud's great influence there. Perhaps more than anything else it was Freud's influence that led Paul away from his doctorate in mathematics to become a sociologist by choice and to organize in Vienna a tiny institute for community studies.

Hovland took his doctorate at Yale, and was fortunate enough to be selected as Clark Hull's research assistant, and later to be Hull's collaborator in some of Yale's most distinguished studies of learning theory. He worked along with a remarkable group, including Don Marquis, Ernest Hilgard, Neil Miller, Robert Yerkes, Kenneth Spence, and Leonard Doob.

Interrupted Careers

Launched on highly promising careers, each of these four men came to a sudden and unexpected turn in their road. Lasswell's experience was in some ways most traumatic. He came back to Chicago as a young teacher but found it necessary to resign and leave only 12 years later, in 1938. The reason was that Robert Maynard Hutchins, Chicago's humanistic President, refused to give him a permanency. Hutchins, his biographers said, "couldn't stand" social science, and Lasswell was not even a good orthodox social scientist. Trained in political science, he studied propaganda, gave lectures trying to reconcile Freud and Marx, conducted lay psychoanalysis, sounded sometimes likes a political sociologist or a political psychiatrist or—perish the thought—even a specialist in political communication, and resolutely refused to be pigeon-holed.

When he decided he had no future at Chicago he loaded all his books and notes into a truck and started for New York. The truck and all its contents burned. So he was without a job, without students, without the materials any scholar needs, including 15 years of research notes. This man, who in 12 years had turned out some of the ablest young political scientists of our day, never had another Ph.D. student during the remaining 40 years of his life, during which he was nevertheless active enough to publish 5 million words. His professorship, when he finally got it, was at the Yale Law School, which did not take social science doctoral candidates. The interesting jobs he found to do in the interim were mostly in wartime communication; in particular he headed the content analysis projects at the Library of Congress and later at Stanford University. So his interest in communication became his career.

Lewin started his great career teaching at the University of Berlin, where his students included some of the best young social psychologists in Europe. Then the shadow of Nazism fell upon him, and he had to leave Germany. In the United States, jobs were few, midway through the great depression of the 1930s, and the most attractive opening he discovered was at an unlikely sounding place: the Iowa Child Welfare Research Station (in Iowa City). But he made himself at home there, and made it *his* kind of place. He attracted a group of bright young doctoral students of a quality equalled few other places in the world. And he went on studying questions of great practical as well as theoretical importance. Increasingly, he focused on problems in group communication; group pressures, group decisions, group morale, democratic vs. authoritarian groups, group patterns as related to communication, and so forth.

If Lasswell had the most traumatic turn of events, Lazarsfeld probably had the most unexpected one. With a university doctorate in mathematics, he went into community studies, learned to do survey research, and wrote his first important book (with Marie Jahoda and Hans Zeisel) on *The Unemployed of Marienthal*, an Austrian village where *everyone* was unemployed. Then Hitler's Reich began to expand ominously toward Austria. In the next 3 years three extraordinary things happened to Lazarsfeld. First, the Rockefeller Foundation awarded him a traveling fellowship to observe social research in the United States. While he was on the American continent, the Foundation decided to establish an office of radio research at Princeton, and offered the headship to Paul. About the time the first exciting studies began to come out of the new Princeton center, he met Frank Stanton, who was then director of research, later president, of CBS. Stanton told him how much research needed to be done on the radio audience, and how much money was available for it. With Stanton's help, and a considerable infusion of CBS money, Paul established the Bureau of Applied Social Research at Columbia University. Only 3 years from Marienthal to the directorship of the most famous media research organization of his time!

Carl Hovland, too, went through an abrupt career change. In 1941 he was considered the most promising young *experimental* psychologist in the United States. Came the war, and in 1942 he became Chief Psychologist and Director of Experimental Studies for the U.S. War Department. In this new job he was doing essentially social, rather than experimental, psychology. He worked with Sam Stouffer, studying morale in the armed services, and his own chief assignment was to examine the effects of a series of troop orientation films. At the end of the war he and Stouffer loaded copies of their data into a truck (which fortunately did not burn, as Lasswell's did) and carted them to Yale and Harvard. Stouffer became head of the Institute of Social Relations at Harvard, and Hovland became head of psychology and founder of the Yale Program in Communication and Attitude Change. He still worked like an experimental psychologist, but now his chief subject matter was the kind of communication studies he had begun for the U.S. War Department.

The Founders' Relationships with Their Students

Each of these four men had a deep influence on students and a seldom-equalled ability to attract some of the best ones. In Lasswell's scant 12 years at Chicago he helped train scholars like Herbert Simon, the recent Nobel laureate in economics, V. O. Key of Cornell, David Truman of Columbia, Ithiel de Sola Pool of M.I.T., Morris Janowitz of Chicago, and many others. Those were his last Ph.D.'s. After that, his influence had to be exerted by writing and by personal contacts. Some of his chief personal influence came through collaboration in research and writing. For example, his chief research assistants in the Library of Congress project were Leites and Eulau; on the Stanford project, Pool and Lerner. The impact of his writing is suggested by the fact that his name appeared on 6 *million* words of scholarly publication. When he died, late in 1978, characteristically three very large volumes on *Propaganda and Communication in World History* were going through the press.

I should not call Lasswell or any of the other three of these men a great lecturer, but each in his own way was a master at dealing with individual students or small research groups. In 1967 Leo Rosten wrote for the *Saturday Review* a hilariously funny memoir on Lasswell as a self-conscious young lecturer, who "smothered rather than informing," and was so ill at ease that he had to talk at a race-track pace and was afraid to leave even a few seconds of the class period empty of sound. Rosten chuckled over the way his old teacher used language to cover up simple ideas, for instance explaining communication as "the fortuitous parallelism of bio-psychic variables." But yet, looking back over 35 years of acquaintance, Rosten concluded that he had "learned more or was encouraged and jolted and inspired to learn more from (Lasswell) than from anyone I ever met."

Lewin's Saturday meetings with his students were known all over the academic world. In Berlin he called them his *Quasselstrippe—quassel* meaning to ramble on, and *strippe* a string. They "strung out" through most of Saturday. In Iowa the same activity came to be called in good midwestern idiom the "Hot Air Club." "The most stimulating experience I have ever had," said Norman Maier, now a professor at Michigan. Everyone could talk. Every idea was listened to and could be challenged. Every problem was looked at as though it were wholly new. "I could hardly wait for one of those meetings," one of his students wrote, "and then I could hardly wait to run out of the meeting and do an experiment." That was the kind of experience that Lewin brought to people like Lippitt and White, Bavelas and Festinger, Cartwright and Dembo, Fritz Heider, and many others whose names we all know.

Under Lazarsfeld, the Bureau of Applied Social Research at Columbia University was no ordinary center of audience research. He was never much interested in *how many* were listening to radio, but always in *who* was listening, and *why,* and *what effect* it had. Therefore he and his Bureau turned very soon to studying the effects, rather than merely the audiences, of the mass media; to the voting studies; and to the comparison of personal with media influence. Through the Bureau came many people whose names you know: among them Berelson, Merton, Klapper, Lowenthal, Herzog, Arnheim, Coleman, Katz.

Hovland's program at Yale may have seemed to an outsider the least spectacular of all these, but that was only until one got to know Carl and the program well. Carl rated far over on the quiet and calm side of the semantic differential. He worked on communication and attitudes as one might expect an experimental psychologist to work—identifying, controlling all the significant variables, testing one or two at a time, trying the most promising combinations, letting theory build. This was the kind of experience he gave Irving Janis, Arthur Lumsdaine, Brewster Smith, Harold Kelley, William McGuire, Herbert Kelman, and many others.

A PERSONAL NOTE

Let me say a personal word about Carl and these other men. The thing I remember best about Carl is indeed his calm and quiteness, but the better you got to know him the more you felt his controlled excitement at making theory. Working with him in designing research was one of the most exciting experiences I can imagine, yet always quiet. "The world's most non-authoritarian leader," some of his students called him. He was the kind of person a student could call "Carl" without the least embarrassment on either side and still with complete respect. Carl died as he lived, quietly. He was cut off early by cancer. He worked on his research until the disease no longer let him work. Then he went home, and quietly, as he did everything else, ended his life.

Paul Lazarsfeld was hearty, humorous, a great entrepreneur. What made him unique, said James Coleman after Paul died in 1976, "was not his involvement with ideas or his involvement with people but his ability to stir the two together." Projects were quick to start at the Bureau, and smoothly run, but because they were surveys rather than experiments it was often five or ten years before Paul was satisfied that the theory had been wrung out of the data and they were ready to be published. In the late 1950s, Paul decided that he would take no more communication Ph.D.s (Elihu Katz was the last one), and went back to studying mathematics and administering sociology. Why, we can guess: He simply stayed much longer than most visitors at Bab elh-Drah. But the Bureau was never quite the same again.

The picture I remember best of Kurt Lewin is of him pacing back and forth in front of the chalkboard, face flushed with excitement, asking, challenging us, "Vot haf ve fergassen?" What variables had been left out of the field, ignored in the typology? Sometimes he said "fergassen," sometimes "fergotten." It didn't matter. We chuckled over his fractured English, but not so much as we might have, because his enthusiasm and his insights carried everyone along with him. One of his statements became a sort of password among his former students. Rising in a seminar to dispute politely what a speaker had said, he is reported to have said, "Can be, but sink absolute ozzer." Thereafter, at an APA meeting whenever we heard someone say to someone else, "Can be, but sink absolute ozzer," we knew two Lewinians were talking. Kurt started a third career, and this might have been greater than either Berlin or Iowa. It was heading a new Center for Group Dynamics at M.I.T. But in less than 2 years Kurt was dead, and what was left of the Center moved to Michigan.

If you read Rosten's marvelous piece on Lasswell, permit me to enter a minority report. I never personally saw any of the stuffiness in him that Rosten describes. The first time I went to see him was at the Center for Advanced Study in the Behavioral Sciences (at Stanford). He pushed aside a mountain of papers and talked with me for nearly 6 hours, forgetting both the cocktail hour and dinner, taking my poor little hypotheses and setting them against a fabulously rich intellectual background.

I was a young scholar in a field that interested him; as such, I had an always renewable pass-key. I found him always approachable, always kind, right up until the week he died, in 1978, 6 million words after he started, with three volumes still in press.

THE NEW INSTITUTES

I have said more than I should and less than I should like to, about these four remarkable men. We can be briefer about the rest of the story, because it will be familiar to most readers. The growing edge of science, during the last several centuries, has been in institutes, laboratories, and centers, often *in* but not always *of* universities. The Cavendish Laboratory at Cambridge is an example of the kind of place I am talking about: Modern physics and molecular biology grew there. On the social side of science, psychology grew largely in German laboratories. In the United States, the first type of institute to appear, before World War I, was devoted to community studies and staffed largely by social workers. In the early 1930s a second type of institute appeared, originating in data rather than problems: commercial consumer studies, public opinion polling studies, radio audience surveys. Institutes like these, said Lazarsfeld, provided "the raw material for the new field of communication and opinion research.

About that time a few institutes were created to conduct social research for its own sake. Most typical of these was Lazarsfeld's own Bureau of Applied Social Research, at Columbia. After the war of 1939–1945, there was another wave of institute-building, growing largely out of government wartime use of empirical research. Examples were Hovland's new program at Yale, Stouffer's at Harvard, and the Michigan Survey Research Center. That brings us through what we called the Age of the Founding Fathers. But there was still a fourth wave of institute-creation, when some universities felt a need to have organized social research, but wanted it to be close to their existing departments and programs. This was how the new institutes of communication came to be.

A great deal of the pressure for these new institutes came from the communication skills departments of universities—first from journalism, then from speech, broadcasting, film, and the like. The doctorate had become a common requirement for heads of journalism schools and departments, and it substituted for long and distinguished news careers in the case of many new young faculty members. As the doctorate became more necessary, more and more of the journalism schools began to offer their own doctorates, so that a prospective teacher or researcher in journalism could earn a doctorate in communication rather than political science, sociology, psychology, or history. That meant that among the graduate courses developed for journalism had to be subjects like the theory of communication, history of communication, research methods in communication, and the like, in addition to courses in theory and method borrowed from other social science departments.

As more and more teachers with research training joined the journalism faculties, these faculties began to develop research groups. Iowa organized a Bureau of Audience Research to study the reading of weekly as well as daily newspapers. Minnesota had a long-continuing research unit. And the name "communication" began to appear in the official titles of journalism schools and departments. At Minnesota and Wisconsin, for example, the name became Journalism and Mass Communication. Illinois organized a Division of Communication. Stanford renamed its Journalism work as the Department of Communication, and soon the programs in broadcasting and film, which had been in Speech, joined Communication.

A number of departments of speech went through a process of cell-division in the course of this movement. The traditional program of teaching public speaking as a branch of rhetoric usually remained the Department of Speech. The younger teachers, trained more fully in social science, in many universities organized a new department often called Speech Communication. At Iowa, this socially oriented Speech group took over the name Department of Communication. More commonly, two departments appeared—one called Speech; the other, Speech Communication.

So far as I know, the first two universities to handle communication study in the European grow-through-institutes pattern were Illinois and Stanford. Illinois founded its Institute of Communications Research in 1947, Stanford an Institute *for* Communication Research in 1956. The Illinois Institute came into being about the same time as the Division of Communication; the Stanford Institute was formed within the Department of Journalism. Both of them had about the same marching orders: Take responsibility for the graduate training in the department, and build a lively research program that will both attract and include doctoral candidates. Both began about the same way, which is not wholly surprising considering that they had the same director.[2] Both Institutes had some senior members of the journalism faculty as members of the institute; at Illinois, these included Fred S. Siebert and C.H. Sandage; at Stanford, Chilton R. Bush and James Brinton. Both very early appointed a distinguished social scientist to their staff. Illinois appointed Charles E. Osgood; Stanford, Nathan Maccoby.

Both institutes also established close relationships with the social science departments closest to their interest. Stanford actually had some-

[2]Editor's note: In fact, the director was Wilbur Schramm.

what more success with this than did Illinois. Some psychologists, sociologists, political scientists, anthropologists, and members of the education faculty came to a number of the Communication Institute meetings, some of them joined Institute faculty in joint research projects, and, without any formal appointments, a nucleus from these departments acted as a sort of graduate faculty in communication, sitting on doctoral committees, joining in the supervision of dissertations, and sometimes offering special courses or modifying course content with the needs of communication graduate students in mind. Both Stanford and Illinois faculty members say that one of the things in favor of this close and helpful relationship was that Communication was able from the beginning to attract a very high level of advanced graduate students, many of whom had new and interesting research ideas, and were able to compete on an even level with the social science doctoral candidates.

This should not be interpreted as meaning that there was necessarily a sharp distinction between universities that ran their advanced communication programs through institutes and those that ran them through research and graduate teaching programs within journalism or speech. Institutions like Wisconsin and Minnesota, to take two examples, preferred not to form separate institutes, but gave the same duties to a graduate teaching faculty, and/or research programs within the departmental structure. The point is, rather, that there was a general movement in communication skills departments toward offering advanced graduate study and degrees, built on theory and research, and drawing upon as much interdisciplinary cooperation as possible within the university. There was also a very strong feeling throughout the late 1940s, and in some places earlier, that journalism and speech, broadcasting and film, should be more active in research. Looking at the products of Lazarsfeld's Columbia Bureau, Hovland's Yale organization, and Lewin's Iowa program, journalism leaders admitted somewhat ruefully that these social science organizations were doing the work journalism ought to be doing—audience study, content study, effects of the mass media, and so forth. In fact, journalists had a certain advantage in such studies, because they had more experience with the media themselves.

It hardly needs saying that in the last 20 years the balance in communication research output has swung away from the social science departments and institutes toward the communication, journalism, and speech institutes and departments. More than 1,000 persons now testify by membership in appropriate research organizations that they are seriously interested in communication research and theory. One book alone (Comstock and Fisher, 1975) lists 2,300 studies on just one aspect of communication research—television and human behavior. A great part of this research has come from the new institutes and programs in communication, for examples of which we need only cite universities like Wisconsin and Minnesota, Syracuse and Texas, the two Annenberg schools at Pennsylvania and Southern California, Georgia, Indiana, Washington, the two major Michigan universities, as well as the pioneers, Illinois and Stanford, which we have already had occasion to mention, and many others.

THE NEXT CHAPTER?

What can we expect the next chapter of this story to be? We have followed the growth of communication study in the United States through the beginnings in different disciplines, the coming of four "fathers" who built up strong interdisciplinary programs within their own disciplines but focused upon communication problems, to the emergence of communication institutes, departments, and research programs, which have taken over much of the responsibility for advanced research and training. What comes next?

You will remember that the village of Bab Elh-Dhra disappeared after about a thousand years, despite its good water and its considerable history. Can we extend that part of the metaphor also to communication study? How much permanency can we really expect of the new communication programs in universities, and to what extent can we expect them to build around themselves the protective walls and boundaries that help to preserve the traditional academic disciplines?

Although the communication institutes, programs, and departments seem very healthy now, and have built up wide interest and membership in their field of activity without giving up the interdisciplinary quality that has always characterized this study, I wonder whether they do not suggest a scenario of change rather than changelessness. I have no idea that the study of communication is going to pass from the earth, as did Bab Elh-Dhra. On the other hand, I should not be greatly surprised if the communication institutes and their parallel structures were to last, in their present form, even as long as Bab Elh-Dhra.

It seems to me significant that the communication research programs have been so successful at keeping themselves and their academic faculties and training as interdisciplinary as they have. What we are now seeing, I suspect, is a phase of academic evolution which will confirm the importance of communication study, and greatly enrich studies of the media and other communication, but not necessarily be the last stage in that evolution. As the social disciplines come to value their exclusivity less and a broader base of theory more, is it too much to anticipate that communication theory and research, along with social psychology, sociology, anthropology, political science, and others might not be absorbed into a more broadly conceived disciplinary study of human society? If this happens, we may anticipate that communication will continue to be seen as the fundamental process of society, but it will be seen as less rather than more separate from the other processes.

And if that happens, is it too much to dream that communication and the other interdisciplinary studies might lead social science toward the long-hoped-for science of man?

REFERENCES

George Comstock and M. Fisher (1975), *Television and Human Behavior: A Guide to the Pertinent Scientific Literature*, Santa Monica, California: The Rand Corporation.

Charles Horton Cooley (1909), *Social Organization: A Study of the Larger Mind*, New York: Scribners.

Marie Jahoda, Paul F. Lazarsfeld, and Hans Ziesel (1971), *Marienthal: The Sociology of an Unemployed Community*, translated by John Reginall and Thomas Elsaesser from the original, entitled *Die Arbeitslosen von Marienthal* ("The Unemployed of Marienthal"), Chicago, IL: Aldine.

Walter Lippman (1922), *Public Opinion*, New York: Harcourt, Brace.

Wilbur Schramm (1980), "The Beginnings of Communication Study in the United States," in Dan Nimmo (ed.), *Communication Yearbook, 4*, New Brunswick, NJ: Transaction.

Chapter 13

The Basic Concepts of Communication and Information[1]

Osmo Wiio
University of Helsinki

INTRODUCTION

Both European and American scholars recognize that Shannon and Weaver (1949) provided the basic paradigm for effects-oriented communication research by setting forth the main elements (source, channel, message, receiver) of a simple, linear model of communication. This model became tremendously popular with communication researchers, enabling the field of mass communication study to "take-off" about 30 years ago. It formed the main paradigm around which the invisible college of communication researchers formed. Less well-known is the contribution by Shannon and Weaver in defining the concept of information as a central notion for the field of communication scholarship. Here, Professor Wiio, an eminent Finnish scholar, takes us back to first principles when he draws an important distinction between the two central concepts of (a) communication, and (b) information. These two concepts trace from Aristotle to the Shannon and Weaver mathematical theory of signal transmission, and to other models of information and communication. Although Shannon and Weaver's concept of the probabilistic model of information has been fruitful in leading to further research, it was never intended to describe linguistic information and human communication. Probabilistic models are not very useful models to describe meaning: Human reasoning is a very open system and the probabilities are not known. A functional system model of information is offered here instead, based on the idea of changes in the state of a control system. To process information (that is the control system) in an open system, energy changes, from the environment and/or from within the system, produce signals. Raw information is extracted from these signals and transformed into information with value. The changes may be kept as stored information. The whole process is a time-bound work cycle of the control system. There is little agreement among scholars about the definition of communication, but the present author offers a definition that is elegant in its simplicity.   *E.M.R., F.B.*

This chapter is about *information* and *communication* in a system. Our main interest here is the human system and the process of communication as behavior. Human behavior is the end result of many different and simultaneous factors. The approach here is General System Theory, which allows a holistic approach to investigating behavior in living systems.

---

[1]This chapter is based upon Wiio (1981).

Each of us is the end result of many different interacting variables. In our cells we have a genetic program which decides whether we are men or mice. Such genetic factors determine, however, only the conditions for our development. Environmental factors mold us to what we are as human beings.

We receive information from the environment through our senses: Light waves stimulate our vision, sound waves our hearing, gasses our smell, chemical changes our tastes, and pressure and temperature our skin senses. All such information can be regarded as forms of matter-energy. The senses collect information and change it into electro-chemical processes in our nervous system. To some degree our senses also select stimuli from the environment. There must be a certain threshold amount of stimuli before we can perceive anything at all; the change in the stimuli must exceed a given threshold before we perceive a change in the input. Much goes on around us which we do not perceive at all. There are sounds we do not hear, and there are electromagnetic waves that our eyes or other senses do not process.

GENERAL SYSTEM THEORY

General System Theory is a frame of reference created mainly by Ludwig von Bertalanffy during the 1930s and 1940s. Later Norbert Wiener's theories of self-regulating machines (cybernetics) were combined with the biological approach of Bertalanffy. The basic principle of the systems approach was given by Aristotle when he said: "The whole is more than the sum of its parts." So systems theory emphasizes the interdependence of the parts of a system.

General System Theory has not escaped criticism (see Churchman, 1979; Bertalanffy, 1968). The following points have been raised:

1. Models are often too general and conceptual.
2. Models may not be wrong but that does not mean necessarily that they are right.
3. It is difficult to define system boundaries.
4. Models are often mere analogies, and hence not very useful to researchers.
5. System models are sometimes used because they are fashionable and not because the research problem or setting would warrant their use.
6. General System Theory is an inflexible and formal intellectual structure which forces reality into an artificial framework.

7. System models are static, and do not allow for rapid change or for completely new approaches.
8. General System Theory claims to be a general frame of reference for all scientific disciplines; this scope may be too broad.

INFORMATION SYSTEMS

The basic requirement for human communication is the ability to process information. Humans are the world champions as overall processors of information. Other animals may win in specialized fields of information-processing: They may be better in interpretation of jungle smells and sounds. However, in remembering, and in combining and transferring of information, we are unique on this planet.

All biological systems are open systems: They cannot survive without exchanging information with their environment. They are constantly interchanging material and energy with their environment. They receive matter and/or energy as their input, process it in cycles into different forms, and export it into the environment as the through-put of the system. Open systems also receive information from the environment to regulate the input and output of the system (this is feedback).

A human being is an open system. He can react to environmental changes in many different ways. He lives in the scorching heat of the Sahara and the chilling coldness of Greenland. He dives to the bottom of the ocean and flies to the moon. He multiplies his strength with machines and enhances his information-processing with technological means like computers.

The boundary of a system separates it from its environment and thus also regulates the openness of the system. Sometimes it is difficult to make a distinction between the constraints on, and the boundary of, a system. In some cases the difference is evident: The skin of a man is his boundary but he has many internal and external constraints which limit his freedom of action. The exact boundaries of a system are not always clear: Are the customers of a business firm inside the system's boundaries or outside?

WHAT IS INFORMATION?

In our conception of information and communication, control systems are essential parts of a system. The control system is a subsystem which regulates and controls the work processes of a system. In a car the steering system, the clutch, the brake, and the gas system form the control system. In a computer the control system consists of the central processing unit (CPU).

Information is something which reduces uncertainty. *Communication* is exchange of information. Most scholars in the field of communication research would have no difficulty in agreeing with the first definition. Just as many scholars, no doubt, would like to change the second definition. A tremendous variety of definitions of the concept of communication have been proposed in recent years.

But very few scholars ever question the validity of the probabilistic nature of the information concept: Information reduces uncertainty. Claude Shannon and Warren Weaver introduced their mathematical theory of signal transmission in 1949. Since then their mathematical information theory has almost become a law of nature. Shannon and Weaver's concept of information, defined as "a measure of one's freedom of choice when one selects a message" (Shannon and Weaver, 1949), has been a fruitful stimulus for much further research. It was never intended to be a measure of semantic information although it has been used for that purpose. Shannon and Weaver stated that "information must not be confused with meaning." Such confusion has prevailed ever since.

If one single definition of information (basically Shannon and Weaver's) has overshadowed all others, just the opposite is true for definitions of communication. No two writers seem able to agree on a definition of communication. Further, there is very little relationship between the definitions of information and of communication: One does not seem to follow from the other.

The Latin word *information* originally meant "the shaping of something", mostly shaping something concrete: stone, wood, leather, etc. It was not a very common word. In fact many large Latin dictionaries do not even list it. Its root is *forma,* form.

"Mathematical information theory" is a misnomer for Shannon and Weaver's theory; their original name is "The Mathematical Theory of Communication" and it is about "signal transmission." It became very popular in a short time because its seemingly precise mathematical approach appeared to open up possibilities for quantification of information (which until then had been impossible). The theory was used with success in electronics for many purposes, from the design of telephone networks to matrices of computer memories.

Information seems to be always a relative concept: If something is known then there is little information. There seems to be agreement that information is a measure of uncertainty. Thus information is dependent on the receiver of the message. Therefore a statement that information is a state or a structure is not enough. Somebody must receive a description of the state.[2]

Information is a change in the state of the control system. A control system determines the states of other systems or subsystems. In this view, the concept of information is not a probabilistic concept but rather a physiological or neurophysiological process variable.

The definitions of information often do not make a distinction between "information-as-uncertainty-reduction" and "information-as-a-change-in-the-state-of-the-control-system."

The tendency is to connect the concept of information only with purposeful communication. However, we feel that information can be exchanged without intention.

TIME AND INFORMATION

Time is such an obvious part of the process of communication that almost all writers in the field have forgotten to mention it, much less to include it in any definitions. However, it can be argued that time is *the* basic element of information. It may even be the only criterion by which information can be universally measured.

Time does not exist independently of events, but is an aspect of the nature of the universe and all that comprises it. Several scholars have suggested (Wiio, 1979; Bruneau, 1979; Whitrow, 1980) that different human cultures apply "clocks" at different paces. The "subjective time" seems to change with age even in the same individual.

Whitrow (1980) suggests that time is a fundamental concept that cannot be explained in terms of something more fundamental." It is the inclusion of time as a variable in communication research that allows us to study communication as process.

DEFINING COMMUNICATION

A conceptual definition of communication rests upon these points:

1. The definitions of information and communication should be considered together.
2. The concept of communication must be compatible with the concept of information.

---

[2]This line of thinking leaves open the question of whether there could be intrapersonal information through introspective processes that do not have a correspondence in reality.

3. Definitions of information and communication should cover as many situations as possible in which information and communication are involved.
4. Definitions should be free of value judgments.
5. Definitions should not be logical tautologies.
6. All elements of the definitions should be definable.
7. The concept of information should be independent from the concept of value or meaning of the information.
8. The concept of communication should be independent from intentionality, reciprocity, presence, and the use of symbols.

In many prior definitions of communication, there is an overt or implicit requirement for reciprocal interaction among the participants in a communication process. In fact the root name of communication (*communis* or "common") implies this two-way process. However, there are everyday communication events where reciprocity is impossible.

A communication system is any combination of two or more information systems. Communication is the work process of a communication system in which signals from any of the information systems create information in any of the other information systems.

Communication is an interchange of information between systems or parts of a system where output information from one or several control systems causes work processes in one or several other control systems. The basic idea here builds in a logical way on the concept of information (as it was defined earlier).

Communication in our sense is an umbrella word for a large family of functions: thinking, speaking, hearing, discussing, printing, dancing, etc. However, I am afraid that this usage creates additional confusion and some strong protests from other branches of behavioral sciences such as linguistics, psychology, etc. Information-processing is a more neutral term to be used for this purpose. Accordingly: *Communication is a special case of information-processing.*

REFERENCES

Ludwig von Bertalanffy (1968), *General Systems Theory,* New York: George Braziller.

Tom Bruneau (1979), "The Time Dimension in Intercultural Communication," in Dan Nimmo (ed.), *Communication Yearbook 3,* New Brunswick, NJ: Transaction.

C. West Churchman (1979), *The Systems Approach and Its Enemies,* New York: Basic Books.

Claude Shannon and Warren Weaver (1949), *The Mathematical Theory of Communication,* Urbana, IL: University of Illinois Press.

G.J. Whitrow (1980), *The Natural History of Time,* Oxford, England: Clarendon Press.

Osmo A. Wiio (1979), "Time and Information: Intercultural Aspects of Human Communication," Paper presented at the World Communication Conference, Athens, Ohio.

Osmo A. Wiio (1981), *Information and Communication: A Conceptual Analysis,* Helsinki, Finland: University of Helsinki, Department of Communication.

Chapter 14

The Empirical and Critical Schools of Communication Research[1]

Everett M. Rogers
Stanford University

INTRODUCTION

The empirical and critical schools of communication research represent two quite different approaches. The former is typified by quantitative empiricism, functionalism, and positivism, while the critical school is characterized by a more philosophical emphasis, greater attention to the context of communication, an early Marxist orientation, and a concern with who controls a communication system. Here we describe the historical rise of these two schools, and their differences in how they view development and communication technology. The critical school tends to be concentrated in Europe, while the empirical school is strongest in the United States. Prospects for greater understanding of the critical school by members of its counterpart, and vice versa, are discussed.   *E.M.R., F.B.*

The world of communication scholarship can be divided for certain purposes into two main schools, based on the nature of their ideology, assumptions, and methods of approaching communication research. These are commonly referred to as the "empirical school" and the "critical school", although this terminology is somewhat of an oversimplification.

While not everyone agrees on exactly what is meant by these terms, nor on who belongs to which school, I believe they offer a set of useful distinctions. The *empirical school* of communication research is commonly characterized by quantitative empiricism, functionalism, and positivism. In the past it has generally emphasized study of the direct effects of communication, while paying less attention to the broader context in which such communication is embedded. In contrast, the essence of the *critical school* is its more philosophical emphasis, its focus on the broader social structural context of communication, its early Marxist orientation (although by no means are all critical scholars Marxists), and a central concern with the issue of who controls a communication system. Critical scholars believe that a theory of communication is impossible without a theory of society, so their scope of analysis is much wider than that of empirical scholars.

---

[1] This chapter appeared in a previous form as Rogers (1981 and 1982).

The purposes of this chapter are (a) to summarize the important intellectual differences between the empirical and the critical schools of communication research, and (b) to propose certain directions through which these two schools might better learn from each other.

THE TERMINOLOGY OF EMPIRICAL AND CRITICAL

In this paper we utilize the terminology of the "empirical school" and the "critical school" of communication. These are the most frequently encountered terms today. Various synonyms have been used in the past, since Paul F. Lazarsfeld (1941) referred to these two scholarly viewpoints as "administrative research" and "critical research." The article in which this terminology appeared was published in a special issue of a journal called *Studies in Philosophy and Social Research,* organized by Lazarsfeld to include representatives of both the critical school, such as Theodor W. Adorno, and the empirical school, like Harold D. Lasswell and Lazarsfeld himself. The terminology for the two schools utilized by Lazarsfeld (1941) in his article seems to have been acceptable to both schools at that time (Lang, 1979). Adorno's colleague, and the Director of the Frankfurt School (to be described shortly), Max Horkheimer (1937, pp. 188–243), preferred "critical school" as a more appropriate label than "Marxist school," which the school had originally considered as its name in the 1920s instead of the Frankfurt Institute of Social Research (Jay, 1973, p. 8).

Lazarsfeld (1941) utilized the term "administrative research" for what I presently call the "empirical school." He did not originally distinguish between administrative research (a) in the service of media institutions' current objectives, and (b) research aimed to modify these objectives (Blumler, 1978).[2] Adorno (1945) referred to these two types of administrative research as "exploitive administrative research" and "benevolent administrative research," respectively.

Certain members of the critical school resent this nomenclature (of an empirical and a critical school) because they claim, quite correctly, that they often use empirical data in their critical analysis. In any event, most critical scholars would agree that a critical viewpoint is the dominant viewpoint of their school, and most empirical scholars would agree that the use of empirical data is a dominant characteristic of their school.

Whatever exact terminology a particular communication scholar may prefer for these two schools, almost everyone that I know feels that at

---

[2]Although Lazarsfeld (1948) later seems to have realized this distinction between the sub-types of administrative research.

least two different viewpoints exist. Most critical communication scholars identify themselves as such. In contrast, most members of the empirical school do not especially think of themselves as associated with any particular "school" of thought, other than with communication research in general. In part this lack of identification with the empirical school is because many empirical scholars (especially those in the United States) do not know of the existence of the critical school of communication research. In any event, when an American researcher is called a "positivist" by a European or a Latin American, the U.S. scholar is likely to be surprised and puzzled; he thought of himself as just a communication researcher, and may not even be sure what a positivist is.

THE EMPIRICAL SCHOOL OF COMMUNICATION RESEARCH

U.S. communication scholars need to be more aware of the European roots of their field. For instance, few U.S. doctoral students are taught to appreciate the important role of Robert E. Park of the "Chicago School" (of sociology) early in the present century. Park was one of the most influential members of the Chicago School from 1904 to 1941, and is credited with founding the sociological study of mass communication in the U.S. and with being the field's first theorist (Frazier and Gaziano, 1979, p. 1). After a background of extensive experience as a journalist, Park earned his Ph.D. in Germany. He then conducted pioneering research and theorizing about mass communication and public opinion, with an emphasis upon the issue of control. For example, Park studied how newspapers control public opinion, and how such public opinion controls newspapers. Park favored qualitative methods of data-gathering and analysis, and was suspicious of statistical methods. "Disdaining formal hypothesis-testing in his own work, he concerned himself with broad theory" (Frazier and Gaziano, 1979, p. 13).

Despite these aspects in common with the present-day critical school, Park was a functionalist who felt that the communication of news in society led to the formation of public opinion, and thus to social changes, in a process of dynamic equilibrium. Park was much influenced by pragmatism, the integration of the concept of evolution as a problem-solving process with the concept of the scientific method as a problem-solving mechanism, within which the individual can develop to fullest potential.

The Chicago School, as led by Park, represented one of the European-influenced roots of present-day social science research in the U.S., through which empirical positivism was oriented to studying and ameliorating crime, prostitution, and other social problems resulting from the very rapid urbanization and industrialization then occurring in the U.S.

(Hinkle and Hinkle, 1954). The Chicago School's interest in using social research to improve society traced especially to the French positivism of August Comte and Emile Durkheim, and to such German scholars as Max Weber and Ferdinand Toennies[3]

Social science research, especially communication research, has changed a great deal since the days of the Chicago School. Research methods have become more quantitative, sampling considerations have facilitated generalization of research results, and research sponsorship has usually become necessary as the nature of scholarly investigation has moved from an individual enterprise to that of a research team. In this process, U.S. communication scientists may have become more closely oriented to the views of the Establishment (as certain European and Latin American scholars claim).[4] These critics stress that the U.S. researchers' preoccupation with persuasion, with propaganda, and with media effects in general, stems from the willingness of the government, private industry, and foundations to fund such studies. Research interest in these topics began under World War II conditions, when a national priority was to be able to understand and counteract Hitler's propaganda, and to use the results of persuasion research for military training purposes.

The emphasis on studying the effects of communication was encouraged by the influence of Shannon and Weaver's (1949) linear model of communication. By concentrating on individuals, the empirical scholars implied that the mass media were a generally positive force in society. The media were likened to an automobile engine that performed useful functions, although it might need tuning-up from time to time (a task in which the effects research could assist). The U.S. was generally a "happy" society during the 1950s and early 1960s, when the effects research came into vogue, and so perhaps it was understandable that most scholars in the empirical school followed a predominantly functionalist perspective. Functionalism postulates a view of society with relatively stable relationships and a tendency toward stability, value consensus, and equilibrium (Hardt, 1979, p. 28). Schiller (1983, p. 24) states:

> Almost always present [in empirical research] is the implicit assumption that things will turn out well. The road is the right one, and the direction taken is promising. Sometimes, in brief periods of doubt, it is admitted that there may be a detour or a few potholes up the road a bit.

---

[3]Later, U.S. communication research was also directly influenced by a cadre of emigré scholars from Germany and Austria: Paul F. Lazarsfeld, Kurt Lewin, and others (Lang, 1979).

[4]For example, Beltrán (1976).

During recent decades, the concerns of empirical scholars broadened considerably from their earlier concentration on direct effects. Such indirect effects as the agenda-setting function of the media are now investigated, for example. And certain scholars have focused on studying the mainly negative effects of mass communication, such as the consequences of television violence upon children.[5]

In summary, the empirical school of communication research is characterized by quantitative empiricism, functionalism, and positivism. In the past it has generally emphasized study of the direct effects of communication, while often ignoring the broader context in which such communication is embedded.

THE CRITICAL COMMUNICATION SCHOOL

Just as communication research in the U.S. grew in part out of the Chicago School of Sociology, and such other social sciences as the social psychology of Kurt Lewin and the political science of Harold D. Lasswell, communication research in Europe grew from the foundations of the Frankfurt School and other social science institutions. The Institute for Social Research *(Institut für Sozialforschung)* was founded in 1923 as a research center dedicated to a critical and Marxist approach.[6] The Institute was associated with the University of Frankfurt and its director was appointed as a professor at the University, but the Institute was able to maintain its financial independence through an endowment provided by a successful German grain merchant. In 1931, Max Horkheimer became Director of the Institute, and it began to attract an outstanding set of German and Austrian scholars: Theodor W. Adorno, Leo Lowenthal, Erich Fromm, Herbert Marcuse, and others. Most of the key figures in the Frankfurt Institute came from backgrounds in prosperous Jewish families, but were committed to a Marxist approach to understanding society. The first Director, Carl Grünberg, stated that Marxism would be the ruling principle of the Institute. However, the Institute staff soon began to ques-

---

[5]In fact, certain empirical scholars of TV violence have acted almost like members of the critical school, as they testified before the U.S. Congress to decrease the violent content in children's watching hours, and to restrict the TV advertising of sweet drinks, candy, and other nutritionally questionable foods. Thus, empirical scholars wish to use communication research to improve society, as do critical scholars; they differ, however, in acting on this position through their research.

[6]An authoritative account of the Frankfurt School is provided by the historian Martin Jay (1973), upon which the present chapter draws heavily.

tion orthodox Marxism, and eventually (in the late 1950s) moved even further away, dropping class conflict as "the motor of history" and replacing it with domination (Jay 1973, p. 256).[7]

With the rise of Hitler in Germany in 1933, Frankfurt became an inhospitable site for Marxist scholars with Jewish backgrounds, and in 1934 the Institute for Social Research moved, after one year in Geneva, to New York, where it was affiliated with Columbia University until it returned to Frankfurt in 1949. During its U.S. period, Adorno and others' (1950) *The Authoritarian Personality* was completed by the Institute staff, with funding from the American Jewish Committee, a book that was to become a social science classic. This investigation utilized empirical data, but generally followed a critical approach.[8]

The U.S. sojourn of the Frankfurt Institute led to a gradual integration of American social science and the philosophy of science into the critical school, and this American empiricism was then introduced to Germany in 1949 when the Institute for Social Research left New York to take up again its association with the University of Frankfurt. Empirical methodology gradually caught on in Europe, in part through the teachings of the Frankfurt School, but mainly as a result of other types of Euro-American contact. Today most European communication scientists utilize a combination of the empirical and critical approaches, possibly with somewhat greater emphasis on critical methods (Blumler, 1980).[9]

Although such key figures in the Frankfurt Institute as Max Horkheimer, Herbert Marcuse, and Theodor W. Adorno are deceased (in 1973, 1980, and 1969, respectively), and others like Leo Lowenthal are retired, the influence of the original Frankfurt School continues, especially in Europe. In fact, the New Left and the radical movements of the 1960s led to a rekindling of interest in critical theory in both the U.S. and Europe (Held, 1980). The modern-day intellectual leader in recasting and remodeling critical theory is Jürgen Habermas, a former assistant in the Frankfurt Institute in the 1950s, who is presently a professor at the University of Frankfurt. Although highly critical of positivism and preferring dialectical methodology over empirical approaches (Jay, 1973, p. 251), Habermas

---

[7]Later, the Frankfurt School became a major force in the revitalization of Western European Marxism in the post–World War II period.

[8]From its early days, the Frankfurt Institute was receptive to using empirical methods. In the 1938 issue of the *Zeitschrift fur Sozialforschung* (the main journal of the Institute), Horkheimer wrote: "Critique of positivism does not prevent us from recognizing and promoting its technical achievements" (cited by Habermas, 1980).

[9]"Recent German work on mass communications has absorbed some of the spirit and techniques of American behavioral science, though it has absorbed it critically and contentiously" (Hardt, 1979, p. 13).

has sought to reformulate critical theory so as to develop a theory of society toward the goal of the self-emancipation of people from domination (Held, 1980, p. 250). It is important for communication scholars to note that Habermas is essentially proposing a communication theory of society (Habermas, 1971, 1975, 1976, McCarthy, 1978; McLuskie, 1977).

To early critical scholars, the central questions were "Who controls communication? Why? To whose benefit?" This concern with the ownership and control of mass media institutions continues to this day among members of the critical school.[10] Perhaps the central questions being asked today by critical scholars about communication are "Why?" or "Why not?" while the central research questions for the empirical school are "How?" and "How much?"

The Frankfurt School, originally influenced by Marxist theory, questioned a mainly capitalistic society, including the role of mass media institutions in society (many of which are organized as capitalistic enterprises). Emphasis was given to the social-political-economic context of communication, and the academic field of communication was not separated from other types of social science research (as occurred after the 1950s in the U.S., as departments, institutes, and schools of communications were launched). Critical scholars feel that empirical communication scholars put too much emphasis upon communication itself, ignoring the holistic context in which communication occurs. Critical scholars argue that to ignore this context is to seriously distort the reality of communication. Because such quantitative research designs as the survey and experiment are individualistic and microanalytical, and hence not able to tell us much about social context, critical scholars often prefer less-structured methods that yield more qualitative data.

One research method utilized by both the empirical and critical schools is content analysis, although they use this method in quite different ways. Empirical scholars utilize content analysis methods to categorize media content into the form of quantitative data, which they then analyze to test certain hypotheses. Content analyses of mass media messages by critical scholars are usually less quantitative (they may be entirely qualitative), and more semiological in nature; the intent is often to uncover the presumed motives of the message-maker. There is often less concern with objectivity, measured by whether another communication researcher would content-analyze the same messages in the same categories.

A well-known example of such research is Dorfman and Mattelart's

---

[10]"Critical scholarship tends to see the primary role of mass media as one of control" (Gandy, 1982, p. 2).

(1971) *¿Para Leer al Pato Donald? (How To Read Donald Duck)*. These critical scholars content-analyzed Walt Disney's Donald Duck comic strip as it was published in Latin American newspapers to show that it contained subtle themes of U.S. imperialism toward developing nations. The researchers imply that such content themes in the comic strip may have influenced its readers. In contrast, empirical scholars are usually very cautious about implying the assumption of an effect, as the empirical scholars believe that most mass media messages do not have much effect (and hence that content data does not equal effect). However, critical scholars often carry out content analysis, not in order to infer effects on an audience, but to make inferences about the message-makers. For example, Dorfman and Mattelart (1971) conducted their content analysis of the Donald Duck comics in order to provide evidence about the imperialistic motivations of Walt Disney and his staff.

Here we see an illustration of the contrasting orientations of empirical and critical communication scholars: (a) empirical researchers emphasize understanding communication effects on an audience, and they conduct content analysis in order to aid understanding of such effects, while (b) critical scholars emphasize understanding the control of a communication system, so they conduct content analysis in order to make inferences about mass media institutions. Here is an example of where empirical and critical scholars might combine their types of research to mutual advantage, such as study of a mass media institution, combined with a content analysis of the messages that it produces, and with an audience survey of these messages' effects. Dorfman and Mattelart's (1971) study might have been broadened by gathering data (a) from Walt Disney Studios about why the cartoon strip's makers utilized themes that the content analysis displayed,[11] and (b) from readers of these comics to determine what effects, if any, they caused. Such a multi-method approach to a research problem is usually superior to using any single research method, but there are few such multi-method researches in communication research.

In summary, the essence of the critical school is its philosophical emphasis, its focus on the broader social-structural context of communication, an original basis in Marxist thought, and a central concern with the issue of who controls mass communication systems.

---

[11]Given the attitude of Walt Disney Studios toward *¿Para Leer al Pato Donald?* including legal action to prevent its publication in English in the U.S., it is doubtful that they would have provided much information about their motivations for message-making, at least to Dorfman and Mattelart. Eventually, an English language edition of this book was published and distributed in the U.S.

VIEWS OF DEVELOPMENT COMMUNICATION AND OF COMMUNICATION TECHNOLOGY

Critical communication scholars have long had a central interest in social class structure as one of their main concepts, as it affects communication, along with the associated concepts of conflict, domination, and dialectic.[12] Such an orientation quite naturally headed many critical scholars toward studying dominance and inequality, especially in international communication. Critical scholars claim that development programs, such as those funded by the U.S., were intended to increase American domination of developing nations. Empirical researchers on development communication are accused by critical scholars of providing assistance to such U.S. cultural imperialism through the gathering of data about the effects of mass media exposure on the attitudes and behavior of the public in developing nations. In the eyes of critical scholars, such researchers have encouraged the expansion of U.S.-owned mass media institutions (like the sale of U.S. television programs and films), facilitated the creation of a mass consumption society through expanded advertising, and assisted right-wing military dictatorships to stay in power.

A basic difference between empirical and critical scholars regards their basic optimism/pessimism about the degree to which mass communication can bring about social change. "In Europe, academics of a Marxist and critical bent especially regard the mass media chiefly as agencies of social control, blocking pathways of radical social change and propping up the *status quo*" (Blumler, 1980). Empirical scholars, especially those in the United States, feel that the mass media can sometimes contribute to social change, such as by providing information about social problems as a first step toward their amelioration. This optimism/pessimism of empirical and critical scholars underlies, in part, their differing viewpoints on the role of mass communication in development. Many critical scholars feel the media are powerful, while most empirical scholars feel that direct media efforts are usually minimal.

Many critical scholars express concern about such new communication technology as broadcasting satellites, computers, and cable television systems, as they are being used in the Third World. Critical scholars claim that such technology is mainly controlled by the multinational cor-

---

[12]Social class was an important concept for early critical scholars in understanding society, although this concept (a) has undergone substantial revision by Habermas (1976, pp. 130–177) in recent years, and (b) always was much more important for orthodox Marxist scholars than for critical scholars.

porations of the U.S. and other industrialized nations, and so it will likely enlarge existing inequalities between the advanced and the developing countries. For instance, Herbert I. Schiller, an American critical scholar, states:

> Given the existing distribution of power, given existing arrangements of control, and given the dynamics of how the Western model operates to extend its influence, in my judgement, the new electronic technology serves exclusively as a conduit for pumping into the developing world all of the various messages and all of the values which, in the long run, inflict the kinds of damage to people that I have heard my colleague [Ithiel de Sola Pool of MIT] here say he deplores. (Pool and Schiller, 1981)

In comparison, many empirical scholars tend to see the new media as offering the potential of decentralized control to the public, both in the Third World and in industrialized nations.

THE GEOGRAPHY OF THE EMPIRICAL AND CRITICAL SCHOOLS

Some observers feel that difference between the critical and empirical schools are due simply to U.S./European contrasts. There *is* a tendency for critical scholars to be European rather than American, and for empirical scholarship to flourish more strongly in North America than in Europe. And to oversimplify greatly, empirical scholars tend to be represented especially in the International Communication Association (ICA), and critical scholars in the International Association for Mass Communication Research (IAMCR). The main strength of IAMCR's membership of somewhat over one thousand is in Europe. In comparison 80 percent of ICA's membership (of about two thousand) is in the U.S. Most ICA members belong to the empirical school.

It is an over-simplification, however, to say that ICA is dominated by U.S. members of the empirical school, while IAMCR's most active members are European critical scholars. For example, one of the noted critical scholars is Herbert Schiller, a professor at the University of California at San Diego, and there are many other U.S. critical scholars. Likewise, several empirical scholars such as Ithiel de Sola Pool (at MIT) and Alex Edelstein (at the University of Washington) are active in IAMCR. The empirical school is well-represented in Europe, and today there are as many empirical scholars as critical scholars in Europe. Further, there are probably more critical scholars in the United States than in Europe, although an exact count is not available.[13]

However, the intellectual leaders of the critical school are mainly Europeans: Armand Mattelart teaches at the University of Paris; Kaarle Nordenstreng is a professor in the Department of Journalism and Mass Communication at the University of Tampere, Finland; and Cees Hamelink is at the Institute of Social Studies, The Hague, Netherlands. Previously we mentioned that Jürgen Habermas, a German, is the key figure today in the second generation of the Frankfurt School; he is a sociologist and philosopher who gives major attention to human communication (not just to mass communication).[14]

Similarly, there is a strong tendency for members of the empirical school of communication research to belong to ICA; many are North Americans. Nationalism obviously effects how communication scholars view the world. For example, we previously implied that the socioeconomic conditions of North America facilitated the implicit assumption of many empirical scholars that mass media institutions only need a little tune-up (from effects-oriented research), rather than a major overhaul. U.S. members of the empirical school are likely to be turned off by the critical scholars' attacks on the U.S. for its disproportionate ownership of such mass media institutions as advertising agencies, magazines, and news agencies throughout the world, and for its multinational corporations that export films and TV programs. Undoubtedly, nationalism is a major barrier, both psychologically and spatially, to any efforts to bring the empirical and the critical schools together.

Neither the empirical nor the critical school is dominant in Latin America today, and it is possible that a kind of hybrid school may eventually develop, in which Latin American communication scholars draw upon the elements from both schools that are most appropriate for the contemporary communication problems of Latin American societies. At present, both the empirical and the critical schools are well-represented in many Latin American nations, and most communication students study

---

[13]In very recent years, a number of signs of the vitality of the critical school in the United States are evident: (a) the launching of a new journal, *Critical Studies in Mass Communication*, by the Speech Communication Association and edited by Professor Robert K. Avery of the University of Utah, in 1984; (b) the founding of the Union for Democratic Communications in 1981, with two hundred members and seven local chapters, and a 1982 convention; and (c) publication of a new annual, *Critical Communication Review*, edited by Vincent Mosco and Janet Wasko, and published by Ablex, beginning in 1983.

[14]Unlike interpersonal communication, mass communication involves public opinion, politics, and political ideologies. Quite naturally then, mass communication is of special interest to European scholars, and especially to critical scholars, while interpersonal communication is much less so (Carey, 1981).

books and other publications written by authors of both schools. Communication schools in public universities in Latin America, for reasons of the socioeconomic status of their student body, tend to emphasize the critical school, while private university schools of communication may stress the empirical approach.

The social-cultural-political conditions of many Latin American nations may encourage communication scholars to borrow certain elements of the critical approach. These are generally not very "happy" societies: Health and nutrition are relatively poor, especially in rural areas and in urban slums; poverty is a very serious social problem; and the mass media are heavily oriented to urban, educated elites. There is a high degree of economic penetration by foreign-owned multinational corporations (especially those headquartered in the U.S.), including American films, television programs, and magazines. Under these conditions, it is not surprising for a communication scholar to question whether the mass media are very functional for his society. At least to some degree, a critical stance is only natural for many Latin American scholars as they look at their society. But many Latin American communication scholars also realize that they are seldom able to convince government officials or politicians to change a communication policy unless they can present empirical evidence about the suggested policy change.

In Latin America, the positivistic potential of quantitative communication research in ameliorating social problems makes a synthesis of certain elements of the critical school and the empirical school seem to be a logical and promising direction for the future. If a synthesis of the empirical and critical approaches is to be forged, it may be most likely to occur in Latin America. And such a Latin American school could have an important intellectual influence upon the future directions of communication research in Europe, North America, and in other nations. For these reasons, it is especially important to watch the future development of communication research in Latin America, particularly in Brazil, where our field has considerable intellectual strength, and where it profits from exchange with both Europe and North America.[15]

TOWARD IMPROVED UNDERSTANDING OF THE CRITICAL AND EMPIRICAL SCHOOLS

Communication scholars of each school are convinced that their viewpoint is superior. For instance, some empirical scholars feel that critical scholars do not really do research, or at least rigorous research, and

---

[15]Sweden is another promising nation where hybrid merging of the critical and empirical schools may be occurring (Rosengren, 1981).

that critical scholars are not objective scientists because of their ideological position. In return, many criticals scholars feel that empirical scholars are too busy gathering data to have time to think about its meaning and its context, that their work lacks theoretical depth,[16] and that many empirical scholars are either extremely (1) naive about the uses to which their researchers are put, or else (2) the empirical scholars are willing tools of "cultural imperialism" being carried out by the U.S. government and by multi-national corporations.

Neither empirical nor critical communication scholars have a very accurate perception of each other, in the opinion of scholars who have fairly extensive contact with both schools.[17] The main reason for these misperceptions of each other is a lack of close contact between members of the two schools. Most critical scholars do not include many (if any) empirical scholars in their personal friendship networks; similarly, the empirical scholars lack much personal contact of a professional nature with critical scholars. The geography of the two schools is one cause of this avoidance pattern (as noted previously); it also means that many critical scholars and empirical scholars do not share a common language. They are unlikely to publish in the same journals, or to be colleagues in the same university department or research institute. Nor are they very likely to belong to the same communication research association; as mentioned previously, the superior attitude of each school toward the other, and the fact that critical scholars often direct their criticisms against empirical scholars, tends to drive the two schools apart. Intellectual antagonism and avoidance maintain and encourage misunderstanding.

---

[16]A team of British critical scholars commented on the effect-oriented research of the empirical school: "The Laswellian formula [*Who* says what to *whom* with *what effect?*] makes sense only as an instrumentalist empirical model for the analysis of short-term effects. Its very dominance has been a permanent and, despite some tokenism to the contrary, a surprisingly resilient block to theoretical thinking about mass communications" (Curran and others, 1979, p. 3).

[17]For example, Lang (1979) points out that the critical school is incorrect in viewing the empirical school as "the product of commercially supported media research cultivated and exported from the U.S.A." Lang reviewed the history of the empirical school to show (a) that the empirical tradition is as much a German as an American phenomenon, and (b) that the empirical school developed as much as a response to broad intellectual, social, and political interests as to the demands of media organizations operated for profit. In the opposite direction, Carey (1979, p. 409) stated: "Unfortunately, this work [European communication research] as yet has had little influence on American social science which remains rather blissfully unaware of European work except that representing modifications Europeans make on essentially American ideas and research." Or as Davis (1980), a U.S. empirical scholar, concluded: "We have tended to dismiss attacks as being politically motivated and based on a misunderstanding of empirical social research. We would like to assume that our critics are refusing to understand our work or are consciously misinterpreting and misrepresenting it."

The empirical school is at present considerably larger than the critical school, whether measured in terms of the number of communication scholars, or the amount of research resources commanded. In addition to their greater numbers, empirical scholars have certain other important advantages over critical scholars: almost all share the common language of English, as well as a common scientific paradigm that guides much of their work.[18] Further, the critical stance of the critical scholars means they are less likely to receive research funds or other types of institutional support from such establishment institutions as national governments, foundations, or international agencies.[19] While the empirical school has several communication research journals devoted to publishing their work, there is not a single journal devoted mainly to publishing critical communication research.[20] No general communication textbooks written from the viewpoint of the critical school are available.

The present discussion of the critical school of communication research suggests several lessons for empirical scholars to consider.

1. Researchers focusing mainly on communication effects cannot afford to ignore the nature of the communication system that is producing and delivering the messages. Who owns and controls this system, and the purposes for which it is operated, are important parts of the communication context, and directly aid the investigation of effects.
2. Ethical aspects of the communication process they study should not be ignored by empirical scholars, even if these aspects cannot be studied with their usual research methods.
3. Communication research should be cast in a wider scope, both in recognizing (a) that research questions of global significance should be emphasized over culture-bound inquiries of national media systems, and (b) that to understand human communication is to understand society, as critical scholars have realized since the beginnings of the Frankfurt School.
4. Greater emphasis should be placed upon policy-relevant research. Herbert Schiller, a U.S. critical scholar, points out: "By and large, communication research in the United States is quixotic. Re-

---

[18]After pointing out that the critical school "finds as yet only a relatively small group of adherents", Hamelink (1980), a European critical scholar, concluded that a more serious problem is that the critical school "has not yet been able to develop a conceptual framework that is sufficiently different from the mainstream of thinking."

[19]As Halloran (1981, p. 29) noted: "Critical research, or at least much of it in many countries, has to survive in what is inevitably a hostile atmosphere."

[20]Although *Media, Culture, and Society*, a journal begun in 1979, comes closest.

searchers study intently a world that does not really matter while ignoring the one that does'' (Schiller, 1983, p. 24).

More generally, critical scholars would urge empirical scholars to adopt a more critical stance toward our field: To continually question the motives of the powerful for communicating with the weak, to stop assuming that most communication is necessarily for the benefit of the audience, and to realize that communication can be conceptualized as leading to a conflict situation, as well as one leading to harmony.

Will the empirical and critical schools move more closely together in their intellectual positions?

> Are they bound to polarize into two quite antithetical and irreconcilable positions, with one camp radically critical of the prevailing mass communication order, while the other willingly or unwittingly upholds it, and each fails to address the predominant preoccupations of the other? Is there no viable middle course of research purpose falling between such extremes? (Blumler, 1978)

In important ways, both the critical and empirical approaches to communication research necessarily entail the other.

> Social theory that is contradicted by empirical research belongs in the realm of ideology, but empirical research that does not recognize implicit assumptions about the nature of society and change cannot lead beyond itself to policies for change. (McAnany, 1981, p. 8)

What could the two schools of communication research do if they really wanted to understand each other better? A first step would be for each school to treat the other with more respect. Without such an attitude, little meaningful information-exchange will occur. The previous rancor and debate between the two schools should be replaced by a realization that each may have much to learn from the other.

Pluralism (the position that all points of view deserve to be heard and considered) must prevail in national and international associations for communication research, in their conferences, and in the journals and other publications that these associations control. These channels could help provide the contact that is needed between the two schools. Unfortunately in the past, these associations, conferences, and publications have tended to play a segmenting, rather than an integrating, role.

The present chapter was written by a member of the empirical school. Perhaps a critical scholar would also like to tell the story from his viewpoint.

In such a way the dialogue might begin.

REFERENCES

Theodor W. Adorno (1945), " A Social Critique of Radio Music," *Kenyon Review, 7,* 208–217.

Theodor W. Adorno and others (1950), *The Authoritarian Personality,* New York: Harper and Row.

Luis Ramiro Beltrán (1976), "Alien Promises, Objects, and Methods in Latin American Communication Research," *Communication Research, 3,* 107–134.

Jay G. Blumler (1978), "Purposes of Mass Communication Research: A Transatlantic Perspective," *Journalism Quarterly, 55,* 219–230.

Jay G. Blumler (1980), "Mass Communication Research in Europe: Some Origins and Prospects," *Media, Culture and Society, 2,* 367–376.

James W. Carey (1979), "Mass Communication Research and Cultural Studies: An American View," in James Curran and other (eds.), *Mass Communication and Society,* Beverly Hills, CA: Sage.

James W. Carey (1981), "Mass Communication Theory: The Critical Dimension," Paper presented at the International Communication Association, Minneapolis, MN.

James Curran and others (eds.) (1979), *Mass Communication and Society,* Beverly Hills, CA: Sage.

Dennis Davis (1980), "Isolation or Dialogue: The Choice Facing American Mass Communication Researchers," Paper presented at the Association for Education in Journalism, Boston, MA.

Ariel Dorfman and Armand Mattelart (1971), *¿Para Leer al Pato Donald?* Valparaiso, Chile, Ediciones Universitarias (reprinted by Siglo XXI, Buenes Aires, Argentina, in 1972).

P. Jean Frazier and Cecillia Gaziano (1979), *Robert Ezra Park's Theory of News, Public Opinion and Social Control,* Lexington, KY: Association for Education in Journalism, Journalism Monographs 64.

Oscar H. Gandy, Jr. (1982), *Beyond Agenda Setting: Information Subsidies and Public Policy,* Norwood, NJ: Ablex.

Jürgen Habermas (1971), *Knowledge and Human Interests,* Translated by Jeremy J. Shapiro, Bostom, MA: Beacon Press.

Jürgen Habermas (1975), *Legitimation Crisis,* Translated by Thomas McCarthy, Boston, MA: Beacon Press.

Jürgen Habermas (1976), *Communication and the Evolution of Society,* Translated by Thomas McCarthy, Boston, MA: Beacon Press.

Jürgen Habermas (1980), "The Inimitable *Zeitschraft für Sozialforschung:* How Horkheimer Took Advantage of a Historically Oppressive Hour," *Telos, 45,* 114–121.

James D. Halloran (1981), "The Context of Mass Communication Research," in Emile G. McAnany and others (eds.), *Communication and Social Structure: Critical Studies in Mass Media Research,* New York: Praeger.

Cees J. Hamelink (1980), "New Structure of International Communication: The Role of Research," Paper presented at the International Association for Mass Communication Research, Caracas, Venezuela.

Hanno Hardt (1979), *Social Theories of the Press: Early German and American Perspectives,* Beverly Hills, CA: Sage.

David Held (1980), *Introduction to Critical Theory: Horkheimer to Habermas,* Berkeley, CA: University of California Press.

Roscoe E. Hinkle, Jr. and Gisela J. Hinkle (1954), *The Development of Modern Sociology: Its Nature and Growth in the United States,* New York: Random House.

Max Horkheimer (1937), *Critical Theory: Selected Essays,* New York: Herder and Herder (published in 1968).

Martin Jay (1973), *The Dialectical Imagination: A History of the Frankfurt School and the Institute for Social Research, 1923-1930,* Boston, MA: Little, Brown and Co.

Kurt Lang (1979), "The Critical Funtions of Empirical Communication Research: Observations on German–American Influence," *Media, Culture and Society, 1,* 83–96.

Paul Felix Lazarsfeld (1941), "Remarks on Administrative and Critical Research," *Studies in Philosophy and Social Science, 9,* 2–16.

Paul Felix Lazarsfeld (1948), "The Role of Criticism in the Management of Mass Media," *Journalism Quarterly, 25,* 115–126.

Emile E. McAnany (1981), "Change and Social Structure in Mass Communication: An Overview," in Emile G. McAnany and others (eds.), *Communication and Social Structure: Critical Studies in Mass Media Research,* New York: Praeger.

Thomas McCarthy (1978), *The Critical Theory of Jürgen Habermas,* Cambridge, MA. M.I.T. Press.

Ed McLuskie (1977), "Integration of Critical Theory with North American Communication Study: Barriers and Prospects," Paper presented at the International Communication Association, Berlin, West Germany.

Ithiel de Sola Pool and Herbert I. Schiller (1981), "Perspectives on Communication Research: An Exchange," *Journal of Communication, 31,* 15–23.

Everett M. Rogers (1981), "L'Ecole Empirique et l'Ecole Critique de Recherche en Communication," *Les Cahiers de la Communication, 1,* 311–326.

Everett M. Rogers (1982), "The Empirical and the Critical Schools of Communication Research," in Michael Burgoon (ed.), *Communication Yearbook 5,* New Brunswick, NJ: Transaction.

Karl Erik Rosengren (ed.) (1981), *Advances in Content Analysis,* Beverly Hills, CA: Sage.

Herbert I. Schiller (1983), "Information for What Kind of Society?" in Jerry L. Salvaggio (ed.), *Telecommunications: Issues and Choices for Society,* New York: Longman.

Claude Shannon and Warren Weaver (1949), *The Mathematical Theory of Communication,* Urbana, IL: University of Illinois Press.

Chapter 15

Communication Research: One Paradigm or Four?[1]

Karl Erik Rosengren
University of Göteborg

INTRODUCTION

Sweden is one nation (perhaps Brazil is another) where the empirical and critical schools of communication research coexist, pluralistically learn from one another, and may be forging a vigorous hybrid. Here a leading Swedish communication scholar sets forth a classification system, borrowed from two sociologists, Burrell and Morgan, on which the empirical school and three alternatives are positioned. This taxonomy is a two-by-two categorization on the basis of subjective-objective orientations, and/ or radical change-regulation, yielding four paradigms: (a) the Radical Humanist, (b) the Radical Structuralist, (c) the Interpretive, and (d) the Functionalist. The latter type, representing objective-regulatory scholars, is the dominant paradigm (which elsewhere in this book is called the empirical school). The intellectual paradox illuminated by the classification and identification of the four paradigms is that the empirical scholars who can give the answers to interesting questions did not ask them, while scholars of the three critical paradigms who asked these questions cannot provide the answers. Professor Rosengren then illustrates the paradox, and how to overcome it, by considering three types of research (that dealing with mass media news, communication and culture, and mass media use). In the case of these three problematics, research methodologies borrowed from the empirical school have been utilized fruitfully to answer important questions raised mainly by scholars in one of the three dissident paradigms. If such borrowing can be effective, both here and in many other possible cases of communication problematics, the author questions whether there really are four paradigms of communication research. Perhaps there is only one.   *E.M.R., F.B.*

There is ferment in the field, no doubt about that. Intellectual ferment: Critical scholars and hard-nosed empiricists vehemently fight each other, disdainfully ignore each other, or cautiously maneuver to find a precarious *modus vivendi*. International ferment: Scholars and social scientists from the Old and the New World meet and marvel at each others' strange ways of thinking; data and theories from, and about, the First,

---

[1]This chapter also appeared in a short version in the *Journal of Communication* in 1983.

Second, and Third Worlds add cultural diversity to the conflicting intellectual perspectives. Political ferment: Radical critics, liberal reformists, and conservative defenders of the status quo use communication research to buttress their political arguments in the debates of the day. The risk cannot be neglected that in the process, the community of communication scholars and scientists will dissolve and be replaced by a number of fighting sects and sectarians (Rex, 1978).

The message has been written on the wall for some time, and serious students of commnication have tried to do something about it. Noting a diversity of perspectives which may show some similarity to the threat of an explosion, the first impulse, perhaps, is to look around and try to produce a description of the situation, a list of the several perspectives, their main proponents and adherents, the way they seem to be going, and where they are coming from. Recently such descriptions have been published, sometimes including also a certain number of prescriptions about what to do and where to go.[2] At least two major attempts were recently made to facilitate the comparative study of a number of such descriptions and prescriptions by some leading communication scholars and scientists from various parts of the world: (a) this book, and (b) a *Journal of Communication* Symposium initiated by the Editor, George Gerbner.

There is ferment in other fields than ours, however, and efforts similar to those in communication research have also been made in other social sciences. Lists of various schools and perspectives have been drawn up, symposia have been convened, anthologies have been published. Especially in sociology, perhaps, such efforts have been numerous.[3] In the sociology of organization an ambitious attempt to move a few steps further was made some time ago by the Anglo-American team of Gibson Burrell and Gareth Morgan (1979).

FOUR PARADIGMS

Realizing the necessity of moving beyond the rather simplistic dualism of criticism–empiricism, Burrell and Morgan started out with a multidimensional property space for schools of thought and research in sociology. The property space was finally reduced to two dimensions called "objective/subjective orientation," and the "sociologies of regulation/radical change." The objective/subjective dimension covers four levels

---

[2]For example, see Blumler (1982), Curran and others (1982), Fitchen (1981), Gitlin (1981), Nimmo and Sanders (1981), Rogers (1982), and Schramm (1980).

[3]See, for instance, Collins (1982), Ritzer (1975), and Short (1982).

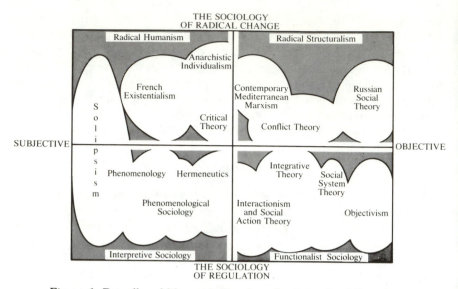

Figure 1. Burrell and Morgan's Typology for Schools of Sociology

of dual assumptions about the nature of social science (in ontology: realism/nominalism; in epistemology: positivism/anti-positivism; about human nature: determinism/voluntarism; about methodology: nomothetic/ideographic). The regulation/change dimension covers seven levels of dual assumptions about the nature of society, some of which are status quo/radical change; consensus/domination; solidarity/emancipation; and actuality/potentiality. These levels are less neatly ordered into a clearcut system than are the categories of the subjective/objective dimension.

Crossing the two main dimensions of Burrell and Morgan (1979), we get a fourfold typology: the Radical Humanist, the Radical Structuralist, the Interpretive, and the Functionalist paradigms. By means of this typology it is possible to classify in a meaningful way the fairly large number of research traditions and schools of thought constituting present-day sociology. Figure 1 presents the two dimensions, the four main paradigms, and a number of schools of thought and research traditions classified in terms of the typology. The location of each school is not exact. At best, it is valid at the level of an ordinal scale—hence the cloud-like contours. The terms used to characterize the various paradigms, schools, and dimensions of the typology could be discussed. Nevertheless, the typology is an ingenious heuristic device. It provides a neat overview of an otherwise bewildering array of schools, traditions, and perspectives.

Burrell and Morgan (1979) use their typology in two ways. First, they characterize in a fairly novel way a number of different schools of sociology (drawing also upon the four plus seven levels constituting the two dimensions of the typology). Second, against this background, they are able to characterize a number of schools of organizational analysis in a way which presumably adds to a better understanding of the field of organizational studies, and possibly will help in developing and consolidating the research carried out within that field.

Comparing Figure 1 with one's own personal impressions of the field of communication studies, one is struck by the similarity. The social sciences represent a number of different disciplines and fields, which have passed through similar phases of development. Sociology together with psychology, economics, and political science form the principal "mother disciplines" of communication studies. Small wonder, then, that there is a striking similarity to be found between our personal impressions of the status of the field of communication research, and the semi-formalized picture of the various schools of sociology (offered by Figure 1).

It would make an interesting task to replicate for the field of communication studies the classification and detailed discussion of the various schools and research traditions which Burrell and Morgan undertook for the field of organizational studies: using, of course, not only the two dimensions of Figure 1, but also the four plus seven underlying levels (or some revised version thereof). In a second step the result of such an exercise of classification could be compared with empirically based maps of the field, obtained by means of questionnaires or citation analysis (Small, 1979; Rosengren, 1968, 1981b). Such maps already exist for the field of scientific communication (White and Griffith, 1981), and for Swedish mass communication research (Höglund, 1982).

Within the scope of this chapter, however, we must be content to note that the vast majority of communication studies have been, and probably still are, being carried out within the intellectual framework of the lower right cell, a framework being continuously criticized and questioned from the vantage points of the other three cells, a critique and questioning which have sometimes led to bitter and sterile quarrels but which no doubt have also been at least indirectly stimulating. The typology of Figure 1, especially if complemented with a citation study, could help us better to understand such discussions, and, thereby, the entire field of communication studies.

A crucial point of the typology is the nature of the dimensions. It is obvious that they are continua—at least within limits. Within the cells, schools of thought can be ordered as being located above or below, to the left or right of each other. The location of each school can be discussed, and so can the relative positions of various schools. Between cells, however, there is less freedom.

Indeed, according to Burrell and Morgan (1979), in the final analysis the lines drawn between the cells represent absolute, qualitatively definite boundaries. In a scholar's way of thinking about social science, at heart he/she is either a "subjectivist" or an "objectivist." One cannot be a little of both. Similarly, in one's thinking about society, at heart one is either a "radicalist" or a "reformist," not something in between. This being so, the fact that both dimensions are based upon a number of "levels" which are supposed to be logically independent, would seem to require either choosing one of them as the touchstone for each dimension, or stipulating the minimum number of criteria to be satisfied in order to locate a given school in a given cell. Burrell and Morgan are not absolutely clear on this point (perhaps because they do not make any clear distinction between what have been called monothetic and polythetic typologies (Bailey, 1973, p. 21). Personally, I would tend to regard the lines between the cells as less absolute than do Burrell and Morgan. Nevertheless I think the fourfold typology remains a useful heuristic device.

More fruitful than using the typology for classification exercises, is to use it as a springboard for reflections on what one can, and cannot, do within different paradigms (in our case the four main paradigms of the typology). This basic question has not been given much attention in the debates of the last 10 or 15 years. These debates amount to a series of attacks directed towards the "dominant paradigm" in the lower right cell of Figure 1 by adherents of various schools of thought belonging to the three "dissident paradigms" to be found in the other cells. The questions raised in these attacks have often been serious enough, that more than once the final result of the discussions has been that research carried out within the dominant paradigm of the lower right cell has been enriched in various aspects.

The strategic situation of the debates has been paradoxical, however. The questions raised from the vantage points of the three "critical" cells were, as a rule, not raised—at least not that vociferously—in the fourth cell. They could have been raised there, but by and large they were not. On the other hand, they can be given answers in that cell, but not—by and large—in the other three cells, especially not in the two left cells, which have a different ontology, a different anthropology, a different methodology, and a different epistemology than the two cells to the right in the typology. The paradox is that; *Those who can give the answers did not ask the questions; and those who asked the questions cannot provide the answers.*

The extent to which the paradox holds true could form the subject of detailed research within the history, sociology, and philosophy of science. The paradox, if accepted, raises two types of questions. The first concerns the past: the genesis of the situation. Why and how did it come about? The second type of question concerns the future: the remedies for an awkward situation. What can we do about it? In my opinion questions of the second type are the more interesting ones.

In the remainder of this chapter I will show how questions raised in one or more of the three "dissident" cells of the typology can be given answers within the dominant paradigm of the lower right cell (as a matter of fact some answers, have already been given, albeit not definitively). I shall discuss three substantive problematics: mass media news, communication and culture, and mass media use. I will show that methodological distinctions and instruments, varying widely in degree of generality but all developed within the dominant paradigm, are helpful (indeed necessary) when trying to answer some vital questions raised within the three dissident paradigms (as well as, partly, within the dominant paradigm). The fact that questions raised in one paradigm may be given satisfactory answers by means of methodologies developed in another paradigm casts some doubt on the alleged incomparability of the four paradigms. Indeed, it may be questioned whether what we have are really paradigms at all.

MASS MEDIA NEWS

An important branch of communication research is the study of news disseminated by the mass media. Within the dominant paradigm, the production, distribution, and reception of news have been described in great detail in innumerable studies usually grouped into a small number of research traditions: gatekeeping, diffusion, international news, etc. Behind such studies one may find, implicit or explicit assumptions about society and social science to the effect that there is an objective reality on which the news media report more or less accurately. The relationships between (1) reality, and (2) the picture of reality offered by the media and received by the public, are patterned in a stable way, and it is for news research to detect and explain these stable patterns in terms of individual psychology, institutional settings, macro-economic restraints, etc.

Criticisms of Empirical Research on News

During the last two decades this type of research has been increasingly criticized from two perspectives. From what could be called a "subjectivistic perspective" it has been maintained that news should not primarily be regarded as more or less accurate reports of an objective reality (if indeed there is such a thing). News reports constitute or create a reality of their own, it is maintained, and it is the task of news research to describe and understand that reality on its own terms. From a politically radical perspective the dominant type of news research has been criticized for ignoring the way in which news is biased on both the national and international scene. Behind the bias lie political and economic structures, and the bias helps to reinforce and maintain these structures. Bias in news serves the powers that be; it works for the *status quo*. It is the task of news research to reveal the bias and unmask the powers behind it, thus helping to bring about a radical change of the whole system.

In terms of the typology of Figure 1, the two types of criticism are based upon radically different assumptions about the nature of society and the possibilities of social science. However, they have borrowed elements from each other, and it is probably not uncommon to find side-by-side in the same study elements from the three paradigms called by Burrell and Morgan (1979) "Interpretive Sociology," "Radical Humanism," and "Radical Structuralism." Only a number of detailed case studies about these types of news research could untangle the precise intellectual origin of the actual arguments used in the various pieces of research.

The subjectivist perspective is, in my opinion, always precarious and especially misapplied in connection with news studies. Brought to its logical consequence this perspective leads to solipsism, as has been pointed out many times, by Burrell and Morgan (1979) and others. Obviously the philosophy of solipsism is not a very good starting point for the study of news. Even those who maintain that news reports constitute a reality of their own must admit that there are other realities available, and that news relates to these realities in one way or another. In fact they admit this indirectly as soon as they use the term "bias," as they often do. For bias in news presupposes something which has been somehow misrepresented. That something is usually called "reality." To demonstrate satisfactorily the existence of bias in news we need:

1. Measurements of "reality."
2. Measurements of news about the same reality.
3. An idea about which relationships between (1) and (2) we are willing to accept as "unbiased."

Thus the "news-as-a-reality-of-its-own perspective" is either misapplied or tends to negate itself if applied in a consequent way. Nevertheless, some of the questions raised by researchers subscribing to that perspective are important. Happily, they meet with no principal difficulties within an objectivist paradigm. In such a paradigm it is quite natural to compare measurements of reality with measurements of reports on the same reality. For some reason, however, such a comparison has not often been made.

A second point concerns the radical perspective. According to the fourfold typology (of Figure 1) there are two variants of this perspective: a subjectivistic and an objectivistic variant. In reality the two are sometimes mixed up, with confusion and lack of clarity as a result. However, when the radical perspective of society is combined with an objectivistic perspective of social science, the differences with the dominant paradigm seem to be manageable. In both paradigms the existence of an objective social reality, in principle accessible by means of scientific research, is assumed. The adherents of the two paradigms also agree about the relevance of values to social science, and they agree about how to regard them. More specifically, they agree: (a) that values and evaluations may influence the type of research that is being carried out—even, perhaps, the way it is being carried out; (b) that the influence of values and evaluations on scientific research should be minimized—to the extent that it is possible to do so; and (c) that values and evaluations should be made the object of scientific research.

Adherents of the two paradigms disagree on assumptions about, and evaluations of, the more precise character of objective social reality. But these assumptions are researchable, and so the difference between radical and traditional objectivists may be less absolute than Burrell and Morgan assume. For psychological reasons it may be true that "one must always be committed to one side more than another" (Burrell and Morgan, 1979, p. 19), but one could still decide under what circumstances one perspective is scientifically more fruitful than another, in the sense that it is able more parsimoniously to explain a greater part of the social reality under study. In areas where empirical research is being carried out within both paradigms, therefore, a confluence will gradually take place. International communication is such an area. The heated debates[4] following the MacBride report demonstrate at least two things: first, that such a confluence between two different research traditions is a very difficult process; second, that it is on its way (Stevenson and others, 1980).

Intra- and Extra-Media Data

Common to the two points made above, on news research within the subjectivist and radical perspectives, is the fact that they both refer to the existence of an objective social reality. An important part of the study of news is the investigation of the relationship between that reality and the pictures of it offered by the news media, which implies a need to relate to each other data about an external reality and data about the media's reports on that reality. To be used as a basis for a scientifically valid comparison, these two types of data must be as independent as possible. Ideally, data about "reality" should stem from sources independent of

---

[4]For examples of these discussions of the MacBride Report, see Part II of the *Mass Communication Review Yearbook*, Volume 3; and the *Journal of International Affairs, 35*(2).

the media, they should be "extra-media data," to be related to "intra-media data" about the news provided by the media.

The terms "intra- and extra-media" data were introduced in Rosengren (1970), and have been used in a number of later studies.[5] More important than terminology, however, is the methodology of relating to each other two types of independent data (one about an external reality, the other about the picture of that reality offered by the media). Such methodology is intuitively appealing and has been re-invented spontaneously many times, by a number of communication scholars and other social scientists, drawing upon a rich variety of sources for extra-media data: historical records (Lewis, 1960; Lippmann and Merz, 1920), people themselves appearing in the news (Charnley, 1936; Scanlon, 1972), planted observers (Halloran and others, 1970; Lang and Lang, 1953), white books (Smith, 1971), surveys undertaken originally for other purposes (Owen, 1957) or especially for the purpose (Rosengren and others; 1975), and official statistics (Rosengren, 1974). As a rule the extra-media data have been used as a standard by means of which the reports of the media have been evaluated and found to be more or less lacking in various ways: accuracy, relevance, balance, bias, etc.

A more interesting way of using extra-media data, however, is to use them in explanatory, causal studies. Radical critics often maintain that the international news flow is to a large extent determined by economic and political structures; this is a causal hypothesis. For "proof," one is usually referred to more or less systematic intra-media data showing or exemplifying that some part of the world is "underrepresented" in the news compared to other parts of the world. Such proof, however, is lacking in at least two respects, both of which can be taken care of by means of extra-media data.

In the first place, such "proof" disregards the obvious fact that some parts of the world are economically and politically more powerful than other parts, and consequently deserve and need to be more fully covered, in positive and negative terms. It would be strange, for instance, if Sweden were continually given as much attention in the news media as the USSR. Using as standards such extra-media data as population, GNP, and international trade data, one may find that a country seemingly given excessive attention in the news may actually be underrepresented with respect to one criterion, while at the same time it may be overrepresented according to another criterion (for an example, see Rosengren, 1977). Such a result should warn us to be cautious when making assertions about under-

---

[5]For examples of studies using the intra-media/extra-media data distinction, see Edelstein (1981), Hicks and Gordon (1974), Nnaemeka and Richstad (1981), Robinson and Sparker (1976), Rosengren (1979), Smith (1971), and Schulz (1976).

or over-representation in the news. The question of under- or over-representation is less simple than it may appear to be at first sight.

In the second place, the pseudo-proof fails to make a necessary distinction between (a) a given country's capacity to produce news events, and (b) that country's capacity to have these news events disseminated over the world. Intra-media data alone cannot handle that distinction. However, using extra-media data about both events and the countries of origin of the news events, it is possible (a) to control for a country's news-producing capacity, and (b) to measure the influence of the country's capacity for world wide dissemination. This procedure was followed by Rosengren (1974 and 1977). The results were not trivial. It was shown that between the two variables such politico-economic factors as population, GNP, and international trade data can explain between one-third and two-thirds of the variation in international political news.[6] The fact that this seems to hold true for countries as different as Sweden, England, and the German Democratic Republic should not make the results less relevant to a truly radical critic of the existing international order of communication.

A methodology developed within the dominant paradigm seems to be able to answer important questions raised mainly within the dissident paradigms of Figure 1. New empirical data collected in the light of further refinements in theory and methodology should make possible a more thoroughgoing understanding of the processes determining the flow and structure of international news, certainly a problematic highly topical in present-day communication research.

COMMUNICATION AND CULTURE

The concepts of culture and communication are inextricably intertwined. Culture, therefore, represents a problematic which is central to communication research of whatever paradigm. Especially in the two radical paradigms of Figure 1, the concept of culture has been a main focus of interest.

Empirical Tests of Critical Questions

From a humanistic Marxist perspective, members of the Frankfurt critical school and their followers—Horkheimer, Marcuse, Adorno, Habermas, and others—maintained that the liberating and emancipatory potential of high culture is continually being debased and neutralized in the mass culture offered by the mass media to the populace of a mass society.

---

[6]Cioffi-Revilla and Merritt (1982) found that actual distance was a less important predictor.

The end result is supposed to be a generally alienated (rather than eman-
cipated and activated) audience.

From a more objectivistic Marxist perspective, members of what
Burrell and Morgan (1979) call a "Contemporary Mediterranean Marxism"—Althusser, Poulantzas, Colletti, and others—maintained that the
mass media together with schools and churches form an "ideological apparatus," one of several "apparatuses of control." The mass media create
and disseminate the ideology, the set of ideas, values, and beliefs which
legitimate the *status quo* and thus help to reproduce the existing social
order, and/or to gradually change it (as needed). The mass media in a
powerful way represent the bourgeois hegemony in society.

It is difficult to put the Frankfurt perspective to a scientifically valid
test, given its abstruse, all-too-Hegelian language. Its truth value rests to
no small extent with the more or less convincing rhetoric of its proponents
and with the credibility of the examples they marshal in support of their
case. The adherents of the radical structural perspective, however, follow
an ontology and epistemology that leads them to an objectivistic, almost
neo-positivistic set of assumptions about social science, which, in principle,
should not prevent them from testing, rather than just illustrating, their
hypotheses. The fact that this testing is seldom done could probably be
explained, at least partially, by the strong Marxist tradition of illustrating
general arguments by means of specific instances.

A classic study of the ideological message of the mass media, a
quantitative content analysis of heroes in popular literature, fitting in very
well with a radical structuralist perspective, was carried out by Leo Lowenthal (1961), who is usually considered an adherent of the Radical Humanism paradigm. Perhaps the lines between the four cells of Figure 1
are less absolute than Burrell and Morgan (1979) themselves would have
it (Bauer, 1969; Block, 1982; Goldmann and Lagerkranz, 1977). The Lowenthal study also shows that the two radical paradigms have a reservoir
of theory on culture which could be, but for some reasons has not been,
made the subject of rigorous empirical study and testing. Recent methodological advances within the dominant paradigm of communication research may facilitate the empirical study of the important questions about
culture and ideology raised within the radical paradigms. Some of the
questions about culture and ideology raised within the radical paradigms
have been asked also within the dominant paradigm, as a result of intra-
paradigmatic developments.

Cultural Indicators

Culture is a macro phenomenon, one to be studied at a societal
level. In Marxist and other theories, culture is often related to other macro
phenomena: economy, politics, and technology. Theories of these latter
areas draw on empirical research using units such as dollars and ballots,

and/or other measures such as economic and social indicators of one sort or another. Until recently, the study of culture has benefited from neither natural units nor generally accepted indicators. During the last decade or so, however, a growing number of cultural indicators have been developed.

The systematic, scholarly study of culture has proceeded at least since the romantic era in the late 18th century and early 19th century, but only in the 1930s did Sorokin (1937–1941) launch a major attempt to measure culture and cultural change in a way comparable in principle to the way other large societal systems were being measured. Sorokin and his associates did not use the term "cultural indicator." Neither was the term used by the team of experts working at about the same time with Ogburn (1933) under a presidential committee, with the task of measuring "Recent Social Trends." Yet it is clear that from the mid-1930s, three types of societal indicators were developed: economic, social, and cultural indicators. Given the large differences in the natural units to be studied, in the theoretical history of the various fields, and in the amounts of statistical material available for analysis, it is only natural that studies using the three types of indicators have proceeded at diferent paces and in different directions.

Economic indicators are indispensable. Yet they do not measure some very important aspects of societal structure and development. This deficiency called social indicators into existence, tapping important dimensions of the social reality falling outside the conceptual space delimited by economic indicators. The study of social indicators had its breakthrough during the 1960s, and was followed since then by a regular and continuing development (Bauer, 1969; Zapf, 1976). Just as limitations in economic indicators, however, called forth the creation and use of social indicators, so limitations inherent in social indicators have called forth cultural indicators.

It is customary to distinguish between "objective" social indicators (measuring objective characteristics of a social structure) and "subjective" social indicators (measuring perceptions and evaluations thereof). A striking result in recent research within the "social indicators movement" is that the relationship between objective and subjective social indicators supposedly corresponding to each other is somewhat problematic, both within and between societies, both cross-sectionally and over time. It is true that some relatively strong positive correlations between objective and subjective social indicators have been found (Inkeles and Diamond, 1980). But on the whole one may conclude that welfare does not necessarily produce well-being, an old insight which is now being corroborated and more precisely expressed by social indicators research.[7]

---

[7]Allardt (1975, 1981), Andrews and Inglehart (1976), Duncan (1975), Easterlin (1973), Stipak (1979), and Wasserman and Chua (1980).

One explanation for the low or absent relationship between objective and subjective social indicators is the fact that what has often been treated as a two-factor problem—objective conditions and perceptions and evaluations of these conditions—is really a three-factor problem. Perceptions and evaluations of objective social conditions are made against the background of knowledge, opinion, and values—in short, against the background of individual expectations (Bénéton, 1978; Merton and Kitt, 1950) as shaped by a common culture.

The implication is that attention should be directed towards the factor ultimately influencing the relationship between objective and subjective social indicators: culture. Just as the scientific study of the economic aspects of society demanded the development of economic indicators, just as the social aspects called for social indicators, so the serious study of culture will ultimately necessitate the systematic and sustained development of cultural indicators. Such development—mainly methodological in its thrust—may lead to a corresponding theoretical and empirical enrichment of the study of culture, not only in the social sciences but also in the humanities. A set of reliable and valid cultural indicators applied over time and space will permit comparative studies of culture at a higher level of precision than before.

Definitions of the concept of culture are legion. Three among them have been more influential than the rest: those definitions presented by Tylor (1871), by Kroeber and Kluckhohn (1952), and by Kroeber and Parsons (1958). All three definitions are somewhat lengthy, and also enumerative rather than criterion-oriented. Vermeersch (1971) forcefully makes this point and suggests a new, criterion-oriented definition. It would take us too long here, however, to try to disentangle the complexities and niceties inherent in such definitions. All the definitions refer to culture as a class of abstract phenomena having material embodiments. Culture is abstract; therefore it can only be indirectly observed. Each single embodiment of culture, of course, can be observed and described in great detail. But culture as such—a class of abstract phenomena—cannot be directly observed. It must be studied by means of indicators.

The term "cultural indicator" was introduced by Gerbner (1969), who has since maintained a regular monitoring activity of American television, developing and applying a number of cultural indicators, the most widespread of which is the "violence profile" (Gerbner and others, 1980). Gerbner's efforts have been widely discussed and criticized, sometimes acrimoniously so (Hirsch, 1980; Hughes, 1980; Gerbner and others, 1981). They have also been replicated, more or less successfully, in other parts of the world (see several articles in Melischek and others, 1982).

Gerbner's approach represents a major step forward, giving increased impetus to the study of culture. In 1980, a session on Cultural Indicators and the Future of Developed Societies was held at the International Communication Association Conference in Acapulco, Mexico. That was the first time representatives of different types of cultural indicators research met to discuss general problems of common interest to all scholars working in the field. Two years later, the Vienna Symposium on Cultural Indicators for the Comparative Study of Culture was convened (Melischek and others, 1982). The papers presented at the Symposium offer testimony that a field of cultural indicators research is emerging, drawing upon the results obtained by Gerbner and his associates, but also upon results, theories, and methodologies from other pioneers in the field. There are at least a dozen such scholars, each grappling with the problem of measuring aspects of culture, and each creating his own set of "cultural indicators" (even if not using that term): Ogburn (1933), Sorokin (1937-1941), Lasswell and Namenwirth (1968), McClelland (1961, 1975a, 1975b), Rokeach (1973, 1974, 1979), Inglehart (1977) and Namenwirth (1973).

Swedish Research on Cultural Indicators

In Sweden an extensive research program on the development of the Swedish cultural climate during the postwar period has been carried on for some years: Cultural Indicators: The Swedish Symbol System, 1945–1975 (CISSS). The program is organized in five independent but coordinated subprojects, run by social scientists and scholars from the Universities of Lund and Stockholm and representing such diverse disciplines as sociology, political science, economics, history, philosophy, and theology (Rosengren, 1981a, 1981c). The interdisciplinary character of the program ensures a stimulating variety of theoretical perspectives, while the common thrust—the development and application of cultural indicators based on quantitative content analysis of postwar Swedish dailies and weeklies—ensures enough common ground to make inter-project comparisons possible and fruitful.

Using references in the daily press to a supernatural reality of a religious nature as indicators of belief and/or interest in such a reality, theologian Per Block (1982) has demonstrated an overall trend to secularization in the cultural climate of postwar Sweden. There is a clear regional differentiation in the trend, and superimposed on it one may discern a cyclical pattern as well as seemingly random variations. The trend should be related to basic developments in the Swedish economy, while the cyclical pattern may have something to do with middle-range developments on the international and domestic political scenes. The seemingly random variations may, at least partly, be related to isolated events in the religious arena of Sweden.

Applying a Rokeachean perspective, historian Eva Block (1982) used references to the values of freedom and equality in editorials of Swedish dailies of the postwar period as cultural indicators. For most of this period, she found a declining trend for the value of freedom, and a rising trend for the value of equality. Towards the end of the 1960s and in the early 1970s, these two trends culminated, stagnated and, possibly, turned into a phase of opposite trends: decline in the value of equality, and an increase in the value of freedom. These results have a high degree of face validity. 1968 was a year of upheaval in Sweden as in many other countries, and in 1976 a bourgeois government took over, after 44 years of Social-Democratic government. The results also raise several interesting questions: Where do such changes come from? What effects do they have? Are they superstructural epiphenomena only, mechanically reflecting developments in the economic–technical base? Is there, perhaps, a certain amount of independence, while the base has the upper hand? Or do the values perhaps affect the base, so that real equality follows an increased salience of the value of equality? These are questions with obvious relevance for the hegemony theories and for the theories about an ideological apparatus of control being developed. But as a rule these theories are not rigorously tested within the Radical Structuralism paradigm. It should be possible to find at least some tentative answers to these questions by relating Eva Block's cultural indicators to parallel social and economic indicators.

The relationships between a cultural and ideological superstructure and other, more "basic" societal systems have been debated for centuries. Assuming a closed society, there are, in principle, four possibilities (Figure 2).

While the debates have been raging for a long time along the ideologically inflamed materialism/idealism axis, it would seem that during the last few years increasing attention has been given to the more realistic independence/interdependence axis. The increased use of cultural indicators in combination with economic and social indicators will spread further light on these intricate problems.

Most societies, however, are not closed, even if some societies do

		Other Societal Structures Influence Culture	
		Yes	No
Culture Influences Other Societal Structures	Yes	Interdependence	Idealism
	No	Marterialism	Autonomy

Figure 2. Four Types of Relationships between Culture and Other Societal Structures. (*Source:* Rosengren, 1981a).

build long, high walls around themselves (Imperial China for example). One should include the economic, political, and cultural environments of a society when theorizing about base/superstructure relationships. Partly in his study within CISSS, partly in other contexts, political scientist Kjell Goldmann (1979; Goldmann and Lagerkranz, 1977) measured the overall political tension in Europe during the postwar period, as well as the degree of polarization in the international political system. The results of these measurements have been related to the Swedish foreign policy debate and also to the data of other subprojects within CISSS (Goldman, 1982). These comparisons clearly show that arguments about the relationship between culture and other societal systems cannot be carried out in an international vacuum. The surrounding environment has an influence and must be heeded.

In another subproject within CISSS, communication researcher Kjell Nowak and philosopher Gunnar Andrén used content analysis of ads in weeklies as a basis for developing a number of cultural indicators, mainly within the economic sector of society. One of their interests concerned equality between the sexes, as manifested for instance in the proportions of the two sexes being economically active (gainfully employed). An outstanding characteristic of postwar Sweden (as of many other countries) has been a strong increase in the proportion of women gainfully employed. In the "society" to be found in the ads of the weeklies, however, the development has been precisely the opposite. The proportion of women gainfully employed shows a slow but steady downward trend (Nowak, 1982; Nowak and Andrén, 1982), a rather startling result to theoreticians of various schools speculating about the relationships between mass-mediated ideology and economic developments.

Several interpretations are possible, cultural independence being one ("autonomy" in terms of Figure 2). Another interpretation could be the speculation that the message of the symbolic environment in this case may actually have delayed the increase in the proportion of economically-active women ("idealism" in terms of Figure 2). However, such an interpretation is difficult to validate empirically, and hard to reconcile with extant theories. To be really convincing, therefore, this problem needs more data and further theoretical development, taking us quite a few steps beyond the rather simplistic hegemony hypothesis. This case illustrates well how the construction and application of cultural indicators—a methodological development undertaken in the dominant paradigm of communication research—may not only give empirical answers to questions raised within other paradigms, but also, hopefully, stimulate new theoretical developments within these paradigms—and within the dominant one.

MASS MEDIA USE

Common to any communication study is the fact that a host of circumstances interact in the communication process or structure under study, a fact which makes all research results contingent on the specific combination of circumstances at hand in the specific situation. The remedies used in the dominant paradigm against this predicament are mainly three: (a) experimental techniques (randomizing, various control designs, etc), (b) replication, and (c) multivariate statistical analysis of one sort or another. In mass communication research, the latter two are more commonly used than the former.

The Interpretative paradigm and the Radical Humanism paradigm as a rule turn to another basic strategy. Their ontology, anthropology, and epistemology lead them towards a *verstehen* approach. By means of empathy and subtle verbal analysis, they recreate as faithfully as possible the individual or systemic communication situation under study. In the paradigm of Radical Structuralism—subject to direct and indirect influences from both Radical Humanism and the dominant paradigm—one may find both strategies applied.

The advantage of the *verstehen* approach is that, if intelligently applied, it may result in brilliant verbal descriptions and analyses, striking the reader as having an inherent quality of obvious truth about them. The drawback is the lack of possibilities for precision, falsification, and replication. Any talented scholar can come up with a widely different interpretation, seemingly equally plausible. The criteria for choosing between the different interpretations are vague. In the multivariate analyses undertaken within the main paradigm, the possibilities for falsification and replication are at hand, but here the drawback has been the difficulty of including more than just a few variables in the analysis, a limitation which the less-formalized *verstehen* approach does not encounter. Each one of the two approaches, then, seems to have its own advantages and drawbacks, more or less balancing each other. During the last decade, however, this situation has changed. A major breakthrough has dramatically increased the power of multivariate statistical analysis.

LISREL and PLS

There are two main traditions in multivariate analysis, the factor analysis of psychology and the path analysis of genetics, economics, and sociology. The factor analysis tradition is concerned with relationships between manifest and latent variables. The path analysis tradition is concerned with relationships between manifest variables. For decades, the two traditions grew independently of each other, until about 1960, when a confluence occurred between the two. Once the confluence was established, further development was very rapid. It is no coincidence, probably, that a substantial part of this process took place in sociology, traditionally turning its janus face towards both micro social psychology and macro political economy (Mullins, 1975). Some very decisive steps, however, were taken at the Department of Statistics at the University of Uppsala, Sweden. Here K.G. Jöreskog and his associates developed the various versions of LISREL (Linear Structural Relations), while, somewhat later, H. Wold and his associates developed PLS (Partial Least Squares). Today, LISREL and PLS represent two main approaches for advanced multi-variate statistical analysis of large sets of manifest and latent variables by means of computer (Jöreskog and Sörbom, 1981; Jöreskog and Wold, 1982; Lohmöller, 1981). In the following section, the two approaches will be schematically presented from a layman's perspective.[8]

Both LISREL and PLS build upon the combination of a measurement, or "outer" model (corresponding to the factor analysis tradition), relating manifest indicators to latent variables, and a structural, or "inner" model (corresponding to the path analysis tradition), relating latent variables to each other. Both approaches build on large systems of equations representing the two types of models. In PLS, the equations are solved by iterations between the two models until the system converges into an optimal solution; LISREL solves the equations simultaneously. LISREL uses primarily the maximum likelihood approach; PLS, the least-squares approach. LISREL demands more assumptions about the original data, while on the other hand it squeezes out more information from them. LISREL is parameter-oriented; PLS, prediction-oriented. They thus complement each other nicely. Since at present PLS can handle a larger number of manifest and latent variables at a lower cost in computing time, while LISREL seems to have a greater capacity for precision in the analysis, it may be a good strategy to start with PLS for an overview analysis ("soft modeling"), and then to turn to LISREL for a more precise and detailed analysis (model testing and modification).

The end result of both PLS and LISREL are usually presented in graphic diagrams containing boxes representing manifest variables (test items, elements of a content analysis, etc), circles representing latent variables (attitudes, dimensions of texts, etc), and arrows representing "loadings" or "weights" of manifest variables on latent variables (the measurement model), as well as what are presumed to be causal relationships between latent variables (the structural model). The arrows correspond to cells in large matrices (originally covariance or correlation

---

[8]A detailed, critical exposition of LISREL and PLS is beyond the present chapter, but see Bentler (1980), Horn and McArdle (1980), and Knepel (1981).

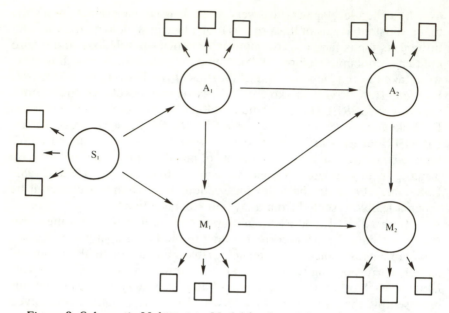

Figure 3. Schematic Multivariate Model for Social Origins and Effects of
    Mass Media Use

matrices of manifest variables), and each arrow can be given a coefficient
representing the loading of a given manifest variable on a given latent
variable (outer, measurement model), or the unique influence exerted by
one latent variable on another latent variable, when the influence from
all relevant variables in the model has been controlled for (inner, structural
model). From these coefficients in turn, the total (direct and indirect) influence exerted by one latent variable upon another latent variable can
be calculated.

Figure 3 presents a conceptual model of the LISREL or PLS type.
It is a relatively small dummy model without coefficients attached to the
arrows, intended as an illustration only (the designations of the latent variables will be explained and used below).

LISREL in particular has been extensively used in sociology and is
now entering adjacent disciplines such as psychology (Horn and McArdle,
1980), political science (Dalton, 1980), and communication studies (Gerbner and others, 1980; Hedinsson, 1981). PLS has been less extensively
used but may be entering its take-off stage. In a few cases PLS and LIS-
REL have been applied to the same original data set (Knepel, 1981, p.
166 ff; Lohmöller and Wold, 1982). While the two approaches offer no
panacaea for the social sciences (Huba and Bentler, 1982; Martin, 1982),
they do present us with new and powerful techniques of analysis. Their

capacity to handle simultaneously a large number of manifest and latent variables is very impressive.

I submit that these techniques will help bridge some of the gaps between the four paradigms of Figure 1. In a way acceptable to the dominant paradigm they make it possible to heed many more of the variables involved in a communication situation, a complexity that could formerly be handled only in the loose and intuitive way preferred by the Interpretative and Radical Humanism paradigms. Some highly interesting and provocative questions raised in the critical paradigms may thus be given answers that are falsifiable and replicable. An expanded version of the model sketched in Figure 3, complete with coefficients attached to the arrows of the (outer) measurements model and (inner) structural model, would represent a decisive step forward, adding precision, testability, and replicability to the vague but vital arguments of the critical schools. The first, more-or-less complete examples of such models have already been presented in mass communication research (Gerbner and others, 1980; Hedinsson, 1981, p. 170 ff), and there are more to come.

Uses and Gratifications

One broad problematic will be discussed: voluntarism vs. determinism; finality vs. causality. This general problematic will be discussed in terms of a specific mass communication research tradition, the uses and gratifications approach.

One level of the subjective/objective dimension of Burrell and Morgan's (1979) typology is represented by assumptions made about human nature: the anthropology, the "models of man" used in the various paradigms. Towards the subjectivistic end of the continuum a voluntaristic model predominates; towards the objectivistic end, a deterministic one. In terms of communication research the deterministic view corresponds to research carried out, for instance, in terms of more or less sophisticated S-R models, while the voluntaristic view to research is carried out, for instance, in terms of symbolic interactionism and the like. Both deterministic and voluntaristic elements of thought are blended in many otherwise rather different research traditions.

In much communication research of the last decade the deterministic view has been gradually complemented with more voluntaristic perspectives. A case at hand is the revived interest in uses and gratifications research (Blumler and Katz, 1974; Windahl, 1981). Partly in opposition to deterministic effects research, uses and gratifications research stresses the individual's capacity to consciously seek, find, and use mass media content fitting in with his/her more or less conscious needs, wants, and requirements. While uses and gratifications research has grown partly in opposition to the more naive variants of effects research, the need for a merger between effects versus uses and gratifications research has been stressed continually (Rosengren and Windahl, 1972; Windahl, 1981).

From a radical perspective, uses and gratifications research has been criticized for neglecting the social class perspective, the politico-economic framework which determines the individual's requirements and his/her way of satisfying them (Elliott, 1974). Uses and gratifications research has been criticized also from a humanistic perspective, strangely enough for overestimating the individual's capacity to express his/her wants and requirements, and his/her ways of satisfying them—the capacity, that is, to answer "yes", or "no", or "maybe" to a number of test items.[9]

By means of their capacity to simultaneously handle a large number of manifest and latent variables, LISREL and PLS are capable of taking care of much of the criticism of the uses and gratifications approach discussed above. The influence of social class may be taken care of either by introducing variables such as income, occupational status, and education, as control variables in the models, or by comparing with each other different models for different social classes, a comparison which LISREL can carry out in a formalized way. The humanist questioning of the individual's capacity for expressing his/her wants and requirements as well as his/her way of satisfying them is taken care of by the measurement model. The weight or loading coefficients can express the degree to which the manifest variables (test items, various questions about gratifications sought and obtained, etc.) are able to express the variation in the latent variables (the attitude, the gratifications sought or obtained, etc.). The capacities of these powerful techniques become especially intriguing when applied to panel data. The combined use of panel data and LISREL and/or PLS will throw new light on the discussion about effects and/or uses and gratifications research, and more generally, on the basic opposition between a voluntaristic and a deterministic perspective.

Uses and gratifications research hypothesizes that the mass media fulfill a number of functions for the individual using them. Somehow the individual senses his/her needs, wants, requirements, and desires, and gets motivated to satisfy them by means of mass media use. It is the task of uses and gratifications research to describe and explain that process as clearly as possible, a finalistic approach based on a voluntaristic perspective. Effects research, on the other hand, hypothesizes that mass media consumption affects the individual indulging in it, more or less irrespective of the motives behind the consumption; this is at bottom a causal approach based on a deterministic perspective.

------

[9]Swanson (1977) provides an overview of criticism directed against uses and gratifications research.

A conceptual model of the type exemplified in Figure 3, in combination with relevant data, helps us realize that both perspectives (media effects versus uses and gratification) may be valid, an insight which immediately calls forward questions about the conditions under which they are valid, and to what extent. In the context of mass media use, it would seem reasonable to hypothesize that a finalistic, voluntaristic perspective is valid primarily in the short run (as might be operationalized in a cross-sectional design while a causal, deterministic perspective is valid primarily in the long or semi-long run (operationalized in a longitudinal design). An empirical LISREL and/or PLS model of the type illustrated in Figure 3 enables us to take a step forward towards the solution of the problem of voluntarism and determinism in the study of media use and effects.

In Figure 3, let circles M_1 and M_2 represent mass media use by the same individuals on two different occasions, and circles A_1 and A_2 some hypothesized correlates of that use (alienation, aggressiveness, an attitude, etc.). Circle S_1 represents a control variable, say socioeconomic status or social class position. The squares in Figure 3 represent manifest measurements related to the latent variables—in this context test items, questions about media use, social class position, and the like.

A uses and gratifications approach would concentrate primarily on the arrows pointing from A to M, while an effects approach would concentrate its interest primarily on the arrow pointing from M to A. The model, then, visualizes the hypothesis that cross-sectionally, in the short run, a voluntaristic perspective would be valid (attitudes, motives, etc. lead to mass media use), while longitudinally, in the long or semi-long run, a deterministic perspective would be valid (mass media use will affect attitudes, beliefs, etc.).[10] The relative role played by the two perspectives will be indicated by the path coefficients attached to the various arrows in the model. The arrows from S represent influence from social class, while the horizontal arrows depict the stability of attitudes and media behavior.

Given a number of models of the kind exemplified in a schematic way in Figure 3, we will know more about the determining effect of social class position on media use and its effects, more about the relative role to be played by a voluntaristic and a deterministic perspective when trying to understand short-term reasons for, and long-term effects of, mass media use. LISREL and/or PLS will help us to integrate, in a combined cross-sectional and longitudinal design, uses and gratifications with effects.

---

[10]In fact, this hypothesis represents an old tenet in mass communication research, that of reinforcement.

The Swedish Media Panel Program

Figure 4 illustrates the present argument. It is a section of a large LISREL model, built on a previous PLS model. The full model will be presented in a doctoral thesis by Keith Roe (forthcoming), to appear in a series of reports from the Media Panel Program (University of Lund) covering the social origins and effects of the media use of children and adolescents from ages 6 to 15 (Flodin and others, 1982; Hedinsson, 1981, Johnsson-Smaragdi, forthcoming; Rosengren and Windahl, 1978; and Sonesson, 1979). The model is a three-wave panel model for the relationship between parent/peer orientation and the use of popular music by boys at the ages of 11, 13, and 15. Parent/peer orientation is an attitudinal variable; popular music, a behavioral variable. Peer orientation and pop music are hypothesized to "go together", with empirical research testing

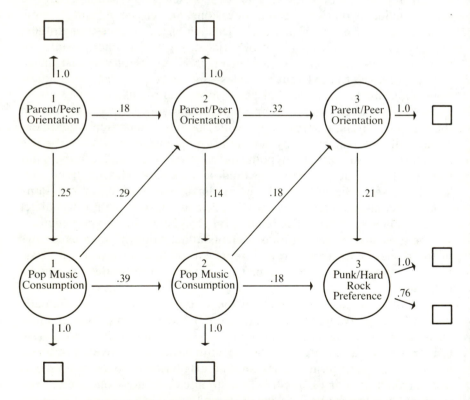

Figure 4. Relationship between Male Adolescents' Parent/Peer
Orientation and Pop Music Use: A Longitudinal Model with
Three Time Points*

* Section of a larger model with 18 latent and 31 manifest variables: Unstandardized solution. X^2 for whole model 372 with 248 df (p = .18; N = 93).

the relationship. The manifest variables of parent/peer orientation and pop music consumption consist of an index and a single question, respectively, while the latent variable of preference for, and knowledge about, punk and hard rock, builds on two items chosen as the constituents of a latent variable (by a factor analysis of a larger number of items). The model thus only suggests the many possibilities of combining manifest variables into latent ones, inherent in the LISREL and PLS techniques. It clearly demonstrates, however, the possibilities of the two techniques—when applied to panel data—to accommodate the "voluntaristic" and "deterministic" perspectives in one and the same model.

Before starting to unravel the process of reinforcement visualized in Figure 4, it should be mentioned that social class exerts no direct influence on either parent/peer orientation or on pop music use and thus is not included in the figure. It does have a strong influence on school achievement and school commitment, however, both of which, in turn, influence, in a complicated way, parent/peer orientation and/or pop music use.

Figure 4 shows that at *time 1* adolescents' degree of peer-orientation exerts a cross-sectional influence on their amount of popular music consumption. Such consumption, in turn, strengthens the degree of peer-orientation at *time 2*, which, again cross-sectionally, leads to more pop consumption, again strengthening peer orientation at *time 3*. So voluntaristic and deterministic processes succeed each other cyclically over time. The "last" variable in the figure is a preference variable, supposedly tapping both attitudinal and behavioral aspects of the use of popular music. The arrows leading up to it suggest that an early use of rather conventional popular music has a tendency to end, through a reinforcement process together with parent/peer orientation, in a preference for, and expertise in, punk and hard rock—the traditions within popular music most detested and despised by the parents.

The process is one of reinforcement. The stability coefficients are relatively low, due to the truly radical upheavals that boys undergo from ages 11 to 15, upheavals which are indeed one of the raisons-d'être for the Media Panel Program in Sweden. In spite of the low stability, the strength of the reinforcement process (as indicated by the coefficients attached to the arrows running between parent/peer orientation and pop music) is considerable. The total, indirect and direct, influence exerted on "parent/peer orientation" by "pop music" adds up to .33, while the total influence in the other direction totals .35. Paradoxically reinforcement processes may be quite strong in spite of low stability. "Reinforcement" may actually result in "change"—in this case from conventional pop music to outlandish punk.

Overall, Figure 4 gives support to the hypothesis that the voluntaristic perspective is valid primarily in the short run, and the deterministic perspective primarily in the long run. However, the opposite combination may exist (the deterministic perspective cross-sectionally, etc.). Indeed, the Swedish Media Panel Program provides data also illustrating that possibility. In this specific case, however, the data tell us the best way of conceptualizing the relationship between the two perspectives (as depicted in Figure 4).

The task of ascertaining under what circumstances this or that combination of the voluntaristic and the deterministic perspective prevails, offers a stimulating challenge to mass communication research. Figure 4 shows that it is possible to accept the challenge. There are good opportunities in the near future to integrate in one study a voluntaristic perspective with a deterministic viewpoint. Finality and causality may be compared. This approach to research will probably affect the relationships between the four paradigms of Burrell and Morgan's typology. Important questions raised within the two radical paradigms can be given answers in a way acceptable to the dominant paradigm.

TOWARD ONE PARADIGM FOR COMMUNICATION RESEARCH

The starting point of this chapter was the observation that the field of communication studies may be fragmented into a number of rival sects. In order to counteract this risk, it is mandatory that we—the workers in the field—realize the situation and get an overview of its main characteristics. The fourfold typology for schools of sociology presented by Burrell and Morgan (1979) can serve as an instrument of clarification. Based on the two dimensions of subjectivism/objectivism, and regulation/radical change, the typology presents us with four main paradigms called by Burrell and Morgan: Functionalist, Interpretive, Radical Humanism, and Radical Structuralism. The three latter paradigms are here called the "dissident paradigms", while the first was called the "dominant paradigm".

Important aspects of the present situation—as well as its history—in the field of communication research can be conceptualized in terms of the typology and its four main paradigms. The polemics raging between adherents of the various paradigms is paradoxical: The three dissident paradigms have raised important questions but, by and large, have been unable to provide any answers. The dominant paradigm, however, could answer the questions, but, by and large, has not raised them.

Three cases illustrating the paradox have been offered: the study of mass media news, the study of communication and culture, and the study of the social origins and effects of mass media use. In all three cases it was shown that methodological developments in the dominant paradigm made it possible to find answers to important questions raised by the dissident paradigms (and often also in the dominant paradigm). The methodological developments ranged in generality from a specific distinction in news research (intra/extra-media data), to a general type of measurement in the study of culture (cultural indicators), to a major breakthrough in advanced multivariate analysis (represented by LISREL and PLS).

The fact that questions raised in one paradigm of the Burrell-Morgan typology can be given answers in another of its paradigms raises some doubts as to whether what we have is really four different paradigms in the strong sense of the word. Are the demarcation lines between the four cells of the typology really as absolute as their authors (and many others) would have it (Burrell and Morgan, 1979, p. 19)?

The dimensions of the typology are highly relevant, and the typology represents a heuristically fruitful device when overviewing much social research of today, including communication research. But it would seem that the two dimensions should to advantage be conceptualized as continua, rather than as discrete variables.

The regulation/radical change dimension in particular does not build upon basically different ontological and/or epistemological assumptions. This dimension is more politically than scientifically valid, mistaking hopes, wishes, and fears for basic assumptions about actually-existing traits of society. The subjectivist dimension, on the other hand, builds more directly upon basic differences in ontology and epistemology. A truly subjective perspective, however, is very difficult to combine with any kind of serious scientific activity: The more extreme variants of existentialism and phenomenology have flourished mainly in literature and non-academic philosophy. There may be a qualitative gap somewhere on the subjectivist/objectivist continuum, but this gap should be located "more to the left" than is implied by the Burrell-Morgan (1979) typology.

If the dimensions of this typology can be regarded as continua, then the general situation in the field of communication research may be characterized as one of pseudoconflicts. From a somewhat different perspective, Kurt Lang (1979) arrived at much the same conclusion. Nevertheless, part of the conflicts concern scientifically valid and relevant questions. Contrary to what is often maintained, however, these conflicts are not always insolvable. Several of the basic assumptions of the paradigms can be formulated as empirically-answerable questions about conditions in actually existing societies, and the fact that some of these questions or hypotheses have their origin in one research tradition and their answer in another should not prevent the community of communication scholars from addressing them seriously and open-mindedly. However, such a feat is more easily said than done.

The main hindrance to such movement probably is the interest which leading representatives of rival schools have vested in demonstrating to themselves, to their followers, and to their opponents that somehow they are radically different. In the long run, however, such claims cannot hold their own against empirical evidence. It is a very positive sign indeed that an increased tendency to empirical investigations has made itself felt during the last few years within the three dissident paradigms (or pseudo-paradigms), especially within Radical Structuralism. To the extent that the same problematics are empirically studied by members of various schools, the present sharp differences of opinion will gradually diminish and be replaced by a growing convergence of perspectives. This chapter presented three examples of such problematics. There are many more around, to be found by those who think that provocative questions deserve sound empirical answers.

Thus there is a strong possibility that ferment in the field of communication research will be replaced by vigorous growth.

REFERENCES

E. Allardt (1975), *Att ha, att älska, att vara,* Lund, Sweden: Argos.

E. Allardt (1981) "Experiences from the Comparative Scandinavian Welfare Study: With a Bibliography of the Project." *European Journal of Political Research, 9,* 101–111.

F.M. Andrews and R.F. Inglehart (1976), "The Structure of Subjective Well-Being in Nine Western Societies," *Social Indicators Research,* 73–90.

K.D. Bailey (1973), "Monothetic and Polythetic Typologies and Their Relation to Conceptualization, Measurement, and Scaling," *American Sociological Review, 38,* 18–33.

R.A. Bauer (ed.) (1969), *Social Indicators,* Cambridge, MA: M.I.T. Press.

Ph. Bénéton (1978), "Les Frustrations de l'Égalité," *Archives Européennes de Sociologie, 19,* 74–140.

P.M. Bentler (1980), "Multivariate Analysis with Latent Variables: Causal Modeling," *Annual Review of Psychology, 31,* 419–456.

Eva Block (1982), "Freedom, Equality, Etcetera: Values and Valuations in the Swedish Domestic Political Debate, 1945–1975," in G. Melischek, K.E. Rosengren, and J. Stappers (eds.), *Cultural Indicators: An International Symposium,* Vienna, Austria: Akademie der Wissenschaften.

Per Block (1982), "Newspaper Content as a Secularization Indicator," in G. Melischek, K.E. Rosengren and J. Stappers (eds.), *Cultural Indicators: An International Symposium,* Vienna, Austria: Akademie der Wissenschaften.

Jay G. Blumler (1982), "Mass Communication Research in Europe: Some Origins and Prospects," *Mass Communication Review Yearbook, 2,* 37–49.

Jay G. Blumler and Elihu Katz (eds.) (1974), *The Uses of Mass Communications,* Beverly Hills, CA: Sage.

Gibson Burrell and Gareth Morgan (1979), *Sociological Paradigms and Organizational Analysis,* London, Heinemann.

M.V. Charnley (1936), "Preliminary Notes on a Study of Newspaper Accuracy." *Journalism Quarterly, 44,* 482–490.

C. Cioffi-Revilla and Richard L. Merritt (1982), "Communication Research and the New World Information Order," *Journal of International Affairs, 35,* 225–246.

R. Collins (1982), *Sociology Since Midcentury*, New York, Academic Press.

J.M. Curran, M. Gurevitch, and J. Wollacott (1982), "The Study of the Media: Theoretical Approaches," in M. Gurevitch and others (eds.), *Culture, Society and the Media*, London: Methuen.

R.J. Dalton (1980), "Reassessing Parental Socialization: Indicator Unreliability Versus Generational Transfer," *American Political Science Review*, 74, 421–431.

O.D. Duncan (1975), "Does Money Buy Satisfaction?" *Social Indicators Research*, 2, 267–274.

R.A. Easterlin (1973), "Does Money Buy Happiness?" *The Public Interest*, 73 (30), 3–10.

Alex S. Edelstein (1981), *Comparative Communication Research*, Beverly Hills, CA: Sage.

Philip Elliott (1974) "Uses and Gratifications Research: A Critique and a Sociological Alternative," in Jay G. Blumler and Elihu Katz (eds.), *The Uses of Mass Communication*, Beverly Hills, CA: Sage.

Richard Fitchen (1981), "European Research," in Daniel D. Nimmo and Keith R. Sanders (eds.), *Handbook of Political Communication*, Beverly Hills, CA: Sage.

B. Flodin, E. Hedinsson and K. Roe (1982), "Primary School Panel: A Descriptive Report," Lund, Sweden, University of Lund, Dept of Sociology, Media Panel Program Report 17.

George Gerbner (1969), "Toward 'Cultural Indicators': The Analysis of Mass Mediated Public Message Systems," *AV Communication Review*, 17, 137–148.

George Gerbner and others (1980), "The Mainstreaming of America: Violence Profile No. 11," *Journal of Communication*, 30 (3), 10–29.

George Gerbner and others (1981), "Final Reply to Hirsch," *Communication Research*, 8, 259–280.

Todd Gitlin (1981), "Media Sociology: The Dominant Paradigm," *Mass Communication Review Yearbook*, 2, 73–121.

K. Goldmann (1979), *Is My Enemy's Enemy My Friend's Friend?* Lund, Sweden: Student-Litteratur.

K. Goldmann (1982), "World Politics and Domestic Culture: Sweden, 1950–1975," in G. Melischek, K.E. Rosengren, and J. Stappers (eds.), *Cultural Indicators: An International Symposium*, Vienna, Austria; Akademie der Wissenschaften.

K. Goldmann and J. Lagerkranz (1977), "Neither Tension Nor Détente: East-West Relations in Europe, 1971–1975," *Cooperation and Conflict*, 12, 251–264.

James Halloran and others (1970), *Demonstrations and Communication: A Case Study*, Harmondsworth, England: Penguin.

E. Hedinsson (1981), *TV, Family, and Society*, Stockholm, Sweden: Almqvist & Wiksell International.

R.G. Hicks and A. Gordon (1974), "Foreign News Content in Israeli and U.S. Newspapers," *Journalism Quarterly*, 51, 639–644.

Paul M. Hirsch (1980), "The Scary World of the Nonviewer and Other Anomalies," *Communication Research*, 7, 403–456.

L. Höglund (1982), "Om Kommunikation och Välfärd," *Nordicom-Information*, 19–25.

J.L. Horn and J.J. McArdle (1980), "Perspectives on Mathematical/Statistical Model Building (MASMOB) in Research on Aging," in L.W. Poon (ed.), *Aging in the 1980's: Psychological Issues*, Washington, DC: APA.

G.J. Huba and P.M. Bentler (1982), "On the Usefulness of Latent Variable Causal Modeling: A Rejoinder to Martin," *Journal of Personality and Social Psychology*, 43, 604–611.

M. Hughes (1980), "The Fruits-of-Cultivation Analysis: A Reexamination of Some Effects of Television Watching," *Public Opinion Quarterly*, 44, 287–302.

R. Inglehart (1977), *The Silent Revolution: Changing Values and Political Styles among Western Publics*, Princeton, NJ: Princeton University Press.

Alex Inkeles and L. Diamond (1980), "Personal Development and National Development: A Cross-National Perspective," in A. Szalai and F.M. Andrews (eds.), *The Quality of Life: Comparative Studies*, Beverly Hills, CA: Sage.

U. Johnsson-Smaragdi (forthcoming), *Adolescents' TV Use: A Longitudinal Study.*

K.G. Jöreskog and D. Sörbom (1981), *LISREL V: Analysis of Linear Structural Relationships by Maximum Likelihood and Least Squares Methods*, Uppsala, Sweden: University of Uppsala, Department of Statistics.

K.G. Jöreskog and H. Wold (eds.) (1982), *Systems under Indirect Observation: Causality, Structure, Prediction*, Amsterdam, North Holland.

H. Knepel (1982), *Sozioökonomische Indikatormodelle zur Arbeitsmarktanalyse*, Frankfurt, Germany: Campus.

A.L. Kroeber and C. Kluckhohn (1952), *Culture: A Critical Review of Concepts and Definitions*, Cambridge, MA: Harvard University, Peabody Museum of American Archeology and Ethnology Paper 47.

A.L. Kroeber and T. Parsons (1958), "The Concepts of Culture and of Social System." *American Sociological Review, 23,* 582–583.

Kurt Lang (1979), "The Critical Functions of Empirical Communication Research: Observations on German-American Influences," *Media, Culture and Society, 1,* 83–96.

Kurt Lang and Gladys G.E. Lang (1953), "The Unique Perspective of Television and Its Effects," *American Sociological Review, 18,* 3–12.

Harold D. Lasswell and J.Z. Namenwirth (1968), *The Lasswell Value Dictionary, Three Volumes*, New Haven, CT.

H.L. Lewis (1960), "The Cuban Revolt Story: AP, UPI, and 3 Papers," *Journalism Quarterly, 37, 573–578.*

Walter Lippmann and C. Merz (August 4, 1920), "A Test of the News," *The New Republic.*

J.B. Lohmöller (1981), *LVPLS 1.6. Program Manual: Latent Variables Path Analysis with Partial Least Squares Estimation*, Munich, Germany: Hochschule der Bundeswehr.

J.G. Lohmöller and H. Wold (1982), "Introduction to PLS Estimation of Path Models with Latent Variables, Including Some Recent Developments in Mixed Scales Variables," in G. Melischek, K.E. Rosengren, and J. Stappers (eds.), *Cultural Indicators. An International Symposium*, Vienna, Austria: Akademie der Wissenschaften.

Leo Lowenthal (1961), *Literature, Popular Culture, and Society*, Englewood Cliffs, NJ: Prentice-Hall.

J.A. Martin (1982), "Application of Structural Modeling with Latent Variables to Adolescent Drug Use," *Journal of Personality and Social Psychology, 43,* 598–603.

David C. McClelland (1961), *The Achieving Society*, New York: Irvington.

David C. McClelland (1975a), *Power: The Inner Experience*, New York: Irvington.

David C. McClelland (1975b), "Love and Power: The Psychological Signals of War," *Psychology Today,* 45–48.

G. Melischek, K.E. Rosengren, and J. Stappers (eds.) (1982), *Cultural Indicators: An International Symposium*, Vienna, Austria; Akademie der Wissenshaften.

Robert K. Merton, and Alice S. Kitt (1950), "Contributions to the Theory of Reference Group Behavior," in Robert K. Merton and Paul F. Lazarsfeld (eds.), *Continuities in Social Research: Studies in the Scope and Method of the American Soldier*, Glencoe, IL: Free Press.

Nicholas C. Mullins (1975), "New Causal Theory: An Elite Specialty in Social Science," *History of Political Economy, 7,* 499–529.

J.Z. Namenwirth (1973), "Wheels of Time and Interdependence of Value Change in America," *Journal of Interdisciplinary History, 3,* 649–683.

Daniel D. Nimmo and Keith R. Sanders (1981), "Conclusion: Constructing the Realities of a Pluralistic Field," in D.D. Nimmo and K.R. Sanders (eds.), *Handbook of Political Communication*, Beverly Hills, CA: Sage.

T. Nnaemeka and J. Richstad (1981), "Internal Controls and Foreign News Coverage: Pacific Press Systems," *Communication Research, 8,* 97–135.

K. Nowak (1982), "Cultural Indicators in Swedish Advertising, 1950–1975," in G. Melischek, K.E. Rosengren, and J. Stappers (eds.), *Cultural Indicators: An International Symposium,* Vienna, Austria: Akademie der Wissenschaften.

K. Nowak and G. Andrén (1982), *Reklam och samhällsförändring*, Lund, Sweden, Student-Litteratur.

C. Ogburn (1933), *Recent Social Trends in the United States, Volumes I–II,* New York, McGraw-Hill.

J. Owen (1957), "The Polls and Newspaper Appraisal of the Suez Crisis."

J. Rex (1978), "Threatening Theories," *Society, 15* (3), 46–49.

G. Ritzer (1975), *Sociology: A Multiple Paradigm Society,* Boston, MA: Allyn and Bacon.

G.J. Robinson and V.M. Sparkers (1976), "International News in the Canadian and American Press: A Comparative News Flow Study," *Gazette, 22,* 203–218.

Keith Roe (forthcoming), *Mass Media and Adolescent Schooling: Conflict or Co-existence?*

Everett M. Rogers (1982), "The Empirical and the Critical Schools of Communication Research," *Communication Yearbook 5,* New Brunswick, NJ: Transaction.

Milton Rokeach (1973), *The Nature of Human Values,* New York: Free Press.

Milton Rokeach (1974), "Change and Stability in American Value Systems 1968–1971," *Public Opinion Quarterly, 38,* 222–238.

Milton Rokeach (ed.) (1979), *Understanding Human Values,* New York: Free Press.

Karl Erik Rosengren (1968), *Sociological Aspects of the Literary System,* Stockholm, Sweden: Natur och Kultur.

Karl Erik Rosengren (1970), "International News: Intra and Extra Media Data," *Acta Sociologica, 13,* 96–109.

Karl Erik Rosengren (1974) "International News: Methods, Data and Theory," *Journal of Peace Research, 11,* 145–156.

Karl Erik Rosengren (1977) "International News: Four Types of Tables," *Journal of Communication, 27,* 67–75.

Karl Erik Rosengren (1979), "Bias in News: Methods and Concepts," *Studies of Broadcasting, 15,* 31–45.

Karl Erik Rosengren (1981a), "Mass Media and Social Change: Some Current Approaches," in Elihu Katz and Tomas Szecskö (eds.), *Mass Media and Social Change,* London: Sage.

Karl Erik Rosengren (1981b), "Measurement of Invariance and Change in the Literary Milieu: Sweden in the 1880's and the 1960's," *Zeitschrift für Literatur-wissenschaft und Linguistik, Beiheft 12: Literaturwissenschaft und Empirische Methoden,* 52–73.

Karl Erik Rosengren (1981c), "Mass Communication as Cultural Indicators: Sweden, 1945–1975," *Mass Communication Review Yearbook, 2,* 717–737.

Karl Erik Rosengren and S. Windahl (1972), "Mass Media Consumption as a Functional Alternative," in D. McQuail (ed.), *Sociology of Mass Communications.*

Karl Erik Rosengren and S. Windahl (1978), "Media Panel: A Presentation of a Program," Lund, Sweden, University of Lund, Department of Sociology, Media Panel Report 4, (mimeo).

Karl Erik Rosengren and others (1975), "The Barsebäck 'Panic': A Radio Programme as a Negative Summary Event," *Acta Sociologica, 18,* 303–321.

T. J. Scanlon (1972), "A New Approach to the Study of Newspaper Accuracy," *Journalism Quarterly, 49,* 588–590.

Wilbur Schramm (1980), "The Beginnings of Communication Study in the United States," *Communication Yearbook 4*, New Brunswick, NJ: Transaction.

W. Schulz (1976), *Die Konstruktion von Realität in den Nachrichtenmedien*, Munich, West Germany: Alber.

J.F. Short (1982), *The State of Sociology*, London: Sage.

H. Small (1979), "Co-Citation in the Scientific Literature: A New Measure of Relationship Between Two Documents," *Journal of the American Society for Information Science*, *24*, 265–269.

R.F. Smith (1971), "U.S. News and Sino-Indian Relations: An Extra Media Study," *Journalism Quarterly*, *48*, 447–458, 501.

I. Sonesson (1979), *Förskolebarn och TV:* (Pre-School Children and TV: With an English Summary), Stockholm, Sweden: Scandinavian University Books.

Pitirim Sorokin (1937–1941), *Social and Cultural Dynamics, Volumes, 1–4*, London: Allen & Unwin.

R.L. Stevenson, R.R. Cole, and D.L. Shaw (1980), "Patterns of World News Coverge: A Look at the Unesco Debate on the 'New World Information Order'," Chapel Hill, University of North Carolina.

B. Stipak, "Are There Sensible Ways to Analyze and Use Subjective Indicators of Urban Service Quality?" *Social Indicators Research*, *6*, 421–438.

D.L. Swanson (1977), "The Uses and Mis-Uses of Uses and Gratifications," *Human Communication Research*, *3*, 214–221.

E.B. Tylor (1871), *Primitive Culture*, Cloucester, MA: Smith.

E. Vermeersch (1971), "An Analysis of the Concept of Culture," in B. Bernardi (ed.), *The Concept and Dynamics of Culture*, The Hague, Netherlands: Mouton.

I.M. Wasserman and L.A. Chua (1980) "Objective and Subjective Social Indicators of the Quality of Life in American SMSA's: A Re-Analysis," *Social Indicators Research*, *8*, 365–381.

H.D. White and B.C. Griffith (1981), "Author Co-Citation: A Literature Measure of Intellectual Structure," *Journal of American Society for Information Science*, *26*, 163–171.

S. Windahl (1981), "Uses and Gratifications at the Crossroads," *Mass Communication Review Yearbook 2*, Beverley Hills, CA: Sage.

W. Zapf (1976), "Systems of Social Indicators: Current Approaches and Problems" *International Social Science Journal*, *27*, 479–498.

Chapter 16

The Beginnings of Political Communication Research in the United States: Origins of the "Limited Effects" Model[1]

Steven H. Chaffee
Stanford University

John L. Hochheimer
University of Iowa

INTRODUCTION

The intellectual history of U.S. political communication research is traced from its origins in the 1940 Erie County study by Paul F. Lazarsfeld and his colleagues at Columbia University, through the more psychological studies of voting centered for many years at the University of Michigan, to the contemporary era of studies by mass communication researchers. The Columbia studies created an image of the limited effects of the mass media on voting behavior, a paradigm taken over more broadly by communication scholars. Chaffee and Hochheimer argue that empirical support from the Columbia studies for the limited effects model was problematic, and was mainly a result of the studies' design and conduct, and the assumptions upon which they were based. The Michigan researches on voting during the late 1950s and 1960s largely relegated the mass media to a minor role. It was not until the late 1960s, when scholars trained in mass communication research began to engage in studies of political behavior, that the limited effects model began to be seriously questioned.   *E.M.R, F.B.*

The basic paradigm for research into the roles of mass communication in political processes has remained largely intact since the earliest major studies conducted in the United States (Lazarsfeld and others, 1944; Berelson and others, 1954). This paradigm projects an image of the "limited effects" of the mass media in the context of election campaigns, an expectation that has had profound influences on the conduct of research on mass communication in Europe as well as in the U.S., in the four ensuing decades. It has also had a considerable influence on public policy, particularly in defending new communication technologies (e.g., television) from governmental regulation or control in the United States. The argument that media need not be controlled because they have only minimal

---

[1]Portions of this chapter were presented in earlier papers delivered to the German Association for Journalism and Communication Research at Münster, Federal Republic of Germany, in 1982; and to the International Communication Association convention at Dallas, in 1983.

political and social impact has been continually reasserted by the broadcasting industry. The now-venerable research on which this argument rests has rarely been subjected to fresh academic scrutiny.

Because the original studies were highly empirical, the analysis of media "effects" has long been regarded as the essence of empirical mass communication research, despite a growing body of work on media uses (e.g., Blumler and McQuail, 1969; Blumler and Katz, 1974), media institutions (e.g., Ettema and Whitney, 1982), working norms of the press (e.g., Tuchman; 1978, Schudson, 1978), and other non-effects themes. Because the early investigators brought a "marketing" orientation to the problem of politics, effects were sought that would take the form of "selling" one candidate or party in preference to another; only to the extent that a medium displayed a strong bias in favor of one side, and then only to the extent that this bias was reflected in the votes of that medium's audience, would more than "limited" effects be imputed to mass communication. Because, as Gitlin (1978) has pointed out, the field of marketing treats all topics of media manipulation homogeneously, it was assumed that what had been found (or not found) for politics would hold more or less equally for other topics, and vice versa (Katz and Lazarsfeld, 1955; Berelson and Steiner, 1964); thus the idea of "limited effects" was extended to the entire range of mass communication (Klapper, 1960).

While current scholars have been expanding the realm of communication research, rewriting much of "what we know" about the importance of mass media, it is essential as we approach a new era in communication technology to reexamine not only the earliest studies but also the assumptions that lay behind them. These basic assumptions, which remain with us to a great extent today, included the following:

1. That the act of voting is a consumer decision equivalent to the purchase of a product in the marketplace. From this assumption comes the definition of "political communication" as a message or campaign that effects a change in people's evaluations of candidates for office. In short, political communication is viewed as a marketing phenomenon, and research on this topic can be interpreted in terms of the study of a marketing problem.
2. That politics and communication can be assessed in contrast to an idealized system, in which all people should be concerned, cognizant, rational, and accepting of the political system, and in which the institutions of communication should be comprehensive, accurate, and scrupulously fair and politically balanced. This kind of assumption grew naturally from the use of "ideal types" in sociological theorizing of the 1930s and 1940s. Imagined ideal behaviors and systems were useful, in the absence of comparative

data, in that they provided a standard for interpretation of empirical observations in early studies.

3. That communication and politics are appropriately viewed from the top or power center rather than from the bottom or periphery of the system. The role of the media was conceived in terms of their effects, what they might do to people, rather than what people might be doing with the media (or without them). Politics was examined in terms of the needs of the political system, in particular the electoral component of that system, and from the perspective of political elites. These media-centric and elite-oriented approaches were quite congenial to the people conducting the studies and the funding sources that supported them.

4. That the processes involved in political communication are approximately equivalent across time and space. There was in the 1940s a growing appetite within social science for theoretical generalizations, broad conclusions about relationships between extensive variables, which were assumed to hold regardless of the empirical boundaries of a particular study. Gradually it was to be recognized that the field would have to settle for "theories of the middle range" (Merton, 1957), but at the beginning the method was to assert a proposition in as general a way as possible. The task of demonstrating the limits beyond which a statement would no longer hold was implicitly left to future research.

THE LAZARSFELD TRADITION

These intellectual assumptions and perspectives were brought into the communication research field most forcefully by the work of Paul F. Lazarsfeld of Columbia University. While they would not be accepted by many researchers today, the original studies based upon them are still treated as benchmarks against which contemporary research is to be compared. These early studies are the main object of our attention here.

In 1940 Lazarsfeld undertook his landmark study of the determinants of voting in the U.S. presidential election campaign (Lazarsfeld and others, 1944). Together with a follow-up study in the 1948 campaign (Berelson and others, 1954), these were the first major election studies to give concentrated attention to the role of the mass media—and also virtually the last for many years thereafter. The limited range of impact ascribed to the media in the Lazarsfeld studies so impressed itself on the minds of most social scientists that the general question of media "effects" on politics was not reopened until about ten years ago. Recently there has been a new flowering of research exploring the role of mass communication in political processes, breaking out of the mold established by Lazarsfeld in a number of ways. But, to a remarkable extent, most of the assumptions of the original studies continue to structure current research.

There have been, to be sure, studies of the media-election nexus that do not fit clearly into this analysis. Some refreshingly new research directions have been taken, and a number of *ad hoc* studies of particular elections across the years have been reported without reference to Lazarsfeld's original work. Journalists have also written a great deal about the role of mass media in politics, typically in ignorance of any empirical research on the topic. Still, the impact of the early studies on today's researchers remains pervasive. A fair measure is the recent *Handbook of Political Communication* (Nimmo and Sanders, 1981). A quick count of entries in the index to this comprehensive volume reveals that Lazarsfeld and Berelson both are cited in more than 40 locations; almost all of these references are to their 1940 and 1948 election studies. A recent analysis of citation networks in *Journalism Quarterly* (Tankard and others, 1982) suggests that those two monographs are the "classics of the field", along with Klapper's (1960) synthesis of the limited effects model.

A MARKETING ORIENTATION

The marketing orientation to research has been so intimately intertwined with much of communication research that it would seem inseparable to many scholars. The search for "effects" of the media stems from the concern of producers of goods to sell their products through the use of advertising, product and packaging design, pricing decisions, and so forth. The most effective marketing is that which realizes the largest increases in sales (i.e., positively influences the buying behavior of the largest segment of the target population). The "effect" of the media is then seen as the intervening factor that induces a more favorable perception of the product being marketed.

The focus of research, in this approach, is to differentiate factors characteristic of people, messages, and media to see where the most effective implementation of marketing techniques might be made. Lazarsfeld's training and basic research orientation made him a pioneering scholar in this burgeoning field.

Although he became known in the U.S. as a member of the sociology faculty at Columbia, Lazarsfeld's basic academic orientation was to the psychology of marketing. In a biographical note to a methodological article in *The National Marketing Review* (Lazarsfeld, 1935), he is described as "a member of the Department of Psychology of the University of Vienna who has been interested in applying psychological principles to the field of marketing research," having "conducted numerous marketing surveys in Europe" and more recently having "tested his principles in the laboratory of American marketing research,"[2] His interest in voting as an example of a consumer decision is evident in his early article. His concern with media came a bit later, in the famous radio audience analyses that he conducted with Frank Stanton, later President of the Columbia Broadcasting System (Lazarsfeld and Stanton, 1942). The 1940 election study was planned as an assessment of the influence of the media on the vote, although when they came to writing up the report the evidence of media impact was considered weak enough that the purpose was broadened to that of discovering "how and why people decided to vote as they did" (Lazarsfeld and others, 1944, p. 1).

THE ERIE COUNTY STUDY

For their 1940 election survey, Lazarsfeld and his associates chose Erie County, Ohio, the center of which is the small city of Sandusky. Their panel design was described in *The People's Choice*, the slim (178 pages) monograph in which they reported their findings:

> Erie County, Ohio . . . was chosen because it was small enough to permit close supervision of the interviewers, because it was relatively free from sectional peculiarities, because it was not dominated by any large urban center although it did furnish an opportunity to compare rural political opinion with opinion in a small urban center, and because for forty years—in every presidential election in the twentieth century—it had deviated very little from national voting trends.

> In May, 1940, every fourth house in Erie County was visited by a member of the staff of from twelve to fifteen specially-trained local interviewers, chiefly women. In this way, approximately 3,000 persons were chosen to represent as closely as possible the population of the county as a whole.

---

[2]Merton (1968, pp. 504–505) ties Lazarsfeld directly to this line of the evolution of American marketing techniques: "As Lazarsfeld and others have pointed out, mass communications research developed very largely in response to market requirements. The severe competition for advertising among the several mass media and among agencies within each medium has provoked an economic demand for objective measures of size, composition, and responses of audiences." Merton continues: "And in their quest for the largest possible share of the advertising dollar, each mass medium and each agency becomes alerted to the possible deficiencies in the audience yardsticks employed by competitors, thus introducing a considerable pressure for evolving rigorous and objective measures not easily vulnerable to criticism."

This group—the poll—resembled the county in age, sex, residence, education, telephone and car ownership, and nativity.

From this poll, four groups of 600 persons each were selected by stratified sampling . . . Of each of these four groups of 600, three were reinterviewed only once each.

(T)he 600 people of the panel were kept under continual observation from May until November, 1940. Whenever a person changed his vote intention in any way, from one interview to the next, detailed information was gathered on why he had changed. The respondents were also interviewed regularly on their exposure to campaign propaganda in all the media of communication—the press, radio, personal contacts, and others. (Lazarsfeld and others, 1944, pp. 3–5)

Thus, as Sheingold (1973) points out, the Columbia research had its analytical focus on decision-making, although the authors concluded that voting was primarily a group process. This led to a research agenda that looks at politics and voting as the sum of individual interactions with the media, "opinion-leaders", and so forth, rather than the social networks through which information and influence flow. Since self-report data are insufficient to study network structures, and since "network attributes are more important than individual attributes in determining the likelihood of new information reaching an individual" (Sheingold, 1973, pp. 714–715), the Columbia research design was largely inappropriate to understanding the dynamics of political behavior, communication flow, and information-seeking within the context of an electoral campaign.

In retrospect it is difficult to imagine what kind of evidence might have satisfied the expectations regarding media impact that led to the Erie County study. Lazarsfeld (1935, p. 35) distinguished between what he called "biological" and "biographical" determinants of an action, and "determinants of the first degree." The latter category might include the "circumstances" under which a decision is made, the person's "purpose", and "all the factors which carry this decision on until it has actually been executed." The task of a survey questionnaire is to ascertain "the *total* motivational set-up of the first degree," by which he meant the immediate motivating factors entering a person's thinking (Lazarsfeld, 1935, p. 36; emphasis his).

It is intuitively obvious that for most marketing decisions, many of these determinants are unlikely to be attributed by a consumer to the mass media. In approaching the vote as a type of consumer decision, Lazarsfeld asked voters in the post-election survey what sources had provided information that led them to arrive at their vote decisions, and which source had been most important to them. More than two-thirds mentioned newspapers or radio as a "helpful" source, while less than one-half mentioned any type of personal source (relatives, business contacts, friends, and neighbors). More than one-half said either radio or newspapers had been the single most important source, but less than one-fourth cited a personal source as important (Lazarsfeld and others, 1944, p. 127, 171). Despite this seemingly preponderant evidence of media impact, the authors concluded that "more than anything else people can move other people." The 1940 study came to be cited as the basis for the two-step flow model of personal influence mediating between voters and the world of public affairs (with the latter treated as one of many commodities to be marketed) (Katz and Lazarsfeld, 1955).

ELECTION CAMPAIGNS: A VERY SPECIAL TOPIC

Unlike most kinds of campaigns, an election campaign consists of competing messages for the opposing candidates; one candidate succeeds only if the other loses. In a marketing campaign, each of the competing brands might succeed to the extent that they capture a share of the market; in most product classes a number of alternative brands can succeed simultaneously. Much of everyday politics is conducted in a similar fashion. For example, oil companies successfully "market" the special interest of deregulation to the extent that they gain some relief from public controls as a result of their constant campaign on that theme. An election campaign is more finite in scope and time, and fits the marketing model much less well than does the ongoing clash and compromise of competing political interests. Generally in politics one would attempt to estimate the total impact of campaigning, but in a two-sided "zero-sum" election contest the result is represented by the net effect—i.e., all those effects favoring the winning candidate, minus those favoring the loser. This approach, which confuses an analysis of the campaign *process* with an analysis of the election *outcome*, constitutes a serious mismatching of research purpose to study design. The news media do not as a rule intend to serve the purposes of only one side in an election contest; rather they strive to illuminate decision-making processes by providing news and information about the candidates.

Although content analyses indicated that both radio and newspaper news coverage favored the Republican Party's cause in 1940, the newspapers (in Sandusky, Ohio, and its environs) were much more heavily slanted in this direction. Lazarsfeld suggested that this difference effectively offered "a medium for each party," although neither radio nor the newspapers were literally "for" the Democrats in Erie County. Changes in favor of the Republicans were almost twice as likely to be based mainly on a newspaper report (31 percent of changers) as on something heard on radio (17 percent). As they had loosely hypothesized, among those changing toward the Democrats the results were approximately the reverse: 30 percent based on radio reports, 20 percent on newspapers (Lazarsfeld and others, 1944, p. 132). These rather large contrasts are especially impressive when one considers that most news coverage, even in local newspapers of that time, was largely standardized wire service material selected according to professional norms of newsworthiness. It must have included a good deal of campaign-related material favorable to each side, regardless of the medium of transmission, and this would have tended to neutralize the net effect of a particular medium leaning toward one side or the other.

At the same time, very slight differences in the same directions were found regarding exposure to these two media, Democrats being slightly more exposed to radio than Republicans, and slightly less to newspapers.[3] The partisan differences in net effects, which were much larger than those in media exposure, were later to be treated as having been theoretically explained by selective exposure factors.

"Selective exposure" was thereafter destined to join the "two-step flow" as the major conceptual basis of the "limited effects" image of media impact (Klapper, 1960; Kraus and Davis, 1976). Neither had shown up as a major factor in the 1940 study, at least not in comparison with the evidence of direct effects—nor did they in any subsequent study. No multivariate comparisons were employed in the 1940 study, nor for many years thereafter (Chaffee and Miyo, 1982). No new measures or analyses appropriate to these questions were added in the 1948 Elmira study. The theoretical terms simply became "facts" independent of their empirical origins or lack thereof.

If a marketing orientation was not pursued very clearly in Lazarsfeld's data-analysis and interpretation, it certainly was in his study design. The vote was taken to be the ultimate criterion variable, as if it were the single most important political act a person can perform. This focus on voting has been followed by many researchers since the 1940s, so it must have some appeal to the democratic ear (Sears, 1969; Mendelsohn and O'Keefe, 1976). Certainly voting is an act of consequence in popular government, but so too are the contribution of time and money to a campaign, personal argumentation on behalf of a candidate, the display of campaign buttons and bumper stickers, etc. Indeed, all of these require more personal investment than does the simple act of casting a secret ballot at the end

---

[3]On an index where means for Republicans and Democrats differed by 5 scale positions, between-media differences within each party were not greater than 1.1 scale positions.

of a campaign. Far more consequential to the political process is organized political activity through groups representing various economic and social interests, as Lazarsfeld later pointed out (Lazarsfeld and Merton, 1948).

For all its importance in the selection of political leaders and the transfer through them of power from one societal interest or class to another, casting a vote is neither a very large event, nor a risky one, in the lives of most people. The political movements for union representation, women's suffrage, and equal political and economic rights for minorities have been important issues in this century's American political history, and involved millions of participants who devoted much more than votes to their causes. These movements involved the formation of large voluntary political organizations such as the Anti-Defamation League and the National Association for the Advancement of Colored People. The roles of mass media communication, both for informing members of such organizations and for disseminating messages to the general public, are crucial in large-scale organized political activity.[4] But in a field survey of individuals that is focused simply on voting, this role is almost totally obscured and politics is reduced to a single act of "the sale and purchase" of candidates when viewed from a marketing perspective.

CONTEMPORARY INFLUENCES ON LAZARSFELD

Much of the research interest in the vote was inherited by Lazarsfeld from the dominant research paradigms that immediately preceded his Erie County study. Perhaps the most important within the academic community was the work of Stuart Rice, a sociology professor at the University of Pennsylvania, who laid the basis for the behavioral movement in political science with his widely used volume *Qualitative Methods in Politics* (1928), and his reader *Methods in Social Science* (1931). Building on the growing interest in the 1920s in the concept of "attitudes", Rice was able to marshal a variety of ecological data to account for various kinds of election outcomes. These books were well known in the major social science graduate departments throughout the 1930s, and Lazarsfeld's reduction of community data to individual-level data through personal interviews was looked upon as a logical extension of the beginning that Rice had provided (Rossi, 1959).

A more immediate influence in concentrating attention on the vote as the main criterion were two books by Louis Bean, *Ballot Behavior*

---

[4]Interpersonal communication, and communication structured along internal lines of organization, are likewise essential for any successful political movement.

(1940), and *How to Predict Elections* (1948). Bean, whose methods constituted refinements and extensions of Rice's, was cited in *The People's Choice,* which contains only seven references to other work related to any aspect of the project. In *Voting,* the 1948 election study report, Bean is mentioned on the second page in a blanket reference along with Samuel Lubell and Louis Harris, well-known public opinion poll specialists.

But the person whose professional conception of research undoubtedly had the greatest influence on the design of the Erie County study was the pollster Elmo Roper. In the 1930s, Roper had built a successful and well-known marketing survey organization that had gradually refined sampling and interviewing techniques for public opinion polling. His firm contributed to the funding of the 1940 research "and he and his staff were most helpful in the planning and execution of the study" (Lazarsfeld and others, 1944, p. v).[5] Roper had built a public reputation by predicting election outcomes in advance, on the basis of sample surveys. It was most logical that a study he co-sponsored would adopt as its goal the explanation of the vote as a primary criterion variable.

From this perspective, the main effect of heavy attention to the news media and the content of the campaign was seen as that of rendering a voter more predictable. Lazarsfeld repeatedly emphasized that unstable voters, and those who voted contrary to their "predispositions", reported quite low levels of campaign exposure. The predispositions were measured indirectly, through demographic correlates: Democratic votes tended to be drawn from blue collar, low socioeconomic status (SES), Roman Catholic families, and those who considered themselves "labor", while the Republicans were supported by white collar, high SES, Protestant, business-oriented voters (Lazarsfeld and others, 1944). The presumed predispositions were not so much psychological as social. They heavily reflected the different class interests served by the Democratic Party of the New Deal and by its conservative Republican opposition, and were presumably translated into votes through communication about these differences. For many voters, this communication doubtless had occurred some years before the 1940 campaign. But each campaign produces new candidates and new circumstances and at least some people might have paid particular attention to the campaign to assure themselves that they were indeed voting in their own best interests.

The communication process by which demographic differences came to be viewed as class interests and in turn were translated into votes was never examined. Had it been, it is likely that mass communication would

---

[5]Other sponsors included the Rockefeller Foundation, Columbia University's Office of Radio Research, and *Life Magazine.* Their influence was not, however, nearly so evident in either conceptualization or execution of the study as was Roper's.

have been an important part of it, especially in connection with the Republican candidate, Wendell Willkie, who was little known to the public prior to his nomination (Barber, 1980) and who had no clear political definition during the campaign (Lazarsfeld and others, 1944, pp. 28–32). Then too, the year of 1940 brought constant news about the recovering economy, and of the war in Europe in which Roosevelt was progressively involving the United States. These factors, which weighed heavily in many voter decisions, were of course dependent upon the mass media for their transmission to people. But news usually cuts several ways, reinforcing, in this instance, both isolationists and interventionists in their views. While the total effect is often large, the net effect is usually quite small. Using multivariate regression analyses (which are common today, but were practically unheard of in 1940) we would probably characterize the role of the mass media in that campaign as an interaction with class-related and interest-related independent variables; as a predictor of the vote, media exposure habits would have little main effect but rather strong multiplicative effects.

Looking across the Lazarsfeld-Berelson election studies as a whole, it is reasonable to conclude that their purpose shifted from the original one of investigating the role of the mass media to that of explaining the direction of the vote (Rossi, 1959). This transition would be completed in the next phase of election research, the national surveys conducted by the Survey Research Center at the University of Michigan (Kraus and Davis, 1976). Before examining these studies, though, we should examine in detail some covert assumptions of the Lazarsfeld research tradition, assumptions that have been accepted with little question in the Michigan series and most smaller-scale studies in the same vein.

THEORETICAL GOALS AND ASSUMED HOMOGENEITIES

Lazarsfeld's group held as their general goal the development of theoretical generalizations about processes that enter into the development of vote decisions. If these scholars' initial ambitions in this regard were unreasonably high, they were soon tempered by the reality of handling field survey evidence (with all its uncertainties and imperfections). Their conclusions were always phrased in terms of general variables, in a fashion extending well beyond the empirical boundaries of their study. Typically these were bivariate theoretical relationships, such as, "The less interest people have, the more variable are their vote intentions" (Lazarsfeld and others, 1944; p. 68), or, "Interest in the campaign invariably increases as the campaign progresses" (p. 77). Bivariate relationships like these were derived from empirical analyses with one or two control variables at most, and then strung into longer sentences to produce more complex theoretical syntheses.

Berelson was particularly fond of cataloging these findings, which came to be called in the phrase of another influential colleague, Robert Merton (1957), "theories of the middle range." This seemingly modest term referred to a broad search for general "laws" of human behavior. The assumption that fundamental laws would be discovered in the highly specific context of a U.S. election campaign must have seemed ludicrous even in those early years of empirical social science.

An appendix of the Elmira study report presents a chart summarizing the evidenciary support across seven studies for more than 200 separate inferences. This approach of cataloging knowledge eventually led to the expansive volume *Human Behavior* (Berelson and Steiner, 1964), which covered a wide range of topics. Most of the generalizations they drew about mass communication have since been disproven in at least some circumstances. It would be difficult for most scholars today to accept such assertions as, "the mass media do not appear to produce substantial . . . reaction to violence" (p. 546), or, "the fuller . . . the interest . . . then . . . the more resistant [the audience] to uncongenial [communications]" (p. 542), in the face of continuing research of the past 15 years.

The error, and it was probably a necessary error in order to get their grand enterprise in motion in the first place, was that Lazarsfeld and Berelson made a number of assumptions about the homogeneity of the elements they were studying. These elements included the basic pieces of an empirical study: people, places, times, and such specifics as elections, vote decisions, media, and political parties. To some extent the concept of "history" as a threat to validity of an inference (Campbell and Stanley, 1966) covers this problem. In studying one election campaign, and then a second, it was hardly outrageous for the investigators to assume that a finding from the first that was replicated in the second would prove to be an enduring generalization, especially if it remained couched in the most general of terms. If history proved these conclusions to be bound to their time (the 1940s), it would be the responsibility of future generations of researchers to demonstrate this limitation by repeatedly testing the propositions produced by Lazarsfeld and Berelson. What happened, though, was quite different. Their findings were accepted by most academics as valid generalizations, and therefore as not standing in need of further testing. Only in recent years, as the number of active researchers in this area has noticeably expanded, have many of the original propositions been subjected to new tests. About as often as not, they have not survived these tests.

There are further difficulties inherent in the assumptions of a homogeneous population, on which the theoretical interpretations of Lazarsfeld and Berelson rested. Each member of their sample was treated as an equally weighted unit, which permitted application of random sampling and statistical models that were then coming into vogue. Lazarsfeld and others (1944, p. 3) asserted that they were studying "the *development* of votes and not their distribution" (emphasis theirs); but evidence of what was important was drawn mainly on the basis of the frequency with which certain behavior patterns occurred. The key analysis, which led to the conclusion that there had been little room for the media to have any impact beyond "reinforcement" of predispositions to vote in a particular direction, was based on a turnover table comparing May and October voting intentions (Lazarsfeld and others, 1944; p. 102–104). Anyone whose stated vote intention had not changed during this time was classified as either "reinforcement" (53 percent of all cases) or "no effect" (16 percent). By contrast, "conversion" from one side to the other was "by far, the least frequent result" (8 percent). It was this interpretation of marginals, coupled with the finding that those classified as "conversion" cases were low in attention to the campaign via the media, that led to the "law of minimal consequences" regarding media effects.

Had not the focus been exclusively on the vote, and specifically on within-campaign changes in voting intentions, and had not each case been weighted equally and relative frequencies been taken as the indicator of theoretical importance, a very different interpretation of the role of mass media could have been derived from the findings of the 1940 study—and of every election study since. Some people certainly weigh more heavily in the political process than others; Lazarsfeld noted the role of "opinion leader", people who influenced other people and who themselves relied heavily on the media for their political information. Much has since been made of the concept of opinion leader, often implying that they are somehow independent of and distinct from other people and the media. Media attention is much higher among those who are more likely to vote, who contribute their efforts to campaigns, and who are at the forefront of organized political groups and movements. Only on Election Day do all voters count equally; even then the non-voters are strongly defined by their lack of attention to the campaign. In the 1940s their lack of interest may have been tantamount to a lack of exposure, but this is not the case today. In the intensive campaigning via television and other media, even people with little political interest or partisan attachment are now reached by a heavy volume of campaign messages (Chaffee and Choe, 1980).

The decision to locate the 1940 and 1948 studies in small cities of the Northeastern U.S. was mainly dictated by economic and administrative imperatives. But in each instance a case was made for the appropriateness of the site selected as representative of the entire nation, almost as if theories of the middle range would emerge from communities of the middle range in terms of size, geographic, socioeconomic, and political characteristics. Erie County, Ohio, had "deviated very little from the national voting trends" (Lazarsfeld and others, 1944, p. 3), and Elmira, New York was close enough to a "normal" American community "to assure a realistic test of the generalizations" (Berelson and others, 1954 p. 10). The Columbia researchers did not assume that these local sites represented valid samples of a homogeneous national political community. But neither did they locate their studies in Harlem, New York; Cambridge, Massachusetts; or Atlanta, Georgia. These would have been more obviously atypical. They also would have provided more evidence of the competing factions, interests, and ethnic groups that exist in the very heterogeneous United States than did Erie County—which was in fact atypical by its very lack of political interest groups.[6] The Columbia researchers also consciously picked communities that were very stable politically. This choice reduced the likelihood of their finding much instability—the within-campaign change they considered a necessary condition for inferring media effects—at the level of the individual voter.

In selecting a single community the researchers also thereby selected its local news media. In the cases of Sandusky and Elmira, these media consisted mainly of pro-Republican newspapers in a stable Republican region, and a small number of (and thus little variety among) low-budget, local radio stations. The homogeneity of media provided in a single site greatly restricts the variance available for study, and consequently restricts as well the possible covariance one may detect between media content and exposure, and other variables. It was not until 1976 that a major election study would be conducted in two sites selected for their constrasting media resources (Patterson, 1980). By this time, with the coming of television and the demise of many local newspapers, there was not sufficient

---

[6]"Local union leadership had not been outstanding or progressive or particularly aggressive and local units were not active in their own state organizations. Labor was not an important influence in the county; the domination of business over labor was freely admitted by local labor leaders . . . labor did not form a political bloc as such, and no group or individual was able to deliver the labor vote. On the whole, the labor picture was apathetic rather than calm . . .

"There were no special interest groups in Erie County wielding important political influence. None of the ethnic groups—Negroes (sic), Germans, or others—formed an organized voting unit. The minority parties were not strong and there was no youth movement in the county (although there was a Young Republican Club). The votes of neither veteran nor fraternal groups could be delivered; and there were too few relief clients for them to be influential as a unit" (Lazarsfeld and others, 1944, pp. 12–13).

between-community variance to make a detectable difference in voter decision-making processes. We can only speculate on the possibility that the seeming imperturbability of voters in Elmira, New York in the volatile election year of 1948 might not have been very indicative of simultaneous events in media-rich New York City, the burgeoning suburbs of Los Angeles, or the Deep South of the "Dixiecrat" revolt against the liberal civil rights platform adopted by President Harry Truman's Democratic Party.

HISTORICAL SHIFTS

Lazarsfeld and Berelson can hardly be faulted for their limited samples of time frames. They happened to be working in the election years 1940 and 1948, and their implicit ahistorical assumption of the homogeneity of times was unavoidable. But subsequent scholars might have been more attentive to some major changes in the elements involved in voting behavior and theoretical statements about it, which occurred in the U.S. after 1948. The media system has, as noted, changed dramatically. Television has replaced radio as the most popular source of news, and cities where competing newspapers of rival political perspectives once thrived have come to be dominated by single (usually centrist) newspapers. Thus the arrays of media available to an individual vary considerably by time and place (Hochheimer, 1982). With a rising level of mass public education should come a concomitant increase in people's capacity to process complex political information. More than one-fifth of all adults—and undoubtedly a higher proportion among those who vote and otherwise participate in politics—receive one of the informative weekly news magazines, *Time* and *Newsweek*. If the "enlightened electorate" presumed by romantic democratic theorists ever existed, it ought to be more likely in the United States of the present day than it was in the 1940s. Berelson and others (1954, Ch. 14) in a somewhat pessimistic final chapter concluded that the voter they had been studying "falls far short" of standards of knowledge, principle, and rationality in reaching a decision. Whether that generalization would be as easily reached or accepted today is at least debatable, but it is certainly true that most people find electoral politics much less engaging an activity than do the researchers who study them. There is an inescapable "elitist bias" in academic evaluations of the intellectual performance of the typical member of society. Most evidence suggests voters have become better informed and more issue-oriented over the decades since the early voting studies (Nie and others 1976), although many would still fall short of an idealized standard.

Certainly American electoral politics has changed since the 1940s. Campaigns are conducted today not by political parties nearly so much as by professional campaign consultants, who specialize in direct mail solicitation, polling, advertising, and media relations. Whether for this reason or others, parties do not loom large in the public mind as they did when the original studies were undertaken. People in the U.S. today are less likely to say they belong to a party, and this measure is a less-strong predictor of the vote, than was the case 30 years ago (Nie and others, 1976). Votes seem to be determined by specific comparisons of candidates on issues, more than they are by party labels. In the studies of 1940 and 1948, the Columbia researchers emphasized how much voters distorted their perceptions of the candidates' positions so as to coincide with personal preferences and partisan allegiances. When the intellectual leadership in U.S. election research shifted to the University of Michigan in the 1950s, these assumptions, conclusions, and interpretations went with it, and party indentification became the core concept in predicting the vote.

THE MICHIGAN TRADITION: PSYCHOLOGICAL EXPLANATIONS

Party identification is a distinctly American way of "explaining" political processes, growing out of the unique political history of the United States. By the time social research began in this century the two-party system had become deeply ingrained in U.S. politics.

In today's era of relatively low allegiance to parties, it may be difficult to recall the deep-seated feelings that were once associated with the term "identification" when it was applied to partisan orientations. Freudian psychology, which stressed the importance of early emotional experiences and subconscious psycho-dynamic processes of adaptation to the outside world, had an enormous impact on American intellectuals of the 1920s and 1930s. The Freudian concept of "identification" was conceived as an affective bonding between the person and an ideal, or another person, or a group, a bonding that is considered essential to the development of a well-integrated personality (White, 1956, p. 200). Harold Lasswell (1930), who was highly intrigued by the possible application of principles of psychopathology to political processes, brought the most extreme version of this view into political science. In an elaborate speculation on the clashes between ego and id that he saw as involved in identification with a nation or a social class, he concluded that the large American middle class was particularly vulnerable to propaganda and suggested "devising expedients of mass management by means of significant symbols which induce the harmless discharge of collective insecurities" (Laswell, 1935, p. 233). There was thought to be, then, a strong need for identification with national symbols of power and with one's distinctive group, and these ties were acquired in an individual's early formative years within the family.

There is no evidence that this view of party identification as a primal force was ever adopted by the early election researchers. Lazarsfeld almost never used the term "identification"; his concept of "party preference" was measured by the self-reported frequency for candidates of each party. Only in the last major interview wave of the last Columbia election study (dated October 15, 1948) was a question asked about the person's psychological orientation toward political parties: "Regardless of how you may vote in the coming election, how have you usually thought of yourself—as a Republican, Democrat, Socialist, or what?" (Berelson and others, 1954, p. 361). This question represented a supplementary measure, near the end of the interview schedule; Lazarsfeld and Berelson were behaviorists.

Angus Campbell, who directed the major national election studies at the University of Michigan from 1948 until the late 1970s, was a psychologist. He viewed the determinants of the vote as psychological in nature, and party identification was pre-eminent among these. He impressed upon the Michigan studies his assumption that the explanation of voting behavior was to be found in the partisan attitudes of individuals (Campbell and others, 1960, pp. 64–75). Noting that Americans' party preferences "show great stability between elections", the Michigan group viewed this consistency as a product of an "individual's affective orientation to an important group-object in his environment," which they called party identification. The party was not viewed so much as representing a consistent class or interest thrust as it was simply a distinctive group in society "toward which the individual may develop an identification, positive or negative" (Campbell and others, 1960, pp. 120-122). This psychological attachment was not considered the same as regularity of voting for one party, although there was a strong empirical correlation between the two. This distinction allowed the central concept to jibe with the basic facts of the times: While the Michigan investigators were studying the 1952 and 1956 victories of the Republican President Eisenhower, they continued to find that most people reported that they considered themselves to be Democrats, not Republicans.

The origins of party identification were not so important in the Michigan studies as was the simple fact that this self-classification measure was a reliable predictor of the vote. When asked what their parents' party preferences had been, voters tended to describe them as consistent—both between mother and father, and between parent and child (Campbell and others, 1960, pp. 146–149). The validity of this retrospective measure was not tested, although it was of some concern. Campbell and others (1960) expressed some skepticism over the notion that party identification was typically learned at a very young age, or transmitted between generations within a family in association with strong emotional linkages to parent–child relations. Instead, they emphasized the many different kinds of political events and experiences that might account for both the acquisition and the later fluctuation of party identification.

IGNORING THE MASS MEDIA

That this fluctuation due to the flow of events might depend heavily on the kinds of political information brought to the person via the mass media did not enter the discussion of the Michigan scholars. From the 1948 study through that of 1972, use of mass media variables were generally limited in the Michigan questionnaires to one item per medium (radio, newspaper, magazine, and television) asking whether the respondent had heard or read any campaign program or story from that source. These experiences were treated as instances of political participation, somewhat weaker than such forms of campaigning as giving money, wearing buttons, or attending meetings, but nonetheless evidence of something greater than total apathy on the respondent's part. *The American Voter*, the highly influential monograph summarizing findings from the 1948, 1952, and 1956 national surveys, devoted only one paragraph specifically to the subject of mass media use during a campaign (Campbell and others, 1960, p. 92).

The message of this research for students of electoral behavior was clear: Party identification and other partisan attitude measures were strong predictors of the vote. The use of mass media was a type of "informal participation" which for a few people constituted "a principal means of relating to politics," but was generally not related to prediction of the vote and hence is of very little theoretical consequence. By relegating media-related activity to the status of a minor mode of political participation, the Michigan studies through the 1960s inadvertently insured perpetuation of the limited-effects model of mass communication. No new data relevant to the question of media effects would be gathered, so no new interpretations could be reached.

THE HYPODERMIC NEEDLE (MAGIC BULLET): A NON-TRADITION

It is often asserted that the limited-effects conclusions of Lazarsfeld and his associates were reached in reaction to an earlier image of the mass media that accorded them very powerful putative effects. The latter is often referred to as the "hypodermic needle model" in skeletal histories of the field (e.g., Schramm, 1971; Reeves and Wartella, 1982). The term "magic bullet" is also sometimes used to describe this supposed naive and long-discredited view. In a popular current introductory textbook, for example, De Fleur and Dennis (1981, p. 502) equate the "magic bullet theory" with both the "hypodermic needle theory" and "stimulus–response theory", defining them as the assumption "that all subjects will receive some critical feature of the message (the magic bullet) that will change them in the same way." This "legacy of fear" of massive media impact, they say, stimulated much of the mass communication research in this century. The studies by Lazarsfeld and others "opened a new era in thinking" by rejecting "the old hypothesis that the media have great power" (De Fleur and Dennis, 1981, pp. 294–297).

This widely accepted version of the field's history does not correspond to the published record as we have found it. Early studies of the impact of motion pictures on young people, sponsored by the Payne Fund in the late 1920s, were quite sophisticated in the complexity of their applied theory, although they were built upon a linear model of media effects (Rogers and Kincaid, 1981). The same film, it was found, affected children differently depending upon a child's age, sex, predispositions, perceptions, social environment, past experiences, and parental influence (Reeves and Wartella, 1982). None of the subsequent investigators of media effects in the 1930s and 1940s ever seems to have proposed a simple, direct effects model in which media content would be accepted and acted upon by large masses of people. The learning theory set forth by Carl Hovland in his experimental studies of propaganda film effects proposed a sequence of direct information inputs, followed by lesser impact at the levels of affect and conation (Hovland and others, 1949). Several of these experiments demonstrated large differences in effects due to intervening factors such as the person's mental ability. Hovland concluded that mass-scale direct effects should not be expected, although considerable impact is possible if a message is carefully designed for its audience.

Lasswell, in his darkest writings on the psychopathological side of politics (1930) and the need of atomized man in modern society for symbols of group identification (1935), considered that media messages that filled this kind of need for an individual would be gladly accepted as therapeutic. Somewhat parallel assumptions were being made in the planning of Nazi propaganda in Germany at the same time (Doob, 1950). This view was only speculation on Lasswell's part, however; his empirical research concentrated on analysis of media content, which reflected his deep interest in the manipulation of symbols.

In any event, Lasswell does not seem to have been on the minds of the early political campaign researchers. He is not cited in either of the Columbia election studies (Lazarsfeld and others, 1944; Berelson and others, 1954), and the only reference to him in *The American Voter* is in connection with individual differences or "personality" variables (Campbell and others, 1960, p. 499).

Although it is Lasswell who is most often cited as the author of a "hypodermic needle" model of direct effects (e.g., Schramm, 1971; Davis and Baran, 1981; Dominick, 1983), it is difficult to find the evidence in his own writing. At the most, this piece of imagery would have had a highly specific meaning in the context of Lasswell's essays of the 1930s. Writing in the depths of the Depression, he saw the threatening political movements sweeping Europe (such as Fascism and Communism) as almost inevitable outcomes of the isolation of the individual in an atomized society.[7] By bringing symbols of nationalism and group identity to such a person, he reasoned, political campaigns via the mass media could be effective because they would be welcomed by the person in the absence of any more satisfying social ties. A hypodermic needle is, of course, a method for injecting medication into an ailing body. Later research stressed the message strategy of "immunizing" a person against propaganda by "inoculation" with a belief defense (Lumsdaine and Janis, 1953; McGuire and Papageorgis, 1961; McGuire, 1964; Roberts and Maccoby, 1973). This extension of the medical metaphor may account for the extent to which the hypodermic needle model became embedded in the literature long after its supposed heyday.

The image of a "magic bullet" is also derived from a medical metaphor, and also seems to have been created as a straw man years after the supposed fact. In this case, the usage of the term represents almost precisely the *opposite* of its meaning in the popular literature on medicine. Far from an image of universal impact, a magic bullet is a specific medication, which hits only those few in the population who are diseased; it is "magic" because it passes through all the others without any effect on them.[8] The direct metaphor is that of a bullet that one could fire into a crowd, which would kill all one's enemies but leave friends and neutrals unharmed. Ironically, a literal magic bullet metaphor would accord rather well with the empirical image of political media effects we have distilled from the long research record since Lazarsfeld. As campaign messages diffuse through a population, they do indeed seem to pass through many people without noticeable impact on their thought or behavior, but it has been repeatedly demonstrated that a substantial minority who are seeking political orientation are affected when the content of the message coincides

---

[7]Elihu Katz, a leading student of Lazarsfeld's, summarized what was "in the air" if not explicitly to be found in the writings of the Columbia scholars, in this passage from a synthesizing article: "Until very recently, the image of society in the minds of most student of communication was of atomized individuals, connected with the mass media but not with one another" (Katz, 1960, p. 436).

[8]The Edward G. Robinson film, "Dr. Ehrlich's Magic Bullet," concerns the search for a cure for syphilis.

with their current needs (e.g., Chaffee, 1978; Weaver and others, 1981).

In sum, there does not seem to have been a general theory of massive media effects that was seriously proposed by empirical investigators of political behavior and mass communication.[9] With the development of new campaigning techniques and strategies, such a time may very well lie in the future (Rice and Paisley, 1981). It would seem, though, that the competitive arena of political campaigning (Chaffee, 1981) lends itself much less easily to this kind of eventuality than is the case with public health, environmental topics, and other activities on which audience predispositions are more likely to coincide with message intent.

THE CONTEMPORARY ERA

The publication of Joseph Klapper's *The Effects of Mass Communication* (1960) marked the watershed of the limited effects model. This highly influential volume weaves together the Lazarsfeld-Berelson middle-range theoretical propositions into one global generalization: The impact of mass media on public attitudes and behaviors, especially those in the political realm, should ordinarily be expected to be minimal. Not until after the 1972 election campaign, in which the media played an unmistakably central role, did additional measures related to mass communication get added to the questionnaires for the Michigan electoral research series (Miller and others, 1974). By this time a number of new currents of political communication research had begun to flow, in other academic settings.

---

[9]Many other writers, generally neither communication scholars nor social scientists, did write extensively about the great power of the mass media and why society should fear them. These popular writings are probably responsible for creating the hypodermic needle model that Lazarsfeld and his colleagues were later credited with destroying. Speculations about powerful media influences have been a major theme in both journalistic and novelistic literature throughout this century. Examples within academic circles include accounts of the role of the Hearst newspapers in crystallizing the Spanish–American War, analyses of Hitler's propaganda warfare, the panic created by Orson Welles's "War of the Worlds" broadcast, and the fear of Madison Avenue advertising effects as expressed in Vance Packard's book *The Hidden Persuaders*.

Scholars entering the field of mass communication research typically encounter these kinds of writings early on, before they begin to study empirical research. Consequently, the phenomenological introduction of the individual researcher to the field is usually one of progression from hypodermic-needle beliefs to a more measured comprehension of how mass communication processes actually work. It requires only a slight leap of inference to confuse this personal experience with the history that the ongoing research field itself has experienced, especially when the small literature on that history describes it in a way that matches one's personal experience. In preparing this chapter, the authors became acutely aware of this kind of confusion in their own earlier experience and thinking.

Throughout the 1960s evidence began to accumulate which suggested that the limited effects image was at best oversimplified and under many circumstances quite misleading. Its most thorough codification (Klapper, 1960) had stressed that there were a number of conditions that might produce strong, direct media effects. Klapper's qualified statements tended to get rounded off in summary treatments by other authors, however, and relatively few academics saw much promise in the study of the political impact of the mass media.

Politics, though, inexorably continued. Campaigns had to be mounted each election year, and it was difficult for researchers to ignore them. In 1958, a gubernatorial candidate in California tried a political gimmick of then-rising popularity, an election eve "telethon." Schramm and Carter (1959) conducted a survey of the potential audience for this program, and found that few of those who listened or called in were not already his supporters. This expensive campaign event failed for lack of an audience, due to selective exposure (and the candidate lost the election to boot). The limited effects model seemed to fit.

Two years later, however, Carter (1962) found a campaign situation that did not provide much opportunity for the audience to select itself according to partisan predispositions: the series of televised debates between John F. Kennedy and Richard Nixon in the fall of 1960. In a then-rare test of the prevailing wisdom, he tested panels of pro-Kennedy and pro-Nixon voters on their knowledge of factual items that each candidate had presented during the course of the first debate. Among those individuals who had watched the entire debate, there was no difference in recall based on which candidate the voter favored. Nixon partisans recalled what Kennedy had said as well as what Nixon had said, as did Kennedy supporters. Katz and Feldman (1962), in their comprehensive review of all studies of the 1960 debates, called this finding "most intriguing."

The more general conclusion from the 1960 debates studies, though, was that they had mainly served as "image-building" events, giving the young Kennedy a chance to demonstrate that he was more "experienced" and had qualities of "leadership", according to various panel studies. The net impact of the debates on the vote was slight, although enough to help Kennedy win a very narrow victory. Even if recall were not selective, and if the two-candidate format limited the opportunity for selective exposure, party identification was still a regnant concept and the debates were treated as a unique exception to the rule of limited effects (Pool, 1963). In retrospect, though, Carter's (1962) finding was not an anomaly, but the beginning of a new wave in mass communication research.

By the early 1960s a number of former journalists were emerging from newly-established doctoral programs in mass communication research in the U.S. A marketing orientation is not particularly comfortable for scholars who view the media through the eyes of reporters, nor is the belief that the media are of little consequence in politics. These news-oriented researchers tend to conceive of the role of the news media as primarily one of informing—rather than directly persuading—people, and consequently have focused increasing attention on the cognitive effects of political communication. For example, McCombs and Shaw (1972) initiated study of the "agenda-setting" power of the media. The "uses and gratifications" served by the media's public affairs content were first investigated by Blumler and McQuail (1969) in Great Britain, and have since been enthusiastically pursued in the United States (e.g., McLeod and Becker, 1974; Mendelsohn and O'Keefe, 1976). The importance of the news media in informing young people of pre-voting age about politics has been demonstrated in several studies (e.g., Chaffee and others, 1970; Hawkins and others, 1979). But even as they diverge from the Lazarsfeld tradition in their selection of dependent variables and conception of the media's role, these recent departures retain many characteristics of the early studies: election campaign settings, large-sample field surveys, predominantly individual-level data-analysis, and the search for enduring generalizations. The debt of contemporary researchers to Lazarsfeld and his colleagues is clear, and it is recognized. The Erie County study remains one of the most-cited sources in political and mass communications research even in the 1980s (Paisley, 1984).

We have dwelt at length on the earliest studies of mass media in U.S. election campaigns, and emphasized the extent to which they have influenced later research. This brief effort at historical scholarship has impressed upon us several conclusions of a historical nature, involving both the history of our field and the extent to which interpretations of research findings should be considered relative to their historical times and places.

HISTORY OF THE FIELD

The "received history" of mass communication research as brought to us in brief prefatory chapters and paragraphs written since 1960 does not correspond to the actual work in the decades of the original studies, if we are to judge from the published record of that time. The earliest studies stressed that media impacts are contingent on personal orientations and accordingly differ from one person to another. No empirical study has, to our knowledge, ever purported to demonstrate a universal, massive pattern of media impact. The "hypodermic needle" and "magic bullet" images represent misinterpretations of metaphors drawn from medicine, and appear to have been "straw men" created some years later as a naive conception against which the limited-effects model could be contrasted. The conclusion that media effects are limited was based on assumptions derived from the field of marketing, and is in the process of being discarded as assumptions more appropriate to the communication functions of public affairs media are applied to research.

The assumption that communication and political influence are unidirectional linear processes has also come under considerable criticism of late. Dervin (1980b) argues that the source-to-receiver image of communication flow may be backwards; in the area of communication and development, Hornik (1980) used the term "feedforward" to refer to the idea that the initiative for a communication program may often lie with the person who is eventually to receive the information. Rogers and Kincaid (1981) point out that the linear perspective captures only one-half of the "convergence" process that comprises communication. Sheingold (1973) contends that the most useful contribution sociology can make to voting research will come from the analysis of the communication networks through which political information flows. From a viewpoint of intellectual history, the early studies—which were designed in ways that precluded the empirical examination of concepts of these more sociological kinds— probably served to retard the development of social theories of political communication even though the studies were often conducted by sociologists.

THE RELATIVITY OF RESEARCH DATA

Empirical research findings need to be interpreted in the context of the historical time and place in which the data were gathered. Estimates of the percentage of individuals who behave in a particular way, or of the strength (or even the direction) of bivariate relationships, should be constructed only very tentatively on the basis of a single study. Whereas the groundbreaking researchers could reasonably give their research monographs generic titles like *Voting* and *The American Voter*, we have found that certain of their generalizations do not hold up in the face of historical change. Today it is becoming common to find time-specific and locale-specific labels attached to the titles of research reports that deal with general variables: "in the Carter–Reagan Campaign", "during the 1984 U.S. Election", and the like. This reflects a new found awareness that quantitative results may differ widely from time to time and place to place, as the conditions of media and politics vary.

It is still quite possible that certain findings will prove to be generalizable. The strong correlation between public affairs knowledge and newspaper reading, for example, seems to hold up consistently in various settings. We would not fault the pioneers of our field for putting forth their intitial results as generalizations, because they assumed that it was understood that these propositions were always open to subsequent test. But now that more than four decades of studies have accumulated, an empirical reassessment of those propositions is long overdue. We have not attempted to reconstruct a set of empirical propostitions in any systematic way in this chapter. We believe that a re-analysis of the underlying assumptions should be the first step in such an undertaking. We expect that some generalizations are indeed attainable, but that many findings will prove to be specific to the conditions of a particular study. Careful comparison of these differing conditions can produce new hypotheses for testing, hypotheses that would help to explain why such very different relationships between similar variables are to be found under different circumstances.

RELATIVITY OF RESEARCH PERSPECTIVES

An additional point we wish to stress is that the "effects" orientation of political-marketing research assumes a fundamentally linear model of communication from source-to-receiver, and a system-down model of politics. These are not the only conceptual possibilities, nor even the preferable ones, as Rogers and Balle suggest in the introductory chapter of this volume.

The source-to-receiver view is unidirectional, seeing the person whose decisions and other behaviors are at stake as the intended target of messages. In a campaign context, messages are studied for their effects upon voter perceptions and behaviors, and how they may influence the outcome of the election. The system-down perspective posits the behavior of the "ideal" or "proper" citizen, and leads to studies of the extent to which the voter approaches the model of behavior established by the scholar. This approach may result from top-down definitions of politics (Lemisch, 1969). The paradigm of politics as voting behavior, a normative and stable process, has remained virtually unchallenged throughout the history of political communication research, even as the focus may have shifted toward cognitive and professional communication criteria. The behaviors of political actors continue to be interpreted almost entirely within the confines of electoral campaigns, as if "politics" consists simply of attempts to attain public office, an activity that is concentrated in the short period prior to each election. There is as yet in the study of political communication no analog to the "convergence" model of communication outlined elsewhere in this volume by Rogers, although some empirical beginnings have begun to appear (e.g., Eulau and Siegel, 1981).

The assumption of homogeneity as to people, places, media, and political cultures that is permitted by the early narrow view of political communication reduces us to a "stipulated static paradigm for research" (Meyer and others, 1980, p. 264). It is ironic that in the United States, probably the most heterogeneous country in the western world, statistical parameters to describe "typical" political processes and "the American voter" have been the object of so much of our research. In a country where voting by 60 percent of the eligible citizens has come to be considered a "heavy" turnout in national elections, more attention might well be given to other, perhaps more profound forms of political communication and action.

A reversal of the conceptions of communication and politics would be an essential step in this direction. Brenda Dervin (1980a, 1980b; Dervin and others, 1982) and Rita Atwood (Atwood and Dervin, 1981), among others, have recently been arguing that the source-message-channel-receiver (S-M-C-R) picture of communication processes puts matters backwards. In line with the psychology of "becoming" (Rogers, 1979), they see people as active creators of their own information, defined as the sense one makes of the world while moving through time and space. The media, from this person-oriented perspective, can be seen as the lenses through which the world is viewed and which structure the ways in which the person makes his or her particular sense of it (Hochheimer, 1982). Similarly, a person-centered perspective would view political socialization in terms of the needs and capacities of the person developing from childhood into adolescence, and thence on into adulthood. For example, Wackman and Wartella (1977) have studied children's reactions to television advertising from such a developmental perspective. Most research on political socialization, however, has assumed that the standard of comparison is a stipulated political system, toward which the young person is expected to become socialized. More person-oriented research, reversing both the S-M-C-R and system-down models, is likely to enrich our understanding of political communication in the future.

The political dynamics of elections vary over time. Sheingold (1973) suggests that the dynamics of the decision-making process lying behind voting also varies with differences in historical situations. The electorate itself changes over time, too. Women, blacks, and people without property were, in various times and places, excluded from voting. Party alignments have shifted dramatically due to changing economic and social conditions. For example, the Democratic "Solid South" that was formed in the wave of post-Civil War Reconstruction has become an increasingly Republican New South in the past 20 years of civil rights struggles, influx of new industry, rising affluence, and, perhaps, media influences.

The media, too, change over time, both as cause and as effect of political, social, and economic change. The content, form, and uses of a medium interact with a changing environment to remain in flux (Williams, 1974). Thus, the search for the political role of the mass media constrains the analysis of communication and of politics. Both are processes; both evolve. We need not remain constrained by the assumptions upon which Lazarsfeld, his colleagues, and their scientific descendants constructed their research. We can learn from the past as we look to the future.

Our broadest recommendation, then, is that the study of historical change should be reintroduced into the analysis of political communication. Politics, in the words of Lord Acton, "is the one science that is deposited by the stream of history." Mass media serve both as a central component in the political process, and as an enduring record of its history. The search for ahistorical theory has unnecessarily impoverished our understanding of that process and of that record.

REFERENCES

Rita Atwood and Brenda Dervin (1981), "Challenges to Social-Cultural Predictors of Information-Seeking: A Test of Race vs. Situation Movement State," Paper presented at the International Communication Association, Minneapolis, MN.

James David Barber (1980), *The Pulse of Politics*, New York: Norton.

Louis H. Bean (1940), *Ballot Behavior*, Washington, DC: American Council on Public Affairs.

Louis H. Bean (1948), *How to Predict Elections*, New York: Knopf.

Bernard Berelson, Paul F. Lazarsfeld, and William McPhee (1954), *Voting*, Chicago, IL: University of Chicago Press.

Bernard Berelson and Gary Steiner (1964), *Human Behavior: An Inventory of Scientific Findings*, New York: Harcourt, Brace and World.

Jay G. Blumler and Elihu Katz (1974), *The Uses of Mass Communication*, Beverly Hills, CA: Sage.

Jay G. Blumler and Denis McQuail (1969), *Television in Politics: Its Uses and Influences*, Chicago, IL: University of Chicago Press.

Angus Campbell, Philip E. Converse, Warren E. Miller, and Donald E. Stokes (1960), *The American Voter*, New York: Wiley.

Donald T. Campbell and Julian C. Stanley (1966), *Experimental and Quasi-Experimental Designs for Research*, Chicago, IL: Rand-McNally.

Richard F. Carter (1962), "Some Effects of the Debates," in Sidney Kraus (ed.), *The Great Debates*, Bloomington, IN: Indiana University Press.

Steven H. Chaffee (1978), "Presidential Debates: Are They Helpful to Voters?", *Communication Monographs*, 45, 330–346.

Steven H. Chaffee (1981), "Mass Media in Political Campaigns: An Expanding Role," in Ronald E. Rice and William J. Paisley (eds.), *Public Communication Campaigns*, Beverly Hills, CA, Sage.

Steven H. Chaffee and Sun Yuel Choe (1980), "Time of Decision and Media Use in the Ford-Carter Campaign," *Public Opinion Quarterly*, 44, 52–69.

Steven H. Chaffee, L. Scott Ward, and Leonard P. Tipton (1970), "Mass Communication and Political Socialization," *Journalism Quarterly*, 47, 647–659.

Steven H. Chaffee and Yuko Miyo (1982), " Selective Exposure and the Reinforcement Hypothesis in the 1980 Presidential Campaign: An Intergenerational Panel Study." Paper presented to the Association for Education in Journalism, Athens, OH.

Dennis K. Davis and Stanley J. Baran (1981), *Mass Communication and Everyday Life*, Belment, CA: Wadsworth.

Melvin L. DeFleur and Everette E. Dennis (1981), *Understanding Mass Communication*, Boston, MA: Houghton Mifflin.

Brenda Dervin (1980a), "Information as a User Construct: The Relevance of Perceived Information Needs to Synthesis and Interpretation," Paper presented at the Research and Educational Practice Unit, National Institute for Education, Washington, DC.

Brenda Dervin (1980b), "Communication Gaps and Inequities: Moving Toward a Reconceptualization," in Melvin Voigt and Brenda Dervin (eds.), *Progress in Communication Sciences, Volume 2*, Norwood, NJ: Ablex.

Brenda Dervin, Thomas L. Jacobson, and Michael S. Nilan (1982), "Measuring Qualitative and Relativistic Aspects of Information Seeking: A Test of a Quantitative-Qualitative Methodology," Paper presented at the International Communication Association, Boston, MA.

Joseph R. Dominick (1983), *The Dynamics of Mass Communication*, Reading, MA: Addison-Wesley.

Leonard W. Doob (1950), "Goebbels' Principles of Propaganda," *Public Opinion Quarterly, 14*, 419–42.

Heinz Eulau and Jonathan W. Siegel (1981), "Social Network Analysis and Political Behavior: A Feasibility Study", *Western Political Quarterly, 34*, 489–499.

James S. Ettema and D. Charles Whitney (eds.) (1982), *Individuals in Mass Media Organizations: Creativity and Constraint*, Beverly Hills, CA: Sage.

Todd Gitlin (1978), "Media Sociology: The Dominant Paradigm," *Theory and Society, 6*, 205–253.

Robert Hawkins, Suzanne Pingree, Kim Smith and Warren Bechtolt (1979), "Adolescent Responses to Issues and Images," in Sidney Kraus (ed.), *The Great Debates*, Bloomington, IN: University of Indiana Press.

John L. Hochheimer (1982), "Probing the Foundations of Political Communication in Campaigns: The Dispersion Process of Media." Paper presented to the International Communication Association, Boston, MA.

Robert Hornik (1980), "Communication as Complement in Development," *Journal of Communication, 30*, 10–24.

Carl I. Hovland, Arthur A. Lumsdaine, and Fred D. Sheffield (1949), *Experiments on Mass Communication*, Princeton, NJ: Princeton University Press.

Elihu Katz (1960), "Communication Research and the Image of Society: Convergence of Two Traditions," *American Journal of Sociology, 65*, 435–440.

Elihu Katz and Jacob J. Feldman (1962), "The Debates in the Light of Research: A Survey of Surveys," in Sidney Kraus (ed.), *The Great Debates*, Bloomington, IN: Indiana University Press.

Elihu Katz and Paul F. Lazarsfeld (1955), *Personal Influence*, New York: Free Press.

Joseph T. Klapper (1960), *The Effects of Mass Communication*, New York: Free Press.

Sidney Kraus and Dennis Davis (1976), *The Effects of Mass Communication on Political Behavior*, University Park, PA: Pennsylvania State University Press.

Harold D. Lasswell (1930), *Psychopathology and Politics*, Chicago, IL: University of Chicago Press.

Harold D. Lasswell (1935), *World Politics and Personal Insecurity*, New York: McGraw-Hill.

Paul F. Lazarsfeld (1935), "The Act of Asking Why in Marketing Research," *National Marketing Review, 1,* 26–38.

Paul F. Lazarsfeld, Bernard Berelson, and Hazel Gaudet (1944), *The People's Choice,* New York: Duell, Sloan and Pearce.

Paul F. Lazarsfeld and Frank Stanton (1942), *Radio Research, 1941,* New York: Duell, Sloan and Pearce.

Paul F. Lazarsfeld and Robert K. Merton (1948), "Mass Communication, Popular Taste, and Organized Social Action," in Lyman Bryson (ed.), *Communication of Ideas,* New York: Harper and Brothers.

Jessee Lemisch (1969), "The American Revolution Seen from the Bottom Up," in Barton Bernstein (ed.), *Towards a New Past: Dissenting Essays in American History,* New York: Vintage Books.

Arthur A. Lumsdaine and Irving L. Janis (1953), "Resistance to 'Counter-Propaganda' Produced by One-Sided and Two-Sided 'Propaganda' Presentations," *Public Opinion Quarterly 17,* 311–318.

Maxwell E. McCombs and Donald L. Shaw (1972), "The Agenda-Setting Function of the Press," *Public Opinion Quarterly, 36,* 176–187.

William J. McGuire (1964), "Inducing Resistance to Persuasion: Some Contemporary Approaches," in Leonard Berkowitz (ed.), *Advance in Experimental Social Psychology, Volume 1,* New York: Academic Press.

William J. McGuire and Demetrios Papageorgis (1961), "The Relative Efficacy of Various Types of Prior Belief-Defense in Producing Immunity Against Persuasion," *Journal of Abnormal and Social Psychology, 62,* 327–337.

Jack M. McLeod and Lee B. Becker (1974), "Testing the Validity of Gratification Measures Through Political Effects Analysis," in Jay G. Blumler and Elihu Katz (eds.), *The Uses of Mass Communications,* Beverly Hills, CA: Sage.

Harold Mendelsohn and Garrett J. O'Keefe (1976), *The People Choose a President,* New York: Praeger.

Robert K. Merton (1957), *Social Theory and Social Structure,* New York: Free Press.

Robert K. Merton (1968), *Social Theory and Social Structure,* New York: Free Press.

Timothy P. Meyer, Paul J. Traudt, and James A. Anderson (1980), "Nontraditional Mass Communication Research Methods: An Overview of Observational Case Studies of Media Use in Natural Settings," in Dan Nimmo (ed.), *Communication Yearbook, 4,* New Brunswick, NJ: Transaction Books.

Warren E. Miller, Arthur Miller, and F. Gerald Kline (1974), *The CPS 1974 American National Election Study,* Ann Arbor, MI: University of Michigan, Center for Political Studies.

Norman H. Nie, Sidney Verba, and John R. Petrocik (1976), *The Changing American Voter,* Cambridge, MA: Harvard University Press.

Dan D. Nimmo and Keith R. Sanders (1981), *Handbook of Political Communication,* Beverly Hills, CA: Sage.

William Paisley (1984), "Communication in the Communication Sciences," in Brenda Dervin and Melvin J. Voigt (eds.), *Progress in Communication Sciences, Volume 5.* Norwood, NJ: Ablex.

Thomas E. Patterson (1980), *The Mass Media Election,* New York: Praeger.

Ithiel de Sola Pool (1963), "The Effect of Communication on Voting Behavior," in Wilbur Schramm (ed.), *The Science of Human Communication,* New York: Basic Books.

Byron Reeves and Ellen Wartella (1982), "For Some Children Under Some Conditions: A History of Research on Children and Media." Paper presented at the International Communication Association, Boston, MA.

Stuart A. Rice (1928), *Quantitative Methods in Politics,* New York: Knopf.

Stuart A. Rice (1931), *Methods in Social Science: A Case Book,* Chicago, IL: University of Chicago Press.

Ronald E. Rice and William J. Paisley (1981), *Public Communication Campaigns,* Beverly Hills, CA: Sage.

Donald F. Roberts and Nathan Maccoby (1973), "Information-Processing and Persuasion: Counterarguing Behavior," in Peter Clarke (ed.), *New Models for Mass Communications Research,* Beverly Hills, CA: Sage.

Carl R. Rogers (1979), "The Foundation of the Person-Centered Approach," *Education, 100,* 98–107.

Everett M. Rogers and D. Lawrence Kincaid (1981), *Communication Networks: Toward a New Paradigm for Research,* New York: Free Press.

Peter H. Rossi (1959), "Four Landmarks in Voting Research," in Eugene Burdick and Arthur J. Brodbeck (eds.), *American Voting Behavior,* Glencoe, IL: Free Press.

Wilbur Schramm (1971), "The Nature of Communication Between Humans," in Wilbur Schramm and Donald Roberts (eds.), *The Process and Effects of Mass Communication,* Urbana, IL: University of Illinois Press.

Wilbur Schramm and Richard F. Carter (1959), "Effectiveness of a Political Telethon," *Public Opinion Quarterly, 23,* 121–126.

Michael Schudson (1978), *Discovering the News: A Social Life History of American Newspapers,* New York: Basic.

David O. Sears (1969), "Political Behavior", in Gardner Lindzey and Elliot Aronson (eds.), *The Handbook of Social Psychology, Volume 5: Applied Social Psychology,* Reading, MA: Addison-Wesley.

Carl A. Sheingold (1973), "Social Networks and Voting: The Resurrection of a Research Agenda," *American Sociological Review, 38, 712, 720.*

James W. Tankard, Tsan-Kuo Chang, and Kuo-Jen Tsang (1982), "Citation Networks as Indicators of Journalism Research Activity." Paper presented at the Association for Education in Journalism, Athens, OH.

Gaye Tuchman (1978), *Making News: A Study in the Construction of Reality,* New York: Free Press.

Daniel B. Wackman and Ellen Wartella (1977), "A Review of Cognitive Development Theory and Research and the Implication for Research on Children's Response to Television," *Communication Research, 4,* 203–224.

David H. Weaver, Doris A. Graber, Maxwell E. McCombs, and Chaim H. Eyal (1981), *Media Agenda-Setting in a Presidential Election,* New York: Praeger.

Robert W. White (1956), *The Abnormal Personality,* New York: Ronald Press.

Raymond Williams (1974), *Television: Technology and Cultural Form,* New York: Schocken Press.

Chapter 17

Toward Integration of European and American Communication Research

Everett M. Rogers
Stanford University

Francis Balle
Université de Paris II

INTRODUCTION

Our theme here is that European and American communication research scholars can learn useful lessons from each other, despite the important differences that exist between the mass media on the two continents. U.S. scholars should emphasize the context of the communication act more than they have in the past, give more attention to policy issues in designing their research, and learn more from the viewpoints of their critical colleagues. European scholars might do well to borrow and adapt models of interpersonal communication, especially in light of the interactive nature of the new media. Thus certain kinds of intellectual strength can derive from closer contact between European and American communication scholars.   *E.M.R., F.B.*

We began this book with an Introduction that stressed the historical roots of communication research in Europe and in America. In the ensuing chapters our contributors have explained the nature of these differences, and the basic similarities today. Here we consider how each side of the Atlantic might learn from the other, and thus move toward a more common approach to communication research. There are those who point out that such closer integration might have intellectual disadvantages, as well as advantages. While we grant that this is so, we feel that the differences are so wide, and the advantages of integration so compelling, that we feel that at least somewhat closer integration is in order. We seek to show some of the intellectual benefits that might derive from greater communality between Europe and America.

DIFFERENCES BETWEEN EUROPE AND AMERICA

A fundamental reason for the contrasts between the communication research that is conducted in Europe and in America is that the mass media systems are quite different on the two continents. Out of these basic differences in ownership, control, and functioning of the media grow many appropriate contrasts in the style of communication research. Obviously, these differences are appropriate. But we feel that many of the differences in communication research are not due to differences in the media. And even when they are, Americans could often learn useful approaches from their European counterparts, and vice versa.

For instance, public ownership and/or control of radio and television systems is a general pattern in European nations, while private, for-profit ownership is most important in the Unite States (today a modest public broadcasting system exists in the United States for radio and TV, and commercial channels are gaining strength in Europe). The trend toward a coexisting public and private broadcasting system in both Europe and in the United States means that research approaches earlier followed in one or the other of the continents may now become useful in the other. The contrasts in ownership and control on the two sides of the Atlantic exist for historical, political, and institutional reasons. These background factors cannot be ignored (rather they should be understood) when transferring research approaches across the Atlantic. Such understanding is part of the context of communication, a context that must be taken into account when investigating a communication problem (as our European colleagues insist).

The different governmental roles regarding the mass media in European nations and in the United States affect the new media of satellites, cable, and microcomputer technology. In Europe, these new communication technologies are generally the direct product of government programs to promote the national development of an information economy. For example, the French government funded R & D (carried out by high-technology private firms) that lead to the manufacturing and sale of the microelectronic equipment used in the videotex experiment at Velizy, near Paris. The French government is similarly involved in an interactive cable system using fiber optics technology today in Biarritz, the Atlantic resort city. The implementation and evaluation of these new technologies at Velizy and at Biarritz are responsibilities of the French government; the purpose of the experiments is to determine the effectiveness of the new technologies for use in France, and for sale abroad. Similar involvement of the national governments in other European countries in experimenting with the new media is common. However, in the United States the major experiments (several dozen are presently under way) on interactive communication technolgies are entirely in private hands.

So the role of the government (a) in the conventional media, and (b) regarding the new media, is quite different in Europe and in the United States. One would expect, as a consequence, greater interest by policymakers and by communication scholars in issues of equality in Europe. In the U.S., where free market forces are the main determinants of the new media, equality will not receive as much attention. Perhaps it should get more attention than it does. Or at the least, perhaps American scholars should attend to the European evaluations of the new media so as to learn important lessons about the social impacts of the new communication technologies on the information-rich and the information-poor.

The new media bring out another important difference between Europe and America: the much greater attention to policy issues by European communication scholars. We feel that it is good, intellectually and politically, for the field of communication research to be involved in policy considerations. There is a detectable trend among many U.S. communication scholars to pay more attention to policy issues in their research. Ultimately this will mean not just a closing section on policy implications in research reports, but a refocusing of the topics of certain studies in the directions of usefulness to policy-makers. And of course to know what these directions are, communication scholars must have contact with policy-makers. Here (regarding the policy emphasis of communication research), we think that American researchers can learn a great deal from their European colleagues. They have found that relevance to policy-makers is an important consideration in planning the directions of communication inquiry; the result is a greater appreciation for communication research due to its utilization in public policy decisions. And our European colleagues tell us that policy relevance need not be associated with any diminishing in the rigor or the intellectual quality of communication research. This emphasis on policy issues is not just a characteristic of European scholars; it is also typified by critical communication scholars (who are primarily concentrated in Europe).

We are beginning to see greater attention paid to the critical communication school in the United States in very recent years. For example, the International Communication Association, long considered a bastion of empirical communication scholars, now has one of its nine divisions devoted to the philosophy of communication (this division includes much more than just critical scholarship). Some very interesting discussions occur at the annual conventions of the ICA in the communication philosophy division sessions, as critical scholars and their empirical colleagues exchange viewpoints. Unfortunately, there are not many other locales in which such an exchange occurs, to the detriment of both the empirical and critical schools of communication research. Certainly the two viewpoints, antagonistically opposed through much of their history, have much to learn from each other. Critical scholars are generally most opposed to such pluralistic interchange, claiming that empirical scholars are trying to subvert the critical school, co-opt its positions, and to take it over under the guise of seeking to understand it. Such attitudes mean that the first step toward mutual understanding must be taken by empirical scholars in most cases; perhaps it will then be convincing in its advantages to both parties, and the exchange will continue. Nevertheless, the basic difficulties in meaningful learning from each other should not be underestimated.

Fortunately for these purposes, Europe provides one site in which the two schools are in some degree of contact. At least in certain nations, like Sweden for example, critical and empirical scholars may be learning from each other. Professor Karl Erik Rosengren, in his contribution to this volume, argues that one school has the most interesting questions for communication research, while the other has the most appropriate means of answering them. Thus there is a natural advantage, intellectually, for at least a minimum kind of exchange between the two schools. We feel that one of the outcomes of closer integration of European and American approaches to communication will be a closer exchange between the critical and empirical schools, simply because of the much greater importance of the critical school in Europe. A consequence of closer contacts between the two continents and the two schools might be greater heterogeneity within U.S. communication research. A comment by many European communication scholars who are well-acquainted with U.S. communication research is its sameness. Certainly in the past, American mass communication researchers have displayed a shared loyalty to one main paradigm for research. We doubt that this intellectual consensus will continue into the future, nor should it. There is today ferment in the field of communication research, and one result will be a greater diversity of theories and methodologies.

However there is one dimension on which European scholars are much more homogeneous than are their American counterparts: In Europe, communication research means *mass* communication research. Due to the historical and political context of European scholarship, an emphasis on interpersonal communication research never developed in much strength. In contrast, these two branches of communication inquiry are about equally represented in the United States; they constitute *the* basic division of the field of communication research. At most large-sized universities, a department of mass communication and a department of interpersonal communication may each exist, and have relatively little to do with each other intellectually. In other U.S. universities with a single communication department, the two specialties usually co-exist in an uneasy alliance.

These U.S. differences between interpersonal and mass communication have some important disadvantages to scholars of communication behavior. Not the least of these problems is that the two types of communication are not so easily separated in everyday life. For example, consider the way in which a mass media organization functions to process news. It is largely interpersonal communication behavior, with reporters interviewing witnesses, passing along the information they obtain to editors, eventually leading to a mass media message that is then disseminated to a mass audience. But then the process of news dissemination again becomes interpersonal, as a newspaper reader, say, tells a friend about some news item. So we see that mass and interpersonal communication behavior can only be separated in a very artificial and arbitrary way.

This intellectual division of the field of communication research is about to become passé, in our opinion, due to the new communication technologies. Their interactivity means that the new "mass" media will function in certain ways that best fit the models of interpersonal communication. For example, a surprise of the Velizy experiment with interactive videotex in France was the formation, within months of the beginning of the new service, of more than 350 common interest groups, each around a bulletin board. Here the electronic technologies provide a convenient means for individuals with a common interest (in sports cars, bee-keeping, or classical music) to exchange information. In every interactive communication system with which we are acquainted, such bulletin board groups quickly form. The participants are complete strangers in the usual sense, in that they do not know each other in a face-to-face manner. But they soon become very thoroughly knowledgeable about each other's special interest. Certainly the study of such electronic groupings must draw on interpersonal communication models. Yet a "mass" medium is involved in the exchange; this is machine-assisted interpersonal communication.

Thus the new media will encourage European communication scholars to give more attention to interpersonal communication than they have in the past. And in the United States, the interactivity of the new media will lead toward a merger of the mass and the interpersonal approaches to communication research.

In summary, important differences exist between European and American approaches to communication research. These differences are beginning to diminish, as the mass media in Europe and America tend to become more alike and as communication scholars on the two continents have more contact with each other.

COMMUNICATION RESEARCH ON THE NEW MEDIA

We see the new communication media as having a powerful influence on the nature of communication research. These new technologies make scholarly research on communication "a whole new ball game," unfreezing this research field from many of its assumptions, paradigms, and investigatory methods of the past. This challenge from the new media is impacting upon the nature of communication research in both Europe and America today. The common realization of these impacts on both sides of the Atlantic is a powerful force toward closer integration of European and American approaches to communication research. That's why "the media revolution" is part of the title of this book, and why the new communication technologies have been a theme of the previous chapters.

The new communication technologies are bringing about major changes in the nature of communication research. The predominantly linear models of one-way communication effects now must give way to convergence models of communication as a two-way process of information-exchange, due to the interactivity of the new media. This interactivity means that a highly-varied content is communicated, instead of the more standard content of print and broadcasting communication in the past. Not only are new theoretical models of communication forced by the new communication technologies, but alternative research methods for collecting and analyzing data are also provided by the new media. For instance, computer-recorded data are often available to scholars when they study interactive communication systems, because the computer that allows for interactivity also keeps a verbatim record of the messages. Often lacking, however, are effective means to utilize such data in scholarly studies of the social impacts of the new media. So the Communication Revolution that is starting to occur today is also a revolution in communication research, involving both methods and models (Rice, 1984).

The linear effects models of mass media effects, most popular in past U.S. communication research, simply do not work very well in assessing the social impacts of the new media. For one thing, the "social impacts" (as the terminology implies) of the new media are much more, and much different from, the simple, direct effects of, say, television on children (that have been investigated in past research). The new media are likely to be much broader and more powerful in the nature of their impacts. For example, one consequence of office automation, it seems from early studies, is a reversal of sex roles in the office. Bosses, traditionally males, are now doing "typing" on word-processors, while secretaries (who usually are female) are using their newly-freed time to take on office management tasks (for example, scheduling meetings, arranging travel plans, etc.) that were the responsibility of male bosses in the past.

Suddenly we are beginning to realize that information is becoming the most important resource in modern society. Thus the study of human communication is indeed becoming the study of society. This realization promises to elevate communication scholars to a crucial role in the new society that is being formed by the Information Revolution. Are they prepared?

Here are four major research directions, each detailed with a series of specific research questions to be pursued, that are of high priority in the study of the new communication technologies.

Computers and Our Children

An estimated 90 percent of U.S. schools today use microcomputers for teaching purposes. About 12 percent of U.S. homes now own a microcomputer (a number that doubled in the past year); one of the major uses is to play video games and to facilitate children's education. Since its beginning less than 10 years ago, the U.S. video game industry gained larger sales (by far) than films or records/music, amounting to over $4 billion in 1982 (Rogers and Larsen, 1984). While the potential of these new technologies for educating our children is tremendous, results to date have been discouraging. Most U.S. schools use microcomputers as an expensive kind of electronic flashcards for simple drill-and-practice exercises. Further, there are not nearly enough microcomputers in the average school for all students to have even a minimum amount of use; the result is thus to widen gender and socioeconomic gaps between the information-rich and the information-poor. Video games are mainly of the "shoot 'em up" variety, offering little more than addictive entertainment; the consequence has been a public outcry against video game arcades by parents (in fact, arcades are banned in certain cities and in some nations). Clearly, here is a communication research topic of the very highest priority. Some important research questions to pursue are:

- What is the process through which schools adopt microcomputers? What problems of implementation are encountered? Why are microcomputers not utilized in schools in ways that would allow their full potential for learning and teaching to be realized?
- Why are microcomputers so attractive to children? How do microcomputers enable schools to reach special audience of children like the learning-retarded, delinquent children, etc.?
- How do microcomputers change the mental processes of children (for example, making them more logical in their thinking, socially alienated, quantitative, etc.)?
- How do microcomputers widen (or perhaps narrow) the gender, ethnic/racial, and socioeconomic gaps between the information-rich and the information-poor?

Computer Impacts on Work

One of the most important impacts on the Information Revolution is on the lives of individuals in their places of work, whether offices or factories.

• What are the social impacts of computer-based technologies (like word-processing, electronic messaging systems, etc.) in the office, such as sex-role changes between boss and secretary, unemployment, heightened work-stress, etc.? How can the technologies be designed/redesigned so as to be more "friendly" and acceptable, particularly for special employees like older females?
• What are the social impacts (for example, unemployment, needs for employee retraining, etc.) of new information technologies like robotics in the factory (and in the home)?
• What social problems (like the invasion of privacy, computer "phreaks" (criminals), technological vulnerability, etc.) accompany the increasing role of computers in society? How might these social problems be avoided or ameliorated?

New Communication Technologies (satellites, microcomputers, etc.) for Development in the Third World

Although the potential of the new technologies for the Third World seems to be very great, at present it is hardly possible to point to examples of the effective use of these technologies in development programs. Why is this so?

• How can the new communication technologies be better harnessed for improving development programs in agriculture, health, education, etc.?
• What are the positive impacts (higher levels of food production, improved health, more widespread literacy, the launching of spin-off high-technology firms), and negative impacts (such as unemployment) of the new communication technologies in the Third World?
• Can microcomputers and other new communication technologies enable Third World nations to leap over the industrial era into becoming information societies (as Jean-Jacques Servan-Schreiber has claimed)? What national and international public policies might facilitate this transition to becoming information societies (for example, in Mexico, Brazil, India, and Singapore)?
• To what extent do the new technologies increase dependency of Third World nations on Europe, Japan, and the United States?

Impact on the Advanced Information Societies

The social impacts of the new information technologies are now being felt most strongly in the advanced information societies like the U.S.,

Japan, France, Germany, and England, and especially in certain high-technology systems therein, like California's Silicon Valley. Investigation of these settings today provides one scenario of the future information society. Although Silicon Valley is a system characterized by dynamic entrepreneurship, continuous technological innovation, and vigorous competition, Silicon Valley is also typified by extreme socioeconomic inequality; pollution, smog, traffic, and other problems of overcrowding and unplanned rapid growth; and by such human problems as family instability, high job stress, "workaholism", and burn-out. But Silicon Valley is a bright spot in an otherwise drab national economy in creating jobs, in generating economic growth, and in contributing toward the U.S. balance-of-payments. So it receives a great deal of special attention from national politicians and from the mass media.

Unfortunately the methods of communciation research do not provide very effective means of understanding the future. Our methodologies are best for looking into the rearview mirror of the recent past, or for understanding the present. One available design for looking into the future is to study the advanced sectors of contemporary society. Thus a look at Silicon Valley today may provide one scenario for the Information Society.

- How might high-technology complexes like Silicon Valley rise in such other locations as Research Triangle (North Carolina), Austin, Phoenix, Portland (Oregon), Kyushu Island (Japan), Munich, and Singapore? What factors (entrepreneurship, the presence of a research university, climate and quality-of-life, and the availability of venture capital) are essential elements in the growth of these high-technology systems?
- What are the workstyle and lifestyle impacts (like burnout, high work involvement, child development problems, high divorce rates, etc.) of high-technology systems like Silicon Valley?
- What are the societal implications of the growing political power of the high-technology industries that produce such information technologies as computers, semiconductors, and video games?
- What are the impacts of two-way cable television in the new "wired" communities of Hi-OVIS in Japan, Milton Keynes in England, Velizy and Biarritz in France, *Bildschirmtext* in Berlin and Düsseldorf, QUBE in Columbus, Ohio, etc.?
- What industrial policies of national governments could best assist information technology industries (especially semiconductors, minicomputers, etc.) in competing effectively with their counterpart industries in other nations (like Japan)?
- How can national public policies aid a rapid transition into becoming an advanced information society, in a way that minimizes

such current problems as high unemployment, a slow rate of economic growth, and an unbalanced balance-of-payments?

We suggest that questions such as these will increasingly occupy the attention of communication researchers in the future. They are quite unlike the main research questions of the past.

THE FUTURE OF COMMUNICATION RESEARCH

What will eventually happen to communication research? Wilbur Schramm (1980, p.82) concludes his review of the history of communication research (see our Chapter 12) by saying: "As the social science disciplines abandon their exclusivity and build their theory on a broader base, I wonder whether we cannot expect communication research and communication study to be absorbed, along with social psychology, sociology, anthropology, and the others, into a more broadly conceived science of human society?" Communication research may thus contribute to a larger behavioral science.

William Paisley (1984) sees the field of communication research "as more likely to be 'absorbed' epistemologically than organizationally." Indeed, this analyst predicts a reorganization of communication research through expansion. The trials and experiments of new communication systems "are affording mass communication researchers their first opportunity in more than three decades to study public use of a new mass medium in the United States."

The new communication technologies are beginning to affect the field of communication research, says Paisley (1984), in several important ways: "Behind communication research stand several Institutions that historically had little in common but are now converging in the 'Information Society'. These include Mass Media, Telecommunications Industries, Computer Industries, and Information Systems and Services." For example, daily we now read of two or more of these seemingly-unalike institutions cooperating in the new communication technologies. An illustration in the United States is provided by QUBE, the interactive cable system in Columbus, Ohio. QUBE is a joint venture of Warner Communications (a conglomerate mass communication firm) and American Express (a credit card and banking firm). Strange bedfellows are being formed by the Communication Revolution. And they will increasingly stand behind communication research. Until quite recent years, computer firms like IBM, Hewlett-Packard, Honeywell-Boole, and Apple would not have been considered communication industries, nor did they think of themselves as such. Thus the changes under way due to the informatization of society are momentous, and especially so for the nature and the role of communication research.

William Paisley (1984) concludes: "No group of social researchers could wish for more than to find their variable at the center of transformations of work, learning, political participation, play, and the other functions of society."

We agree.

REFERENCES

William Paisley (1984), "Communication in the Communication Sciences," in Brenda Dervin and Melvin J. Voigt (eds.), *Progress in the Communication Sciences, Volume 5*, Norwood, NJ: Ablex.

Ronald E. Rice and associates (1984), *The New Media: Communication, Research, and Technology*, Beverly Hills, CA: Sage.

Everett M. Rogers and Judith K. Larsen (1984), *Silicon Valley Fever: The Rise of High-Technology Culture*, New York: Basic Books.

Wilbur Schramm (1980), "The Beginnings of Communication Study in the United States," in Dan Nimmo (ed.), *Communication Yearbook 4*, New Brunswick, NJ: Transaction.

Appendix A

Some Communication Research Centers in Europe

I. Belgium

Centre d'Études des Techniques de
  Diffusion Collective
Institut de Sociologie de l'Université
  Libre de Bruxelles
Avenue Jeanne 44
1050 Brussels, Belgium

Centre de Recherche sur les Arts de
  la Communication (C.R.A.C.)
Université de Liège
Place du XX Août 32
4000 Liège, Belgium

Centre de Recherches sur la
  Communication en Histoire
  (U.C.L.)
Collège Erasme
Place Blaise Pascal 1
1348 Louvain-la-Neuve, Belgium

Département de Communication
  Sociale
Université Catholique de Louvain
Ruelle de la Lanterne Magique 14
1348 Louvain-la-Neuve, Belgium

Departement Communicatie
  Wetenschap
Katholieke Universiteit te Leuven
Van Evenstraat 2a
3000 Leuven, Belgium

Pers en Communicatie Wetenschap
Vrije Universiteit Brussel
Pleinlaan 2
1050 Brussels, Belgium

Pers en Communicatie Wetenschap
Universiteitstraat 8
9000 Gent, Belgium

Bureau d'Études de la R.T.B.F., Cité
  R.T.B.F.
Boulevard A. Reyers 52
1040 Brussels, Belgium

Centre d'Information sur les Media
  (C.I.M. asbl)
Galeries Agora
Rue Marché aux Herbes 105, bte 6
1000 Brussels, Belgium

Centre de recherche, d'Étude et de
  Documentation en Publicité
  (CREDOP)
(Union Belge des Annonceurs asbl)
Rue des Colonies 28, bte 7
1000 Brussels, Belgium

Centre de Recherche et d'Information
  Socio-Politiques (CRISP)
Rue du Congrès 35
1000 Brussels, Belgium

Coopérative Internationale de
  Recherche et d'Action en Matière
  de Communication
Secrétariat
R.T.B.F. Liège
Palais des Congrès
4020 Liège, Belgium

Groupe de Recherche Appliquée en
  Communication Šociale et Opinion
  Publique
Groupe RECOS asbl
Avenue R. Vandendriessche 71
1150 Brussels, Belgium

II. Denmark

Nordic Institute
University of Arhus
Niels Juelsgade 84
DK-8200 Arhus N, Denmark

School of Journalism
Halmstadgade 11
DK-8200 Arhus N, Denmark

Sozialwissenschaftliche Fakultät
Universitaet Hohenheim
D-7000 Stuttgart 70, Federal Republic
of Germany

Institut fuer Publizistik
Universitaet Hamburg
D-2000 Hamburg, Federal Republic of
Germany

III. Federal Republic of Germany

Institut fuer Publizistik
Westfaelische Wilhelms-Universitaet
Bispinghof 3/E
D-4400 Muenster, Federal Republic of
Germany

Institut fuer Kommunikations- und
Politikwissenschaft
Universitaet Erlangen-Nuernberg
D-8500 Nuernberg, Federal Republic
of Germany

Institut fuer Publizistik
Johannes Gutenberg Universitaet
Mainz
D-6500 Mainz, Federal Republic of
Germany

Institut fuer
Kommunikationsforschung
Universitaet Muenchen
Geschwister-Scholl-Platz 1
D-8000 Muenchen 22, Federal
Republic of Germany

Institut fuer Publizistik
Freie Universitaet Berlin
D-1000 Berlin 33, Federal Republic of
Germany

Institut fuer Publizistik
Universitaet Bielefeld
D-Bielefeld, Federal Republic of
Germany

IV. Finland

Department of Journalism and Mass
   Communication
Tampereen Yliopisto
Box 607
SF-33101 Tampera 10, Finland

Department of Journalism and Mass
   Communication
Helsingin Yliopisto
Alexandersgatan 7
SF-00330 Helsinki 33, Finland

V. France

Institut Français de Presse et des
   Sciences de l'Information—UER
   94
Université Paris II
83 bis, rue Notre-Dame-des-Champs
75006 Paris, France

Département d'Etudes et de
   Recherches Cinématographiques
Université Paris III
13, rue de Santeuil
75231 Paris Cedex 05, France

Centre d'Etudes Littéraires et
   Scientifiques Appliquées (CELSA)
Université Paris V
77, rue de Villiers
92523 Neuilly, France

Unité Pluridisciplinaire des
  Techniques d'Expression et de
  Communication (UPTEC)
Université Bordeaux III
Domaine Universitaire
33405 Talence, France

Institut d'Expression et
  Communication
Université Grenoble III
Domaine Universitaire
Saint-Martin d'Hères
BP 25 X Grenoble 36040 Cedex,
  France

UER des Sciences des Langages et
  des Moyens d'Expression
Centre Pluridisciplinaire de
  Recherches Sémiologiques
Université Lyon II
86, rue Pasteur
69365 Lyon Cedex 02, France

UER—Journalisme—Centre
  Universitaire d'Enseignement du
  Journalisme
Université Strasbourg III
10, rue Schiller
67083 Strasbourg Cedex, France

UER—Sciences de l'Expression et de
  la Communication
Université Toulouse III
118, route de Narbonne
31077 Toulouse Cedex, France

Institut d'Histoire de la Presse et de
  l'Opinion
Université François-Rabelais
8, place Foire-Le-Roy
37000 Tours, France

Institut des Sciences et Techniques de
  la Communication (ISTECO)
Université Paris Nord—Paris XIII
Avenue Jean-Baptiste Clément
93340 Villetaneuse, France

Centre Audiovisuel de l'Ecole
  Normale de Saint-Cloud
92210 Saint-Cloud, France

Centre d'Etude d'Opinion
Maison de la Radio
116, avenue du Président Kennedy
75016 Paris, France

Centre National d'Etudes de
  Télécommunications
BP 1266
2, rue de la Mabilais
35013 Rennes Cedex, France

Centre National du Cinéma
Service de l'Action Culturelle et de
  l'Information
12, rue de Lubeck
75734 Paris Cedex 16, France

Centre d'Etudes Transdisciplinaires
  (Sociologie—Anthropologie—
  Sémiologie)
6, rue de Tournon
75006 Paris, France

Conseil Français des Etudes et
  Recherches sur l'Information et la
  Communication
83 bis, rue Notre-Dame-des-Champs
75006 Paris, France

Institut National de l'Audiovisuel
21, boulevard Jules Ferry
75011 Paris, France

VI. Great Britain
Audio Visual Media Research Group
Institute of Educational Technology
The Open University
Walton Hall, Milton Keynes
MK7 6AA, England

Centre for Mass Communication
  Research
University of Leicester
104 Regent Road
Leicester, LE1 7LT, England

Centre for Contemporary Cultural
  Studies
University of Birmingham
PO Box 363
Birmingham, B15 2TT, England

Centre for Television Research
University of Leeds
Leeds, LS2 9JT, England

Centre for Journalism Studies
University College
34 Cathedral Road
Cardiff, CF1 9YG, Scotland

Mass Media Unit
(Glasgow University Media Group)
Dept. of Sociology
Glasgow University
61 South Park Avenue
Glasgow, G12 8LF, Scotland

Centre for Communication Studies
University of Liverpool
Chatham Street
Liverpool, L69 2BX, England

Primary Communication Research
  Centre
University of Leicester
University Road
Leicester, England

VII. Iceland
Faculty of Social Sciences
University of Iceland
Reykjavik, Iceland

VIII. Netherlands
Department of Mass Communication
Catholic University of Nijmegen
Postbus 9108
6500 HK Nijmegen, Netherlands

Department of Mass Communication
University of Amsterdam
Oude Hoogstraat 24
1012 CE Amsterdam CE, Netherlands

Audience Research Department,
  National Radio and Television
  Service
Postbus 10
1200 JB Hilversum, Netherlands

Department of Mass Communication
Free University of Amsterdam
Koningslaan 31–33
175 AB Amsterdam, Netherlands

Department of Mass Communication
University of Utrecht
Kromme Nieuwegracht 15
3512 HC Utrecht, Netherlands

Department of Extension Education
Agricultural University of
  Wageningen
Hollandseweg 1
6706 KN Wageningen, Netherlands

IX. Norway
Institute for Press Research
University of Oslo
Boks 1093
Blindern
Oslo 3, Norway

Center for Mass Media Research
University of Bergen
Christies gt 15–19
N-5014 Bergen U, Norway

X. Spain* (by Miguel Urabayen)

A. C. Nielsen Company
Luchana 23
Madrid, Spain

Alef
Cinca 19
Madrid, Spain

Asociacíon de Editores de Diarios
  Españoles (AEDE)
Espronceda 32
Madrid, Spain

Asociacíon Española de Licenciados
  en Ciencias de la Informacíon
Plaza del Callao 4
Madrid, Spain

Asociacíon de Revistas de
  Informacíon (ARI)
Orense 39
Madrid, Spain

Asociacíon Española de Prensa
  Tecnica
Balmes 200,
Barcelona, Spain

Bernard Krief
Reina Victoria 72
Madrid, Spain

Centro de Investigacíon Sociológica
  (CIS)
Pedro Teixeira 8
Madrid, Spain

Consulta S. A.
Hermanos Becauer 7
Madrid, Spain

Data S. A.
General Oraa 70
Madrid, Spain

Eco
Alcalá 96
Madrid, Spain

Emopública
Capitán Haya 56
Madrid, Spain

Facultad de Ciencias de la
  Informacíon
Universidad Autonoma
Barcelona, Spain

Facultad de Ciencias de la
  Informacíon
Universidad Complutense
Madrid, Spain

Facultad de Ciencias de la
  Informacíon
Universidad de Navarra
Pamplona, Spain

Facultad de Ciencias de la
  Informacíon
Universidad del País Vasco
Bilbao, Spain

Federacíon de Asociaciones de la
  Prensa de España
Plaza del Callo 4
Madrid, Spain

Gallup S. A.
M. Carmen del N. Jesús 14
Madrid, Spain

---

* *Note:* In Spain, communication research is conducted by (a) university schools of communication (called "information science" in Spanish), (b) professional associations, and (c) by private firms that conduct market research and public opinion studies.

Instituto DYM S. A.
Rda. S. Pedro 28–30
Barcelona, Spain

Metra Seis Marketing
Po de la Castellana 86
Madrid, Spain

Oficina de Justificacíon de la Difusión
(OJD)
Alcalde Sainz de Baranda 35
Madrid, Spain

Sofemasa
Torre de Madrid 3–11
Madrid, Spain

Unión de Periodistas
Silva 30
Madrid, Spain

XI. Sweden

Chair of Mass Communication
University of Gothenburg
Box 5048
S-402 21 Göteborg, Sweden

Stockholm School of Journalism
Gjörwellsgatan 26
S-112 60 Stockholm, Sweden

Gothenburg School of Journalism
Box 31 147
S-400 32 Gothenburg, Sweden

Center for Mass Communication
Research
University of Stockholm
S-106 91 Stockholm, Sweden

PUB
Swedish Radio and Television
S-105 10 Stockholm, Sweden

Department of Theatre and Film
Box 27062
S-102 51 Stockholm, Sweden

Department of Literature
Division of Press Research
Helgonabacken 12
S-223 62 Lund, Sweden

Nordic Documentation Center for
Mass Communication Research
(Nordicom)
Box 5048
S-402 21 Göteborg, Sweden

Appendix B

Some Major Centers for Communication Research in the U.S.

Institute of Communications Research
and the Department of Speech
  Communication
University of Illinois
Urbana, Illinois

School of Journalism
Indiana University
Bloomington, Indiana

School of Journalism and Mass
  Communication
and the Department of Speech and
  Theatre Arts
University of Iowa
Iowa City, Iowa

Department of Communication
University of Michigan
Ann Arbor, Michigan

Department of Communication
Michigan State University
East Lansing, Michigan

School of Journalism and Mass
  Communication
and the Department of Speech
  Communication
University of Minnesota
Minneapolis, Minnesota

School of Journalism
University of North Carolina
Chapel Hill, North Carolina

Department of Communication
  Studies
Northwestern University
Evanston, Illinois

Department of Communication
Ohio State University
Columbus, Ohio

Annenberg School of Communications
University of Pennsylvania
Philadelphia, Pennsylvania

Department of Communication
Purdue University
Lafayette, Indiana

Annenberg School of Communications
University of Southern California
Los Angeles, California

Institute for Communication Research
Department of Communication
Stanford University
Stanford, California

Newhouse School of Public
  Communications
Syracuse University
Syracuse, New York

Department of Speech
Temple University
Philadelphia, Pennsylvania

School of Communication
University of Texas
Austin, Texas

School of Communications
and the Department of Speech
  Communication
University of Washington
Seattle, Washington

Mass Communications Research
    Center
School of Journalism and Mass
    Communication
and the Department of
    Communication Arts
University of Wisconsin
Madison, Wisconsin

Department of Communication
University of Utah
Salt Lake City, Utah

Name Index

A

Abel, Elie, xiii, 150, 163
Adorno, Theodor W., 193, 196, 220, 223–224, 234, 245
Agnew, Carson, 133
Ahluwalia, M., 145, 148
Alavi, Hamza, 145, 148
Albert, Pierre, 10
Allardt, E., 247, 262
Althusser, Louis, 246
Anders, Wolfgang, 109, 132
Anderson, James A., 295
Andrén, Gunnar, 251, 265
Andrews, F. M., 247, 262
Antola, Livia, 163
Arnheim, 205
Aron, Raymond, 83
Atwood, Erwin, 157, 164
Atwood, Rita, 292–293
Avery, Robert K., 229

B

Bailey, Kenneth D., 240, 262
Bair, James H., 116, 131
Balle, Francis, ix, xii, xiii, 1, 80, 291, 297
Ball-Rokeach, Sandra, 139, 148, 190, 197
Baran, Stanley J., 286, 294
Barber, James D., 277, 293
Barthes, Roland, 9
Bauer, Raymond A., 201, 246–247, 262
Baughman, James L., 192, 198
Bavelas, Alex, 205
Beal, George M., 201
Bean, Louis H., 275–276, 293
Beavin, Janet H., 112, 133
Bechtolt, Warren, 294
Becker, Lee B., 289, 295
Beltrán, Luis Ramiro, 222, 234
Bénéton, Ph., 248, 262
Bentler, P. M., 253–254, 262–263
Berelson, Bernard, 2–4, 16, 205, 267–270, 277–281, 283, 285, 287, 293, 295
Bergson, Henri, 87
Bertalanffy, Ludwig von, 213, 217

Bertrand, Claude-Jean, xiii, 19, 21, 32, 42
Blin, Bernard, 8
Block, Eva, 246, 249–250, 262
Block, Per, 249, 262
Blumler, Jay, xiii, 185–188, 191, 196–197, 220, 224, 227, 233–234, 237, 255, 262, 268, 289, 293
Bodem, Helmut, 116, 131–132
Bogart, Leo, 8, 16, 67
Bohlen, Joe M., 201
Bombardier, Denise, xiv, 166, 176–177
Bourdieu, Pierre, 9
Boulding, Kenneth, 201
Brandt, Stefan, 115, 131
Breitrose, Henry, xiv, 19, 68
Brinton, James, 208
Brooks, Tim, 67
Bruneau, Tom, 216–217
Burgoon, Judee K., 67
Burgoon, Michael, 67
Burrell, Gibson, 236–240, 242–243, 246, 255, 260–262
Bush, Chilton R., 201, 208

C

Campbell, Angus, 283–285, 293
Campbell, Donald T., 278, 293
Cantril, Hadley, 147–148, 201
Cantor, Muriel, 137
Capra, Fritjof, 138, 148
Carey, James W., 185, 187, 197, 229, 231, 234
Carlson, Anton, 202
Carter, Richard F., 288, 293, 296
Cartwright, D., 201, 205
Case, Donald, 133
Casey, 201
Cayrol, R., 197
Chaffee, Steven H., xiv, 2, 16, 191, 197, 267, 274, 279, 287, 289, 293–294
Chang, Tsan-Kuo, 296
Charters, W. W., 12, 16
Charnley, M. V., 244, 262
Chapan-Delmas, Jacques, 85

SUBJECT INDEX

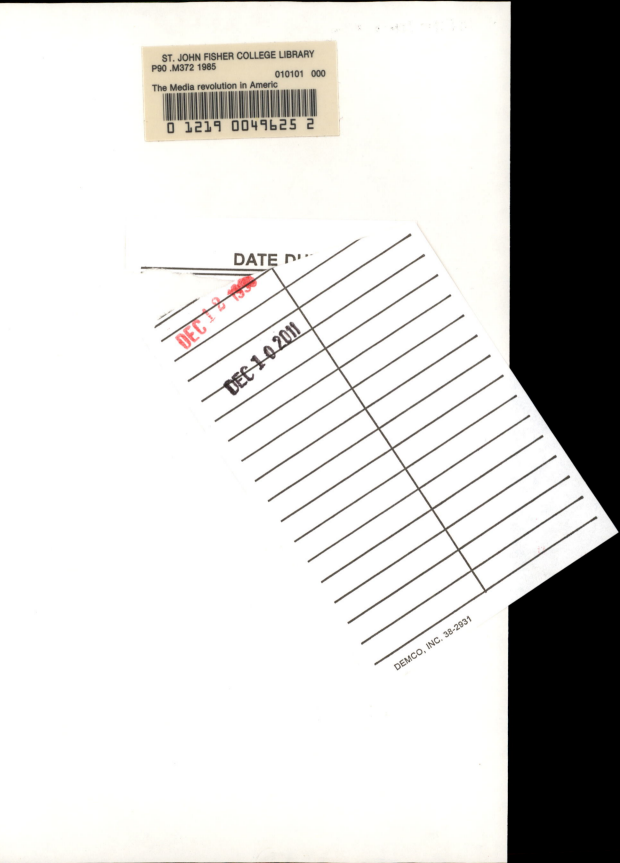

DATE DUE

DEC 1 2 199

DEC 1 0 2011

DEMCO, INC. 38-2931